JESUS WINS THE SERIES

Bill Medley

JESUS WINS THE SERIES

THE BOOK OF REVELATION EXPLAINED AND EXPLORED

VOLUME 1

Bill Medley

WHINE PRESS

Unless otherwise indicated, Scripture taken from the Holy Bible, NEW INTERNATIONAL VERSION®, NIV® Copyright © 1973, 1978, 1984, 2011 by Biblica, Inc.® Used by permission. All rights reserved worldwide.

© 2020 Bill Medley

ISBN 978-0-6484159-0-9

All rights reserved. No part of this publication may be reproduced, stored in a retrieval system, or transmitted, in any form, by any means, electronic, mechanical, photocopying, recording or otherwise without the prior permission of the publisher.

Cover Design by Andrew Clarke Studios

Published by Whine Press, Melbourne, Australia

Printed by Ingram Spark, Melbourne, Australia

Reprinted 2023

ACKNOWLEDGEMENTS

Thanks to those who took part in proof reading. Special thanks to Jayni Manners for countless hours of proof reading, corrections and transposing the sermons into text, but also for providing the inspiration to tackle this work in the first place.

To my beloved Diana
my best friend always

Contents

1. Jesus Wins (Revelation 1:1-8) 11
2. The First and the Last (Revelation 1:9-18) 23
3. The Seven Lampstands (Revelation 1:19-20) 35
4. Ephesus (Revelation 2:1-7) 45
5. Smyrna (Revelation 2:8-11) 55
6. Pergamum (Revelation 2:12-17) 65
7. Thyatira (Revelation 2:18-29) 75
8. Sardis (Revelation 3:1-6) 87
9. Philadelphia (Revelation 3:7-13) 97
10. Laodicea (Revelation 3:14-22) 107
11. Four Main Views (Revelation 4:1-2) 119
12. The Throne Room (Revelation 4:1-8) 131
13. Laying Down Your Crowns (Revelation 4:8-11) 141
14. Why God Created the World (Revelation 4:11) 153
15. The Sealed Scroll (Revelation 5:1-4) 163
16. The Lion and the Lamb (Revelation 5:5-7) 175
17. The Golden Bowls (Revelation 5:8) 185
18. God's Personal Love (Revelation 5:9-14) 193
19. The Four Horsemen (Revelation 6:1-8) 203
20. A World Under Judgment (Revelation 6:8) 217
21. The Saints Above (Revelation 6:9-11) 227
22. The Wrath of the Lamb (Revelation 6:12-17) 237
23. The Seal on the Forehead (Revelation 7:1-3) 247
24. The 144,000 (Revelation 7:4-8) 257
25. The Great Tribulation (Revelation 7:9-14) 267
26. The Great Reversal (Revelation 7:15-17) 279
27. The Silence in Heaven (Revelation 8:1-5) 287
28. The Seven Trumpets (Revelation 8:6) 297
29. Hail and Fire (Revelation 8:7) 309
30. A Third of Blood and Water (Revelation 8:8-12) 319
31. Out of the Abyss (Revelation 8:13-9:12) 329
32. The 200 Million Troops (Revelation 9:12-21) 341
33. The Colossus (Revelation 10:1-6) 353
34. The Sweet and Bitter Scroll (Revelation 10:7-11) 363

1
Jesus Wins
(Revelation 1:1-8)

Beasts! Dragons! Ten-headed monsters! Forget your computer games! What more could you want than this? This is big! This is Revelation! But this is going to be hard. Because when it comes to interpreting the book of Revelation there are many different schools of thought, all of which claim to be right. There are Preterists, Historicists, Futurists and Idealists. There are the pre-tribulation, post-tribulation and mid-tribulation views. And to top it off we have the different millennial views: A-mill, Pre-mill and Post-mill. In fact, you might want to pulp-mill the whole thing after you see how Christians are divided over these issues!

Isn't it ironic that a book called 'Revelation' (*revealing*) is a book that seems so hard to understand and causes so much debate over what might be hidden in its prophecy? The first words of the book are 'The revelation'! But is it a revelation or a frustration?

There are devout Christians throughout the ages who have held to all the four major interpretations as well as other variations. Perhaps the Lord put this book at the end to test us not so much on whether we have the right view, but how we handle something the Lord values more highly—unity.

> Make every effort to keep the unity of the Spirit through the bond of peace (Eph. 4:3).
>
> By this everyone will know that you are my disciples, if you love one another (John 13:35).
>
> Accept the one whose faith is weak, without quarrelling over disputable matters (Rom. 14:1).

Love for one another is placed higher on God's agenda for his people than whether we have superior knowledge on *disputable matters*. But Christians have been anything but unified over this book.

So why write another book about Revelation when it has been the subject of so much division in the church? The more I studied the differing views of Revelation and the conflicts they have caused (some people have even used their view of Revelation as a test of whether you are a faithful Christian—or not!), the more I thought 'this is not worth it!' I have too much to do in the work of the gospel to be adding to disagreements among Christians. I'll just skip it! Is it worth causing possible contention and distracting us from the gospel? I was ready to shelve this work until something hit me in a fresh way. Right in the opening passage we read:

> Blessed is the one who reads aloud the words of this prophecy (1:3a).

Jesus gave this revelation and says those who read it will actually be **blessed!** Wow, how could I hold back a blessing from you, even if I only get you to read the book of Revelation? But wait! There's more.

> ... and blessed are those who hear it and take to heart what is written in it ... (1:3b).

You are even more blessed if you hear it and **take to heart what is written in it.** Do I want you to be blessed? Yes! Then let's get into this book! Right from the opening words this book says it's ...

> The revelation from Jesus Christ, which God gave him to show <u>his servants</u> what must soon take place (1:1).

Who are **his servants?** His people. Not just the super-theologians, but all his people! But how could it be a blessing to *all* his servants when they come up with different views? Could a child get anything out of it? American theologian Vern Poythress thinks a 12-year-old could. He told a story that has been repeated so many times in so many variations that I'm not sure of its origins, but it goes something like this: Some theological students saw a janitor reading the book of Revelation and thought they could help him, so they asked him if he understood it. He said, 'Yes.' Astonished they asked, 'Well, what does

Revelation mean?' And he replied, 'Jesus is gonna win!'[1]

The four major views of Revelation are so different, but they all have this central theme: *Jesus wins*. If you get that, you will know more than a whole lot of theologians who haven't figured this out yet.

Revelation is also filled with word pictures. It's good for children. It stimulates the imagination like no other book in the Bible. It is about Jesus, the conquering King. We are going to see that picture from the start, when Jesus' eyes are like a blazing fire and his face shines like the sun. Later in the book he is mounted on a white horse and coming with the armies of heaven. There are cosmic wars with beasts, demons, and all kinds of creatures. And we are going to peer into the very throne room of God himself. This book is amazing and has everything. It's a blessing to everyone who reads it! We can't lose! As Poythress says, the big picture is, 'Praise the Lord, cheer for the saints, detest the Beast and long for the final victory.'[2]

This is the most exciting book ever written! It starts by saying ... **The revelation from Jesus Christ** ... It's a *revelation*. It is unveiling and revealing things. Think about how the book of Daniel reveals to us spiritual powers behind the scenes of history that aren't visible to us. Or in Job, where we find it is Satan behind Job's catastrophes. In Daniel and Job, we see spiritual powers of darkness opposing God. Ephesians teaches there are invisible principalities and powers at work opposing God. We think it is a battle against people (flesh and blood), *but it's spiritual warfare*. We thought it was Judas who opposed Jesus, and it was, but Satan entered Judas. We thought it was Pilate and Herod who conspired against Jesus, and it was, but there was spiritual warfare behind that. Well, Revelation, like no other book, pulls back the curtain on this reality. We see what is going on behind the scenes. But there is also something else behind it. Someone above it! Far greater than all. Jesus! Jesus is not losing this battle. Jesus wins.

The apostle John is writing Revelation from prison on the Greek island of Patmos. I will argue later that the best evidence for the date of writing is during the reign of the Roman Emperor Domitian, from AD 81-96. Domitian was an Emperor who demanded people call him lord and god. What did that mean for Christians? Well, this book is written to strengthen them when they were under great

---

[1] Vern Poythress, *The Returning King*, P & R Publishing, 2000, p. 14
[2] Ibid, p. 13

persecution, when even their lives were on the line. The persecution against Christians had intensified by this time because Christianity was no longer considered to be a sect of Judaism. Now they were an illegal religion, so they were not only under persecution from the Jews, but also from the Roman Empire.

This is a letter to those Christians. And its message? Hold on! Don't give up! There is a bigger picture. Jesus is on the throne. He is reigning now, and he wins! Hold fast to your testimony! This is what the book of Revelation tells us. Even though it looks like evil is winning, Jesus is in control! He is reigning. But more than that. He has a plan. Jesus is coming back! So be ready.

But how is this relevant to *us now*, we who read and hear and take it to heart? We should see new revelations in here too. Revelations of Jesus, and Jesus himself *revealing* what the Father gave him.

And are we supposed to take Revelation literally? That's one of the big questions we are going to look at. What is to be taken literally and what is not? Here is your first test! When it says in the first verse God gave this revelation to show **what must soon take place,** do we take that literally? Did that have any meaning to those first readers? Did any of this really take place *soon* for them? Or is it all at least a couple of thousand years off? Are there things we should be able to see unfolding near to their time as well as ours?

The book itself says it's a **prophecy** (1:3), which means it is predicting things of the future. But it's also a letter to a specific people. Ancient letters had the writer's name at the start, followed by the recipients, rather than signing at the end of a letter. (They were obviously smarter than us, as we haven't figured out how illogical it is to fumble to the end of a letter to see who it's from.) So after the opening prologue, this letter starts with the writer ...

> John, To the seven churches in the province of Asia: Grace and peace to you from him who is, and who was, and who is to come, and from the seven spirits before his throne ... (1:4).

This verse tells us the letter is from **John,** and he is writing it **to the seven churches** in Asia Minor (western Turkey). So this letter must be relevant to these seven churches. The Book of Revelation was written to them. Also, the consensus among the early church fathers including Justin Martyr, Irenaeus, Clement of Alexandria, and

Tertullian is that the *John* writing this is John the apostle. Justin lived in Ephesus where John ministered, and he also lived among people who would remember John. Irenaeus was a disciple of Polycarp (Bishop of Smyrna) who was a *disciple* of John. And he says John the apostle wrote Revelation.

John doesn't even begin by saying John, an apostle, as Paul might. He doesn't have to. Everyone knows who he is! He is the last living apostle and it is unnecessary to identify himself any more than simply 'John'. Pardon the analogy, but when we say 'Elvis' we don't ask 'Elvis who?' Not if we have any culture about us.

John is writing to *the seven churches*. Is the number seven to be interpreted literally? Of course. But is he only referring to those churches? Is it only a blessing to them, or to all who read it? We will investigate that later as well. However, we can start with the knowledge that John is writing to Christians going through persecution. They are being challenged to remain faithful as witnesses and follow the example of their king ...

> ... and from Jesus Christ, who is the faithful witness, the firstborn from the dead, and the ruler of the kings of the earth ... (1:5).

This verse reminds the first readers that their King has gone before them as **the faithful witness** and conquered. In the original language, the Greek word for *witness* is similar to our English word *martyr*. Jesus is that faithful witness who gave his own life. He is also the beginning of a new creation as the **firstborn from the dead,** reminding all who faithfully follow him that they will also be raised from the dead. This verse also tells Christians that as they (including you) go through persecution, don't forget this one thing—Jesus is also **ruler over the kings of the earth!**

In Ephesians 1:21-22, we learn Jesus is head over everything for the Christian church. It doesn't simply say he is the King who will judge at the end of history, but that he reigns throughout history, *in this present age*. Jesus is Lord. He is the one who is calling the shots—now! This is what 1:5 says. Jesus is *ruler over the kings of the earth!* It is present tense. He rules them now! And Christians going through persecution don't forget this ... he rules over Emperor Domitian. When it looks like evil is winning ... hold fast! Your king still reigns.

Even today the church in many parts of the world is going through serious persecution. But what about us in the Western world? Our church is looking dilapidated. Persecution in the West? Nah, we don't have it. But in fact, the church in the West is being persecuted so subtly it's crumbling before our eyes and we can't even see it. Attacked by a far subtler enemy. Worldliness has walked right into the church and taken over. Later in this book of Revelation we will learn just how that has happened. But don't worry. Jesus' church will not fall. Jesus will keep her. Don't look to the left or to the right at the unfaithful—hold fast! Your king still reigns. Jesus wins! And that thought makes John burst into praise.

> To him who loves us and has <u>freed us from our sins by his blood</u> … (1:5d).

He **freed us.** How? **By his blood.** The cross! Praise God. Until you have believed in the cross you are not free. You are enslaved. Headed for the very judgment described in this book because your sin is still stuck to you. But if you have believed in the cross, you are now free to serve him. How?

> … and has made us to be <u>a kingdom and priests</u> to serve his God and Father—to him be glory and power for ever and ever! Amen (1:6).

This is a quote from the Old Testament (OT). Revelation relies a lot on the OT. John is a devout Jew. He knew his OT Scriptures. We need to know them as well if we are going to understand Revelation, because there are many references to it. The words *a kingdom of priests* mark a very famous turning point in the OT, where God addresses his people, Israel.

> Now if you obey me fully and keep my covenant, then out of all nations you will be my treasured possession. Although the whole earth is mine, you will be for me <u>a kingdom of priests</u> and a holy nation ... (Exod. 19:5-6).

God's plan way back at the Exodus was that his people would be a kingdom of priests. Now here in 1:6 John is saying something very similar to the churches—*you* are now **a kingdom and priests.** We will also explore this later.

But if Jesus is winning now, how come there is so much evil going on? How come it seems like Jesus is not winning in a lot of places?

Well, Revelation answers that too. We are going to learn that Revelation teaches no one gets away with anything! There is an end coming, and evil was not being ignored at all. Indeed, every deed will be examined.

> 'Look, he is coming with the clouds', and 'every eye will see him, even those who pierced him'; and all the peoples on earth 'will mourn because of him.' So shall it be! Amen (1:7).

Coming with the clouds is typical OT language for God coming in judgment. Revelation here is drawing on the book of Daniel.

> In my vision at night I looked, and there before me was one like a <u>son of man</u>, coming <u>with the clouds of heaven</u>. He approached the Ancient of Days and was led into his presence. He was given authority, glory and sovereign power; all nations and peoples of every language worshiped him (Dan. 7:13-14a).

Who was coming on the clouds in judgment in Daniel 7:13? One like the Son of man. It's Jesus! That's what 1:7 is saying. **Look he is coming with the clouds, and <u>every eye will see him, even those who pierced him</u>; and all the peoples of the earth will <u>mourn</u> because of him.** The *piercing* and *mourning* is also drawn from the OT, from the Book of Zechariah.

> 'And I will pour out on the house of David and the inhabitants of Jerusalem a spirit of grace and supplication. <u>They will look on me, the one they have pierced</u>, and they will <u>mourn for him</u> as one mourns for an only child, and grieve bitterly for him as one grieves for a firstborn son' (Zech. 12:10).

How can they *look on me, the one they have pierced?* In Zechariah it is God speaking! God will be pierced and mourned for as an only son? *Now* we know it is Jesus, God the Son, who was pierced. He is *coming with the clouds,* **and every eye will see him,** and *mourn because of him.*

Every eye will see. They will mourn. Not only those at the crucifixion, who rejected their own Messiah, but all those throughout history who have rejected the Son of God. Those who called him a mere man, a good man, a great teacher, or a prophet, but no more. Those who claimed to love him but continued to rule their own lives. They will mourn when they see him. They will *look!*

'Look, he is <u>coming with the clouds</u>,' and '<u>every eye will see him</u>,' (1:7a).

Look! There is that shock! The clouds of judgment. If you are old enough to remember the 9/11 terrorist attacks, when the Al Qaeda terrorists flew planes into the twin towers in New York City, it was quite surreal to watch it on television. Perhaps we have been conditioned by so many violent movies that it seemed hard to believe it was really happening. The United States was under attack! But it seemed like it was just some action movie. Yet the terrifying, gut-wrenching thing was—it *was* real! When 9/11 hit, wherever you were, whatever you were doing, you stopped and looked at the screen. It sent shockwaves throughout the world.

Even though only about 3000 people died out of seven billion on the planet, it affected every one of us. In fact, our lives haven't been the same since. You can't go through airports without that security check. The whole world has changed since that day. But compared to the twin towers, you ain't seen nothing yet! What is it going to be like when the *Lord comes on the clouds*? The shock! Can this be real? There is no escaping. How long before this happens? Whenever it is, it's a whole lot closer now than it was when John wrote this 2000 years ago, and this book is leading up to just that!

Every eye will see him. In 1:14 it says his eyes are like blazing fire. It's not just that every eye will see him, but he will see *you*. He will look right into your heart. This is how Jesus describes it:

> There will be signs in the sun, moon and stars. On the earth, nations will be in anguish and perplexity at the roaring and tossing of the sea. People will faint from terror, apprehensive of what is coming on the world, for the heavenly bodies will be shaken. At that time they will see the Son of Man coming in a cloud with power and great glory (Luke 21:25-27).

With the 9/11 terror attacks, the whole world was in shock. *Terror and perplexity* at our vulnerability. What kind of terror will be struck in your heart when you *look up* ... if you are not ready to meet him? The terror will be so great that men will faint. How many macho men do you know who faint from terror? How terrifying must it be when men *faint* from terror?

There is a close to history. This is Revelation! What we are introduced to here in the opening is just a taster of where we are headed. No matter how much it looks like evil is winning, Jesus wins.

He will bring every deed into judgment, including every hidden thing. And it might seem surreal like the twin towers collapsing, but it will be really happening. Every eye will see him. How will every eye see him from all parts of the world at the same time? We don't know, but …

> … as lightning that comes from the east is visible even in the west, so will be the coming of the Son of Man (Matt. 24:27).

If the creator of lightning can make it shoot across the sky from east to west, then he can make himself visible blazing across the sky and *every eye will see him* (1:7). So, *blessed are those who read this book and take it to heart* (1:3). Not just read it and hear it *but take it to heart*. There is an urgency about this. Jesus will return. Every eye will see him. Not just a couple of planes flying into buildings. The explosions. The collapse of buildings. But the whole world! *Every* eye. Terror! A fearful day for those who did not know him. It's described in more detail later in Revelation …

> Then the kings of the earth, the princes, the generals, the rich, the mighty, and everyone else, both slave and free, hid in caves and among the rocks of the mountains. They called to the mountains and the rocks, 'Fall on us and hide us from the face of him who sits on the throne and from the wrath of the Lamb! For the great day of their wrath has come, and who can withstand it?' (6:15-17).

Nowhere to run! Nowhere to hide! Look! On the clouds. Every eye will see. A day of terror. How will you survive? This is how. It's right here in the opening … *To him who loves us and has freed us from our sins by his blood* … (1:5b).

His blood represents his death on the cross. All who have repented of their sin and trusted in what Jesus has done on the cross to take that sin away are free. On Judgment Day he sees you as spotless. How? Judgement Day for your sin has already passed for you. When? At the cross. That's why you are free. Because God is just, and you can't be punished twice for the same crime. If your sin has already been punished on that cross you are free by the blood of Christ, and your perseverance in the faith will be worth it. That's the book of Revelation. Persevere in faith. Hold fast against evil, because in the end, Jesus wins.

The book of Revelation is also a warning. God is love. He sent his Son to save us. He took the harshest of all torture, the cross. But if you reject that pardon after so many warnings and say, 'No, he will not be my king, not over my life', then what happens? Then you must take the penalty yourself.

Revelation tells us it all happens so quickly. How would your life be different if you knew Jesus was coming back in one month? What would you change? What would you quickly want to get rid of, or start doing? Write that down. Be like the shrewd manager. Think about those things you are clinging to that you know you need to change. How do I speak to my spouse? Is there anyone I haven't forgiven from the heart? Any habits of the eyes you need to change, or covetousness? How much time will you spend in front of the TV, computer, and phone over the next month? Will you find time to pray and read your Bible? How am I serving Jesus in his church? Am I a part of Jesus' commission in discipling? Whatever you can write on that list might be reasons why you are not *taking this to heart* (1:3). And the time left might not be a month!

Surely you are not one of those scoffers, who say, 'When is this coming?' No, you say. But if you are holding something in the closet, if there is some deliberate sin on your list, then you are, in effect, a scoffer. 'He's not coming back yet, I've got time to change that later.' That is like the foolish virgins or the lazy steward. But God is not mocked. If you are not doing something about it now, it might not be any different when *every eye will see him!*

So here we are, at the start of Revelation. The scene is set. Jesus is revealing things. It's going to be a blessing to all who read it and take it to heart. It's going to make sense of what is going on in the world. It will give you reason to persevere in your struggles, your pain and trials. Whatever you are going through, your fight against temptation, heartache or loneliness, Jesus will show you *what* is happening, *why* it is happening, and what is *going* to happen. It's a prophecy. And the point of it all is this: in the end, Jesus wins. Are you with him or not?

'Look, he is coming with the clouds,' and 'every eye will see him, even those who pierced him'; and all peoples on earth 'will mourn because of him.' So shall it be! Amen (1:7).

Study Questions

1. How can people with different views of Revelation all be blessed?

2. Who was Revelation written to and for what purpose?

3. What ways could you defend the deity of Christ from 1:1-8?

4. From the description of Jesus in 1:5, name four characteristics that should encourage readers in their walk both in the first century and today.

5. Rev. 1:5 says you are freed from your sins. In what way are you freed and what are you free to do?

6. What is the significance of 1:6 calling the readers 'a kingdom and priests'?

7. Will knowledge of the OT be of significance in understanding the book of Revelation? Why?

8. How can every eye see Jesus on his return when our planet is a sphere?

9. What things would you change if you knew Jesus was coming back in one month?

2
The First and the Last
(Revelation 1:9-18)

When John was writing Revelation, the Roman Emperor was Domitian. He was regarded as a ruthless ruler, tyrannical according to his own Senate. The Roman historian Suetonius says Domitian, unlike his predecessors, demanded he be addressed as *dominus et deus* (master or lord and god).[3] This might be why there was such intense persecution of Christians under Domitian. Christians would be required, like others, to call the emperor lord and god. And if they didn't? Well, John wouldn't do it. So here he is, in a prison on the island of Patmos, and the reason is given ...

> I, John, your brother and companion in the suffering and kingdom and patient endurance that are ours in Jesus, was on the island of Patmos <u>because of the word of God and the testimony of Jesus</u> (1:9).

John, an old man now, is imprisoned in a cave on **the island of Patmos.** He has outlived all the other apostles. Today Patmos is a small island with a population of about 3000. But in John's day it was more like an Alcatraz, a small prison island. It has a rocky shoreline, and there was no possibility of escape by swimming anywhere. Patmos is about 60 miles (100kms) off the coast of Turkey.

John had testified about Jesus throughout his life. It's now late in the first century, in the AD 90s. When John first met Jesus, he was only a young man. He was the disciple whom Jesus loved. He laid his head on Jesus' chest at the last supper. How do you picture John? Leonardo DaVinci's *Last Supper* portrays him as an effeminate fellow, which the book *The DaVinci Code* picked up on, suggesting he was really a woman. Perhaps you picture John with his head lying on

---

[3] Suetonius, *The Lives of the Caesars*, Book 8: *Domitian* 13

Jesus' chest, and you think 'there's a nice young fellow'. But when John left his fishing business to follow Jesus, he was an aggressive young man. When the people of a Samaritan village wouldn't welcome Jesus, what do you think the reaction was from this 'nice young man' John, and his brother James?

> ... but the people there did not welcome him, because he was heading for Jerusalem. When the disciples James and John saw this, they asked, 'Lord, do you want us to call fire down from heaven to <u>destroy them</u>?' But Jesus turned and rebuked them ... (Luke 9:53-55).

John's loving Christian reaction to these people who wouldn't welcome Jesus was — "Smoke 'em Lord!" Burn them alive! Let's get them! This is John. Is it any wonder Jesus nicknamed John and his brother James the 'sons of thunder'? This is John, the proud, aggressive young man. Remember it was John and his brother who came with their mother to request they could sit one on the right and one on the left, when Jesus came into his kingdom. John wanted to be up there, exalted! And what was Jesus' reply to him? 'Can you drink the cup that I will drink?' 'Yes, we can drink it.' 'Yes, you will drink it,' said Jesus.

And through the years, sure enough, John learned to drink the cup of his master. He learned the way of suffering. He learned humility rather than aggression. You see it in his other writings. He learned the way of love. It's John who records Jesus' words, 'By this everyone will know that you are my disciples, if you love one another' (John 13:35).

Jesus told John and his brother when they wanted to be in those exalted positions, 'Whoever wants to become great among you, must be your servant' (Matt. 20:26). The way of a servant, the way of suffering, was the cup the Lord would give John. Now here is John on Patmos, and instead of bravado and self-exalting, now he speaks to Christians about **patient endurance** and being a **companion in the suffering** in the face of persecution, and that these things **are ours in Jesus.**

Perhaps John reflected there in that cave, decades after Jesus told him, 'you will drink my cup', as he outlived and *out-suffered* his fellow apostles. He had been concerned about 'sitting above' them ... and now he *was* sitting above them, but Jesus' way! The way of suffering. Can you drink the cup John? Yes, he said. And he did. He lived longer to suffer longer than any of them.

Now, a much humbler John writes to encourage his younger fellow Christians to drink the 'cup of Jesus'. This is what Revelation is about. It's written to Christians facing persecution under Domitian, suffering for Jesus as a *companion in the suffering and kingdom and patient endurance that are ours in Jesus*. What is ours in Jesus? John is saying, 'Fellow Christians, we've got the kingdom, we've got the king of the kingdom who gave his life for us, and we've got forgiveness.' That's great John. But what else have we got in the kingdom? An added extra bonus feature. We've got *suffering!* Are you jumping for joy over that one? Because that's also what we've got. And we've got *patient endurance*. Suffering and patient endurance. Christian, are you listening to this, says John? You want the kingdom, you love Jesus, and you want all the beauty of that kingdom. Have you been feeling sorry for yourself? Why do I have to go through all this suffering and endurance? Well, John says, 'I'm your companion. If you will come with me in Jesus' kingdom, you will have to suffer.' Do you really want *all* you get in the kingdom? Do you really want *all* of what you have in Jesus?

Don't listen to those false teachers who tell you, 'Come to Jesus and it will be easy.' If you want to be John's companion it's going to take *suffering* and *patient endurance*. Have you been thinking there is something wrong with you because you've been suffering? Others don't seem to go through what you do? But you don't know their private lives. Finish the race. Don't give up. John says he is your companion—*in the suffering and kingdom and patient endurance that are ours in Jesus.*

But how will we have to suffer? That's why it helps to read the letters to the churches in Rev. 2-3. We suffer by being faithful in our witness, by not giving in to compromise. Easy? Not so easy! How much of the world has crept into your life? Are you looking 'out there' for the martyr's stake? Suffering is right in front of you. In the home, at school, at work, in your church, or in your mind! Not giving up, not going the world's way is tough!

When we maintain a faithful witness, and are attacked by the powers of evil, false teaching, or temptation, enduring is conquering. And if you stand for Jesus, you will be isolated. You might even find yourself on the island of Patmos *because of the word of God and the testimony of Jesus.* It's a two-hour sailing trip from Patmos to the neighboring island of Samos. You can't swim out from there. They put John in a cave. That's where he was when Jesus gave him this *Revelation*. Want to know what this *revelation* is all about? Being in the kingdom means *suffering* and *patient endurance!* Losing is winning. Conquering is testifying to Jesus through your trial and pain. Jesus is conquering to the ends of the earth. He is winning and will win in the end. But you have to get through next week … in your home, or at work! Revelation will answer that, but first John says 'listen to me fellow companions' …

> On the Lord's Day I was in the Spirit, and I heard behind me a loud voice like a trumpet, … (1:10).

The Lord's Day. When John was a boy, the Lord's Day according to the OT Scriptures was a *Saturday* Sabbath. But since the Lord rose from the dead Christians began to meet on his resurrection day (Acts 20:7, 1 Cor. 16:1-2), which John here calls the Lord's Day (1:10). It's the first day of the week, which is Sunday. The first day of the week was when the disciples first saw Jesus raised. Then Jesus appeared again to the disciples exactly one week later, on the Lord's Day, in the morning and evening. Then the Holy Spirit came on the day of Pentecost. He came down in power when? Pentecost was on the Lord's Day (Sunday, the first day of the week). This is why Christians set aside Sunday for worship. So here is John, worshiping Jesus, in a cave, on the Lord's Day.

Now immediately John anticipates a message from God because he says **I heard behind me a loud voice like a trumpet.** In the OT when there was a great pronouncement they got the trumpets out. But John thinks, wait, this is a voice. A loud voice! How loud? Like a trumpet! When John was worshiping in that cave he might have been thinking of his fellow Christians in those churches (many scholars believe John ministered in Ephesus and the surrounding areas), and how they were holding up under the strains of persecution. Perhaps he was praying for them. We know John's greatest joy in his salvation was to see his children walking in truth (3 John 1:4). But while he was worshiping, he would have got a shock as he heard this great voice. Like a trumpet!

> ... which said: 'Write on a scroll what you see and send it to the seven churches: to Ephesus, Smyrna, Pergamum, Thyatira, Sardis, Philadelphia and Laodicea' (1:11).

John knows the selection of these churches is not coincidence. These were the churches in that area of Ephesus where he had been their Pastor. He knew them well. And John immediately recognizes the order of the churches because he knows the geography of the area. If you see them on a map in Asia Minor they follow in a line. A circuit. If John writes to these seven churches as instructed, the order would make it possible for the postman to deliver them all in a row.

But in the midst of this encounter John is still wondering, who is this telling me to write? Dare he look around at a voice so loud and powerful, like a trumpet? Torn between finding the courage to look and being compelled to look John says ...

> I turned around to see the voice that was speaking to me. And when I turned I saw seven golden lampstands, ... (1:12).

Immediately these sights would have been familiar to John from when he was a boy schooled in the OT Scriptures. **Seven golden lampstands.** He would understand the connection. The OT temple! This was like the rebuilt temple mentioned in Zechariah.

> He asked me, 'What do you see?' I answered, 'I see a solid <u>gold</u> lampstand with a bowl at the top and <u>seven</u> lamps on it, with <u>seven</u> channels to the lamps' (Zech. 4:2).

Then John sees someone in the midst of those lampstands ...

> ... and among the lampstands was someone like a son of man... (1:13a).

John immediately connects this with the **son of man** from the book of Daniel 7:13-14. There the *son of man* comes with the clouds and approaches the Ancient of Days. But there is more to connect this son of man with Daniel ...

> ... dressed in a robe reaching down to his feet and with a <u>golden sash</u> around his chest. His head and hair were white like wool, as white as snow, and his <u>eyes were like blazing fire</u>. His feet were like <u>bronze glowing in a furnace</u>, and his <u>voice was like the sound of rushing waters</u> (1:13b-15).

John would be wondering where he has seen this kind of garb before. Look at the sash around his waist. It is like what the high priest was required to wear, but it's golden. This is greater than the high priest. John would recognize this as coming from the book of Daniel. It was one of his favorites he studied as a young Jewish boy in Sunday school (sorry, Saturday school). At least Daniel is one of Revelation's favorites ...

> I looked up and there before me was a man dressed in linen, with a <u>belt of fine gold from Uphaz around his waist</u>. His body was like topaz, his face like lightning, his <u>eyes like flaming torches</u>, his arms and legs like the <u>gleam</u> of <u>burnished bronze</u>, and his <u>voice</u> like the <u>sound</u> of a multitude (Dan. 10:5-6).

Now John realizes this same figure from Daniel is right before his eyes. And just like Daniel's figure, his ...

> ... <u>eyes were like blazing fire</u>. ... His <u>feet were like bronze glowing</u> in a furnace, and his voice was like the sound of rushing waters (1:14-15).

A voice like the sound of rushing waters? John would have recognized two great OT pictures from Ezekiel's vision of God.

> When the creatures moved, I heard the sound of their wings, like the roar of <u>rushing waters</u>, like the <u>voice of the Almighty</u>, ... (Ezek. 1:24).

A voice like the sound of rushing waters? That's the way John could best describe the voice he now hears (1:15). It wasn't just the similarity to Ezekiel for John. He was well familiar with the sound of rushing waters crashing against the shore while living in his little prison cave there on Patmos. But this is a voice!

In fact, in this there is so much brilliance that these precious metals, fiery eyes, and a face shining like the sun are only trying to describe in human terms the indescribable. **Eyes like blazing fire,** that is, eyes that can look right into your heart! **Bronze glowing** in a furnace. And his **head and hair were white like wool, as white as snow.** Again, John remembers ...

> As I looked, 'thrones were set in place, and the Ancient of Days took his seat. His clothing was as white as snow; <u>the hair of his head was white like wool</u> (Dan. 7:9).

The Ancient of Days takes his throne and his *hair is white like wool*. Daniel's vision is of God himself on his throne. Now the son of man in John's vision has hair like the Ancient of Days. And that's not all.

> In his right hand he held seven stars, and coming out of his mouth was a sharp double-edged sword (1:16).

Roman soldiers had a short, tongue-like sword, but John recognizes this sharp double-edged sword as God's judgment sword. Again, John remembers his OT Scriptures ...

> ... He will strike the earth with the rod of his mouth ... (Isa. 11:4).

Isaiah is referring to God as judge! But wait! John is seeing these features in the son of man. *He* is Judge. The Ancient of Days has the white hair, stately and from eternity. But now these are attributed to the son of man. Daniel's prophecy had laid out four kingdoms. Daniel was seeing a vision of the future when a king, a human being, one like a son of man, would come after the kingdoms of Babylon, Medes and Persians, Greece, and the Romans. This new kingdom would last forever. This king will have all authority and power over all peoples. This one like the son of man from the book of Daniel (7:13-14), who was given all authority, is now before John's eyes. *It's him*. It's now. He's here! The King of the kingdom!

But how can this king, this 'son of man', have attributes of the Ancient of Days—God the Father—when he is the 'son of man'? Then John remembers the words of Jesus that John wrote in his gospel, when the apostles were gathered together in the upper room and Philip asked that question.

> Philip said, 'Lord, show us the Father and that will be enough for us.' Jesus answered: 'Don't you know me, Philip, even after I have been among you such a long time? Anyone who has seen me has seen the Father. ...' (John 14:8-9).

The enigma of the Trinity: Father, Son and Holy Spirit, all one God and yet three distinct persons. Separate persons and yet so close they are one essence. But wait, this means the son of man, the Son of God is ... God. This is the LORD Almighty described from Daniel! The One coming with the clouds of heaven (1:7). Every eye will see him!

So in response John says …

> When I saw him, I fell at his feet as though dead. Then he placed his right hand on me and said: 'Do not be afraid. I am the First and the Last' (1:17).

Again, with John's OT knowledge he recognizes those words …

> 'This is what the LORD says—Israel's King and Redeemer, the LORD Almighty: I am the first and I am the last; apart from me there is no God' (Isa. 44:6).

No wonder the Jehovah's Witnesses (JWs) don't appear for about another 2000 years. If Christians knew their Scriptures, they would see this is one of those classic texts the JWs can't handle because they deny Jesus' deity. But here Jesus says **I am the First and the Last.** There is no other God! A clear reference to the only eternal God. Ask the JW who is the First and the Last in 1:17 and they usually say it must be God the Father, Jehovah. But we must ask, but when did Jehovah ever die? Look at the next verse!

> I am the Living One; I was dead, and now look, I am alive for ever and ever! And I hold the keys of death and Hades (1:18).

It's Jesus! Jesus is the Savior, Lord and God! Jesus is the *son of man* from this vision. And he is right before John in all his glory! The First and the Last! He is the glorious Son of God! And he has the keys … **And I hold the keys of death and Hades.** He has the very keys of death and the grave. How? He has overcome death for us. He was dead and is now alive forever. Have you ever heard anyone say they have encountered and seen Jesus? 'Yes, Jesus and I had a chat at my bedside and I told him a few things.' Is that the same glorified Jesus whom John encountered? When John (the disciple whom Jesus loved, the one who was a more intimate friend than perhaps anyone on earth) sees Jesus in glory, he falls at his feet as though dead. That's a real encounter with Jesus.

So which Jesus do you believe in? The First and Last? God? When we worship, which Jesus are you worshiping? Think about how Jesus is worshiped today. The way we speak about him. My buddy? My mate? The way we sing about him. Is it the same Jesus whom John is describing here? We won't see Jesus with a literal sword coming out of his mouth any more than as a lamb (as he is described later). But you will literally see him for what that sword stands for. You will see he is the Judge of the universe, the Lord of glory, so terrifying in all his glory that John is on his face in fear. Yet he is the same Comforter, the same friend, yes, he is indeed all those things. But you can only really appreciate those aspects of his character when you have entered into this. The God and Judge of the universe is the same One who says these beautiful words, **'Do not be afraid.'** They are the words Jesus uttered to reassure John that he need not fear. Jesus is with him always. Look at the same words he will say later …

> These are the words of him who is <u>the First and the Last</u>, who died and came to life again … <u>Do not be afraid of what you are about to suffer</u>, … (2:8,10).

Do not be afraid of suffering in this world. I am the God who is the First and the Last! I suffered before you. I went through death, but behold, I'm alive! You don't have to be afraid. I've got the keys over even death itself. If only we can just grasp this reality with John! If only we can experience this! Pray you can live here in this by faith. We can't see it now, but with the veil lifted to expose the reality, John saw this. Jesus is alive, and we will see him in all his glory. He is living and marching towards the end of the earth, and he is going to close history. We will see Jesus as the Judge of the universe. And just as John saw, we will also want to fall at his feet as though dead. We will fall down, because every knee will bow and every tongue will confess. He is the one who went through that very personal love on the cross, when he took our sins personally in his body when he became sin for us. He became us at our worst on that cross. And he knows you so intimately, also what you are going through right now. He puts his right hand on you and says, 'Do not be afraid. I have overcome. I have got the keys! If I can beat death and hell, don't you think I can beat what you are going through right now? Do not be afraid of what you are suffering.'

We need to live with our eyes on our destination—Jesus. Our destination is not whether we are successful. It is not whether we are meant to be happy all the time, or whether we are meant to have the perfect relationships, health, the right job, or enough money and pleasure. No. This is the goal! Destination—Jesus! We will meet the glorified Jesus. Just like John, we will hear his voice …

> Do not be amazed at this, for a time is coming when all who are in their graves will hear his voice and come out—those who have done good will rise to live, and those who have done evil will rise to be condemned (John 5:28-29).

John's experience will be our experience. John's vision will become our reality. We will hear Jesus' voice and rise. We will come out of the grave! We will all see what John saw in vision. The glorified King with eyes of fire and a face shining like the sun.

This is where history is headed. This is where your life is headed. For some, when they see the risen Jesus it will be like John's experience, awesome and yet exhilarating, as he places his hand on you. 'Get up. Don't be afraid. It is I. The living one.' But for many others it will be a terrifying day that will only continue in shock and terror as those eyes like blazing fire pierce the heart and expose that you never really knew him. You never really walked with him.

So, who will be rejoicing? John's companions. Companions in Jesus' kingdom. Cleansed by their King of the kingdom. Companions who trusted in what he had done at the cross and repented of their sin. Also companions of John in what? *I, John, your brother and <u>companion in the suffering</u> and kingdom <u>and patient endurance</u> that are <u>ours in Jesus</u>, ...*

Those who suffered and endured. Those who wouldn't give in to the lusts and pleasures of this world. Those who continued through patient endurance, forgiving those who hurt them, but didn't give up walking with Jesus. Those who when they had fallen into sin didn't just say, 'Oh well, we are all sinners.' Instead, they came back again confessing and repenting to this Savior, then went on suffering and enduring. Those who suffered, not in the same way as John did on the island of Patmos, but with their own difficulties, whether it be with sickness, loneliness, harassment, bullying, or difficult people in their lives. Those who endured despite temptation in the face of these things with patient endurance. Those who put up with persecution in the home or in the workplace because they stood for Jesus. Those who found their sufficiency in Jesus. Theirs is the kingdom! *They* are John's companions! And they will see this.

When I saw him, I fell at his feet as though dead. Then he placed his right hand on me and said: 'Do not be afraid. I am the First and the Last. I am the Living One; I was dead, and now look, I am alive for ever and ever! And I hold the keys of death and Hades' (1:17-18).

REVELATION 1:9-18

Study Questions

1. What difference do we see in the character of the apostle John from when he was first called by Jesus in the gospels?

2. How does John empathize with those to whom he is writing?

3. If all Christians suffer and have to endure, how might this differ for us from the way John suffered and how might it be similar?

4. Why does John highlight that it is the *Lord's Day* and what is its significance and origin?

5. Is there any significance to the order of the churches John is given?

6. If John is to correctly interpret the features of the 'son of man' vision, which book(s) of the OT will he need?

7. How would you explain to a JW from this text that Jesus is God?

8. How could this text shape the way you worship Jesus?

9. How could encountering the Jesus of this text shape your trust in him?

10. Compare your destination to face Jesus with your earthly goals. Are they compatible?

3
The Seven Lampstands
(Revelation 1:19-20)

What happened to the apostle John when he saw Jesus in his glory? Did he go up and shake Jesus' hand? Give him a 'high five'? No. He was awestruck. He was on his face. It wasn't 'Jesus is my buddy'. Even the disciple whom Jesus loved was on his face in fear and terror in the presence of the risen Lord in all his glory.

Yet John also experiences that this Lord Almighty is the same compassionate friend he remembers. Jesus places his right hand on him and says, 'Do not be afraid' (1:17). The Lord who is the First and the Last, God himself in the person of the eternal Son, comforts John. That means it is God who tells John to 'write' this text of Revelation.

How do you know the Bible is God's word and specifically the book of Revelation? One answer: God came in person and told us. It is Jesus who tells John to ...

> Write, therefore, what you have seen, what is now and what will take place later (1:19).

This is God who is telling John to write down **what you have seen** (in the Rev. 1 vision), **what is now** (what is going on *now* in John's time in the letters to the churches in Rev. 2-3) and **what will take place later** (in what follows in Rev. 4 revealing the future from John's time).

But it's complex and hard to understand because it's filled with strange imagery. Look at the vision in Rev. 1. The son of man is dressed in all kinds of shining brilliance: face, clothes, white hair, and a sword coming out of his mouth. How can we understand it? How did John understand it? Remember John is an old man now, and like all of us, when we get older the memory starts to fade. It will be the times of youth we remember best. A big part of John's youth would have been spent in the synagogue studying the Torah, the prophets and the Psalms. So, by standing in John's shoes with his Jewish OT background, we could figure out the sword represented the judgment authority of God. His strange appearance and the clothes he was wearing we could see was like the son of man and Ancient of Days in the book of Daniel, which related to priestly and kingly garb.

However, unlike the other symbols, this mystery of the golden lampstands must be important because it is directly explained to us. Why is this mystery so significant that it gets an explanation? It's because if we understand this mystery, it will give us a clue to understanding much of the book of Revelation and understanding history itself.

When John saw the imagery of the lampstands, he thought of the temple with its lampstand and seven lamps. But what exactly do the seven stars and seven golden lampstands represent? It was the lampstands that John first saw when he turned around (1:12). What are they? A mystery in biblical language is something previously hidden now revealed. Now Rev. 1 finishes with Jesus revealing to John the meaning of these lampstands.

> The mystery of the seven stars that you saw in my right hand and of the seven golden lampstands is this: The seven stars are the angels of the seven churches, and the seven lampstands are the seven churches (1:20).

Rev. 1:12 said the son of man is *in* the midst of what? The lampstands! What are the **seven golden lampstands? The seven churches!** *Jesus is in the midst of his church!* Even individual churches. That is how Jesus identifies himself when he begins the first of the seven letters to the seven churches ...

> To the angel of the church in Ephesus write: These are the words of him who holds the seven stars in his right hand and <u>walks among the seven golden lampstands</u> ... (2:1).

He walks among his churches! We are told the seven stars are angels of the churches. The word for *angels* in the original Greek language can also mean *messengers*. Some say it could mean the pastors of those churches, that is, earthly messengers, and that's possible. But 67 out of 67 times in Revelation the word *angel* refers to *heavenly angels*. So, the angels are representatives of these churches (either earthly pastors, or more likely, angels above). Either way, Jesus holds *them* in his hand! He holds the church representatives above in heaven and he is in her midst on earth.

The seven lampstands are the seven churches and they are to be a light to the world. The OT temple had a single lampstand with seven lamps. In the tabernacle there was one lampstand with seven lamps. But in Christ, the church is shining a light in the world and spreading. Unlike Israel, one visibly united nation, here are seven separate lampstands. The churches are spreading. Just as the glory of the Lord dwelt in the temple with the one lampstand and seven lamps, the Lord *himself* dwells among these seven lampstands—his churches!

This is the mystery revealed. But why seven churches? Do we take that number literally? It must be literal because the Lord tells John to write this to seven literal churches (1:11). And what follows in Rev. 2-3 are seven letters to those seven literal, historical churches of John's time. Why these seven churches? There were other important churches in the same area which are not mentioned, such as the Colossian and Hierapolis churches. But only seven are mentioned. Is this number *seven* conveying something beyond just those literal seven churches? With John having been trained from a young age in the OT Scriptures, he would see the significance. Seven is the biblical number of completeness. Seven days made up the creation week. Seven days make up our normal, complete week. In the OT, seven is the number of times required for sprinkling in cleansing rituals. Seven thus brings completeness in cleansing. Complete punishments were seven times. So *seven* is the number of completeness in the Bible.

> And the words of the LORD are flawless, like silver purified in a crucible, like gold refined <u>seven times</u> (Ps. 12:6).

> <u>Seven times</u> a day I praise you for your righteous laws (Ps. 119:164).

The number *seven* occurs 54 times in Revelation. Seven churches, seven lampstands, seven stars, seven angels, and seven spirits of God. Do seven spirits of God (1:4) mean we fall four spirits short in the Trinity? No. It's just that seven signifies the completeness that represents the Holy Spirit. Seven spirits of God equal God's complete Spirit. Later we will come across seven seals, a lamb with seven eyes and seven horns, seven angels blowing seven trumpets, seven angels dispensing the contents of seven bowls full of the final seven plagues, seven thunders of voices, seven mountains, seven kings, and a beast from the sea which has seven heads. Are you getting this yet? Seven is the number of completeness and fullness. 'Sprinkle the blood seven times,' the priests were told in the OT. Did they literally have to sprinkle the blood seven times? Yes! But it was symbolizing something more than just a literal seven times. It symbolized completeness.

So when Jesus says so powerfully in 2:1 that *he is the one who walks among the seven golden lampstands* (the seven churches), he is saying that what is true of those literal seven churches is also true of his complete church. The seven lampstands represent the entire church of Jesus. This means that when he addressed this book to the seven churches (1:4), it was also to his complete church. As if to underline this, at the end of the letters to the individual churches in Rev. 2-3 we read this little formula: *Whoever has ears, let them hear what the Spirit says to the churches* … that is, *churches* plural. So it's not just a message for that individual church, but for *all* the churches. The same formula is used at the end of the letter to Ephesus (2:7), Smyrna (2:11) and Pergamum (2:17). So the letters are to seven literal churches, but they are also to the wider church.

So the mystery is revealed! Jesus is in the *midst* of his churches! Individually, and all his wider church! So what follows in the letters to the churches speaks specifically to these historical churches, but also speaks into all in the church in the future and is a blessing to all who read it (1:3).

So, the first mystery of Revelation is solved. Jesus holds the church representatives in his hand above and walks among the churches below. This is where Revelation is headed. As it unfolds, we will see a cosmic war between the powers of darkness and Jesus' church. The good news is that *Jesus is in the midst of his church during this*. This is the reassurance, that although his church will suffer, Jesus wins. Why? Because he is among his churches. Because he is with us!

So Jesus is in the midst of his suffering church in John's day, under persecution from Emperor Domitian. But does this have relevance for today? In the Western world, we just don't experience that kind of persecution. But in many countries persecution is part of Christian life *and death!* So we need this mystery revealed as much as ever. Is Jesus really with his church? Where was Jesus during the bleak Middle Ages? Was the book of Revelation for them? Was Jesus in the midst of his lampstands then? The lampstands were burning low indeed. The Roman Catholic stronghold even withheld the Bible from the people and put it on the list of forbidden books officially in AD 1229. Was Jesus in the midst of his lampstands then? Were there no believers while the gospel of grace was suppressed? Did the gates of hell prevail against Jesus' church?

A little church history lesson might help. The Lord had his people, individuals and movements during that time. For example, have you heard of the Waldensians? They were not known by that name originally. This group of devout Christians was founded by a man called Valdes in about 1170 (later known as Peter Waldo). The Waldensians preached faith in the atoning work of Christ and stood against the unbiblical doctrines of Rome. The Waldensians proclaimed *there must be a preaching of the word of God.* Valdes even had the NT translated into the language of the people back in the 1100s. This bright light was being shone in one of the darkest periods of the church over 350 years before the Reformation. The Waldensians were brutally persecuted. Revelation was *also* written for them. Jesus was in the midst of his lampstands even when the lamps were burning at their lowest.

We will learn in the letters which follow that Jesus is not always happy with his churches, even bringing a rod to his church. Indeed, that is what happened at the Reformation. Finally, the sword that comes out of Jesus' mouth cracked like a whip across his church in the world and split her right down the middle—hence the Reformation in the 1500s. Jesus is in the midst of his lampstands! French philosopher Voltaire (1694-1778) said the church would not last. Even recently one commentator wrote in a newspaper that the church would be 'dead within 50 years'. I felt like writing in reply, 'No, you will be dead in 50 years, but the church will never die because Jesus is in the midst of his lampstands!'

The unbelieving world sees the failings of the church with a critical eye, and these seven letters to the seven churches tell us Jesus also sees her failings, and he is more grieved than anyone. But he never gives up on his church. He gave himself up for his bride and he will see her through to the wedding banquet.

But Jesus being in the midst of the lampstands is bigger than just the survival of the church. What does that mean to you now, Christian? It means that when you gather with fellow believers at your local church that *Jesus is there!* In the OT sanctuary the glory cloud signified the presence of God. Do you think all that OT stuff was just for show? The same Lord still meets his people. He's in their midst now.

This also gives perspective to Jesus' words, *'For where two or three gather in my name, there am I with them'* (Matt. 18:20). This promise of Jesus is in the context of the church carrying out church discipline. Because of that some have said this promise of Jesus must apply *only* when the church is involved in discipline.[4] But would that mean that as soon as the elders change from praying or discussing church discipline to other areas of ministry that Jesus leaves the building? We can answer that by letting Scripture interpret Scripture. Rev. 1:12-13 and 2:1 can interpret Matthew 18:20 for us. Jesus is among his people. That is his promise. He is not *limited* to church discipline, but rather the point of Matthew 18:20 is that *even* in a situation of church discipline, *even* in that painful, difficult process, *he is still there. Even* when you are down to only two or three elders to carry it out, it's okay … Jesus is among you. Why? Because Jesus is always among his lampstands.

So what does this mean for people who fall away from the church, or who don't attend regularly? Are they just drifting away from church life? No, it's really Jesus they are drifting away from. When they leave the fellowship of a local church, they are not just leaving some institution set up by man. They are leaving Christ. They are walking away from Jesus, who is among his lampstands. Being part of the church is more than some theoretical, 'I am a believer, so I belong to the wider church anyway.' Rev. 2-3 shows real people attached to real local congregations (lampstands), where God's people gather, and Jesus meets with them. This was John's point when he wrote in his first epistle about those who left the church …

---

[4] John MacArthur, *The John MacArthur Study Bible*, Word Publishing, 1997, p.1426

> They went out from us, but they did not really belong to us. For if they had belonged to us, they would have remained with us; but their going showed that none of them belonged to us (1 John 2:19).

Leaving the church is leaving Jesus. What did Jesus die for?

> ... Christ loved the church and gave himself up for her ... (Eph. 5:25).

Jesus died for the church! The lampstands! His great desire was to give himself up not just for individuals, but also for a people. The Lord said through Moses, 'Let my people go so that they may worship me.' But come on Moses, why couldn't your people worship where they were? They were called out as a people, to gather together. The plan of Jesus who hung on that cross was to gather a people to be a kingdom of priests, a people called out who would worship him together, and then in heaven forever. We will get to that in Rev. 19. A great multitude.

The goal of the cross is Rev. 21, the new heaven and new earth, where the church will all be gathered together. Heaven is all about Jesus in the midst of the seven lampstands, that is, his complete church forever. For now, we can't all gather together because we are scattered throughout the world, but we seek to do *your will on earth as it is in heaven* by worshiping together. We are seven golden lampstands branching out. But we have this mystery unfolded. The same *son of man* is walking in the midst of his lampstands until we are all gathered together one day. This is the foretaste of that day. The apostle Paul said ...

> Don't you know that you yourselves are God's temple and that God's Spirit dwells in your midst (1 Cor. 3:16)?

The Holy Spirit dwells within each Christian, but that is not what Paul is talking about to the Corinthians. When Paul said *God's Spirit dwells in your midst*, in the original Greek language the word *your* is plural, meaning the *whole church*. The word *midst* is not in the original. So Paul literally says the Spirit is in *you, church* at Corinth! How? Jesus is there! By his Spirit, Jesus is among you, as he is with all his lampstands. Our fellowship and closeness as a church family is not restricted to Sunday worship, but it's no coincidence that John is having this vision on the Lord's Day. The day Jesus rose. Hence, we gather together. If you really are a Christian, this day of meeting together will mean so much to you. This is where we meet with Jesus on his day. To worship him!

Have you seen by faith what Jesus died for? It's his church! (Eph. 5:25). Some treat the church like a supermarket where you get stuff. Do you understand that church is not about you and what you get out of it? Have you seen how Jesus died and rose and longs to meet with his people, and for them to be one, worshiping *him!* I've noticed that those who struggle the most spiritually are often those who find it difficult to regularly attend church worship. It's crucial we are fed on the word of God preached, but that is not the most important reason. You could stay at home and listen to *Sermon Audio*. Some go to church to feel uplifted in singing his praises. But what if you don't get anything out of it? Well, then you go to church for fellowship. But what if that doesn't help you?

None of these things come close to your greatest loss when you don't attend worship. The most important thing! You miss Jesus! Our primary reason for attending church services is to worship Jesus who is there! He is in the midst of his lampstands. He is everywhere of course, but he comes in his special presence into his lampstands! This is his heart and concern. His lampstands. This is where we commune with him! We take communion with him as well as with each other. Baptism is not just about 'me and my profession of faith', but a visible sign of the cleansing of Jesus that joins you to the church. That's why we don't do private baptisms (whenever possible). It defeats the whole purpose. Do you want to be where the action is with Jesus? Jesus is in the midst of his local churches!

New-agers say Jesus is just one of many great religious prophets and each person needs to develop their Christ-consciousness. Others say they have Jesus in their heart, so they don't need his church. But they all have a Jesus of their own making. The Jesus of history gave himself up for his church and he walks among his churches.

It comes down to this. Do you really love Jesus? Do you love what he loves? Do you love his church? He cares about her when she is weak and sinning. Do you? Or do you complain about Jesus' bride? She doesn't live up to what she should be? Get specific. Do you have a problem with *people* in the church? People in churches sin, so do you leave or distance yourself? But who are you distancing yourself from? Jesus! Whatever you did to the least of these brothers and sisters of mine you did it to me, said Jesus. He is in her midst. Not getting enough out of church? It's Jesus who is not enough for you. Some get so fed up with the church they leave her and say, 'I'm still a believer, but I have given up on the church.' If that ever happens to you, it's time to question not whether the church has failed you, but whether Jesus' lampstand been removed—*from you!* That can happen, as we will see in the following letters. The church is not as pure as it should be. People fail. There are even hypocrites in the church. As we delve into our seven churches we will see most of them have difficulties, and those difficulties mostly are the people. These lampstands are filled with sinners. But only those who are truly part of a lampstand are able to forgive and persevere with the church, because that is what Jesus does. He doesn't remove himself.

The lampstands have also been given a mission. They are not just to be together one day a week. The people are equipped and sent forth. We are part of Jesus' family, part of a mission together. What are we? *A lampstand!* We are meant to shine! You are sent forth into your workplace, school, home, and neighborhood to shine!

> Therefore go and make disciples of all nations, baptizing them in the name of the Father and of the Son and of the Holy Spirit, and teaching them to obey everything I have commanded you. And surely I am with you always, to the very end of the age (Matt. 28:19-20).

How is Jesus with us always? He is the *son of man* who is in the midst of his golden lampstands! This is the great commission. He is building a family. He could have just shouted his gospel down from heaven. Instead he uses people who are in his family to build a bigger family, and he goes with us.

So be part of the church and its mission. Get involved in Bible studies and discipling groups. Help with the work. Join prayer meetings. Be at your church every Lord's Day, not just because it makes you feel good or for the fellowship, not even just because he commands you, although he does that too (Heb. 10:25). Nor just because it feeds you and helps you, as it is meant to. None of these are the primary reason to be part of the church. The most important reason is that if you believe in Jesus, you will worship him and believe by faith that he is there! In the midst of his lampstands.

The mystery of the seven stars that you saw in my right hand and of the seven golden lampstands is this: The seven stars are the angels of the seven churches, and the seven lampstands are the seven churches (1:20).

Study Questions

1. Why might the symbols of the lamps and stars be explained in Rev. 1, but not all the other symbols?

2. How could we use 1:17-19 as an apologetic to defend the Bible as the word of God?

3. What are the three periods of time in 1:19 that John is to write?

4. What evidence is there that the number seven might mean more than seven literal churches?

5. Why is the mystery of the lampstands so significant for you, for worship, for the wider church?

6. Give an example of a group whose lampstand still shone in the Middle Ages. Give two distinctives of their beliefs.

7. What is the primary rule of interpretation of Scripture and how might that rule be applied to Matthew 18:20?

8. How could you respond to someone who says they believe in Jesus but don't attend a church?

9. How could you respond to someone who says they have given up on the church because hypocrites in the church have hurt them?

10. What does the church gathering and Jesus in her midst point towards in the future?

11. Give several reasons why Christians should be part of a local church. What is the most important one?

4
Ephesus
(Revelation 2:1-7)

Can God give a word to an individual church, there in the first century, and still be speaking beyond that into the future, even to us? Remember 1:3 says this book is a prophecy. This book is able to speak into the future because it is God himself who is speaking to individual churches and to us. And here is a crucial point. To understand the book of Revelation as a whole, we need to understand what was going on in these seven churches. I know you are hanging out for all the seals and bowls and beasts, and you could always skip all this boring stuff in these letters and go straight to Rev. 4. But the fact is, if you take the time to read these letters it will help you to understand the whole book of Revelation. And wait a minute! *All* Scripture is God breathed, so we just might get something out of these letters too!

John starts with a letter to the church at Ephesus.

> To the angel of the church in Ephesus write: These are the words of him who holds the seven stars in his right hand and walks among the seven golden lampstands: ... (2:1).

We learned in 1:13 that Jesus is the one who walks among the seven lampstands, which are the churches. At the time of writing, late in the first century, Ephesus was the largest and most important city in Asia Minor with a population of about 250,000. It was connected to major cities of Asia Minor by highways and was the first port of entry for someone going inland in Asia Minor to any of the other churches. So Ephesus would have naturally been the first church on the postman's route from Patmos, where John was writing from prison.

The church at Ephesus was an important one and central to the apostle Paul's mission. He used Ephesus as a base to preach into Asia

Minor. He also wrote a major letter to the Ephesians. Many scholars believe the apostle John also lived and ministered at Ephesus. Remember Ephesus from the book of Acts? Paul caused a riot there. It was a leading city in commerce, trade guilds and banking. Greek geographer and philosopher Strabo wrote in the first century that Ephesus was the largest commercial center in Asia Minor.

Ephesus was also a spiritual center. It was called the 'temple warden' of the great goddess Artemis (Roman 'Diana'). The temple was considered one of the seven wonders of the ancient world. Look up a photo of the Parthenon in Athens and see how tiny people are next to it. The temple of Artemis was *four* times larger than the Parthenon! It was the largest building in the Greek world. Paul was there for at least two years in the lecture hall of Tyrannus. Ephesus is where Timothy was when Paul wrote his two letters to Timothy.

The church at Ephesus was completely surrounded by a pagan culture. The city was also famous for magic and sorcery, so much so that the phrase 'Ephesian letter' was an ancient term for a magic formula. Some of these magic scrolls (Ephesian letters) have survived to this day and are held in London and Paris. But back in the first century, when God touched the hearts of people in Ephesus while Paul was preaching the gospel, not all these magic scrolls survived ...

> A number who had practiced sorcery brought their scrolls together and burned them publicly. When they calculated the value of the scrolls, the total came to fifty thousand drachmas (Acts 19:19).

This is what was happening when people were being converted. But not everyone was happy about those conversions because it affected local trade. There were silversmiths in Ephesus who manufactured miniature shrines of the temple of Artemis. This was a major business. Literally thousands of priests and priestesses served in the area of the temple of Artemis. Daily life revolved around temple worship. When the apostle Paul was there and people were being converted and burning their scrolls, they forsook all those shrines, the business plummeted, and a riot broke out. Christians came under great persecution in Ephesus. They experienced hardships, but they persevered. So Jesus firstly tells John to *commend* these Ephesian Christians. He knows what they have gone through.

> I know your deeds, your <u>hard work</u> and your <u>perseverance</u>. I know that you cannot tolerate wicked people, that you have tested those who claim to be apostles but are not, and have found them false. You have <u>persevered and have endured hardships</u> for my name, and have not grown weary (2:2-3).

Not only did they endure hardships from outsiders, they were also on their guard against *false teachers* who tried to infiltrate the church. They were willing to stand for the truth! This was the resolve of the Ephesians who had obviously taken heed from what Paul said. The last time Paul saw the elders at Ephesus he left them with this warning they never forgot:

> I know that after I leave, savage wolves will come in among you and will not spare the flock. Even from your own number men will arise and distort the truth in order to draw away disciples after them. So be on your guard! Remember that for three years I never stopped warning each of you night and day with tears (Acts 20:29-31).

Now this letter to the Ephesians from John comes about 30 years after Paul first warned them. And Jesus commends them saying **I know your deeds, your hard work and your perseverance. I know that you cannot tolerate wicked men, that you have tested those who claim to be apostles but are not, and have found them false.** These Ephesians were the real deal. They put their faith into hard action and 30 years after Paul warned them they are still holding fast. They guarded their doctrine. They persevered in it. Not only from the time when Paul ministered there and when John pastored there, but also into the second century. We know that from historical records. A letter written to the Ephesian church by the early church leader Ignatius (who died about AD 107), showed that the Ephesians continued to resist the corruption of false teachers.[5]

What might have struck the Ephesians receiving this letter in Revelation (and should strike us), is that Jesus is watching you at your local church! He says to these people *I know your deeds*. When you are doing things wrong, you know he is watching you. But here we see Jesus also notices when you hold fast doing right. He is pleased. And that is what he is saying here to this church. According to Ignatius, the Ephesians continued with their sound doctrine and didn't

---

[5] Ignatius letter to the Ephesians 1:1, 9:1, 11:2

tolerate false teachers.[6] These were high commendations, especially this one from Jesus himself in Revelation. Yet for all their hard work and perseverance, Jesus says next …

> Yet I hold this against you: You have forsaken the <u>love</u> you had at <u>first</u> (2:4).

Scholars debate as to what exactly was the **love they had at first.** Is it their *first love* as in when we are first converted, or is it *first love* in importance? Is it *love* as in witnessing to the world, or is it *love* for one another? Or *love* for God?

Perhaps scholars are trying to be too clever? The text doesn't specify what is meant by *first love*, so rather than looking so close as to dissect one definition, perhaps we should stand back and ask, 'How can you separate any of these?' Surely they are intertwined. Our first love in importance is Jesus and the cross, and the way he saved us. This love is often most heartfelt when we are first converted. And of course, when you have a true love for Jesus first, you love others, so you proclaim Jesus and his cause, which is the gospel going forth! It all comes under our first and foremost love of Jesus! The first love can include all these things. How can you extract just one? So Jesus says, *yet I hold this against you: You have forsaken your first love.*

But surely if the Ephesians have their doctrine right and have made such serious efforts that Jesus himself can say such wonderful things as: *You have persevered and have endured hardships for my name, and have not grown weary,* then shouldn't that count for more than those churches which have weak doctrine and don't persevere? Surely this little reminder about love will need no further comment. But then Jesus goes on to say …

> Consider how far you have fallen! <u>Repent</u> and do the things you did at first. If you do not repent, I will come to you and <u>remove your lampstand</u> from its place (2:5).

Wow! **Repent** and go back to your first love or what? *I'll* **remove your lampstand!** What does that mean? Does it mean they won't even be a church anymore? No matter what the faults of the other six churches, Jesus doesn't say this to any of the others. What about

---

[6] Ibid

those who *have* fallen for false teachers? What about those whose morals need rebuking? What will Jesus tell them? As it turns out, he also tells them to repent, but none of them are rebuked quite like this. If you don't go back to the things you did at first, you won't be a true church anymore. Is this too harsh? Remember, this is the church which stands for truth.

Think back to Paul's letters. He doesn't rebuke the Ephesians as he does the Galatians, the Colossians or the Corinthians. Paul's Ephesians letter covered more than one church in the area of Ephesus, but if those Ephesians can soak in Paul's letter to them, look at where they must have stood on doctrine. Right there in Ephesians 1 Paul begins with the doctrine that everyone else finds so difficult. Predestination! Chosen from before the foundation of the world. In Ephesians 2 he talks about being dead in sin until being made alive in Christ, and there are also the doctrines of grace alone and faith alone. The Ephesians never baulked at any of that. They stood for truth and rejected false teachers. It's obvious the church at Ephesus was just like ours!

And they persevered. They patiently endured. So why do they get the most serious threat of all the churches? *If you do not repent I will remove your lampstand?* Why so severe? Because they knew better! With more knowledge comes more responsibility. It's all through the Scriptures. Knowledge puffs up; love builds up (1 Cor. 8:1). Pride yourself in how much you know, and you will be held *more* accountable ... *From everyone who has been given much, much will be demanded; and from the one who has been entrusted with much, much more will be asked* (Luke 12:48). The Ephesians had knowledge and had been entrusted with the most important thing of all—their first love. Jesus. They have so much going for them, as Jesus continues ...

> But you have this in your favor: You hate the practices of the Nicolaitans, which I also hate (2:6).

We are not absolutely certain who the Nicolaitans were, but with the next church (Smyrna), the Nicolaitans are equated with idolatry and the sexual immorality of the teachings of Balaam (2:15). The 'practices' of the Nicolaitans seems to be that of professing Christians who still partook in some of the culture, lifestyle, and promiscuity of those around them, such as in the city of Ephesus.

The Ephesians were surrounded by temptations and these Nicolaitans were saying some involvement with the values of Ephesus and its ways were okay.

There are so-called Christian teachers around today who promote the teachings of the Nicolaitans. They say it's okay to engage in the world's way. As long as you make your decision for Christ, you can go with the world's pleasures, language, morality, and so on, 'as long as you love the Lord'. Jesus said the Ephesian church didn't tolerate those false teachers. He said *you tested* false teachers (2:2). If anything characterizes the wider church today, it's that there is little or no testing of teachers. There are dynamic speakers and great communicators! Ask Christians why they excuse their false teaching, and they say, 'Well, yes … but this preacher also has lots of good things to say.' There is a serious lack of testing. There are not many churches today bold enough to carry out tough biblical things like church discipline. How many take the Scriptures seriously in our moral practice? Ah, but that is not us! We are like the church at Ephesus. We hold fast. We shun worldliness and immorality. We have sound doctrine and reject moral compromise with the world's practices. Surely Jesus is pleased with us?

But even if you have all that, Jesus says … *Yet I hold this against you: You have forsaken the love you had at first. Consider how far you have fallen! Repent and do the things you did at first. If you do not repent, I will come to you and <u>remove your lampstand from its place</u>.*

Wow! We had all the right beliefs and practices and yet Jesus was not happy. Would Jesus really remove a lampstand? It happened here in Ephesus. Centuries later it was overrun by Islam and ceased to exist. Jesus removed a lampstand by taking the church away.

But there are different ways Jesus can remove a lampstand. Churches may have many people attending, great music, and a great vibe, but is Jesus there? I went to a funeral at a church filled with about 1000 people and the Pastor was ready to be bold. He talked about heaven and hell and the need to be saved to get to heaven. Great! He gave a full 20-minute sermon. Bold. Direct. But he didn't mention Jesus or the cross, sin, or the gospel! He did say you must prove you are filled with the Spirit by talking in tongues to be able to get into heaven. Works to get to heaven? I'm sure my mainstream Pentecostal friends would be as horrified as anyone. Big church. No gospel. Jesus has left the building! Lampstand not there. When we test teachers, it's not just what they say, but what they leave out.

But we Ephesians are not like that. We stand firm on the gospel. We stand firm on the word of truth ... but wait. You are the ones that Jesus is writing to, not them! He is saying he will remove his lampstand from us in the church at Ephesus, not the false teachers! Why? The problems were not with those unbelievers 'out there'! It was we in here who held fast to the truth and endured hardship. What was the problem? ... <u>*You*</u> *have forsaken the love you had at first.*

How could we miss it? Maybe we've been too busy finding fault in others. Have you forgotten the height from which you have fallen? Remember when you first saw the light? You were willing to lose everything. Do you remember what you did when you were first converted? You were so keen to come to church and join the Bible study. You wanted to invite your friends and family to join as well. And you were willing to lose anything that stood in the way of honoring Jesus. You were like those of the earlier Ephesian church who were willing to burn their old sorcery scrolls worth 50,000 drachmas (Acts 19:19). That's a lot of drachmas! A drachma was about one day's wage, which makes 50,000 drachmas as much as $10 million today. When they were converted they were ready to give up everything for the Lord. Their money, their time and their lives!

They were on fire for the Lord and ready to lose all! But now, years later, another letter arrives. You're still the best with your doctrine. And you're still enduring hardships for Jesus. But *you have forsaken the love you had at first.*

Can you identify with this? You believe all the right things. Your doctrine is sound. Outwardly you maintain good morals. But have you forsaken your first love? All those wrong priorities just crept back in? Before you left the world behind. But where are you now? Are you still growing in that first love? The Ephesians' massive burning of such valuable books reminds us that all those things of this world will one day be burned up.

> But the day of the Lord will come like a thief. The heavens will disappear with a roar; the elements will be destroyed by fire, and the earth and everything in it will be laid bare...That day will bring about the destruction of the heavens by fire, and the elements will melt in the heat (2 Peter 3:10,12).

Think about the priority of where you spend your time and money. Then picture where you are headed in a few short years. We must all appear! Appear where? Before the judgment seat of Christ who is the First and the Last. The same One whom John saw and fell on his face before him. Have you lost sight of that day and feel quite at ease because you have persevered and have all your right doctrine? There was a time when you threw all caution to the wind, but now even coming to church every week is not the same. It's all just going through the motions. And there are other things that come up.

You once made a commitment to Jesus, 'I gave my heart to the Lord.' Is that commitment now like those who make marriage vows but then forget them? Think about how you treat your spouse compared to when you first met. The way you spoke and acted. You went out of your way to be nice. And you made vows before God. Is it still there, or have your marriage vows been forgotten?

So what happened to your *first* love? Are you a traitor to your vows? Do you still share the gospel, or has that grown dim with rejections? D.L. Moody had a lady say to him, 'I don't like the way you do evangelism.' He asked her how she did it and she said, 'I don't.' So Moody said, 'Well, I like the way I do evangelism better than the way you don't do evangelism.'[7]

Have you become good at criticizing others but don't do much yourself? What sort of light are you shining? Is the lampstand shining? Do the people in your life see you as different? Have they heard the gospel from you? Have they had an invitation from you? Are you part of the mission? Or have you forsaken your first love? Are any of us so prideful in our stand for truth that we dismiss this letter as speaking to someone else? What can we do? Only one thing! Repent! *If you do not repent* ... (2:5). At least this implies that if you *do* repent he won't remove the lampstand.

> Whoever has ears, <u>let them hear</u> what the Spirit says to the churches. To the one who is victorious, I will give the right to eat from the tree of life, which is in the paradise of God (2:7).

Can you hear? **Whoever has ears** assumes not everyone is going to

---

[7] http://www.itslikethis.org/d-l-moodys-style-of-evangelism/

hear! Some will 'hear', but not really hear. But to the ones who *hear* and *are victorious*, they get access to the *tree of life* and *paradise!* The great reversal of Genesis 3, when mankind was expelled from paradise and the tree of life, to God being with his people again! Have you pictured eating from the tree of life in paradise? Revelation will climax with that picture of the tree of life and every tear being wiped away by the Lord himself, who will be with us. Have you got that first love? No use getting through those beasts and bowls if we don't make it to the tree of life.

God created this world knowing he would administer justice to most people who ever lived and mercy to only a few. The path is narrow said Jesus. Hell is right, just and fair. It's God doing right. You didn't even realize it, but there you were on the edge of the Abyss. Like Frodo waiting to throw that ring into the burning volcano, but it was *you* who was to be thrown in. *Along with everyone else!* But God decided to do something extraordinary ... to send his Son to save people. And he sent his Spirit to convict people, so they would put their trust in the Savior Jesus.

But why should you be included in that? You shouldn't! Except for one thing ... grace. God placed people and circumstances in your life that turned you to Jesus! He came to you. You didn't seek him! He sought you! He is our first love!

Look at what God is saying to you ... *I will give you to eat of the <u>tree of life</u> in <u>paradise</u>*. Paradise restored. We are going to be in paradise forever. It all seems so theoretical now, but the tree of life speaks of full restoration. It won't be long now. We are dying. Do you know anyone who died recently? Every time that happens we get a jolt of reality. Life is short. And on the other side ... It's forever...

Are you better than the billions who have passed on who never made it? Why were you saved? How were you saved? The torture of Jesus. The *cross*. Have you forsaken your first love? Does it no longer stir you into being part of his mission? Have the magic scrolls you burned when you first believed been replaced with other things of the world? We can read this passage and think it is talking about someone else, but only to our own peril. This is prophetic. This is scary. But this is the beauty. It's also a warning. It gives you opportunity to repent! To the one *who is victorious* he will take you into a garden. Paradise.

Whoever has ears, let them hear what the Spirit says to the churches ...
Study Questions

1. In what ways had the church at Ephesus proven to be faithful? (Including back to the time of the apostle Paul's ministry.)

2. What things was the city of Ephesus known for that would be a temptation or clash with the Christian life?

3. What were the practices of the Nicolaitans?

4. What are the different ways we can understand the 'first love' the Ephesians had lost?

5. Why might losing their first love be so harshly rebuked by Jesus, when he could commend them for sound doctrine and resisting compromise?

6. How might Jesus remove his lampstand from a church?

7. What are some of the ways you might have lost your first love?

8. How does this text speak of restoration?

9. What sort of things might you need to do to rekindle the preciousness of salvation?

5
Smyrna
(Revelation 2:8-11)

The apostle John was imprisoned on the island of Patmos because he had testified to Jesus. Now Jesus visits John in his affliction in that cave. Jesus dictates seven letters for John to send to seven churches in Asia Minor where John had ministered. The second letter was to the church at Smyrna.

Smyrna was the second largest city in Asia Minor, about 37 miles (60kms) north of Ephesus. So we picture the postman sailing from Patmos, delivering the first letter to Ephesus, then trekking on to Smyrna. We are still in the area of modern-day Turkey. In fact, Smyrna is still there today as the third largest city in Turkey. Today it is called Izmir.

At the opening of each of these letters to the different churches, Jesus identifies himself by drawing on the descriptions given of him in the vision which John saw in Rev. 1. But Jesus chooses details from the vision which relate to his specific message to each individual church. For example, in the first letter to Ephesus, Jesus is the one who walks among the golden lampstands (2:1). We have already learned in 1:12 that Jesus is the one walking among the golden lampstands. What was the significance of this to those in Ephesus? Jesus says to them, *'I know your deeds ... I know that you can't tolerate wicked men ...'* I know you! And I know that you have forsaken your first love. How does he know all that? He's there walking in their midst!

Now in his letter to the church at Smyrna Jesus identifies himself again from the vision in 1:17-18, where he pronounced he was the First and the Last, who died and rose again ...

> To the angel of the church in Smyrna write: These are the words of him who is the <u>First and the Last, who died and came to life again</u> (2:8).

Why is this title significant to the church of Smyrna? Because they were a suffering church, persecuted even to death. Now the Lord, **the First and the Last, who died and came to life again,** will tell them to hold fast, even to death. They can be assured of deliverance even through suffering and death by the one who not only can see from *first to last*, but who has conquered *death and come to life again!* Then Jesus continues ...

> I know your afflictions and your poverty—yet you are rich. I know about the slander of those who say they are Jews and are not, but are a synagogue of Satan (2:9).

The world sees Smyrna's material **poverty,** but Jesus says they have spiritual richness. So here is the end to the prosperity gospel. Jesus doesn't say, 'I know you have poverty, but I will give you material wealth.' He knows their suffering, but it doesn't always mean he will take it away or that they have done wrong. They are in poverty and suffering, yet Smyrna is one of only two out of seven churches that *doesn't* get rebuked. Later we will see a contrast with the church at Laodicea who thought they were rich (which they were in the worldly sense), but Jesus has a different view of riches. Which church is closer to you? Poor materially and rich spiritually, or rich materially and poor spiritually? Smyrna has the true riches, yet they are materially poor.

They are also slandered by **those who say they are Jews and are not, but are a synagogue of Satan.** First century Jews who rejected Jesus called it blasphemous to acknowledge Jesus as Lord. Jesus says he knows the Smyrnians have endured, being slandered and spoken of as blasphemers. Jesus is saying something significant here. Not all those who say they are of Israel are truly Israel. True descendants of Abraham are those who have the *faith* of Abraham, who believed in the Messiah to come. Those who oppose the Christ, even if they are ethnic Israelites, are not merely neutral, but *a synagogue of Satan.*

In the first century, the Jewish religion was recognized as a legitimate religion within the Roman Empire. As long as Christianity (founded by Jews) was considered a Jewish sect, there was no problem. But after Emperor Nero's crazed attacks in the AD 60s, Christianity came under suspicion and Jewish opponents were incensed that they were losing many Gentile God-fearers to

Christianity. God-fearers were Gentiles who hadn't become full Jews but worshiped Israel's God. Many of these people were now embracing the Jewish Messiah Jesus. So Jewish opponents were only too happy to point out to the Romans that Christianity was *not* a Jewish sect but a separate religion, which made it illegal! The Romans should stamp them out! So persecution was now not only from the Jews, but also from Rome. They will put you in prison…

> Do not be afraid of what you are about to suffer. I tell you, the <u>devil</u> will put some of you in prison to test you, and you will suffer persecution for ten days. Be faithful, even to the point of death, and I will give you life as your victor's crown (2:10).

Did you notice there is someone else other than Romans and Jews behind their suffering? **The devil will put some of you in prison!** The devil stirs up people against the people of God. Why do you get upset with your friends, even loved ones, who ridicule your faith? The battle is not against flesh and blood (it's not them), but powers of evil in the heavenly realms stirring them up. So don't be afraid. Why? Jesus is Lord. And he says … **I will give you life as your victor's crown.**

The *crown* could have resonated with the people of Smyrna in several ways. Smyrna was a city that competed with Ephesus as the largest in Asia Minor, and was said to be the most beautiful, with its picturesque buildings on the rounded top of the hill of Pagos. This rounded top was known as the 'Crown of Smyrna'. But Smyrna was also famous for its athletic games. So there is also the imagery of a crown wreath for the victor. That would be familiar to them. So what is Jesus saying? You may miss out on earthly crowns, but have I got a crown for you! What crown exactly? The reward! A better reward! Your victor's crown!

But the people of Smyrna will still have to suffer. How? It seems trade unions have a longer history than you might have thought. Trade guilds were a part of the normal work life in each industry in Smyrna, and membership in each trade guild incorporated compulsory pagan rituals as part of everyday work life. If you were not willing to bow to Caesar as Lord then you would find yourself out of your trade guild and out of work. Smyrna was a center for Emperor worship! What does a Christian do? There were no unemployment benefits. If you were out of work, it could mean starvation. *Poverty!*

We don't have that kind of suffering today in the West. But does that mean Christians don't suffer in their workplace? What about pressure in jobs where employers are cutting corners ethically and even fellow employees expect you to compromise? 'What do you mean you can't go along with that? Everyone else is doing it and if you don't toe the line you'll make it worse for us all if you tell the boss you can't do it.'

But in Smyrna you could face prison or even death. Is this relevant today? If the seven churches are speaking into church history, are there examples of the church at Smyrna today? Persecution? More than ever! It might be under the pressure of militant Hindus in India, or tribal or Islamic forces in Africa, or closed Muslim countries in the Middle East, or in China under communist pressure. Christianity is under persecution as never before. There are many Christians suffering horrible torture today in ways that are best not repeated here. The church at Smyrna is with us today in spirit. *Be faithful unto death.*

Jesus told the church at Smyrna *I know your afflictions* ... I know! I know what you have gone through. But **do not be afraid of what you are about to suffer.** What he is saying is, don't be thrown. It's part of the plan. He is the First and the Last and knows the beginning from the end, and there *is* a plan! Jesus is saying he could see what the Smyrnians were going through, but he could also see a little further ahead to the *victor's crown*. It will all be worth it.

But if Jesus 'knows' and loves us, why let us go through it? Isn't that one of the great questions of our whole existence? Atheist scholars have argued that if God was able to create a world without sin in the Garden of Eden and intends to do it again in the new heaven and new earth, then why couldn't he skip the whole problem of evil and suffering in between?

Firstly, that question assumes God can't bring about a victory and *greater good* from all that has gone wrong, than if he had gone straight from the Garden of Eden to Paradise. But if he is the First and the Last, who has a plan of the whole picture, he could do that. Despite man's rebellion against God in the beginning (which sent this world into death and suffering), God did the impossible. He used that evil choice of man to display his love and glory in an even more profound way than could have otherwise ever happened. This is not to suggest that God needed evil to show how good he is. Let's make that absolutely clear. God is never the author of sin. Sin is something that is *against* God. Man's choice to rebel was real and devastating. It was *man's* choice, and yet in God's sovereignty above that, his plan was to do good, *despite* the evil choice of man. Not only is God more glorified, but also the richness of the relationship between man and God could never have been the same if God had not let history unfold. We see a glimpse of this principle in the story of the sinful woman, when Jesus had to tell Simon the Pharisee a story to get through to him.

> 'Two people owed money to a certain moneylender. One owed him five hundred denarii, and the other fifty. Neither of them had the money to pay him back, so he forgave the debts of both. Now which of them will love him more?' (Luke 7:41-42).

The answer is, of course, the one who was given the greater pardon. If love is God's greatest gift, then humankind's ability to experience that love depends on history unfolding. The sinless angels who never experienced the fall or suffering will share heaven with us. Yet they will *never* experience heaven to the same richness in their relationship with God in the same way redeemed human souls will. They never experienced what it is to be saved out of what is so richly deserved, through God giving up his Son for them. They will never experience the transforming process that suffering brings. They will never have the *crown!* But for you who go through the suffering, *Jesus will give* **you life as your victor's crown.**

Also, this letter to Smyrna teaches us that if you suffer, it does not necessarily mean the Lord is not pleased with you. Even Jesus was perfected through suffering. But wasn't he already perfect?

> In bringing many sons and daughters to glory, it was fitting that God, for whom and through whom everything exists, should make the author of their salvation perfect through what he suffered (Heb. 2:10).

If Jesus was already perfect, how can he be made perfect? Suffering was a process that perfected his role as our great High Priest (Heb. 2:17). It enabled Jesus to sympathize with our weaknesses and say *I know your afflictions*. Our suffering enables us to be conformed to his likeness (Rom. 8:29). So how are you going to be transformed into the likeness of the Son of God? What did the Son of God go through? *Suffering!* Affliction! How much more will we be perfected and receive a more glorious crown if we are transformed into *his* likeness through suffering!

But the question is still asked, 'If God knew he would have to put up with so much evil and throw many into hell just to save some, is it really worth it?' Even if he *can* bring good out of it, is it worth the process? The only answer to that is 'the cross'. The cross says *God* thought it was worth it! The cross removes the idea that God is playing an arbitrary game with history and with suffering. *I know your suffering*. He meant it! God sent his only Son into this evil world to experience the greatest suffering ever. He took the full weight of what evil deserves, the eternal wrath of God, so that his people could overcome death and hell and instead receive that rich crown.

I know your suffering is not theory. Jesus *knows* your suffering. God knows. Couldn't God have achieved all this some other way? Jesus asked that question. He said if there was any *other* way God could achieve this, then he wanted out. *My Father, if it is possible, may this cup be taken from me* ... (Matt. 26:39). But the silence from heaven was deafening! There was no other way. God used the greatest suffering and evil ever perpetrated, the murder and forsaking of God's own eternal Son, to bring about the greatest good ever. So, is he also able to bring good out of suffering in our lives? Yes, and more. There is that crown! God is working something of eternal value. A crown that is of such a glory it far outweighs our sufferings and *will make them seem light and momentary* when we receive that crown (2 Cor. 4:17). Greater is your crown because you have held fast through the afflictions. So, what is the message? *Don't give up!*

> Do not be afraid of what you are about to suffer. I tell you, the devil will put some of you in prison to test you, and you will suffer persecution for <u>ten days</u>. Be faithful, even to the point of death, and I will give you <u>life as your victor's crown</u> (2:10).

What is the **ten days?** Did the church at Smyrna have to suffer intensely for ten days before they died? There may have been some literal, short-term time of intense persecution in Smyrna. Remember the main tool we have for understanding Revelation is Scripture itself, especially the OT. We noted earlier that one of the most alluded to OT books in Revelation is the book of Daniel. From the start, Daniel and his three friends were tested how long? *Ten days.* It is mentioned twice in Daniel 1:12-15. The test was whether they would cave-in to the pagan religion around them when they were ordered to eat the king's rich food. That was a sign of loyalty to the king. This is what the church at Smyrna was facing. Will you align yourself with Caesar, or will you stand up for Jesus? If you want to be in the trade guilds then you have to honor the guardian deities in the festive meals. Or will you hold fast to Jesus, even if it means being poor materially, or even unto death?

And what about us? Are we prepared to lose a job, money, or more to stand up for Jesus? Some in Smyrna did. You may have heard of the famous early church leader, Polycarp. He was the Senior Pastor (Bishop) *at Smyrna!* He became Bishop in AD 115. As a younger man, Polycarp was a disciple of the apostle John himself. And here is John writing this book of Revelation and a specific letter to Smyrna from Patmos. Polycarp may well have been in Smyrna as a younger man when this letter from John arrived at his church (Polycarp would have been in his 20s when this letter arrived). It seems these words from Jesus, written by John, must have stayed with Polycarp in his older age. *Do not be afraid of what you are about to suffer ... Be faithful, even to the point of death, and I will give you life as your victor's crown.*

Those words must have burned deep in Polycarp's heart because years later as an old man he was arrested for being a Christian. His account is recorded by the early church fathers and also appears in ancient church historian Eusebius' *Ecclesiastical History*. All Polycarp had to do was to give a token acknowledgement of Caesar as Lord, and he would have been released. Perhaps Polycarp recalled John's Revelation letter to Smyrna, from many years earlier ... *Do not be afraid. Be faithful even to death.* The ancient fathers gave this account.

> After Polycarp was arrested he was brought into the great amphitheater in Smyrna. Thousands of people were there to watch. They sat Polycarp in a chariot and urged him to say Caesar was Lord. What harm can there be in that, they said. The ruler reminded Polycarp of his great age and he urged him to deny his Christian faith: 'Revile Christ, and I will release you.' But Polycarp famously replied, 'Eighty and six years have I served him, and he has never done me wrong; How can I blaspheme him, my King, who has

saved me? I am a Christian.' The ruler then cried out to the crowd, 'Polycarp has confessed himself to be a Christian.' The crowds yelled, 'Let him be burned!' When they went to fasten Polycarp to the stake for burning he said, 'Leave me thus. He who strengthens me to endure the flames will also enable me to stand firm at the stake without being fastened with nails.' As the woodpile was lighted Polycarp bravely spoke a final prayer to his God and then the flames consumed him. He died in AD 156.[8]

Polycarp was faithful to the Lord unto death. He received his crown!

Before we start feeling sorry for people such as Polycarp, we need to remember the fires that Polycarp went through only lasted for a brief moment. When the people threatened to burn Polycarp at the stake, one of his enemies said ...

> 'I will have you consumed with fire unless you change your mind.' Polycarp replied, 'You threaten fire which burns for an hour and is soon quenched; for you are ignorant of the fire of the coming judgment and eternal punishment reserved for the wicked.'[9]

Do these words of Polycarp help us see whom we should really feel sorry for? Polycarp would have remembered Jesus' words when he read that letter to his church in Smyrna ...

> Whoever has ears, let them hear what the Spirit says to the churches. The one who is victorious will not be hurt at all by the second death (2:11).

The lake of fire is the **second death** (20:14). Eternal hell! Polycarp was victorious. He was burned, but only for a short time. And for him there was no second death. God is holy, just, and *eternal*, which is why if we have sinned against God, hell must be eternal. God cannot stop being holy, just, *or* eternal, and sin does not stop being sin. The second death is the remedy for justice. And Jesus has given you, the reader, a direct invitation to escape the second death. **Whoever has ears, let them hear!** No wonder this book is a blessing to all who read it (1:3). We are so caught up in the different views of millenniums and interpretations of Revelation that we miss the big picture! Avoid the second death!

The head of the church, Jesus, has gone through the second death

---

[8] Eusebius, *Ecclesiastical History*, Book IV chapter 15
[9] Ibid

in our place and calls us through suffering to a crown of life! *Jesus wins!* Are you ready to suffer for Jesus? Or are you so comfortable that you've lost sight of what your life is about? Unless Jesus comes back first, we will all experience the momentary first death. But repent and believe so you cannot be harmed by the second death!

Those who are victorious are those who don't give in to the pressure of the trade guilds, to the spiritual attacks and temptations. Satan is behind those temptations, whether they be sexual temptation or covetousness, materialism or financial temptation. Whatever temptation it is, the devil is behind it. So will you stand for Jesus? Will you go through affliction and receive the victor's crown? *Are you ready to suffer for Jesus?*

Many brothers and sisters are being tortured even now. But in the West, we say, Smyrna has nothing to say to me. I am not persecuted. But remember, if you really are a Christian, you will be persecuted in some way (2 Tim. 3:12). Stand up for Jesus and you will be put down. It might not be to death, like for some in Smyrna, but there are different ways we can suffer. There may be the temptation to compromise, or to not stand as a Christian for fear of embarrassment. More and more that pressure is on in the workplace. It's not just the obvious ethical issues, but even pressure to go along with the dirty jokes, bad language, gossip, lies, or cheating. There are different kinds of ways Christians are under pressure.

The devil wants to take that crown away from you. Jesus says, *I know your afflictions, I know what you are going through.*

But if Jesus knows your afflictions, why doesn't he stop it? Because he is working riches. He says, 'I know your afflictions, and I have a crown that's waiting for you. It's beautiful, and it lasts forever. And I am building that crown for your particular reward for you right now.' He also said …

> 'Blessed are you when people insult you, persecute you and falsely say all kinds of evil against you because of me. Rejoice and be glad, because <u>great is your reward in heaven,</u> for in the same way they persecuted the prophets who were before you (Matt. 5:11-12).

Great is your reward! You are one chosen by Jesus to persevere for his name! He is with you. He knows what you are going through. He *knows your afflictions and your poverty—yet you are rich!* How rich? All the riches of Christ (Eph. 3:8)! Have you really seen the riches? This is bigger than anything you go through. A crown! You escape the second death and have Jesus forever. So hold fast!

Do not be afraid of what you are about to suffer ... Be faithful, even to the point of death, and I will give you life as your victor's crown (2:10).

Study Questions

1. Jesus identified himself in these first two letters from particular aspects of his appearance in the vision in Rev. 1. What are they and how do they relate specifically to the first two letters?

2. What are possible ways that resisting compromise might cause the Christians of Smyrna to become materially poor?

3. Why is the prosperity gospel in conflict with this letter to Smyrna?

4. If this text is about holding up under persecution, even to death, how relevant is that to the church today?

5. How does that apply to you?

6. What does Jesus say about the unbelieving ethnic Jews in Smyrna? Why such a harsh characterization?

7. Why had persecution increased from the Roman Empire by this time?

8. Who is behind the persecution in Smyrna? Can you think of suffering you have experienced where you have overlooked the enemy?

9. How would you respond to someone who asks if God is all powerful why would he allow suffering even of his own people?

10. What are some ways God is doing good in your life through trials?

6
Pergamum
(Revelation 2:12-17)

As with the letters to the other churches, Jesus opens with his self-identification. This is where he draws on some part of the vision John saw of him in Rev. 1, which relates to the message he has for that particular church. And now we come to Pergamum, which has been involved in moral compromise. How does Jesus identify himself?

> To the angel of the church in Pergamum write: These are the words of him who has <u>the sharp, double-edged sword</u> (2:12).

Remember the vision of Jesus included a sharp double-edged sword coming out of his mouth. It symbolizes the judgment sword of God. Here Jesus opens this letter to the church at Pergamum, reminding them he is the Lord who is Judge. He will have the judgment victory over Satan. But judgment begins with the house of God, when his people stray!

Jesus begins commending them. Even when they have been persecuted, they didn't give up on the Lord. They **remained true to my name.** They had their own martyr at the church, Antipas, who was put to death, yet they still stood up for Jesus.

> I know where you live—where Satan has his throne. Yet you remain true to my name. You did not renounce your faith in me, even in the days of Antipas, my faithful witness, who was put to death in your city—where Satan lives (2:13).

I know where you live, says Jesus. I know you live right in the middle of the toughest battlefield—where Satan has his throne. Once again, we see who is behind the persecution. Our struggle is not against flesh and blood. It's Satan! He is behind the persecution. This is where Satan has his throne—where Satan lives. That is Jesus' way of saying Pergamum is a central city in Asia Minor for the Roman Government. It's also the capital of the whole region for Emperor worship. They were an educated lot at Pergamum. They had the second largest library in the world with 200,000 books or parchments. We get our English word *parchment* from the linguistically complex translation of the word Pergamum. Pergamum was the first of the cities in Asia Minor to build a temple to a Roman ruler (Augustus). Pergamum was proud to call itself the 'temple warden' of a temple specifically dedicated to Emperor worship.

We have looked at the other churches in Ephesus and Smyrna, where Christians were under pressure to compromise with pagan practices that permeated trade guilds and the financial, economic and general aspects of social life. And it *was* pressure. If you stood for the Lord, you might be putting yourself out of the basic means of living. But when it comes to Pergamum, the center for Emperor worship … double it! This is where Satan lives! Pergamum is where he has his throne!

If you don't acknowledge Caesar as Lord, you are committing high treason against the Empire! The battle was fierce **where Satan has his throne**. The congregation members at Pergamum could say Satan has such a stronghold in that city that it looks like Satan is winning. 'Satan managed to even orchestrate the death of our hero of the faith, Antipas. Murdered for the faith', **put to death in your city … where Satan lives.** And where Satan lives … there are a variety of gods worshiped there. There was a great hill behind Pergamum with many temples. Not least of all, the throne of Zeus, the chief of the Greek gods. Right there in Pergamum the giant altar to Zeus, 120ft x 112ft (40m x 37m), overlooked the city. Zeus might be the chief of gods in the minds of many who lived at Pergamum, but it is not Zeus on his throne, he is just an idol. What did Paul say to the Corinthians? Idols are nothing, but there are demons behind them. Well, Pergamum has more than just any demons behind their idols. Satan himself! His throne!

Another of the famous gods worshiped in Pergamum was Asclepius, the god of healing. Pergamum has been described as the 'Lourdes' of the ancient world, where people came to be healed. And what do you think Asclepius' image was? A serpent! Oh yes, Christians in Pergamum knew this is where Satan lived. But they managed to ... *remain true to my name. You did not renounce your faith in me, even in the days of Antipas, my faithful witness, who was put to death* ... Commended by Jesus and yet ...

> Nevertheless, I have a few things against you: There are some among you who hold to the teaching of Balaam, who taught Balak to entice the Israelites to sin so that they ate food sacrificed to idols and committed sexual immorality (2:14).

Pergamum, you have the opposite problem of Ephesus. Remember the conservative church in Ephesus? They watched their doctrine closely but they had forgotten their first love. Love for Jesus. Love for others. Love for the lost. They had good doctrine, but they sat on it. Well, the guys at Pergamum weren't like that. They stuck their necks out to witness for Jesus, even to death. But when some of their preachers brought questionable teaching thrown in with the gospel, they made excuses. 'Yes, some of the teaching is not right, but we don't want to quench the Spirit because these guest preachers also teach some good things. Who are we to judge?'

Just like the teaching of Balaam of old. What exactly was that? Balaam would ...**entice the Israelites to sin so that they ate food sacrificed to idols and committed sexual immorality.** That was part of the pressure at Pergamum, where every part of life was infiltrated with false worship. Even the food they ate was offered up to the gods. It was finding its way into the church's worship life, as one or two of their preachers would say it was okay to go along with the worship practices around them, as long as you still confessed Jesus in your heart. Sexual immorality was part of temple worship and life in pagan Pergamum, where Satan lives. The church had some preachers who were not so stringent on doctrine, and when you let false teaching in, compromise with morality often follows.

So at one extreme you had the church at Ephesus, so concerned about doctrine that they forgot their first love and commission to be reaching a lost world. But at the Pergamum church, their hearts were so open to the lost world around them; their hearts were too open! Openness to the **teaching of Balaam** meant openness to compromise in worship and sexual immorality.

The culture in Pergamum was overwhelming the church. It was part of everyday life. Does this sound familiar? Sexual references all over the place, even on billboards as you walk down the street. It was in entertainment in the Greek theatre and the way people lived. In fact, you were ostracized if you didn't go along with them. If you didn't, you could even be seen to be 'attacking freedom'. And, 'Why should you expect to get a job within our trade guilds if you didn't give credence to the indigenous spirituality.' Yes. Satan had his throne in Pergamum.

The pressure was more than just constant. You grew up with the culture. So the church at Pergamum had a couple of preachers saying, 'Our worship has to be relevant to the world to reach these people.' So their worship and their lifestyle soon began to resemble the world. And as to sexual purity, they were teaching that if you make your 'decision for Christ', you are under grace not under law, so it didn't matter as much how you lived. What followed at Pergamum was compromise in sexual purity with those justifying it saying, 'We are free in Christ!'

But not everyone thought this was good. Jesus said **you have people there** who hold to the teaching of Balaam, suggesting not all were compromising. There must have been some who stood firm. Perhaps they even suggested some sort of church discipline for those who were straying, but there was never enough support for that because these preachers would say, 'We have to show love, not judgment. We can't be constantly preaching against sin and sexual sin. We are all sinners saved by grace. Besides, if you can't get into the culture, if you don't meet people where they are at, how else can we reach them?'

Remember these seven churches represent the complete church. Yes, these letters literally speak to the original seven churches, but they also speak into the future church from John's day. Is this speaking into our day?

In Pergamum, the world was creeping into the church. Where could this apply today? Are we a church where we aren't converting the world, but rather the world is converting us? We still stand up for many things. We have people who stand up for Jesus in public! And if everything is not quite right with our teaching, at least we aren't like those hard-nosed, doctrinally-pure types who have lost their first love and don't have any effective witness in the world. We are not stuffy or boring, and our preachers may not play hard line with purity, but they still have the Spirit, and a prophetic voice.

The pressure was also on in work life in Pergamum, where every trade guild had worldliness and pagan worship built into it. Either you go along with the rituals or you don't get work. If you want a job and the trade guilds demand you have to say Caesar is Lord, you go along with it ('just as long as you believe in your heart Jesus is Lord ... that's the main thing'). When workmates blaspheme or tell dirty jokes, you don't tell anyone you are a Christian. It's okay, as long as you believe in your heart. Otherwise people will make fun of you. Who wants to be seen as anti-intellectual because you believe God created the world, instead of the popular views of origins? Who wants to be called a bigot against equality because you are not open to redefining marriage? Who wants to be ridiculed as 'religious' and 'taking away a woman's rights' because you stand against abortion? And your 'friends' say you are not free. Christianity is too restricting.

Christians at the Pergamum church never went fully into the world around them, rather the world kind of crept in to them. They weren't as sexually immoral as the promiscuous girls and guys in the city around them. They didn't dress in the same promiscuous ways, well not *as bad* as the world. 'We aren't as modest as some would want, but you have to be where other people are to reach them.' The Christians at Pergamum wouldn't go as far as the world. And that made them feel secure. *You have people there who hold to the teaching of... sexual immorality*. They never slept around with different partners, so it didn't seem so bad that some had sex outside marriage—as long as you were committed to the one person. Sure, some of them played around with pornography, but they were nowhere near as bad as the world around them. The great excuse they had was, 'We must be a true church because we have real Christians among us, not everyone or everything here is that bad.' So much so that Jesus himself could say ... *you remain true to my name. You did not renounce your faith in me.* Surely if you have real Christians in your church, then it can't be that bad? And yet the sword of Jesus' mouth is about to fall upon you Pergamum. Your teachers are going along with the world ...

> Likewise you also have those who hold to the teaching of the Nicolaitans (2:15).

Preacher 'Nicolas' taught that compromise with worship and sexual immorality was okay, as long as you had the blood of Christ. So what is the message if in your church you have stood up for the faith, even in face of great opposition, but you have compromised with the world in your worship and sexual immorality? What if you are playing around with pornography or having sex outside marriage? What if there is just a hint of sexual immorality? What is Jesus' message to you?

> Repent therefore! Otherwise, I will soon come to you and will fight against them with the sword of my mouth (2:16).

This is serious. This is eternally serious. Jesus' sword of judgment that comes from his mouth is a double-edged sword! Where else do we read that?

> For the word of God is alive and active. Sharper than any double-edged sword, it penetrates even to dividing soul and spirit, joints and marrow; it judges the thoughts and attitudes of the heart (Heb. 4:12).

The word of God! It judges. We need to come back to the word of God in the church! In our worship! We are called to worship the Lord in reverence and awe (Heb. 12:29). You can't presume that because you have stuck up for Jesus in so many other ways that the sword will not fall upon you Pergamum ... if you are in conflict with the word of God. You can't be a follower of your preacher! If your preacher allows a little compromise in—flee! Follow the word of God. Jesus says on the Day of Judgment hypocritical teachers will be cut to pieces (Matt. 24:51). What will be your end if you followed them? The double-edged sword! The word of him who is Judge is our only supreme rule. Examine the word. Read it. Listen to it preached faithfully and test all preachers by it. So what is Jesus saying? If you are compromising ... Repent! In case you missed it, he says:

> Whoever has ears, let them hear what the Spirit says to the churches (2:17).

The Spirit inspired the word. If you can hear the word of God, then—*Listen!*

These seven letters are fascinating because Jesus is writing to his individual churches and says to them he is walking in the midst of them (his lampstands). What is fascinating is that Jesus has a personal interest in each of his local churches. Jesus puts up with the horrible things that go on in his churches, and he has a plan to wrap it all up on the Day of Judgment. It's easy just to dismiss this with, 'No church is perfect, and we are all sinners.' Or, 'As long as we all get into heaven, what will it matter if some are slacker than others? Who cares?'

These letters show us Jesus cares! He is concerned when we compromise. Now! He is grieved at what is going on in his local churches when we stray. He is concerned about our worship and our lifestyle. He is right in the midst of your local church. He knows what you are going through ... *I know where you live—where Satan has his throne.* He can say, 'I know where *you* live! I know Satan lives there, in that world around you.' In other words, Jesus says he knows what you are up against. He knows the culture that surrounds you. He knows what temptations oppress you. 'I know where you live.' But do *you*? Do you know what culture you are living in and how it can seduce you? Because none of that is an excuse for compromise. You are in the world of Satan, but you cannot be of it. If you are to truly hold fast to light Satan will oppose you. Expect it. But if you don't repent, then it will be me who opposes you, says Jesus. *I will soon come to you and will fight against them with the sword of my mouth.*

What does Jesus mean when he says he will fight against them? The sword of his mouth is Jesus as Judge, but does that only mean at the end of time? A church can be judged now. It could mean the church is diminished or split, or that it doesn't have any influence in the world anymore. But it could also mean a church could still have great numbers without people really walking with Jesus. Doctrine is played down, so the gospel itself becomes watered down and has no power. Satan has got in. Can we see Pergamum today? A place where living and worshiping in holiness are no longer important? Have we been given up to ourselves? Has the judgment sword come early?

But this letter is not a final condemnation. It's a warning before it's too late. This is for you even if you have compromised with the world and sexual immorality. He doesn't give up on those who are truly his. He calls them again ...

> Whoever has ears, <u>let them hear</u> what the Spirit says to the churches. To the one who is <u>victorious</u>, I will give some of the <u>hidden manna</u> (2:1).

To those who **hear** *and are* **victorious** he promises **hidden manna.** This is not manna the world can offer. Jesus said he is the true manna from heaven (John 6:32-33). So for the faithful who 'miss out' on the world's pleasures and practices, the Lord will reward them when he reveals all, including that *hidden manna.* He is the manna that came down from heaven. Wait on him!

> ... I will also give that person a <u>white stone</u> ... (2:17c).

A **white stone** was used to signify the casting of a favorable vote or acquittal (Acts 26:10). A black stone was guilty. A white stone was also used as an admission pass to an occasion. We are acquitted in Christ! Free entry into the wedding supper of the Lamb! Repent and you get the white stone!

> ... I will also give that person a white stone with a <u>new name</u> written on it, known only to the one who receives it (2:17d).

A **new name?** Whose name? It could be a new name for us, but we will see as Revelation unfolds it is more likely the name of the Lord. That's what he also says to the church in Philadelphia ...

> ... and I will also write on them <u>my new name</u> (3:12).

He says the same thing towards the end of Revelation: *They will see his face, and <u>his name</u> will be on their foreheads* (22:4). If you are one of the Lord's, you will have *his name.* That is, those who *are victorious* (2:17). The only question you have to ask is: 'Have *you* got his name?' Only he knows, we are told in Rev. 19.

> His eyes are like blazing fire, and on his head are many crowns. He has a <u>name</u> written on him that <u>no one knows but he himself</u> (19:12).

But this book is called Revelation, and we have that secret name revealed to us ...

> On his robe and on his thigh he has this name written: KING OF KINGS AND LORD OF LORDS (19:16).

The unbeliever can read that name and yet it remains *hidden* (secret) to them. It's only *revealed* to those who are truly his, who truly know Jesus as their King of kings and Lord of lords. Who gets that name on a white stone? Only those who are victorious. Those who don't compromise in worship or sexual immorality. Those who remain true to Jesus' words.

Study Questions

1. In what way does Jesus identify himself from Rev. 1 to this church, and how does it relate to them in particular?

2. What are some ways 'Satan lives' in Pergamum?

3. What does the Pergamum church have in its history that Jesus commends them for?

4. What is the contrast between Pergamum and Ephesus?

5. What are the two main ways Pergamum compromises?

6. How could Pergamum's experience apply today to Christians in the workplace and public arena?

7. How can we detect false teachers in the church, and in what ways could false teachers encourage sexual immorality?

8. When Jesus says he will judge them with the sword of his mouth, is he talking about the Day of Judgment or before then?

9. Which church do you think you are more likely to make error with? Ephesus or Pergamum?

10. What are the three rewards for those who overcome, and what do they mean?

7
Thyatira
(Revelation 2:18-29)

Once again Jesus introduces himself to the church by choosing a portion of the Rev. 1 vision which relates to the particular issue he wants to convey to that church. Last time, with the church at Pergamum, Jesus wanted to convey he was the Judge, ready to judge his church because they were involved in compromise with their worship and sexual immorality. So Jesus identified himself as the one who had the sharp, two-edged sword proceeding from his mouth. In other words, he would judge his church if they did not repent.

Well lo and behold, the church at Thyatira had the very same problems. So here is Jesus as Judge again, but this time the judge who can see right through them.

> To the angel of the church in Thyatira write: These are the words of the Son of God, whose eyes are like <u>blazing fire</u> and whose feet are like burnished bronze (2:18).

Jesus was described in 1:13-15 as one with *eyes of fire* and *feet of bronze*. Bronze metal work was a major industry in Thyatira. They were famous for their bronze, and the industry had a major trade guild for bronze workers. Here Jesus is saying he is the one with feet of **bronze** that can trample down the wicked. The **eyes are like blazing fire** of the Judge. Those at Thyatira in the bronze industry kept 'trade secrets' on their bronze production. As we progress, we will see more of the 'deep secrets' at Thyatira.

Thyatira is about 37 miles (60kms) from Pergamum (where we were last time). Picture the postman leaving the island of Patmos. The first port is Ephesus, then Smyrna, then Pergamum, and now Thyatira. The cities are geographically in sequence. Thyatira was a smaller city, but it was quite a center of trade. Remember Lydia, the first convert in Philippi in Acts 16? She was originally from Thyatira. She was a businesswoman and her trade was dealing in purple cloth, which was a major industry product of Thyatira, an expensive 'royal' purple cloth (from a dye in sea snails).

In his address to Thyatira, Jesus identifies himself again from the wording of the vision in Rev. 1, only this time he says he is the **Son of God,** which is different from 1:13, where he is the son of man. This seems to be a deliberate difference, because in the context of his letter to Thyatira he alludes to Psalm 2, where the Son of God will rule with an iron scepter and dash them to pieces like pottery. And what do we read at the end of this letter?

> ...that one 'will rule them with an iron scepter and will dash them to pieces like pottery' ... (2:27).

Psalm 2 predicts the Son of God would be the final Judge. So here is Jesus in this letter identifying himself as a fulfillment of Psalm 2! Jesus is the promised Son of God from the OT speaking now to his church in Thyatira.

But the Son of God title is also one that has significance for the people of Thyatira because in their city the patron god of Thyatira, Apollo Tyrimnaeus, was supposedly the son of God, that is, the son of Zeus. The Roman Emperor was also referred to as the son of Zeus. So Jesus opens up this letter as a challenge: To which 'Son' of God will you submit? Over to you, church at Thyatira. To which son will you show your allegiance? But before we get into that, we need to see what good things Jesus has to say about this church.

> I know your deeds, your <u>love</u> and <u>faith</u>, your <u>service</u> and <u>perseverance</u>, and that you are now <u>doing more than you did at first</u> (2:19).

They show their **faith** in works, in outreach. They have **love!** They persevere in outreach despite opposition. And their **service** is that they care for the poor. But more than this, they are growing in these things ... **you are doing more than you did at first.** What else could you ask for? We could only hope that on the Day of Judgment *we* could receive such a commendation from Jesus.

What a contrast to the church at Ephesus, which was doing less at the end than it was in the beginning with its first love. The cold church at Ephesus was meticulous in doctrine, but the people had lost the most important thing of all. Love. Love for the lost, love for one another, and especially love for Jesus. Their lampstand was not shining. How different was the church at Thyatira? This church was filled with love and good deeds. This church was reaching out and had **perseverance.** How many churches can be described this way?

Yet Jesus, the one walking amongst your lampstand as your Judge with eyes like blazing fire, says you have something seriously missing. What could it be? It's doctrine! It's their teaching!

> Nevertheless, I have this against you: You tolerate that woman Jezebel, who calls herself a prophetess. By <u>her teaching</u> she misleads my servants into sexual immorality and the eating of food sacrificed to idols (2:20).

These things pertain to doctrine—Christology, Jesus' exclusiveness, doctrine of man, sin, and sanctification. Do we really need all those big words? Well, yes. Now we can understand the seriousness with which Jesus takes doctrine. At first this church is looking as commendable as you get, yet by the end of it he speaks as the Judge giving a warning to repent or else …

He says they let people into the pulpit without testing their doctrine! And you say, 'Oh, but they have the Spirit.' But you don't have the Spirit if you neglect the most Spirit-filled place in the world. The Bible! Are your preachers teaching from the Bible, or is it teaching that mixes the word of God with other teachings from here and there?

Jezebel was an OT figure, so there must have been some preacher at Thyatira whose doctrinal teaching was so bad that by way of analogy she could be compared to the Jezebel of old, who enticed her husband Ahab and Israel into gross sin. Presumably in Thyatira this woman's name was not literally Jezebel. And it's not that all her teaching was wrong. She must have been a good speaker and still had good Christian things to say. She must have referred to the Bible, or they wouldn't have had her in the church in the first place! They are a Christian church commended by Jesus! *Nevertheless, I have this <u>against you</u>: <u>You</u> tolerate that woman Jezebel, who calls herself a prophetess.…*

But don't just blame it on the woman! It's *you.* *You* put up with her! Some issues at Thyatira were the same as those at Pergamum. Each industry was tied to their respective trade guilds which demanded workers give homage to their patron deities, and in Thyatira there was a guild for almost every trade. On festive occasions you had to pay homage to those deities or you would be out of the guild. In that case you would be out of work. On these festive occasions, part of the expected accompanying practice was immorality. What do you do? You have to provide for your family. Do you bow down a few times a year so you can still feed the little ones? How do you juggle this? Well, into this tension along comes a teacher. The Right Reverend Jezebel, who says you can have both. No tension! Freedom in Christ!

We can easily look at the church in Thyatira and say, 'Yes, if I lived in those ancient times I would stand for Jesus.' But we are faced with this now! We are in an increasingly pagan society with demands from friends, family, and work. Financial pressures make it hard to trust, to simply give our tithe, and reject work or our own pleasures that conflict with our walk with the Lord. And single life has its loneliness and pressures with sexual temptation that society bombards us with. We are living it now!

With Jezebel's teaching, it's easier to get into the world and get along with the world—and to reach the world! You can avoid the problems with the trade guilds, and social and work life. No longer will your friends and family think you are a stick in the mud! So they welcomed this preacher. She has a new style of teaching that really sits so well with us. It feels right. We don't want to alienate people! We want to reach them! She speaks into the reality of our lives. She professes Christ and refers to the Scriptures. Freedom in Christ!

But it's not only what Reverend Jezebel was saying, but once again, *what she was leaving out*. **By her teaching she misleads her servants into sexual immorality.** Was it that she left out the hard teaching on sin and its seriousness? What about teaching on repentance? Misleading people into false doctrine is as simple as not including the essentials of the gospel, which is the holiness of God and the bad news about sin, which goes before the good news of forgiveness and repentance unto life. A new creature in Christ cannot go back to darkness. If it's that subtle, how can we discern a false teacher? Answer: Read the word of God and look out for false teachers, not just by what they say, but what they leave out!

Are we having déjà vu? This is almost the same message that Pergamum received. Thyatira's problems are the same as Pergamum's! Compromise in worship and sexual immorality. Is it wasted space? Jesus doesn't think so.

> Whoever has ears, let them hear what the Spirit says to the churches (2:29).

He says it again in the plural, for *all* churches. So why the repetition? Since it is a real message to real churches in Pergamum and Thyatira, maybe it's just coincidence that it worked out to be a little redundant for the rest of us, since this church literally has the same problems. Maybe. Or could it be this word of God speaks as it often does in repetition to highlight a point? The problems that hit churches can often be centered on those two issues—compromise in worship and sexual immorality, coupled with a lack of testing of those who are teaching in the church. Add to that a lack of church discipline when people stray.

Overall, the book of Revelation comes down mighty hard on false prophets. What we have here is a problem which has plagued churches for 2000 years—morality, and a lack of testing of teachers and doctrine. People don't open their Bibles and read for themselves.

The Bible is clear on sexual immorality. Sex is given by God as a good thing in its God given context, marriage between a man and woman. But when used wrongly, it will keep more people out of heaven than we can imagine ... because we were warned! Over and over again. Here again in Thyatira!

> I have given her time to repent of her immorality, but she is unwilling (2:21).

He has **given her time,** implying this has gone on for some time and no one has done anything about it. It also implies the Lord doesn't wait forever. The warning has been left unattended. This is a book of revelation. A warning book. A Day of Judgment book. 'Oh, but I didn't know, Lord.' 'Yes, you did,' he says. 'I put it in writing!'

> So I will cast her on a bed of suffering, and I will make those who commit adultery with her suffer intensely, unless they repent of her ways (2:22).

Bed of suffering is a metaphor for sickness or some kind of judgment. We know sexual immorality often brings its own self-inflicted sicknesses and suffering. But what about those committing adultery with her? Was that literally? Possibly, as we often see false teachers involved in immorality. But this could also be referring to those who went along with her in what the OT would call adultery, meaning spiritual adultery. There is a price to pay ...

> I will strike her children dead (2:23a).

Presumably **her children** meant people who have followed her ways, as opposed to 'children of God', they are 'Jezebel's children'.

> Then all the churches will know that I am he who searches hearts and minds, and I will repay each of you according to your deeds (2:23b).

The book of Revelation heads towards the end of all things where the dead are judged according to the things they have done (20:12). A terrifying thought for those who demanded justice from God saying, 'Why doesn't God do something about evil?' They never imagine that he does, but far more than they will ever want, *even searching hearts and minds!* **I am he who searches hearts and minds, and I will repay each of you according to your deeds.**

Does that mean believers will be judged in the same way? Aren't believers saved by faith? Yes, but faith without works is dead, and those truly entrusting themselves to Jesus will exhibit faith in the way they live and the choices they make. Did you listen to Jesus? Did you listen to what the Spirit is saying to the churches? *He searches the heart and mind.* His eyes are like blazing fire, so he knows if you are committing spiritual adultery. Is there any immorality going on in your life?

Those *eyes of fire* look right into the deepest part of your heart. Even more than we look at our own hearts. After all, what is the unbeliever's great cry to justify their sin? 'God knows my heart.' But that is the bad news. God *does* know your heart! In fact, he knows it a whole lot better than you, because if you really knew your own heart you would never use that as an excuse. You would confess sin and repent of it, not excuse it. You would see the self-righteousness that is behind it. 'I will go along with the Lord where it suits me, but where it interferes too much, well, God knows my heart.' But that is choosing your own morality. I will be king! I don't have to be like those gung-ho Christians who go to church every week or abstain from this or that (in this case sexual immorality, maybe pornography). But whatever it is, I don't have to worry because, 'God knows my heart.' You might be able to hide from yourself, but not from the One who *searches hearts and minds with eyes like blazing fire*. He warned us and put it in writing!

So faith takes Jesus and the word of God seriously. Are you serious about doctrine? This is also primarily what Jesus is on about here. Teaching. Do you take the word of God seriously? Many people follow teachers rather than God's word. Since Reverend Jezebel is on trial here, let's look briefly at the subject of women preaching in worship services. It's not central to the gospel. It's only secondary compared to the essentials of the gospel, such as Jesus' death, resurrection, deity, and our repentance and faith. On that scale, let's rate it as one out of ten in importance. But as far as God speaking plainly in his word … it gets ten out of ten. How clear is this?

> I do not permit a woman to <u>teach</u> or to assume authority over a man … (1 Tim. 2:12).

The latest NIV translation has the word *assume* next to authority, as though that might accommodate the 21st century enlightened thinking on this subject, which stretches the use of the word that simply means to *have* authority[10]. But even if the word could be stretched, it still wouldn't help that case because Paul also said in the same sentence, *I do not permit a woman to <u>teach</u> over a man!* Can't twist that one (though many will still try).

But here we can use this as a case study on our attitude to the word of God. Instead of trying to twist it, we should enter into why God said it in the first place. We know the Lord never taught that men are superior to women. In fact, the same apostle Paul said male and female are equal in Christ (Gal. 3:28). We know male and female are

---

[10] *The Greek New Testament, Fourth Revised Edition* Ed. Barbara Aland, Kurt Aland, Johannes, Karavidopolous, Carlo M. Martini, Bruce Metzger, (D-Stuttgart: Deutsche Bibelgeselllschaft, 1998) Dictionary p. 28

made equally in God's image (Gen. 1:27). But the idea of roles in relationship is something God has within himself. The Son is in submission to the Father (1 Cor. 1:28) and yet is fully equal to the Father (John 5:18). Nor is the apostle Paul against women in ministry. The Scriptures have many ministries for women, including teaching! Titus 2:4, women are to *teach* other women! Could this be because the Lord sees there are some subjects where women are more suited to teaching other women than male teachers?

In fact, the qualifications for an elder in 1 Timothy 3 preclude most *men* from eldership. But 1 Timothy 2:12 is God's word in the context of instructions on worship in the church, not in the world. So we should not be bothered if a man has a female boss or a female political leader. The church is to reflect the order of God himself, just as our marriages are to reflect Christ and his church.

But what do people say about this instruction to the church? 'Oh, but you have to understand the context of women in that culture and what the apostle Paul really meant ...' But in 1 Timothy the apostle Paul gives the context and says it's nothing to do with culture. He says it has to do with Creation. The woman was deceived, not the man. This tells us the man was more culpable and sinned more willfully. *He* was the one given the direct instruction. He *wasn't* deceived. He was there and should have taken his God given role and protected his wife.

It would take another book to refute every imaginative way people find to ignore this part of the word of God, and even then there are always new ways emerging. But none of them start with God's word or the Bible's worldview that our first sin was pride *(you too can be like God)*. So, the *pride* of fallen humans assumes 'leadership' must mean 'superiority'. With that assumption, through the ages, men have abused Jesus' model of male servant-leadership and turned it into something as though the leader is 'superior', and women have coveted that position of 'superiority' and want equal rights to the 'superior' roles. Both have it wrong. God doesn't say leadership is superior. Only the pride of the human heart assumes that. Instead, Jesus says whoever is leader must be servant of all. Furthermore, the reason for roles is about pointing to God, not us. God has no problem with different roles and equality within himself, Father, Son and Holy Spirit.

If God had wanted there to be no arguments, what else did he need to add to that 1 Timothy text to make it clear? 'I do not permit a woman to teach or have authority over a man—*And I really mean it!*' But what is the response of Christians to this compromise these days, as the world encroaches and demands so-called 'equality'? 'Well, I know this really knowledgeable godly preacher and he (or she) says it's okay for women to teach over men.' Yes, but did you test that against the word of God? 'Oh, but they have this long explanation from the Bible, and God is doing lots through women teachers, and besides, every church goes along with it, so it can't be that bad.' Well, not everyone goes along with it. Nor did everyone go along with Jezebel at Thyatira.

> Now I say to the rest of you in Thyatira, to you who do not hold to her teaching and have not learned Satan's so-called deep secrets, 'I will not impose any other burden on you, …' (2:24).

What were **Satan's so-called deep secrets?** Was it an unhealthy interest with the devil and his ways, beyond what Scripture tells us? Was it some supposedly unknown thing about the devil? Were they specialists at delivering demons from under your couch, but not focusing on Christ? Or were the 'deep things of Satan' referring to false teachers who claim, 'The Lord is leading me', when he wasn't? Here we are, 2000 years on from this letter to Thyatira, and people are still looking for that 'extra' knowledge. The *secrets!* It's as rampant and enticing in Christian circles as ever. Thyatira is alive!

Today everyone wants a personal word from the Lord, just for me. It tickles our ears to hear someone say, 'I've got a word for you from the Lord'. But how do you know it's from the Lord? Well, it's the deep things of God that no one else can give you. Does that mean it's from Satan? Not necessarily. It could simply be from our own spirit (Ezek. 13:3). Even devout Christians get caught up in this. We have this penchant for extra knowledge. Where does that come from? It's straight out of the garden! *Eat of the fruit and you will be like God!* Having what? *Extra knowledge!* And when she saw it was desirable for *gaining wisdom* … It's in us! Knowledge and wisdom beyond what God has given us in his word!

But if you want to know where the real *deep secrets* for a Christian are, they are found in *Christ, ... in whom <u>are hidden all</u> the treasures of wisdom and knowledge* (Col. 2:2-3). We have *all* wisdom in Christ and learn of him through the word of God given to you! He put it in writing!

But we say it's not enough. We are always looking for something extra. Even the Book of Revelation works like that for some people. Jesus said no one knows the time of his return. It will *not* come from your careful observation. 'Yes, but we have this interpretation of Revelation that can tell us the secrets of when it's going to happen.' There are also all those hidden secrets of Satan in the Illuminati. Conspiracy theories, or the hidden secrets of your personal future. Knowledge. A personal word from the Lord. If we had more secrets, then …

But the true hidden treasure is this. *The fullness of all wisdom and treasure is in Christ.* And he has put in writing all the fullness of what he wants to say to us — in his word. There are no extras. Nor should we take anything away from it, like the Jezebels. The trick of the devil today is to get Christians caught up looking for an extra word here, a course there, or a new teaching, just to keep you away from where *all* the real treasure of wisdom and knowledge is found. *In Christ and his word!* How many people caught up looking for these extra things are really spending time reading his living word? If you want to know where the secrets are, where you will find real knowledge and wisdom, then read your Bible!

There are no deep secrets. If we are sinners who face a judge who sees every heart and mind, and repays us according to what we have done, then we are all gonners. We need a Savior. It's so mathematically simple. Get caught breaking the law. The Judge says there is a fine to pay according to what you have done or go to jail! But good news! Jesus pays the fine! The cross. The eternal fine. Paid in full! For all who will believe in him.

Do you want to know how to recognize a false teacher in the church today? They leave out the cross! Sermon after sermon, good Christian stuff and you are listening to the details, when the elephant in the room is this. Where is the cross? Leave it out and *that is* false teaching! That is our Thyatira today.

But not all of you were enticed by that false teaching. So, what is Jesus' instruction to you? *Only <u>hold on to what you have</u> until I come* (2:25).

Just hold fast to Jesus and his word and find contentment in that ...

> To the one who is victorious and does my will to the end, I will give authority over the nations— that one 'will rule them with an iron scepter and will dash them to pieces like pottery'– just as I have received authority from my Father (2:26-27).

Between false teachers within the church and evil rampant outside, it seems like evil is winning, but all those who thought they were getting away with it aren't getting away with anything. They will not only see they were wrong, but **he will dash them to pieces like pottery.** Rev. 2:27 is a quote from Psalm 2. Long ago in history, at about 1000 BC, Psalm 2 gave an answer to that great question. How can God reverse evil? How can God allow it? Well, here is that picture reiterated centuries later in the book of Revelation, that one day Jesus will have the complete and utter victory over evil. He will *smash* it down. In fact, he is able to overturn the deeds of evil and give such victory to those who suffered. They are lifted so high it will be incomprehensible. And ...

> I will also give that one the morning star (2:28).

Jesus refers to himself as the **morning star** in 22:16, so here that authority and reigning with him is confirmed. So **morning star** here means sharing in the Messianic victory. Look at the reward that waits. It's incomprehensible, some of the things Jesus promised to those who *are victorious*. Authority with Christ. To the one who is victorious, there is exaltation over everything that ever opposed you, but in ways that we haven't even begun to comprehend.

However, being victorious implies in the meantime we will have to take up our cross. It will be tough. But we don't chuck in the towel and go with enticing teachers who tell us what we want to hear. We stick to the word of God. Through many hardships we enter the kingdom.

Whoever has ears, let them hear what the Spirit says to the churches.

Study Questions

1. In what way does Jesus identify himself from Rev. 1 in this letter, and how does it relate to Thyatira?

2. How does Jesus allude to the OT in relation to himself in this letter, and what is its significance?

3. What other allusions are there to the OT in this letter, and why is he drawing on them?

4. What is the point of the repetition in the Bible? What factors are repeated in this letter to the church at Thyatira that were in the previous letter, and how is it relevant to the contemporary church?

5. What are the points of commendation from Jesus? What do these have to say to the church today?

6. What pressures exist in the church today to compromise, and why would they be enticing?

7. In what part does this letter address the question of 'Why does God allow suffering and evil?'

8. If we are truly saved by faith and not by works, how can there be a judge who searches our hearts and minds?

9. How might we be tempted to look into Satan's deep secrets today?

10. Where are the hidden treasures to be found?

8
Sardis
(Revelation 3:1-6)

Have you ever heard people complain that Christians don't have anything written by Jesus? After all, the NT is written by Jesus' followers. Well, there is a good reason for that. The whole point of having four gospels of the same essential stories and teaching is that they are independent witnesses. We also have the early history in the book of Acts and the NT letters testifying to Jesus. The Christian faith stands on historical grounds and testimony of various witnesses and eyewitnesses who were with Jesus. This provides a far more substantial historical validity than if a person is just doing his own writing.

Mohammed, the founder and prophet of Islam, lived about 600 years after Jesus. He claimed to have a vision from an angel. Who was there to see it? Only Mohammed. Mohammed himself even doubted the source of the angel visiting him at first. Was it an evil source, or good? He finally concluded it was good, but who can testify for him? What eyewitnesses were there?

Joseph Smith, the founder of Mormonism, claimed in the early 1800s to have had visitations from God and angels. Who was there to see it? It's just Joseph Smith's word and his subsequent writings.

But Jesus' record is one of public events. Miracles not done in a corner but in the open, in public, recorded by eyewitness both friendly and hostile. The greatest miracle of all was that after Jesus was publicly executed, he rose from the dead. We also have a record where it is not merely Jesus writing what he did or said, but eyewitnesses willing to lay down their lives, testifying to what they saw—Jesus risen from the dead! Some of these eyewitnesses were former unbelievers (James and Jude, see John 7:5), even former enemies of Christ, like the apostle Paul, who had murdered Christians in an attempt to eradicate Christianity (Acts 22:4). Yet Paul ended up writing more letters of the NT than anyone. So instead of one man writing about himself, we have eyewitnesses, even former skeptics who testify to Jesus' life and teaching.

So we don't have anything Jesus wrote himself. Or do we?

Here we are launching into the fifth of seven letters written in the book of Revelation that Jesus personally dictated to his beloved disciple John. This is the letter to the church at Sardis. Jesus says to John ...

> To the angel of the church in Sardis write: These are the words of him who holds the seven spirits of God and the seven stars ... (3:1a).

Jesus again identifies himself from the vision in Rev. 1. This time from 1:4, *the seven spirits of God*. Remember, the idea of *seven spirits* is not a new teaching of the Trinity, but the number seven represents completeness. Just as we are looking at seven churches which represent the whole church, the seven spirits mean the complete Spirit of God. So Jesus sends forth his Spirit. Why does he open with this to the church at Sardis? This church was well known as a living active church.

Jesus starts this letter the same way he does writing to the other churches. Let's not forget that even though those letters were sent to each individual church, all the letters are sent as a whole to all the churches. Rev. 1:4 tells us the whole book is addressed to all the churches. So the people at the church at Sardis would have already read the first four letters just as we did. They are familiar with the wording when Jesus starts with this letter to Sardis, *I know your deeds* ... because that has been Jesus' way of introducing his commendations of 'good deeds' to the churches. *I know your good deeds*. So, if you are sitting there in your pew in Sardis, listening as this letter was being read out to the congregation (which is what happened when letters arrived in these early churches), you would have been proudly sitting there, waiting for your commendation from Jesus. Waiting proudly, because you know your church has a reputation for being alive! You are waiting on the edge of your pew for this compliment from Jesus when he starts, I know your deeds ... but then he pulls the rug out from under you ...

> I know your deeds; you have a reputation of being alive, but you are dead (3:1b).

What? **Dead?** But everyone knows we are alive! This is a total shock to this church. And it will take an incredible amount of God given grace and humility for us to get anything from this letter, because if you are anything like the people in this church, you are so confident this has to be speaking to someone else that you won't even think it could be you. After all, you are even known by *others* for being alive. You have a reputation!

So now we know why Jesus chooses to identify himself with the *seven spirits of God and the seven stars*. Jesus is the one who supplies the Spirit of God to those who ask. Why this description from Jesus? Because the people in Sardis are not asking! They don't even suspect they are lacking in the Spirit because they have a reputation for being alive. They don't even suspect they are dead!

How serious is this? Sardis is the only church of any of the seven that is described as dead. Sardis is also only one of two churches of the seven which are given no compliments. If there is any similarity it's with the church at Ephesus, where the church was doctrinally excellent but with no effective witness to the world. The word was not going forth from the church or individuals. Their lampstand was burning low. So Jesus deliberately identifies himself as the one who can give the Holy Spirit!

People flock to churches with a big reputation, famous for outreach, famous preacher, famous for their music, and famous for their size and work. Famous for the Holy Spirit! Everyone is excited about joining this big, happening church, even when they are not happening themselves. That's where the rot sets in. Eventually the church becomes filled with people wanting to *be* served rather than to *serve*. Of course *we* would not fit this description. That's the scary part. The people of Sardis didn't even suspect it. What is Jesus' word to them?

> Wake up! Strengthen what remains and is about to die, for I have found your deeds unfinished in the sight of my God (3:2).

There is still a chance! **Wake up!** Sardis was a wealthy city, famous for its impregnable walls that were on a virtually inaccessible hill. Its people took great pride in that. Sardis was the old capital of Lydia, the 'Overseer of the Hermus Valley'. There was a pride in the people of Sardis in their own strength and reputation. They lived in a city confident that no one could attack. Who could climb the hillsides that were almost straight up and down, about 1500ft (500m) high? There was only one entrance, which could be easily manned, because it was narrow. They were so confident in their own security, they were terribly overconfident. In 549 BC, Cyrus the Persian king came with his army. The king of Sardis had been warned not to be too confident, but even when Cyrus' army showed up on the plains below, they were not concerned because it seemed impossible to scale those walls. Greek historian Herodotus wrote ...

> 'At a place where no guards were ever set, a soldier climbed the rock and other Persians followed in his track, until a large number had mounted to the top. Sardis was taken while it was asleep!' [11]

Wake up! But as history wore on, Sardis went back to sleep with confidence in its own reputation as an impregnable fortress. And it all happened again! In 218 BC, the Seleucid king Antiochus the Great managed to do the same thing. The proud people of impregnable Sardis were what? Caught asleep! It's said these attacks came at night. Like a thief! Were the watchmen asleep? One crack in the rock wall was enough for rock climbers to surprise the proud sleepers.

In AD 17 there was an earthquake that destroyed parts of Sardis. The impregnable city was caught out again. And now, like the city, the *church* at Sardis was confident it had a good reputation. Some real gospel work had been done in the past. Maybe they were like Ephesus in that they had forgotten their first beginnings.

> Remember, therefore, <u>what you have received and heard</u>; hold it fast, and repent. But if you do not wake up, I will come <u>like a thief</u>, and you will not know at what time I will come to you (3:3).

Is Jesus alluding to the history of those attacks on Sardis? Rock climbers like thieves scaled the walls. They needed to go back to what they received, obey it, and repent. Go back to your basic teaching. You received the very word of God. A church needs to constantly look at the Bible. 'Oh, but we already study the Bible. We already love our doctrine.' *Yes, but are you living it, or are you dead?* Remember what you received, obey it, and repent! Otherwise he will **come like**

---

[11] Herodotus, Histories 1.84.1-5

a thief. Unexpectedly! This is reminiscent of Jesus' words ...

> But understand this: If the owner of the house had known at what time of night the thief was coming, he would have kept watch and would not have let his house be broken into. So you also must be ready, because the Son of Man will come at an hour when you do not expect him (Matt. 24:43-44).

Here Jesus is talking about the final judgment. But in the letter to Sardis, is he talking about the final judgment or of a partial judgment in their lifetime? He kind of leaves us hanging, and possibly for the good reason this is what judgment is like. You are not expecting it! It's like those in Sardis who were not expecting Cyrus' men to climb that wall. Like a thief! So unexpected!

> Yet you have a few people in Sardis who have not soiled their clothes. They will walk with me, dressed in white, for they are worthy (3:4).

Rev. 14:4 talks of those who have not defiled themselves with women. That could be what he means here, **not soiled their clothes**. But there were the other problems in ancient Rome of idolatry with the trade guild demands on work life. It was a question of livelihood and being able to avoid being totally outcast both socially and financially. Keep your head down at work, go along with skimping on the boss' time and take advantage of the perks, not just because everyone does it, but because they have pressured you, so if you stick your head up you will spoil it for everyone else. Move with the world. So they compromised with signing up to the trade guild demands. Burn a little incense to Caesar ('I don't really think he is a god, so what difference does it make?') You do have to feed the family. But before you know it, you have become like the world around you and your witness has died. They are dead in Sardis. They don't tell the gospel *or* live it! It doesn't get any more serious.

But praise God there were a few who *have not soiled their clothes*. **They will walk with me, dressed in white, for they are worthy.** Worthy? How? White represents purity. Not compromising with the world in sexual purity, in worldliness, even in literal clothing, the way we dress, or in our entertainment.

Where is Sardis today? Where is the church in need of 'going back to what it had received'? Today in the church we debate what is *soiling of clothes* based on the world's standards. Christian reviewers of movies lament how it's so hard to rate movies because what was rated 'R' before is now rated 'M', so how can you tell? Well how about not using the world's ratings at all! All they prove is that the world *has* no solid ratings. It continually shifts its values downward as we head into paganism. Christianity has a written rating system that hasn't changed in 2000 years. Just use Ephesians 4:29-5:13. God's ratings are: no coarse joking, not even a hint of sexual immorality, and no bad language. God has made it so simple to rate movies. Just run them by *his* rating test.

Another debate between Christians has been how much of graphic descriptions of immorality or bad language should a preacher use if it is in the context of teaching. You would think God has made it really hard for us to figure it out in some subjective guesswork manner. We are like the world. One opinion here, one there. But God has not left us to guess. He made it clear.

> Do not let any unwholesome talk come out of your mouths ... (Eph. 4:29).

How easy is that? What about when I am quoting what someone else said? *Do not let it come out of your mouth.* What about when I am trying to relate something in a realistic manner to non-Christians? *Do not let it come out of your mouth.* It's the same thing with sexual temptation. *Not even a hint.* What about just looking at images? *Not even a hint.* What about getting close to someone? *Not even a hint.* Don't soil your clothes!

But there are some of you who haven't soiled your clothes ... you're not so comfortable. You miss out on some 'fun' stuff. You are willing to put up with ridicule to shine a light. You stay pure and fight temptation. You lose income. You stay faithful to the church. You're willing to be embarrassed. You invite people to church and get ridiculed. You stand up for Jesus' gospel in front of even family and friends who tried to make you choose between them and Jesus' moral standards. You're willing to have your reputation *tarnished* ... you don't care about your reputation.

How much does reputation mean to you? The people of Sardis worried about their reputation. They had a *reputation for being alive* (3:1). That was more important to them. Who is the one you want to have a good reputation with? Look at this …

> The one who is victorious will, like them, be dressed in white. I will never blot out the name of that person from the book of life, but <u>will acknowledge that name before my Father</u> and his angels (3:5).

Here is Jesus, saying the same thing as he did in Matthew …

> Whoever acknowledges me before others, I will also acknowledge before my Father in heaven. But whoever disowns me before others, I will disown before my Father in heaven (Matt. 10:32-33).

Who will stand for Jesus? It's back to witnessing again. Reputation with whom? The world, or Jesus? If you proclaim Christ, he will proclaim you. If you disown him, he will disown you. What an amazing thought! If you are one who stands up for Jesus, the Son of God will personally speak to the Father for you. That is the reputation I want. This letter to Sardis is telling us what Jesus said in the Sermon on the Mount. Not everyone who says they are Christian is going to make it. *Narrow is the road that leads to life and only a few find it.* Jesus says there are only a few who haven't soiled their clothes. Many will come on that day saying, 'Lord, Lord, didn't we do all these good things in your name.' But he comes like a thief. They're climbing your walls Sardis and you are asleep, not realizing your time is running out. Not everyone is going to make it.

Only **the one who is victorious … will be dressed in white**. There is a hardship we have to endure. You might be struggling right now. You might have a spouse who is so difficult you are ready to chuck it in. What is the answer? *The one who is victorious … will be dressed in white.*

You might continue to fight lust of the eyes. *The one who is victorious … will be dressed in white.*

You might have to face the race alone, loneliness. *The one who is victorious … will be dressed in white.*

Work life is pressured, how can I keep going? *The one who is victorious … will be dressed in white.*

You might struggle with rebellious children. *The one who is victorious … will be dressed in white.*

Perhaps you cannot see any way out of a financial crisis. Seek first

His kingdom and all these things will be added. *The one who is victorious ... will be dressed in white.*

You might feel you have no one who can relate to your situation. *The one who is victorious ... will be dressed in white.*

You have had enough and just want to go home to be with the Lord. Not yet! *The one who is victorious ... will be dressed in white.*

You might feel the more you witness to others the more isolated you become. *The one who is victorious ... will be dressed in white.*

Perhaps you are not bothered by anything. You are comfortable. But maybe you are dead! Only ... *The one who is victorious ... will be dressed in white.*

You might think the Christian faith could be a bit more flexible, after all, most Christians these days don't take this holiness thing seriously. But don't stain those garments! Yes, most professing Christians are comfortable. But what is the warning? *Reputation* for being Christian and alive—but you are dead! Don't stain those garments! Only *the one who is victorious will be dressed in white.*

What will your church look like on that day? I want to see every churchgoer I know in white on that day. I don't want to look out and see some from my church with stained garments. It will show up on that day. Who will it be on that day that misses out? Picture your local church. Who will stand out with the stained clothes? You might be living a comfortable, quiet, compromised life now, but on that day, it will be painfully obvious who is wearing the stained garment. Everyone will see.

So who can be victorious? Later Jesus is victorious (17:14). But here it's those who follow him who also must be victorious. How? How can you be dressed in white? We get the message later on in ...

> ... 'These are they who have come out of the great tribulation; they have washed their robes and made them white in the blood of the Lamb' (7:14).

We see the connection in Sardis. *Yet you have a few people in Sardis who <u>have not soiled their clothes</u>. They will walk with me, <u>dressed in white</u>, for they are worthy.* Who is worthy? The only way you can be worthy is if you have washed your filthy rags white in the blood of the Lamb. If you have not been victorious in any of these or other areas, repent! This is the message here. Wake up! Throw yourself on the mercy of the blood of the Lamb and turn from your sin. The cross of Jesus takes away our sin. If you really know Jesus' cross it should do what? Wake you up! And make you want to bring every single one of these areas where you have been dead to the cross of Christ. Repent, and be washed clean and made white in the blood of the Lamb.

If you have not been a witness for Jesus, it's not too late. Wake up! Repent! And if you do?

> ... I will never blot out the <u>name of that person from the book of life, but will acknowledge that name before my Father</u> and his angels (3:5b).

The names are written from before the foundation of the world. It's mentioned all the way through Revelation (13:8, 17:8, 20:12, 15). It climaxes near the end with the contrast between those whose sins are recorded in books and those with washed robes. Their names don't appear in the sin record. Their names are written in the book of life.

If your name is written in that book, here is the promise and guarantee—if your name is there, it stays there forever. It won't be erased. It is guaranteed. **It will never be blotted out.** If you have been called, even if you are one of those with a reputation for being alive but have little spiritual witness in the world, even if your lampstand is almost snuffed out, if your name is there you will be moved to wash your stained garments! If your name is in the book of life, then it is there now. If it's not there, it never will be.

So is your name there? If it's in the book of life and you have been dying, then you will hear what the Spirit is saying to the churches. You will hear what Jesus wrote to you. Wake up!

Could you be in a Sardis church? Are there any Sardines out there? Stained garments? Something smells a bit fishy? The lampstand is getting dimmer and dimmer. There were only a few at Sardis who would wear white. Only a few who heard.

Sardis had a strong Jewish population, as well as its Roman heritage, yet there is no sign of persecution from either. The church is comfortable. At peace. Is that you? You're not persecuted because you don't tell the good news? Jesus says he *holds the Spirit*, waiting to supply. Are you seeking him for the Spirit? Do you attend the prayer meeting at your local congregation? Are you serving in your church? When you don't have the Spirit, it's because you don't ask!

Yet you have a few people in Sardis who have not soiled their clothes. They will walk with me, dressed in white, for they are worthy. We simply cannot be comfortable in the fact there are people around us just as slack as us. We have a lampstand to shine, but is it happening? Sardis was comfortable and relied on reputation but slept while they were overtaken. They didn't even have time to put on their make-up. If you want something written by Jesus personally, if you have a reputation for being alive but are not, Jesus himself wrote this letter for you. Wake up! Repent. *He who is victorious will be dressed in white.*

Study Questions

1. Why don't we have any writings from Jesus himself?

2. What is the significance of Jesus' self-identification from Rev. 1? What do the 'seven spirits of God' mean?

3. What are some characteristics that distinguish the church at Sardis from the other churches?

4. What parallels could we find historically with the city of Sardis and the church there?

5. What are some of the ways Christians could 'soil their clothes' today?

6. If we are saved by faith in Christ, what is the call to be victorious?

7. How do you know your name is written in the book of life?

8. If the people of Sardis are overconfident, how do you know you are not?

9. What does it mean to be dressed in white?

9
Philadelphia
(Revelation 3:7-13)

As we have pictured the postman who left John on the island of Patmos, we noted the seven churches are geographically in a big circle in Asia Minor. So the postman was heading from Ephesus to Smyrna, Pergamum, Thyatira, Sardis, and then he arrives at Philadelphia, about 75 miles (120km) east of Ephesus (where we started).

We can picture the pastor of the church in Philadelphia reading aloud the letter which arrived from the apostle John the following Lord's Day. It was a letter penned by John, but it's actually a letter from Jesus, dictated to John. So they listen with hearts in their mouths.

> To the angel of the church in Philadelphia write: These are the words of him who is holy and true, who holds the key of David. What he opens no one can shut, and what he shuts no one can open (3:7).

The people in the congregation at Philadelphia said, 'Yes, Jesus **holds the key of David.** We regularly read the OT Scriptures here and our pastor preaches it, so we know Jesus is quoting Isaiah.'

> I will place on his shoulder the key to the house of David; what he opens no one can shut, and what he shuts no one can open (Isa. 22:22).

In its OT context (in Isaiah's time), it was Eliakim who was a steward over the house of King Hezekiah and had the 'key' or authority to allow people (or not) into the king's presence. So that's it! Jesus is saying *he* holds the key to get into *the* King's presence. Heaven itself! *Jesus* holds the key of David. David was the king, but he was a type of the greater king to come who said ...

I will give you the keys of the kingdom of heaven ... (Matt. 16:19).

For the people of Philadelphia, they would be saying, 'This is what we needed to hear. We have been under persecution from Jewish people who rejected Jesus as their Messiah. They said *they* had the key to the Davidic kingdom and could exclude us and shut the door on us.' And they did, just as Jesus predicted would happen to Jewish Christians ...

> They will put you out of the synagogue; in fact, a time is coming when anyone who kills you will think they are offering a service to God (John 16:2).

This is what was happening at that time in Philadelphia, when the church received this letter from Jesus. During the synagogue service Jews would pronounce a curse on Christians, leaving those who were Christian Jews to either pronounce a curse on themselves or leave the synagogue. They knew what it was like to say, 'They shut the door on us!' But Jesus says he can open that door and **what he opens no one can shut, and what he shuts no one can open.** They had been struggling with opposition and weakness, but Jesus is saying to them it's okay. I know your weakness, but you still stood up for me. I've been there with you. I have noticed every little effort ...

> I know your deeds. See, I have placed before you an open door that no one can shut. <u>I know that you have little strength</u>, yet you have kept my word and have not denied my name (3:8).

Like city, like church. In Jesus' letter to the church at Sardis, he used the background history of the city to speak to the church. When the people of Philadelphia read Jesus' words, **I know you have little strength,** they would immediately recognize that Jesus is referring to the 'weakness', of the city. It was well known that a massive earthquake destroyed the city of Philadelphia decades earlier in AD 17. Even though it was rebuilt, the city itself was weakened and diminished in number because people were concerned about future earthquake risk, so many lived in outer regions rather than in the city.

Their church also had little strength because they were persecuted. Jesus says I know you have *little strength*, but **you haven't denied my name.** Jesus says, 'I see you are under persecution from unbelieving Jews, but it's okay. I open the doors.' And this little church with little strength was still there 12 centuries later. In fact, there is said to be a small church there today. We notice that other churches of the seven (apart from Smyrna) had their lampstands removed literally, or received rebukes of all kinds, but not Philadelphia. It lasted longer than most of the others. Jesus opens doors, and keeps them open. But there is someone else involved ...

> I will make those who are of the synagogue of Satan, who claim to be Jews though they are not, but are liars — (3:9a).

Even though it's *people* who persecute the church, **Satan** is always behind it. Satan hates the church and uses and stirs up whomever he can. In this case there was a Jewish community in Philadelphia. Ignatius was an early church leader (about AD 35-107) who wrote to the Philadelphians (Philadelphian letter 6:1). He lived during the time when Philadelphia received this letter from Jesus. Ignatius speaks of a conflict between the church at Philadelphia and the local Jewish community. But Jesus is saying just because the persecuting Jews have the ethnic background, that doesn't make them true Jews.

Here is Jesus, the most famous Jew in history who knows the history of Israel. He knows only a small percentage of them were faithful to their God. But now, in Jesus' time, even though the first Christians were Jews, most Jews rejected their Messiah, just as the majority had rejected their God throughout history. Jesus affirms salvation is of the Jews. They are God's chosen. But if the Jews reject their very own Messiah (just like many of the Israelites of old rejected their Lord), although they claim to be Jews, they are not in the true spiritual sense. Jesus says he has the key to the house of David! To the members of the church at Philadelphia, both Jews and Gentiles who have believed in the Jewish Messiah, Jesus says that at judgment he will vindicate his true ethnic Jewish people as well as Gentiles who have embraced the Jewish Messiah.

> ... I will make them come and fall down at your feet and acknowledge that I have loved you. Since you have kept my command to endure patiently, I will also keep you from the hour of trial that is going to come on the whole world to test the inhabitants of the earth (3:9b-10).

He will **keep you from the hour of trial** could be interpreted in a couple of ways, depending on your view of end times. Christians differ on their view of end times and interpreting the book of

Revelation, with good reason. It's difficult! But the bigger message of Revelation is not difficult. It is not negotiable. *All* Christians agree ... Jesus wins!

But depending on your view of how the end times come about, this verse could be referring to a time when Jesus raptures Christians from the earth followed by the tribulation and then the beginning of his millennial reign, a 1000-year reign on earth before the final judgment. This is the predominant view held by most Christians throughout the world today. It is the Futurist Rapture view. In this case there is a rapture of Christians from the earth and *unbelievers* are left behind to go through the tribulation, hence the *Left Behind* series. If that is your view, then this is a good verse to take hold of because Jesus says he will *keep you* from the trial, while the unbelieving world undergoes a tribulation.

That is one possibility for understanding this verse. But there is another. When Jesus says he will *keep you from* the trial, he uses a phrase that is used on only one other occasion in the whole NT where the same original Greek words are used together in that combination. The other occasion also comes from the lips of Jesus and is also in John's writings.

> My prayer is not that you take them <u>out of the world</u> but that you <u>protect them from</u> the evil one (John 17:15).

Protect them from is literally the same phrase in Greek as at 3:10. In John's gospel, the *keeping you from* is a protection *through* the trial, not removal from it. Keeping you, protecting you through attacks from the evil one. So 3:10 may also be understood to mean Jesus *keeps us* not to avoid the trial, but to be kept *through* it.

First and foremost, 3:10 must have a relevance and fulfillment in Philadelphia in the first century ... *I will also <u>keep you</u> from the hour of trial*. It's an *hour* of trial for the Philadelphians. There must have been a short time of intense persecution, like that which Jesus said was going to come upon the church at Smyrna. Remember back in 2:10 ... *you will suffer persecution for ten days*. This indicated a short, sharp period of persecution. Here in 3:10 we are told this trial would come on **the whole world.** The known world was under the authority of Roman Emperor Domitian who demanded that he be worshiped. Faithful Christians did not give in to that. Intense persecution ensued at Smyrna.

But here is the clincher that should make us think carefully before using 3:10 as evidence the church is taken out of the tribulation. The persecution that the church at Smyrna experienced would have been the same at Philadelphia, in fact, throughout the *whole known world*. The unbelieving Jews (*the synagogue of Satan*), were only too happy to 'dob in' Christians, remembering a lot of those Christians were Jews. Christianity was not an officially sanctioned religion. The Jewish religion at the time was legal and approved by the Roman Empire. So the Romans persecuted the Christians. Was the church at Philadelphia removed from the tribulation? No. They were kept from falling in it. Jesus kept them. What would not make sense is if Philadelphia was removed from suffering the tribulation (by being raptured out), while the church at Smyrna was told to endure it even to death! He was *not* taking them out of it (2:10). Why would Jesus take one church out and leave others in it? So it would seem that 3:10 refers to Jesus keeping Philadelphia in the sense that he is with them, *keeping them* through their tribulation.

The test came on the whole world in Philadelphia's time, but as we have looked at before, the seven churches points to the complete church and this letter finishes with that formula that tells us Jesus is speaking to all the churches (plural), *Whoever has ears, let them hear what the Spirit says to the churches*. So prophetically these letters speak into the history of the church. Which church today fits the description of the church at Philadelphia? Apart from Smyrna, Philadelphia is the only church out of the seven which doesn't get a rebuke from Jesus. So every Christian denomination claims, 'The church at Philadelphia must be us!' But Jesus is not referring to a denomination. He is referring to the persecuted church that doesn't deny his name. That would suggest it's not so much a Western-world church today, at least not yet.

Persecution comes in waves. 'Hours' of testing have come throughout history. We have already mentioned Domitian, but it didn't stop there. The most severe persecution in the early centuries came under Emperor Diocletian from AD 284-305. Then there was more persecution with the formation of Islam in about AD 600. The Islamic invasion conquered two-thirds of the 'Christian' world. Then the Roman church of the Middle Ages burned Christians at the stake for translating the Scriptures or standing for Christ. On into the 20th century, the atheistic institution of communism tried to eliminate Christianity. There is even more persecution going on today. What is the common denominator of these persecutions?

The people of the earth are tested with this. Which God will you follow? When the test comes, most people will go with the flow. 'Why should I lose my life? I can serve better if I'm alive.' But Jesus said whoever saves his life will lose it. Those who are not his will capitulate under testing. But if you are one of his who endures patiently, *Jesus will keep you through it.*

Because we don't see much in the West of what is typical in other lands, we don't realize how much persecution of Christians has escalated. It's a world under a test! Recently I was asked to conduct a funeral service for a young man, shot, murdered in Sudan, along with six others, killed for being Christians. For the Sudanese community this is an all too common occurrence. They know what it is to be under a test.

And though we don't see much persecution in the West (to the extent it occurs in other lands), the West knows something of the test. If you stick up for the values of Christ on marriage, abortion, or euthanasia, if you say Christ is the only way, you are no longer simply politically incorrect, you may even be breaking the law. A bigot! Someone who uses hate speech! Already there are laws that test us to see who will stand for Jesus. But to those who don't deny his name, *Jesus will keep you through it.*

We need this message. If 3:10 is saying the tests come on the whole world, and that we have to *live through* the test rather than be *taken out of it,* then we need to know this. We need to know that *Jesus will keep us through those trials.* Didn't he promise he is able to work all things together for the good of those who love him? But what is the context of that famous passage? Just before Romans 8:28 it's all about suffering. Look at Romans 8:18-27 *I consider our present suffering!* Even the creation is groaning in travail. But God works it all for good for his people in the midst of evil and suffering that is coming on the earth, but *not* by taking them out of it! John opened with this at the beginning of Revelation when he said *I, John, your brother and companion in the suffering and kingdom and patient endurance that are ours in Jesus* (1:9). If you want to be a companion in the kingdom, well then here it is! Suffering! But wait. Jesus says he will keep you through the hour of trial. Hold on ...

> I am coming soon. Hold on to what you have, so that no one will take your crown. The one who is victorious I will make a <u>pillar in the temple</u> of my God. Never again will they leave it. I will write on them the name of my God and the name of the city of my God, the new Jerusalem, which is coming down out of heaven from my God; and I will also write on them my new name (3:11-12).

You will be a **pillar in the temple.** What does that mean? Does he mean 'you're going to have to stand still and not move or the whole temple in heaven will fall down?' Revelation will take us to a heavenly temple in the New Jerusalem. God and his people form the temple (Rev. 21-22). But we are told elsewhere in the NT that *the church* is the temple of God with God in their midst. You are the temple Paul says.

> Don't you know that you yourselves are God's temple and that God's Spirit dwells in your midst? (1 Cor. 3:16).

Eph. 2:20-22 says *you are the building, the temple of God*. Heb. 3:6 *we are his house* ... This is how you become a *pillar* in God's temple—if you are one of the Lord's people. The Philadelphians suffered earthquakes more than any of the other cities, and their dwelling was unstable, so this promise of a permanent dwelling as a pillar in God's temple would have been a comfort. This life has no security. But you will be a pillar in my temple.

Jesus finishes the letter with that same formula, *Whoever has ears, let them hear what the Spirit says to the churches*. Again, this reminds us he is not only talking to Philadelphia, but to all seven churches and the complete wider church. So this is speaking to us now. *Whoever has ears* implies not everyone can hear. Only those who are victorious (3:12). Not everyone will be a pillar. Not everyone's going to heaven.

Why not? Why not embrace the one who has the key of David? The key of heaven? Why wouldn't you hear what the Spirit is saying? Well, most hear it deep in their heart but suppress it with self-righteousness. 'I don't need a Savior.' If you know your own heart then you know the selfishness and the pride, but there comes a Day of Judgment when every secret thing is shouted from the heights. Most people don't want to think about that, so they suppress it. They don't hear what the Spirit is saying. They stop up the ears of their own conscience. They suppress the truth with a healthy dose of self-righteousness. 'Well, at least I'm not as bad as some people,' or the ultimate self-righteousness, 'I've tried to be a good person and my good deeds outweigh my bad.' No one would use that line in any other setting. You wouldn't steal a new iPad from a store and when you get caught try to justify it by saying, 'It's okay, I've been in here lots of times, bought lots of stuff, and never stolen a thing. And I've always been a good person. Doesn't that count for anything?' No number of good things can make transgression disappear.

If you talk to people from non-Western cultures and other religions, they are often humbler than Westerners. Have you ever talked to a Muslim about God? I mean the devout follower who wrestles with their inner thoughts. Many of them will tell you, 'I don't really know if on the Day of Judgment I will be going to heaven or not.' Why? They know what's inside. Talk to the Buddhist. I don't mean the Western pretenders. I mean the real Buddhist who is meditating hours each day, desperately trying to free himself from the desires that well up in him that he believes will cause him suffering. It's in his teaching.

> If it's suffering you fear, if it's suffering you dislike, Just do no evil deeds at all – for all to see or secretly. Even a flight in the air cannot free you from suffering, after the deed which is evil has once been committed.[12]

Deep down the human heart knows there is evil inside. You can stop up your ears and use the good old Aussie self-righteousness, 'I'm a good bloke. I try to do the best I can.' But talk to the Hindu who has really gone deep in his inner heart. Their most famous devotee Mohandas Gandhi said towards the end of his life in his autobiography ...

> Where is there a wretch so wicked and loathsome as I? I have forsaken my Maker, so faithless have I been. For it is an unbroken torture to me that I am still so far from Him, who, as I fully know, governs every breath of my life, and whose offspring I am. I know that it is the evil passions within that keep me so far from Him, and yet I cannot get

---

[12] Buddhist Scriptures, (London: Penguin Books, 1959), p.83

away from them. [13]

Anyone who is honest with him or herself knows the self-righteous approach is self-deceit. If God is what Jesus said to the Philadelphians, that he is **holy and true,** then as a holy and true judge every deed will be brought into judgment, including every hidden thing. So where will you stand on the Day of Judgment? How can you be *victorious?* How can you be a pillar in the temple?

You need a righteousness other than your own, other than *self-righteousness*. Self-righteousness cannot open the door to heaven. Later Revelation says no sin can enter heaven (21:27). How can you enter through that door? The gates of hell are the only ones open to you. You need the one who holds the *key* of David.

Jesus went to Judgment Day in advance for you! He smashed those gates of hell and opens the door of heaven that no one can shut on you. He went to the cross to provide a righteousness by taking the penalty of your sin in advance, to take away your sin! Forever. On the Day of Judgment, he looks on you and what does he do? He *opens the door of heaven and no one can shut it on you.* The gates of hell cannot stop you entering heaven. He has the key of David!

What about Satan attacking (3:9)? He is the accuser who tells you the door is shut. Look at what a sinner you are. The gates of hell have closed on you, but Jesus says ... *I have placed before you an open door that no one can shut. I know that you have little strength ... I know you are weak. I know you.* I have been intimately involved in your life and I know your weaknesses. I know you wonder if you will enter heaven or not. This is Jesus speaking to you saying, 'I know!' *I know you have little strength.* How can you know whether that door is open for you? Jesus said it's those who **kept my word and have not denied my name.**

The testing that comes on earth means many will *not* keep his word and will deny his name. They are too embarrassed to stand up and be counted as one of those 'church-going types'. They deny him. But to his people he says, 'I know you'. And ... *what he opens no one can shut.*

What if you have *not* been keeping his word? What if you *have* denied his name? What if you have *not* been victorious? Here is the beauty. This is the simplicity of this message if you listen to what the

---

[13] M. K. Gandhi, *An Autobiography, The Story of My experiments with truth.* (Hardmonsworth, 1927) Introduction

Spirit is saying to the churches. *Repent!* And the door *is* still open to you. If you have been involved in some deliberate sin that you know you need to deal with, then deal with it! Bring it to that cross where Jesus is punished for your sin and be cleansed. *What he opens <u>no one can shut</u>...* How do you know if you are one of the chosen? Easy, if you can listen ... *LISTEN to what the Spirit is saying to the churches* (3:13)!

If you are listening now then the Spirit is at work in you now. Go through the door now! *What he opens <u>no one can shut</u>.* Enter by faith. It's not about your past record! He wipes away the record against you, even now. Jesus has the key to the door. It is his cross. You are free! *Whoever has ears, let them hear what the Spirit is saying to the churches.*

Study Questions

1. Where is Jesus drawing on the OT for his identification as the one who holds the key of David? How does this relate to Jesus in its OT context?

2. How were Christians in Philadelphia literally shut out?

3. What historical background helps us understand what Jesus means about the church having little strength?

4. Why is this a helpful text if your theology includes a rapture of Christians before the tribulation?

5. Give two reasons why that text might be understood differently?

6. Where could this test upon the whole world be seen today? And where might it be manifest in the Western world?

7. When the apostle Paul says God works all things together for good, what is the context we need to understand of that verse?

8. Why would the metaphor 'pillar' of God's temple be used?

9. What are some of the ways Westerners and other religions express

self-righteousness?

10. If we have sinned grievously, how can we be sure the door will be opened for us to heaven?

10
Laodicea
(Revelation 3:14-22)

If you look at a map of Turkey in ancient times you will see the location of the seven churches and how we have been following John's postman's route in a big circle through Ephesus, Smyrna, Pergamum, Thyatira, Sardis and Philadelphia. The last church we come to in that circle is Laodicea, which is about 100 miles (160km) east of Ephesus, just south of Philadelphia where we were last time. They save the best till last, don't they? Philadelphia was second last, and they were commended as a good church. That might have been what the Laodiceans thought as they read through the other letters before they got to theirs, because the Laodiceans were a well-established confident group.

As a city, Laodicea was known for its medical school and ophthalmology, including a locally produced world-famous eye salve (keep that in mind in Jesus' letter to them). They had a world-renowned export business of textile trade in black wool (woolen tunics). Most of all, Laodicea was well known for its wealth. Three major highways met there, and it was financially affluent, renowned as a major banking and finance center. It was commercially prosperous. The rich folks lived here. Laodicea was like Melbourne's 'Toorak' or Sydney's 'Darling Point'. It had the usual trappings of a wealthy city with theatres, a stadium, and gymnasiums with baths.

In AD 60 there was a massive earthquake that brought devastating damage to Laodicea and other cities. Sardis and Philadelphia were also hit, and the Emperor provided financial assistance to rebuild their cities. But to show how financially strong and confident Laodicea was, they not only refused the financial help, but even gave aid to neighboring cities to rebuild. As the Roman historian Tacitus records, Laodicea recovered *itself* from earthquake.[14] And from this letter it seems this spirit of confidence in their own prosperity carried over into the Christian church, because Jesus is not merely alluding to the worldly people of the city when he writes 'to the church in Laodicea' and says later, You say, <u>'I am rich; I have acquired wealth and do not need a thing</u>' (3:17). They had self-sufficiency! Does he mean material self-sufficiency or spiritual? Or both? Jesus opens his letter.

> To the angel of the church in Laodicea write: These are the words of the Amen, <u>the faithful and true witness</u>, the ruler of God's creation (3:14).

As he has done previously, Jesus introduces himself to this church using a portion from the Rev. 1 vision, but this time as what? **The faithful and true witness.** Here Jesus is the faithful and true witness. What is Jesus getting at? Hold that thought. But if the Laodiceans thought Jesus was going to commend them they are in for a shock …

> I know your deeds, that you are neither cold nor hot. I wish you were either one or the other! So, because you are lukewarm—neither hot nor cold—I am about to spit you out of my mouth (3:15-16).

As Jesus has done with the letters to the other churches, he is alluding to a familiar situation in that city. Laodicea was a thriving commercial center, but for its *water supply* the town had water piped in from nearby Denizli about 6 miles (10km) away, but the water was filled with mineral salts, so by the time it reached Laodicea it ended up lukewarm and filled with sediment. It would make you sick and want to spit it out. In the neighboring cities the water supply was good. Hierapolis had hot springs and their hot waters were known for their medicinal effect. Colossae had water that was cold and pure, good for drinking. But Laodicea only had access to lukewarm water … want to spit it out…errghhh.

Jesus is saying, Laodicea, you are like your water! This is an extraordinary reaction from Jesus to a church. It's not like any other in all the accounts of the gospels. Jesus is not angry or upset, but actually says they make him sick to the point of throwing up. Why? They are lukewarm. Lukewarm in relation to what? The two main

---

[14] Tacitus, Annals of Imperial Rome, 14:27

issues commended or rebuked in the other churches have been compromise with the world and their witness to the world. Your lampstand is supposed to shine! And here is Jesus, the one who walks in the midst of the lampstands, and he introduces himself to this church as what? **The faithful and true witness!** As opposed to what? **Lukewarm!** Those who are *not* faithful and true in their witness! They are not sharing the gospel!

But how can Jesus say they would be better off cold than lukewarm? No doubt he wishes they were 'hot', but how is cold even better? Those who are cold to Jesus, those who outright reject Jesus don't bring shame on the witness of Jesus as much as hypocrites. Hypocrites are far more sickening. And don't we feel that? Isn't it more sickening to hear of a pedophile priest supposedly representing the name of Christ, than a crime from the world?

How did Laodicea get to this point? Notice a couple of things missing that other churches had. In Laodicea, there was no persecution. No Jewish persecutors like Smyrna and Philadelphia. No hassle from the Roman government that other churches had. No false teachers infiltrating like Nicolaitans or Jezebels. In fact, it's all so cozy and comfy. Why? You don't tend to get too much persecution when you are lukewarm. Good, quiet, little lukewarm Christians who don't offend anyone. But Jesus says he wants to **spit you out of his mouth.**

We have learned that these churches speak into history. Which church would Jesus be talking about in history if the Laodicean church speaks into our day? Materially comfortable, lack of faithfulness, lack of witness, confident in themselves.

> You say, 'I am rich; I have acquired wealth and do <u>not need a thing</u>' (3:17a).

Perhaps the most striking thing about all this is: What a different view heaven has of a church from the view of the church below. We have looked at the other churches which saw themselves as weak and poor. Poor old Smyrna. *I know your afflictions <u>and your poverty</u>—yet you are rich* (2:9)! Smyrna thought they were poor and downtrodden. But heaven's assessment? You are rich! On the other hand, Laodicea thinks they are strong and established. Heaven's assessment?

> … But you do not realize that you are wretched, pitiful, poor, blind and naked (3:17b).

Heaven sees it all differently. Compare the Western church to the church in Africa, China, or India, that Westerners might think of as 'weaker'. 'We have the structures. We can afford the best in theological education, so we are so much more biblically literate.' But *we* may not be as strong as we think.

Laodicea was also confident because of their financial security, and one element that could have contributed to the decline of the church in the West is financial security. We have so much material wealth we have come to rely on it. We no longer have to pray for our *daily* bread, we can store up our *retirement* bread. We acquire wealth to take care of our future, so we won't have to 'worry'. But before we know it, we have been caught up in a generation that can't see itself. We live in homes literally twice the size of that which our grandparents lived in, but it's not enough. And we give far less than Christians in previous eras. We give to the poor only from our surplus. We focus our money on security rather than how can we use worldly wealth to gain friends in heaven, for mission, and to be a *faithful and true witness*.

Heaven's assessment ... *you do not realize that you are wretched, pitiful, poor, blind and naked*. So which church is the Laodicean church today? Who are these rich folks? Surely not us! Google the 'Global Rich List' and on the minimum Australian wage, you are in about the top 1½% richest people in the world! If you are on a full pension in Australia you are in the top 11%. This is not to trivialize the financial struggles some go through, but much of the world is more concerned about basic necessities such as daily bread and a roof over their head and wouldn't consider spending money on entertainment, or clothes, or cars, or this or that, the way we do. A guest Sudanese preacher at our church recently spoke of his visit to Sudan, driving past two little boys walking on a flat dusty road. It was 20 miles either way to the nearest village. The boys were just walking, hoping the next village might have some food.

The Christian church used to be the one who cared for the poor. The church can't afford to do that anymore because people don't give as much, so the church has handed most of that over to the government. We are so comfortable we have forgotten our calling. We look at the third world church and their struggles and syncretism with tribal beliefs that creep into lives of Christians, and we question how many of them are really Christian? But are they asking the same question of us? They look at us in our affluence and wonder how far we are away from Jesus who had no place to lay his head; the same Jesus who told us to store up treasures in heaven and care for the poor. We might be asking on that day, 'When did we not feed you, when did we not clothe you?' And we will hear, 'When you did not do it to the least of these, you did not do it to me.' So does the African church look at the Western church and wonder 'are *they* really Christian?' Well, are we? Are we the Laodicean church? The Christians in Sudan lose their lives. You can get jailed, beaten, or even worse when you share the gospel in parts of China, India and Africa, as well as the Middle East. But we are afraid to invite people to a church service or Bible study in case we get embarrassed! Are we a faithful and true witness? Or more to the point, have we even thought about it at all? Lukewarm?

Jesus says he is the ruler of *all* creation (3:14). So how did you get on that rich list? You didn't get yourself on it. Jesus got you there. What do you have financially? Whatever it is, it comes from the hand of the ruler of all creation, and it can just as easily be taken away. It's no coincidence if you are in the top 1½% richest people in the world. Jesus gave it to you. And Jesus said to use worldly wealth to gain friends for eternal purposes, for his kingdom (Luke 16:9). Jesus doesn't begrudge you having a home, transport, providing for your family, buying the things you need, or even taking a holiday (check the OT festivals, there are many). Jesus, the ruler of all creation, gave them all to you. But what is heaven's view of where you are? Jesus says you cannot serve two masters. You cannot serve God and money. Are we the Laodiceans? Are we living in defiance of Jesus? Storing up treasures on earth? Gotta improve our lot? It's expected in the culture we live in, isn't it? That's was what the Laodiceans thought! And they couldn't see it. How could they miss it? How can you think you need nothing, and yet heaven sees you as *wretched, pitiful, poor, blind, and naked?* The answer is because they were surrounded by wealth and they had become like the culture around them. But heaven sees it differently. *You say, 'I am rich; I have acquired wealth and do not need a thing ...'*

Yes, at least we are not like the world. We don't worship idols. We don't swear, don't have drug addictions, and don't visit brothels. You won't find us drunk on the streets. In fact, you won't find us on the streets at all. We don't tell the gospel. We stay in our nice homes. We don't need a thing. *But you do not realize that you are wretched, pitiful, poor, blind and naked.* You say, 'I'm not as bad as people in the world.' But who has influenced whom? Is the church more like the world, or the world more like the church?

One theological interpretation of these seven churches is the Historical approach. In this view, each church represents an age of church history. The first church at Ephesus is the apostolic age, then Smyrna up to the AD 300s etc., through to Laodicea, the last age from AD 1900s. We don't need to go into the veracity of that view now, but the churches' problems are given in an order that could build up ... the final one, Laodicea is the complacent church. As John Stott said, there is nothing closer to the contemporary church than this *lukewarm* church.[15] Look at the age we are living in. Never before have we seen such comfort and laxity. Who is Jesus referring to? Worship the Lord in reverence and awe? Lukewarm in witness and purity. Laxity in materialism. Lukewarm morals. Are *we* really Christians? Or are we lukewarm Laodicea?

We can't tell if we are close to the return of Jesus, but has there ever been a time when the church has been more self-sufficient? We need nothing, and yet the church is so lukewarm in holiness, moral practices, and witness. The church in Australia is constantly boasting of big things. Prophesying even of great things. 'We'll take this country for Jesus. We have the Spirit more than ever.' It's fascinating that this is one of the arguments used in the Western church to introduce things to the church that are largely unknown for the last 2000 years until this age. Flippant worship practices, emphasis on music performance and volume over worshipers worshiping, theological triumphalism, and the prosperity gospel. The argument is that the Holy Spirit is working in this late age through *society* to teach us what he never did in the last 2000 years. We have finally arrived. We are the age that has been able to gain what we need when the church for the last 2000 years was never able to figure it out. We can have health, wealth, and Jesus without repentance. We live under grace not under law, so it doesn't matter if divorce, pornography, and immorality are as common inside as outside the church. We have it all. All the things those lesser Christians through the ages never did.

Jesus is knocking on the door, but Jesus has been squeezed out of

---

[15] John R. W. Stott, *What Christ Thinks of the Church* (Grand Rapids, MI: Baker Book House, ©1990, 2003).

his own church. Jesus is not preached. Instead the preacher's topics are on 'felt needs' rather than our desperate need of the cross and the resurrection, the gospel of repentance. We need a return to the words of *the faithful and true witness*. The Bible! Is it central in your church? Obeying it, reading it, hearing it explained. Or should we fill up more time with music and testimonies and self-help stories? Should we come to church and do our bit and return home to our worldly comfort without a thought for Jesus' witness in our lives? Am I faithful, or are there sins I am clinging to? 'It's okay, Jesus forgives, just cruise along. I am rich!' But Jesus says, you are in trouble and you don't know it!

> I counsel you to buy from me gold refined in the fire, so you can become rich; and white clothes to wear, so you can cover your shameful nakedness; and salve to put on your eyes, so you can see (3:18).

Where are the true riches? It's the parable of the lost treasure. We have lost sight of the transforming power of the gospel that calls us to trust that God will be with us if we are faithful witnesses. He will provide for us materially too as we trust in him. The lukewarm church seems to have these three things that go hand in hand—material comfort, a lack of witness in the world, and lukewarmness in moral purity. And Jesus says ... **I counsel you to buy from me gold refined in the fire** ... that is the gold which might come through serious testing. Purification from every blemish is the biblical idea of gold being refined. Getting sin out of our lives. That is why he says **white clothes to wear**. It's a picture of purity. Unstained. Walking with Jesus. Remember the few at Sardis who had not stained their clothes who received white clothes (3:4). It seems the Laodiceans had already stained their clothes. Lukewarm in purity. They were famous for their black wool, but they needed white clothes. Most of all, they needed healing salve for their eyes because they were blind to the trouble they were in! That salve you are famous for Laodicea isn't doing it for you.

What if *you* have been lukewarm? Is it too late? Is it all over? Jesus will spit you out of his mouth. Vomit you up. Deny you on that day. What if you are one of these pretend Western Christians who gives no thought to where your money goes, except on yourself? What if you have lost sight of what you are supposed to be doing as a church in this short time before Jesus comes back (such as witnessing to the world)? What if you are not walking in white clothes, but have a secret sin you have not let go of? What is Jesus going to do? Spit you out? No, that's not the last word.

Here we see the amazing compassion of Jesus. Yes, if that is you, then you have been fooling yourself. But Jesus didn't say he spits you out, he says, 'I am *about to...*' He hasn't done it yet! It's a warning. Instead of bringing judgment, in love, he comes to call you back. Most won't listen. But to those he loves ... he gives a day of grace.

> <u>Those whom I love</u> I rebuke and discipline. So be earnest, and repent (3:19).

Those whom I love. Not everyone will be earnest and repent. But if you are one whom Jesus loves, even if you have been lukewarm, you will hear. Jesus will never spit out a true Christian, but he will rebuke you. How do you know if you are really a Christian if you have been lukewarm? Answer: You will **be earnest and repent!** If you are really his, he will not give up on you, but he may discipline you and seek you ...

> Here I am! I stand at the door and knock. If anyone hears my voice and opens the door, I will come in and eat with that person, and they with me (3:20).

This has to be one of the most famous and well-used evangelism texts ever. Jesus stands at the door of your heart, knocking, just waiting for the unbeliever to open the door and let him in. I hate to burst the bubble on a couple of million evangelism sermons, but this verse is not speaking to the unbeliever! Jesus is not standing knocking at the door of your heart. Where is he? He is standing knocking at the door of your church! It is *we* in the church he is speaking to! Here you are, comfortably singing Colin Buchanan, 'Here I am, I stand at the door and knock, rat a tat tat', and you're thinking Colin is singing about those unbelievers outside. But all along you did not realize— it was *you!* He is speaking to the church! To *you,* lukewarm Christian!

Could you be the lukewarm Christian who thinks you are okay and <u>do not need a thing</u>? *But you do not realize that you are wretched, pitiful, poor, blind and naked?* Have you never been taken aback by the strong warnings of Jesus? 'Not everyone who says Lord, Lord will enter the kingdom' (Matt. 7:21). Only a few find it. Jesus said these words to the believing community of the day. 'Only a few'. Not everyone who goes to church makes it. But of one thing you can be certain. The lukewarm are *not* among the few. The unrepentant lukewarm are not going to make it.

This is the day of grace to wake up! This is not the Day of Judgment. Jesus still stands at the door and knocks. He is still there, but not forever. When he spits you out, it's too late. But this is a wake-up call. People say they don't like the harsh warnings. All that fire and brimstone stuff in the Bible. But the harsh warnings are the most loving thing of all. The world hates fire and brimstone warnings. They say, 'At least the Buddhists don't have fire and brimstone warnings.' But if you read the Buddhist Scriptures, they have a more gruesome hell than anything in the Bible.[16]

Now there is a question for you. If you believed Buddhism is true with its gruesome hell, why isn't the Dalai Lama telling everyone? Why isn't he preaching fire and brimstone? Instead it's, 'Don't worry, you can find your way in any religion.' The Buddhist Scriptures say all other teachings are false.[17] So, if Buddhism was true and other religions false, does that mean I would only find that out when I end up in their gruesome hell because they didn't want to offend anyone with fire and brimstone preaching? So, I would end up in hell saying, 'Why didn't the Dalai Lama warn me about this?' But a warning of danger is love ... if you take hold of it. Those whom I *love* I rebuke.

The invitation is a glorious one—come and eat with me. **If anyone hears my voice and opens the door, I will come in and eat with that person, and they with me.** Notice the intimacy? The Lord will sit down and have a meal with you! All the riches you can gain in this world are nothing compared to eating with Jesus. Let go of the fleeting things of sin, for we are headed to the great feast with the Lord himself. If you are one of the few, this is your calling. To eat with Jesus! Eternal glory.

So, what are you living for now? To know the Lord and serve him? To live by faith? To make friends for eternity? To use worldly wealth for the advancing of the kingdom? To be part of the witness of the

---

[16] Buddhist Scriptures, Translated by Edward Conze, (London: Penguin Books, 1959), p. 224-226
[17] Ibid, 192

church? There is work to be done! We need to renounce lukewarmness, walk in holiness, engage in discipling, join a Bible study, invest time in people, and be a faithful and true witness. How do you do one to one evangelism? Easy. Turn off the TV and computer! Put down your smartphone! Give people the time of day! Spend an hour a week giving unconditionally to someone in your life to earn the right to share the gospel with them or to invite them to a special church service. Volunteer for the work of the kingdom when no one else does. If we were less concerned about buying more stuff, we could fund more gospel work and feed the poor. If we were less lukewarm morally, we could testify with credibility and people would listen more. If we were less lukewarm worrying about what people thought, and more concerned about the one who is the faithful and true witness, we could witness to the world!

> To the one who is victorious, I will give the right to sit with me on my throne, just as I was victorious and sat down with my Father on his throne (3:21).

This is a promise we still haven't got our heads around. This is bigger than we can fathom. Ruling with Christ. Sitting with him **on his throne.** You who forsook worldly status will be lifted up!

> Whoever has ears, let them hear what the Spirit says to the churches (3:22).

Can you hear lukewarm Christian? Can you hear? Only when we truly see ourselves as wretched, pitiful, poor, blind, and naked are we lifted up. The world has a wrong view of itself, but we have been given eyes to see, a salve to heal our eyes to see ourselves as we really are. A broken and contrite spirit the Lord will not despise. 'Lord have mercy on me, the sinner.'

Here I am! I stand at the door and knock. If anyone hears my voice and opens the door, I will come in and <u>eat with that person</u>, and they with me (3:20).

Study Questions

1. Give two reasons why this church might have expected a positive review from Jesus.

2. What is the reason for Jesus' self-identification to this church?

3. Give at least two ways Jesus' comments to the church relate their city's history.

4. Where might we see a 'Laodicean' church today?

5. In what area of our lives could we be overconfident, that may not be pleasing to the Lord?

6. What does Jesus mean when he says we should 'become rich'?

7. Why does Jesus want us to buy gold refined in fire?

8. If those 'lukewarm' are spat out, how is this letter positive to those who are lukewarm?

9. What way has this text been commonly misunderstood and misused?

10. What practical ways might you change from being lukewarm to hot?

11
Four Main Views
(Revelation 4:1-2)

Now we are into the good stuff. Rev. 2-3 was okay but starting to look a bit too 'down to earth'. A bit too churchy. Where is all that cosmic stuff, with battles of Armageddon and beasts and credit card implants in our wrists that we have been anticipating in the book of Revelation? Well, this is the beginning of it. Apocalypse now! (Although I will argue we need the foundation of those church experiences to help us understand the rest of the book.)

Now we have hit a great turning point in the book. John the apostle has received another vision, this time of heaven, but for us on earth who have debated over this book of Revelation for 2000 years, our understanding all hinges on these two words at the beginning and end of 4:1—*After this ...*

> After this I looked, and there before me was a door standing open in heaven. And the voice I had first heard speaking to me like a trumpet said, 'Come up here, and I will show you what must take place after this' (4:1).

After this could also be translated *after these things,* because it's plural in the original Greek language. But what does *after this* mean? After what? Well, this is truly a major turning point of the book, and depending on your point of view, it could be a departing point of the book. Or departing of friendships amongst us, unless we remember the one thing we all agree on? Jesus wins!

There are four main interpretations, or views, that Christians have of Revelation. I won't be able to do justice to every variation of each one, so bear with me if I don't go into full detail. There are four main understandings of *after this.*

There is the Preterist approach (events occur pre-AD 70), the Historicist approach (chronologically specific events from John's time and onwards, throughout the church age), the Futurist approach (everything from Rev. 4-19 is going to happen in a future seven-year period), and the Idealist approach (what happens in John's time describes what happens in 'principle' throughout history, rather than specific, single, historical marking points).

You might wonder which of these four approaches I go with? ... The answer is: I go with the correct one! But then I have noticed everyone else does too. No matter what their view, it's the correct one. And that's the trouble. People have been so dogmatic in the past, as though this very difficult book was as simple and clear as the Bible's teaching on the resurrection, or deity of Christ, or any other essentials of the Christian faith. When I first read the Bible as an unbeliever and finally got to Revelation, I remember thinking that if I had started with this book rather than read it at the end I would have given up on Christianity as just too wacky and difficult. Frankly, some of this can be a bit tricky, so we need some humility in this. And when we get to heaven you can tell me, 'I told you so'.

As I said at the beginning, perhaps the Lord gave us this book at the end because he is more interested to see how we can show charity towards one another when we disagree over non-essentials of the faith, rather than to see who could get it all figured out. Some have never come to grips with the fact that our interpretation of eschatology is not of first importance in the Christian faith. We actually have it in writing from the Lord what are the things of first importance.

> For what I received I passed on to you as of <u>first importance</u>: that Christ died for our sins according to the Scriptures, that he was buried, that he was raised on the third day according to the Scriptures ... (1 Cor. 15:3-4).

These are the things of **first importance!** Not one mention of our millennial views or interpretation of Revelation. They don't appear on Paul's list of things of first importance. We have it in writing from God that there are things of *first importance* we dare not compromise if we are to remain true to the faith, and there are also disputable matters which we should not judge one another over (Rom. 14:1). So as long as we keep it in that perspective, it doesn't mean we shouldn't try and get to the bottom of Revelation, because God has given it to us for our blessing (1:3). And even if we have a different understanding, it should not affect our fellowship in Jesus.

We will first look at the Preterist approach. The word 'Preterist' comes from Latin meaning 'everything has been'. Everything that happens in the book of Revelation took place before AD 70 and describes the lead up to the destruction of the Jerusalem temple by the Romans. This approach has the advantage of a simple, clear, and literal meaning to the last words of 4:1, *what must take place after this*. This view also requires the book to be dated before AD 70, which is cause for debate because most (but not all) scholars believe Revelation was written sometime in the AD 90s. (I'll address that point later.) But for the Preterist, the judgment described in Revelation is the temple's destruction in AD 70. However, some evangelical Preterists also include a final judgment on Jesus' return.

Then there is the Historicist approach. Historicists (and some Futurists) divide the seven churches into ages, so the church in Ephesus is the apostolic era, Smyrna the persecuted age from 300 and so on. According to this approach we are now in the last age, which is the Laodicean church. The Historicist believes details of Revelation can be traced to specific people or events chronologically throughout history, up to the end. And if you examine some of the better Historicist writings, some of their efforts appear quite impressive. The difficulty is that there is no consensus even among fellow Historicists. They almost all differ and most tend to draw heavily on their own particular generation. So depending on when you live, one Historicist might see the Beast or Antichrist as Nero or Adolf Hitler, another as Attila the Hun. (I'll be making my case for Oprah Winfrey. Sorry Oprah, you just happen to be in my time.) The Historicist is the least popular view today because if Revelation was a straight chronological history it would not be debated. We would see each event unfold clearly through history, but it hasn't always been so neat.

However, despite its shortcomings, there is still something we can learn from the Historicist. There are key figures and events that fit with parts of Revelation.

In fact, I will argue that all the views offer something, and perhaps that is why Jesus told us Revelation would be a blessing to all who read and hear and take it to heart. All the views can't be fully right at the same time, but in all of them Jesus wins!

The Futurist approach has two main variations (with and without the rapture before the tribulation), but with both of these 4:1 is most crucial. All the events from 4:1, *after this*, are at some time in the future from us, hence 'Futurist'. In this view 4:1 is not taken literally. *What must take place after this* ... does not mean immediately after what was happening for John and the churches in the first century, but is projecting forwards at least 2000 years. So it's *after this* age of the church, a seven-year tribulation begins.

The Futurist view originates from a Roman Catholic Spanish Jesuit Francisco Ribera, in 1585. He formulated this view in an attempt to counter the popular view held by the Reformers that equated the Papacy with the Antichrist. The Reformers used the Historicist approach. Ribera countered this view of the Pope by placing all things in the future in order to exonerate the Pope. Protestants rejected Ribera's approach and didn't touch it for about 250 years, until Samuel Maitland picked it up in 1826. Then it was taken up with the introduction of Dispensationalism and the Futurist view of J.N. Darby from 1830. He introduced the idea of the rapture before a seven-year tribulation. This is the most popular view today. This is the idea that sometime in the future the church will be raptured from the earth, and after the rapture, what is written in Rev. 4-19 occurs during that seven years. Unbelievers (who are not raptured) are left behind to go through the seven-year tribulation, thus the *Left Behind* series. (There is also a variation with the rapture occurring three and a half years into the tribulation.) If you hold to this view you are in the company of most Christians.

Most Futurists with a pre-tribulation rapture explain that John being called to **'Come up here, and I will show you what must take place after this'**, is in fact conveying the idea that the whole church is taken up before these events that follow *after this*. John 'comes up' to heaven, prefiguring what happens later to all Christians. Personally, I can't imagine how anyone reading this text (without being prepared in advance) could ever see what happened to John as meaning the whole church will be raptured. One reason I don't agree with this view is that it makes everything from Rev. 4-19 irrelevant to the first readers and all Christians throughout history, because everything that happens in those chapters is in a future time where there will be no Christians left on earth to see it. They would have been raptured out of it. So for this Futurist view, Rev. 4-19 is interesting prophecy about what will happen when all Christians are removed from the world, and the events have no direct relationship to anyone in the Christian church.

The pre-tribulation rapture Futurists correctly note that the word 'church' is not mentioned during Rev. 4-19, as evidence that all the Christians have left the building.

But when we listen to what John says: he told us at the beginning that he was writing to the churches. That is, the whole book of Revelation is written to the churches, not just the individual letters (1:4). John said he was writing to them all in their tribulation (1:9). Unless we are bringing in ideas from outside the text, we should be asking, 'Where has John said in Rev. 4 (or anywhere else in Revelation) that he is no longer addressing the churches?' The burden of proof should surely be on those who say the church is not mentioned, to give any good reason why John suddenly switched at Rev. 4 as to whom he is speaking.

Furthermore, is there any reason why the many mentions of 'God's holy people' and 'redeemed' throughout Rev. 4-19 are not speaking about the church? On what basis can you say that in 6:11 the *fellow servants* yet to be killed on earth are not Christians in the church? Or the prayers of God's people in 8:4? Or those who were not to be harmed because they had the seal of God in 9:4? Or those brethren accused day and night by the serpent in 12:10? Are they not all Christians, part of the church? What about those who 'hold to the testimony of Jesus' in 12:17? Isn't this why John said he was writing, to exhort God's holy people to persevere in 1:9? He repeats the same phrase as if he is talking to the same people later in 13:10 and 14:12! Who are God's holy people attacked in 13:7, killed in 13:15, and those who don't receive the mark in 13:17? Who are the ones who stay awake and keep their clothes on in 16:15? And who are God's people whose blood the woman in 17:6 is drunk on because they bore testimony to Jesus? It's only if we bring presupposition as to when this woman exists can we come up with the idea that those saints, those Christians, are not part of the church.

Where did John say he is switching from addressing the churches? When does he say 'the people of God' no longer applies to the church? If there were no presuppositions driving our thoughts, and we approached this as it is written, we might say the church (Jesus' people) is mentioned *all the way through* Rev. 4-19! The fact that the actual word 'church' doesn't appear has no more weight than the JW argument that the word 'trinity' doesn't appear in Scripture. If the concept is taught, it's there!

Now if the church is raptured out at Rev. 4, at the very least this dampens the wonderful promise of 1:3, that there is a 'blessing' in this book for all who read it, if it's not relevant to the church. It also prevents the first readers or any Christian for the last 2000 years being able to take literally the opening of this prophecy, that *the time is near*, and prevents them taking the words of 4:1 literally i.e. what happens *after this*. But if, on the other hand, this prophecy speaks to all God's servants (1:1), including God's servants over the last 2000 years, then indeed these different events have been unfolding and *the time is near* from when those first readers read those words, *after this*.

Now we want to say something good about the Futurist view, partly because so many hold this view, and I'm hoping if you are one of those people, you will still love me 'after this'. But also because the Futurist upholds the imminent return of Jesus. Jesus wins! In this way Futurism highlights the apocalyptic end where Revelation is headed, the future judgment, where some other views water down or miss this crucial point. There is a real future judgment and it's not confined to the temple destruction of AD 70, so I'm also not going with a strict Preterist view.

The fourth main approach, the Idealist, looks to a fulfillment in every age of 'principles' recurring throughout history, rather than confining the figures and events to a single historical time or event. However, unless the Idealist approach includes a build-up to a climax of judgment, then it is missing the highlight of this book too. So I am taking the Idealist view with that modification, and even borrowing a little from the others along the way, seeing this as speaking into our lives now while still emphasizing the build-up to the end.

So how will we understand these words of Revelation at this turning point in 4:1? What happened *after this?* John has a new vision and says, **'After this I looked, and there before me was a door standing open in heaven.'** So after the down to earth trials and lives of the churches right there in John's time, he now looks from his day to see what happens *after this*, and on into history. There is no mention of a delay of unspecified thousands of years from *after this*. Simply, literally, **what must take place after this.** So instead of Rev. 4 onwards having no relevance to the first readers or any readers throughout history down to us, what takes place *after this* speaks from John's time, peering forwards into history down to us today.

We will end up borrowing a bit from the Historicist because we can find literal historical examples of what is described in Rev. 4-19, but we don't want to be limited to single events and people. We will borrow a bit from the Preterist because these events and figures have to represent events from the first century, which literally occurred for those original seven churches, otherwise how does this book have relevance to them? They are told it's going to show them *what must soon take place* (1:1). They are told reading this book will be a blessing to them. So, it must speak firstly to them. And we won't entirely discount the Futurist, if for no other reason than that I would hate to be responsible for ruining the living of whoever is writing all those *Left Behind* books. And as always, I want to stand with the Futurist's emphasis that the book of Revelation is headed towards a climactic future judgment. Today is the day to believe in Jesus!

First and foremost, I'm looking at the words of Jesus' promise at the beginning.

> Blessed is the one who reads aloud the words of this prophecy, and blessed are those who hear it and take to heart what is written in it, because the time is near (1:3).

This will be a blessing and relevant to everyone who reads it, including us, including those first readers in those seven churches, and throughout the ages. It's near. It has meaning for you now!

This second vision John has (4:1) is something entirely different in that the first vision has to do with the earth. John wrote the letters to earthly churches. But now John sees the perspective of heaven. **'After this I looked, and there before me was a door standing open in heaven.'** This is different. This is a heaven's eye-view. This is the heavenly camera angle. A totally different shot. We are looking behind the curtain to the one who controls everything. That is why 4:1 ends with, **I will show you what <u>must</u> take place after this.** The word in the original Greek language translated *must* is often used in the context of coming from the divine source. It's a *must* because God said so! It's not up for debate. Not maybe, it's a *must*. The Divine *must*. So take careful note of what happens in Revelation because it *must* happen! God has laid it out. Every single thing that is recorded in this apocalypse must happen, just as it is recorded. It's not *maybe*, depending on what man or Satan does. We can know with certainty what will happen in the future from what *must* happen. He said the same thing at the very start of the book.

> The revelation of Jesus Christ, which God gave him to show his servants what <u>must</u> soon take place (1:1).

Who are his servants? His people. What must happen, *must happen soon* for the first readers, but also for us too. How will that work? Remember Revelation is written to Christians undergoing persecution under the Emperor Domitian. It is written to strengthen them to persevere, and it continues to do this throughout history, as seven is God's number of completion. So a message to the seven churches speaks to the complete church, including us today.

And amazingly, instead of becoming irrelevant to those churches which first received it, what follows is just as relevant to them as the individual letters they received. In fact, the opening seven letters to the seven churches set the scene. We have seen real churches under real persecution, lukewarmness, temptation to compromise, and real challenges from false teachers. The seven churches were everything from strong, to weak, to dead. Try and picture yourself as a Christian in one of those seven churches to whom John was writing. You are downcast with temptations from the world around you. You feel pressure to compromise and buckle under the world, the devil, and persecution. But what happens next? What is the first thing that John saw in his next vision? He sees into heaven! And what does he see?

> At once I was in the Spirit, and there before me was a throne in heaven with someone sitting on it (4:2).

Who does John see? It is none other than God! The Christians in those churches would be saying, 'this is the same John who wrote to us and told us we were lukewarm, under attack from false teachers, persecuted. In Smyrna we are in poverty because we don't compromise, and we are told to persevere unto death. Will we make it?' Well now John gives them the answer. A word picture and a glimpse of what? Look at this. We are going to see that the one on the throne is none other than the Lord God!

He is not an absent deity. How this was needed for John as he tried to encourage those churches. It's the Lord. He is on the throne! If ever there was a time when we need to see what John saw, it's today. John can say, it's okay church at Ephesus, and hey Smyrna I know your perseverance under threat, but look who it is on the throne. The church in the West today has the world demanding you give in and compromise, and it looks like the church is crumbling. It's weak. Lukewarm. In some places, dead. Is the world winning? Are we giving in and becoming irrelevant. But look who is on the throne!

This is a peek into where the real control room of the universe is. Can you see how important this is to those first readers? Can you see how important this is to us and every age of the church? This is not just a future history that has no relevance to us today. This is alive and speaking as a living word into the church all the way through to the Day of Judgment! If you could get a look into heaven now and see this! The *after this* is going on now. The Lord is there now. He is ruling from heaven now. You can see him there in John's vision. It's okay. He is on the throne. The Lord reigns!

We have seen in the letters to the churches how the church is going, its struggles and attacks. That is Act 1. But now we are seeing Act 2. It's the same story, but from above. This is a peek behind the scenes. After the chaos in the churches below we will see a scene of serenity, peace, and joy. Control. Power. The world is not out of control. The Lord is on his throne. Let the earth tremble. *Be still and know that I am God.* This is heaven's perspective!

Long before Hollywood got the idea of the film director cutting from the battle scene to the quiet calm of the General's office where he plans the battle, we have in Revelation these different camera shots of the 'meanwhile' scenes. We have seen what it's like for the church on earth. But now, cut shot to the scene in heaven. We are going to see different camera angles and perspectives of history building all the way to the end. The wars, the struggles, and the satanic opposition the church is experiencing on the front line all the way up to the end. But wait! Look who is at the controls! We are going to see what is going on in heaven while there is chaos below. And this is the foundation which strengthens and blesses all who read this part of Revelation. While you thought things were so bad here on earth, take a look at heaven! Take a look at who is on the throne! The Lord is there!

John is actually told **Come up here.** He was in the Spirit, so even though it's a vision, it's a real experience for John. He hears the same voice he heard from the first vision in Rev. 1 whisper, *Come up here.* John, you're not gonna believe this. Only it's a loud trumpet voice so it's, COME UP HERE!

So John climbs up and gets a peek into the control room of the universe. Who does he see at the control desk? It's the Lord! John actually gets a peek into heaven and it's a beautiful sight. You thought from your camera angle of life on earth it was just chaos and enemies having a field day, but from the heavenly camera angle it's a scene of every single creature of every description bowing down. They are all bowing down. They are all subject to the one on the throne. Beam me up, Scotty. This is the room I need to see. I am living down here in trial, but everything is not only created by this one and bowing down to this one, but everything and everyone has their every move and existence and being in this one.

The word *throne* is mentioned 40 times in Revelation, compared to only 15 times in the rest of the NT. And *throne* is used 13 times in only 11 verses in Rev. 4. What is the message? The *throne!* The *throne!* The *throne!* Look who is on the *throne!* He is controlling the universe. Power! It's like a child wakened, frightened in the middle of the night, who needs to know that mum and dad are there. 'It's okay, you can go back to sleep.' Relief. Security. Someone is in control whom we can trust. This is not a dream. It's real. It's the Lord himself!

We will see there is no detailed description of God. He is beyond description, but he is there all right. This is what John needed. This is what you need as you wonder what will happen tomorrow. This is what you need if you are suffering serious illness. This is what you need if you are failing right now in your fight against temptation; if you are struggling and don't know where you will find the strength to resist; if you feel enslaved in your life and see no light; if you are lonely or weighed down by the people around you; if you have financial struggles; or if you are struggling in your marriage and are maybe near the point of doing what you never thought you would do—walking out. Or when things go wrong; you lose a job; or a loved one. Or if you feel your life is going nowhere. No plan. You need a glimpse of what John saw. And you have it! Jesus told John to pass it on to you so that all who read this and take it to heart would be blessed. How? By seeing that the Lord is on his throne!

We need to see what John is seeing. Look at it. Read it. Take it to heart and be blessed (1:3). This is for us now, not just the future. From that first peek into heaven John was never the same. And we will never be the same if we *take this to heart*. What else did John see in this throne room? We will have to move on to the next exciting episode of John's revelation.

Study Questions

1. What are the four main views of Revelation?

2. Name at least two Scriptures that would caution us against dividing with Christians with a different view of Revelation. What is the significance of this for Christian fellowship?

3. How does each view understand the words 'after this'?

4. Is Rev. 4-19 relevant for the church? Why or why not?

5. Is the church mentioned in Rev. 4-19?

6. How might this vision encourage John, his first readers, and us, as Christians today?

7. What is one area all the different evangelical interpretations of Revelation agree on?

12
The Throne Room
(Revelation 4:1-8)

A peek into heaven? Into the very throne room of God? Who could ever hope for such a thing? We left John at the very door of heaven, and he sees one on the throne.

> At once I was in the Spirit, and there before me was a throne in heaven with someone sitting on it (4:2).

That someone is God Almighty. What is it like in the throne room? This time we get to look around the room as the camera pans across it. John gets a glimpse of what is happening from the heavenly perspective. There is no mention of a lapse of time for John, but *after this* he looked up and saw the Lord on his throne, now!

John wrote this prophecy down during a time when the ruler of the known world on the earthly throne was Caesar, Emperor Domitian, who demanded to be called lord and god. But now John looks into heaven and sees that it is not Caesar who is lord and god. Emperor Domitian is not on the throne! It is the Lord!

How John and his readers needed to see what was happening 'now'. It matters who is on the throne. Under Emperor Domitian, some paid the ultimate penalty because they did not bow down to call Caesar lord and god. It matters who is leading a country. Whether a country be democratic, communist, or fascist, who is the leader in control? It matters if you are in the Middle East and have a dictator killing your own people. It matters if you are in the West and have leaders who want to enact laws which defy God. It matters who is in control. Who is really on the throne? If we could just see that. Above all earthly powers there is a greater power, although we can't see him. But if we accompany John as he sneaks a peek into this throne room, we can take a photo because John has given it to us in word pictures.

At once I was in the Spirit, and there before me was a throne

in heaven with someone sitting on it. John is not the first one to have a vision of the throne room. Look at this similarity from eight centuries earlier (and notice the same song John is hearing in 4:8, the Lord is holy, holy, holy).

> In the year that King Uzziah died, I saw the Lord, high and exalted, seated on a throne; and the train of his robe filled the temple. Above him were seraphim, each with six wings: With two wings they covered their faces, with two they covered their feet, and with two they were flying. And they were calling to one another: 'Holy, holy, holy is the LORD Almighty; the whole earth is full of his glory.' At the sound of their voices the doorposts and thresholds shook and the temple was filled with smoke ... Then I heard the voice of the Lord saying, 'Whom shall I send? And who will go for us?' And I said, 'Here am I. Send me!' (Isa. 6:1-4, 8).

Isaiah is commissioned as a prophet. In Revelation, John is also commissioned as a prophet to convey this prophecy, Revelation. So he too is escorted into the very throne room of God. So picture John. The hairs on the back of his neck are standing up. (Remember he is old, so he has hair on the back of his neck, losing it from where wants it and growing it in places he doesn't want.) John is sweating. He is in awe. And this is just a peek. Look at what John sees on the throne:

> And the one who sat there had the appearance of jasper and ruby ... (4:3).

Apart from these precious stones, there is not much at all in the description of God himself because God can't be described. Everything and everyone around him are all described, but not God. John would have recognized these precious stones as alluding to the theophanies in the OT, just like Ezekiel 1:26, 28; 9:2; 28:13. These stones like **jasper** and **ruby** are meant to convey the glory of the LORD in picture language, because quite simply, there is no language that can fully convey the glory of the LORD. But take note of this. Picture that throne right in the middle of heaven. And it says in a circle around the throne is what?

> And the one who sat there had the appearance of jasper and ruby. A rainbow that shone like an emerald encircled the throne (4:3).

A rainbow? Why a rainbow? It's not a gay pride flag. We are not going to use 21st century culture to interpret it. What would John, a first century devout Jew, use to interpret? The Bible! What sign did God give in the sky after Noah's flood? The rainbow. God's covenant sign of mercy, his grace, **encircled the throne.** So, you have the LORD on the throne, and a rainbow encircling the throne, like a target with the colors around the center.

> Surrounding the throne were twenty-four other thrones, and seated on them were twenty-four elders. They were dressed in white and had crowns of gold on their heads (4:4).

What would this mean to John? Who exactly are these 24 elders? There have been all kinds of interpretations offered, everything from astrological stars to representatives of 24 prophetic books of the OT. Some say angels, and we can imagine this from the letters to the churches sent to angels who represented them. They certainly are heavenly representatives of something. Why 24? All the way through Revelation we need to keep one thing in mind to help us interpret correctly, lest we go off on our own tangent. Who has written this down for us? Who is receiving this Revelation? John. A first century devout Jew. What would it mean to him? What would he be drawing on for understanding? Again, the answer is the Bible. If we think elders of the OT, how many tribes of Israel? There are 12. And how many elders of the NT (how many apostles)? Again, 12. In that light it's not too hard to see these 24 elders as representatives of the OT and NT together. Especially if we let the book of Revelation do its own interpreting when we read later about the city of God …

> It had a great, high wall with twelve gates, and with twelve angels at the gates. On the gates were written the names of the <u>twelve tribes of Israel</u> … The wall of the city had twelve foundations, and on them were the names of the <u>twelve apostles of the Lamb</u> (21:12, 14).

Together 24 representatives of the redeemed people of God, 12 from the OT and 12 from the NT. In other words, the whole people of God are represented there. What did we learn back in 1:6?

> … and has made us to be a kingdom and priests to serve his God and Father—to him be glory and power for ever and ever! Amen (1:6).

Remember that was an allusion to the famous statement God made about Israel in Exodus 19:6, that God's people, the Israelites, would become a kingdom of priests. Here in Revelation he says it is fulfilled in the people of God, both the OT and NT. Kingdom and Priests.

Remember in the seven letters to the seven churches how those who were victorious were promised a reward? What do you think those people sitting in those churches reading this for the first time were thinking when they got to Rev. 4? Remember Sardis? Those who were *victorious* would be *dressed in white* (3:4). Here in Rev. 4:4 the elders are **dressed in white.** And those who were *victorious* at Smyrna (2:10) and Philadelphia (3:11), were promised crowns. What are these elders wearing? **Crowns.** Then Laodicea. Those who were *victorious* will reign with him (3:21). What happened to those promises? Well here they are. The people of God represented by these 24 elders, not merely there, but on **thrones, seated on them, dressed in white and wearing crowns** (4:4). All those seven churches could relate to this. Now it's here for the people of God who were *victorious*.

Psalm 8 says the LORD made people under him as vice-regents over the earth. Now in heaven the redeemed people of God have thrones. It's incomprehensible. What does it mean? A vindication over enemies? A victory? It's strange indeed. God's people on thrones! So you have the LORD on his throne at the center, surrounding him is the rainbow, and then surrounding that, the 24 thrones. What is the message for John's first readers? Look! They made it! Persevere. It's waiting for you too. I want to see it! The throne room! They got there! Phew! But more! Full vindication and glory. Then...

> From the throne came flashes of lightning, rumblings and peals of thunder. In front of the throne, seven lamps were blazing. These are the seven spirits of God (4:5).

Now John sees what Isaiah was on about! This is the same brilliance and glory that Isaiah saw. John also remembered Daniel 7:9-10 and Ezekiel 1:26-27, which both have the idea of fire after mentioning the throne. The wording here is also from Ezekiel 1:13. It's all so mind-blowing in splendor and sovereign power. The seven spirits of God. Remember the number seven signifies completeness. Seven days in a week, etc. So this is the Holy Spirit of God in his fullness.

And **from the throne came flashes of lightning, rumblings**

and peals of thunder. Think of how awesome and terrifying is the God of the OT. At Mt. Sinai, everyone trembled before the LORD (Ex. 19:16-19). Isaiah was also undone in the presence of the LORD. This is the *throne room of God!* This is the one who evokes thoughts of his judgments with lightning and fire lamps blazing. But what a wonderful thing to see that rainbow surrounding the throne. He is also the God of grace and hope. This is God in heaven right now, and we are given a picture here in the last book of the Bible like no other. A hidden camera as it were, in the very throne room itself.

> Also in front of the throne there was what looked like a sea of glass, clear as crystal (4:6a).

What is a sea doing there and why so calm? Rev. 15:2 tells us more about that sea and its allusion back to Moses at the Red Sea and the deliverance of God's people from evil. The sea often represents evil in the OT, but there is no evil in heaven. Notice two things. First, it's not a sea. It **looked like** **a sea of glass.** Secondly, it's a subdued and peaceful symbol. On earth, it might look as though evil is chaotic, like the roaring sea, but in heaven this representation is 'chill out man', it's all under control. The LORD is clearly in control. No sin can enter it. Pure, calm, like a sea of glass.

> In the center, around the throne, were four living creatures, and they were covered with eyes, in front and in back (4:6b).

Notice it's **four living creatures.** This gives us a hint because we know in the Bible the number four is often used to speak of the Creation in completion. There are the four winds of the earth and four corners or quarters of the earth. So here the four living creatures represent all creatures of earth.

> The first living creature was like a lion, the second was like an ox, the third had a face like a man, the fourth was like a flying eagle (4:7).

The **lion** is the king of the jungle, the king of wild animals. The **ox** is the most powerful of the domestic animals. Humans, intelligence, **man** rules the earth. And the **eagle** is the most majestic of the flying creatures.

> Each of the four living creatures had six wings and was covered with
> eyes all around, even under its wings (4:8).

John and his first readers knew their Bibles and would have thought of Ezekiel 1. The creatures were **covered with eyes** to show they see in all directions. Here the creatures from every direction 'bow down' to the Lord.

Notice these strange creatures are said to be *like* a lion, *like* an ox etc. So, through these symbols we see the representatives. Don't expect to get to heaven and see weird monster creatures with strange eyes all over them. When we get to Rev. 5 and see Jesus, we don't expect he will literally look like a lamb with seven horns and seven eyes. Nor will Jesus look like he did in Rev. 1 with a sword coming out of his mouth. This is apocalyptic literature. Visions of symbols conveying literal truth immediately recognizable, if what? If we know our Bible! John did! These symbols meant a lot to him. We can interpret these symbols from the OT, especially that other great apocalyptic book, Daniel, which also represented great literal truth with symbols.

But what do these creatures and the elders represent in these symbols in Rev. 4? Every single part of creation bows in submission to the one on the throne! If only we could see what John saw in this scene! To actually see that throne—the very source of the power of the universe. If we could see the rainbow surrounding the throne and those 24 elders representing us, the people of God, right across the spectrum from days of old. The OT to NT.

But what is it with those creatures and all those eyes going every which way? Every creature, every action, in every direction is in submission, planned, and directed from that control room. The throne room of God! Once you see that, you realize every detail is under his control. No wonder there is not a single sparrow which falls to the ground apart from his will.

What if you could see that rainbow signifying God's covenantal love and grace right there in heaven now, and we could see everything is planned? We know it in words. *'For we are God's handiwork, created in Christ Jesus to do good works, which God prepared in advance for us to do'* (Eph. 2:10). Yes, the words say the Lord has mapped out the plan of your life and *prepared* your works in *advance*, but what if you could see what John saw? What if you could see an actual glimpse into heaven's control room with all those creatures? What if you could see a picture of God controlling every good work in advance? How that would change you! Then you would let go of worrying about tomorrow. Then you would be bold to serve the Lord! Then you would be motivated to fight through your trials! Because they are all part of a plan! What do you have to fear? He has it all prepared in advance from that room you saw. If only we could get a peek of that picture in heaven.

But don't you see that's what this book of Revelation is? A book of word pictures like no other in the Bible. Right at the end of the Bible Jesus gave this vision to John, to give to you, believer. You see what John saw. Look at it more closely. Jesus says blessed is everyone who reads this and takes it to heart. See yourself there represented. The 24 elders representing us, the people of God right across time. And the creatures, every creature, and every action, down to every single direction—look at all those eyes! *All bow down!* He is in control. All is in submission to him! By faith and with the aid of this word picture you can be like John. 'Come on up' and have a peek into where your life is being controlled. The enemies of temptation, oppression, and fear can't win. They are subject to this control room.

What we are seeing here is the great theme of Revelation unfolded. It looks like Satan and evil are winning down below. But look into the control room. Look who is on the throne. This is what we will learn as we delve into Revelation, as it unfolds the future history. Jesus wins over Satan and evil. The story has already been written. It was a plan all along.

This book is written to those churches in Asia Minor as they suffer trials and persecution. Some are falling for temptation, some have forgotten their first love, others are poverty stricken and persecuted. So what is the one thing they need from here? Is it to put the rest of Revelation away because it is not written to them? No. What they need most of all is to see what happens *after this* (4:1). They need to see this throne room. If they can just get a glimpse of it, if you could just get a glimpse of it and actually see the control room ...

Who is on the throne? The LORD is at the controls. If you could see him pushing those buttons on your day tomorrow, if you could see him pushing the buttons for next year, on what you will be doing, that trouble you thought you had, who you will marry, or what job you will have, or how you will get through the next big hurdle you face. If only you could get a glimpse into that throne room. Well this has to be one of the most exciting parts of the word of God and no doubt that is why the Lord left it till last. Here it is. Revelation!

Whether you are there in the first century under persecution, or now 2000 years later battling troublesome people at work, trouble in your marriage, trouble in your family, under attack from without or within, when accidents happen, when you are fighting a serious trial or you are tempted to go back to regrets of things gone wrong, a relationship, or a lost loved one, a lost job, a test … there is nothing in all creation that does not have its very being and every move controlled from that room. Where did the apostle Paul get the idea of saying all things work together for good for those who love him? From the same Spirit who gave us this. The control room!

I felt this myself with the recent news that several pedophile priests were convicted. How can they have gotten away with that evil in the name of the church? And we, who are the church, are being slandered. Is it out of control? Maybe the authorities didn't catch you, but it's just been logged into the computer above. He will deal with it.

Our perspective is that evil is winning, and our lives are out of control. Heaven's perspective is that no one will get away with anything and God's people are in his care. And this Revelation is going to tell us *what must take place*. From this point in Revelation (4:1), listen carefully. Take notes from here. It's all in here. It *must* take place. He controls all things. But before we head into the tribulation chapters, the first scene—Act 1, is set. The foundation is that no matter how fierce the battle gets after this, don't forget, the Lord *reigns*. We need Rev. 4 first as the foundation, which sets the theme of Revelation. The Lord is on the throne. This is something the Christian needs through all of life, whether through persecution, trial, health issues, temptation, or despair.

Everyone who reads this and takes to heart what is written in it is blessed (1:3). So unbeliever, blessed are you if you read this book and take it to heart. How many unbelievers say, 'If I could just get a look at the other side, then I could believe.' Or, 'I don't believe in the afterlife because no one's ever been there and come back to tell us.' Well, as a matter of fact someone has! There is one in history who has come back from death (not just some seconds or minutes of 'clinical death', but really dead). He gave this revelation to John, and at the beginning of this book, identifies himself as the firstborn from the dead (1:5). Jesus! God himself went through death and came back. Jesus, who went up to heaven, now brings John, his beloved disciple up to get a look at what it's like on the other side! If you want a peek, here it is!

Now if you are an unbeliever, what do you notice about heaven? Surrounding the throne were twenty-four other thrones and seated on them were twenty-four elders. The believers have their rich crowns. Rewarded! What else do you notice about heaven, unbeliever? You are not there! You are not represented. A forgiving God? Yes, but also God who is the judge. From the throne came flashes of lightning, rumblings and peals of thunder. This is the God who the unbeliever faces. The God who thunders. He is a saving, forgiving God, but he did it at the greatest cost. We will see more of that in Rev. 5, the Lamb who was slain. God gave his own Son that whoever believes in him! Believes that he was slain, for me, even me. That's not, 'I believe there is a God out there,' but rather, 'I believe my sin was nailed to the one who was slain.' That is the difference between belief and unbelief—humility. Whoever humbles himself before the holy, holy, holy God, instead of complaining to God about the evil in the world, will say, 'I am part of that evil.' 'God have mercy on *me* the sinner. I am part of the sin of this world.' Your eternal destiny depends on whether you humble yourself before the Savior and entrust your life to him, or whether you want to keep your crown for yourself. 'I'll have my own crown. It's my life, I will be Lord!'

Can you see yourself in this book of Revelation? It looks into the future. You are in there. Everyone is in there. Either you are around the throne worshiping with your crown, with joy and delight, or as we will see further in this book, you will see yourself receiving due penalty according to the things you have done. What about those murderers and rapists and evil people? Yes, they meet justice, but not just them. Everyone who is not washed clean by the Lamb who was slain will receive due penalty, 'according to what they have done' (20:12). It all turns out so fair because God is pure and exact in his judgments. He is holy, holy, holy. Unbeliever, you will receive exactly what you deserved. Why? Because you got to peek into the throne room. You saw him in his holy, holy, holiness. You saw he was at the center, but you wanted to stay at the center of your own life. You passed up forgiveness! You passed up the rainbow. The covenant love of God. You passed up the most amazing love! The Son who was slain in your place!

Holy, holy, holy is the Lord God Almighty, who was and is and is to come (4:8).

Study Questions

1. There are many authorities ruling in life, but what is the significance of who is on the throne?

2. How does this text connect with Isaiah 6 for John?

3. Why are there so few details about God and why is a rainbow surrounding him?

4. Why are there 24 elders?

5. The elders are on thrones, dressed in white and are wearing crowns. Why was this significant to the first readers of Revelation?

6. What does the thunder and lightning in 4:5 represent?

7. Why is the sea in 4:6 symbolized that way?

8. What do the four creatures represent and why all the eyes?

9. Should we expect to see creatures that look like that in heaven one day? Why or why not?

10. In what ways could this scene encourage us going through trials?

13
Laying down your crowns
(Revelation 4:8-11)

We are still in the throne room of the living God in heaven. We have seen how John is like the little boy who has snuck his way up to get a peek into the royal throne room of a powerful king. We have been looking at this throne room. The next chapters will go on to describe the tribulation. The 'revelation' this book reveals is that two kingdoms are at war, and though they seem like equal and opposite rivals, Rev. 4 is crucial in reminding us who is actually on the throne, as we peer into the very throne room of God. We will see they are not two equal kingdoms. Jesus reigns! Jesus wins! And Jesus is winning, through the tribulation!

Rather than this all happening at some distant future time, this is real for John and it is real for us. It is what John needed to see when he received this revelation while Emperor Domitian was pressuring John's parishes in those seven churches to bow down to him and his world. It was what those first readers needed as they endured persecution. It is what Christians through the ages needed when the weight of the world, flesh and the devil were against them. It reminds us that as we go through tough times, we are meant to go through this. Through many hardships we must enter the kingdom (Acts 14:22). It must happen. But the Lord is at the controls in heaven!

This brings us to the question of the structure of Revelation. Do the letters to the seven churches have any bearing on the rest of the book? Is it just a coincidence the way Revelation starts off with letters to real churches and then goes into the visions? Or do those letters teach us something on how to understand what follows? What is the plan of this book of Revelation? Do the letters just relate to the first century? Is it that we can at least read Rev. 1-3 and get some sense out of this strange book, but then in the following chapters launch into totally unrelated, cosmic, multi-headed beasts and galactic scenes that have no relationship to those first readers, so that neither they nor we can make sense of them because it's all irrelevant to the church?

We have been saying all along the whole book is written to those seven churches, not just the letters (1:4). If we forget that, then Revelation seems funny in its set up. It starts off with these relatively down to earth letters and then immediately goes into this weird imagery. Or is there a connection? Are those first readers meant to look at these chapters through the introduction of the very letters sent to them? And indeed, into the future history? Are we meant to see there are more of the same struggles of the church all the way to the end, so that you in the church in every era can find yourself in there? The curtain is pulled back on these battles. The curtain is even pulled back on heaven itself.

Can we truly say everyone who reads the words of this prophecy will be blessed (1:3), because it speaks to all his servants in every era of the church? What did Jesus tell us at the very start of the book? It is for his servants … (1:1). It's alive for us. The Lord is on his throne in the midst of our trials and tribulation.

But if it is meant to be a blessing to all his servants throughout the ages and has relevance to all of us, then why is it so difficult? Why do we have so much trouble understanding it? Take a look at what we have seen in Rev. 4. You have heaven and the One on the throne, but grotesque looking creatures with eyes all over them. Is that literally what heaven looks like? Could a child understand all this with such complexity? Can grown-ups? Even Sunday school children would be able to tell us the rainbow in 4:3 is a sign of God's promise of mercy. So how come children can figure out what the rainbow means? Because since they were little, many of them have been taught the story of Noah and the flood in the OT. It will stay with them for the rest of their lives.

So, what if you were brought up as a Jewish boy in the first century? Not only is Noah and the rainbow familiar to you, but also these creatures with eyes all over them are just as familiar. You would immediately recognize that the creatures covered in eyes are also in Ezekiel 1. These creatures conveyed God as able to move and be in every direction and location and that he is all seeing. Also these creatures worship God, who has control of their every direction and action. What if that jasper and carnelian in 4:3 immediately conjures up the precious stones alluding to the theophanies in the OT (Ezek. 1:26, 28; 9:2, 28:13)? And what if the book of Daniel was familiar to you? These signs are alive for John who was brought up on the OT. They are not grotesque or strange figures any more than the rainbow is to our children. They are symbols which represent great OT truth. When we get to Rev. 5 and see a Lamb who was slain on the throne, for us, like John, this is more familiar territory. We know Jesus will not literally look like a slain lamb with seven horns in heaven, but we don't have to think twice about what or whom the lamb represents. We know it is a symbol and we know it represents Jesus. How? If you have been taught the gospels from childhood, you know they tell us Jesus was the Lamb of God slain for our sins. The symbol is not grotesque but speaks clearly of that truth. So how come Revelation is so full of these symbols?

Shouldn't we take the Bible literally? Yes. Do we take Revelation literally? Of course. Just as we take poetry in Psalms literally as poetry. We take Jesus' parables literally as parables. We take historical accounts literally as historical events. We take metaphor for what it is. When Jesus says, 'I am the gate, whoever enters through me will be saved', we know it's a metaphor. Jesus is not saying he is literally a gate! We take the whole Bible literally in each genre it is written. We take Revelation literally for the type of literature it is. It's apocalyptic, like the great cosmic images in Daniel, parts of Ezekiel and Isaiah. So yes, we take it literally as it presents itself. And how does it present itself right from the start?

> The revelation of Jesus Christ, which God gave him to show his servants what must soon take place. He <u>made it known</u> by sending his angel to his servant John (1:1).

When Jesus says he **made it known,** the Greek root word in the original language is a word that means *sign*. Jesus is saying he will *make it known by signs*. John used the same root word when he spoke of making known through miraculous signs in his gospel (John 2:1-11), when Jesus turned the water into wine, he told us this was the first miraculous sign. It's the same word in John 12:33 when Jesus spoke in metaphor that the son of man will be lifted up to 'show' the kind of death he would die. He spoke in metaphor, to 'show' or 'symbolize' what he meant. When 1:1 opens with Jesus saying he would 'show' *what must happen* and *make it known*, that means by *signs* or *symbols*. So right at the outset we are told to expect symbolic language in this book.

In fact, if we take the whole Bible into account from the ancient Greek translation of the OT (the LXX or Septuagint), there is only one other occurrence in the Bible where these two words in 1:1 'show' and 'made it known' are used in that combination together. The only other occurrence is in Revelation's favorite OT book, Daniel! It occurs in the second chapter when Daniel was revealing to King Nebuchadnezzar what must take place. He 'showed' Nebuchadnezzar what must take place and 'made it known'. How did he do it? In strange imagery through symbols. So what Daniel did in apocalyptic symbols, John is saying right from the outset that this book contains the same kind of literature as Daniel—things of apocalyptic nature through signs or symbols. It's perhaps even more telling that John had at his disposal another more common Greek word he could have used at 1:1 to convey the words *made it known*, but he didn't choose that one because it wouldn't have conveyed the concept of making it known through signs or symbols.

With that in mind we can look at each passage and ask, 'What does this sign or symbol represent?' But most importantly, 'What should we use to interpret those symbols?' Surely the same thing John did! If we are grounded in the Bible we will be looking for answers to those symbols in the Bible, especially the OT.

Ironically, many who say we should take the symbols of Revelation literally don't take the simple words at the end of 4:1 literally, *what must take place after this*. So why do I take that literally? In that context, there is no symbolism or imagery or allusions to the OT. He simply says, 'I'm going to show you what must take place after this.' If we take it plainly and literally, what would it mean to John and his seven churches in the first century? *After this* would naturally mean immediately *after this*, and could be reaching much further forwards as a view of history up to the end.

That's how I will be approaching Revelation. Taking seriously those words *after this*, because the plain wording in the context of that sentence does not suggest there is anything symbolic about it. But when the text speaks in imagery, I should be expecting symbols to convey literal truth (particularly looking to the OT to interpret the meaning of those symbols, using Scripture to interpret Scripture).

So now we continue to look into the throne room of God. The whole of creation testifies that the Lord is worthy. He is so incredibly pure, heaven calls out holy, holy, holy (4:8). We need to pause on that. The spontaneous response of heaven from every creature is to exclaim God is holy, holy, holy. The unbeliever doesn't even try to grasp the holiness of God. Even believers can't comprehend how pure God is. But by faith we know that God, in whom there is only pure light, must judge and punish all sin. And only when we are face to face will we see just how right and good and fair hell really is. If you've ever had a tinge of doubt that maybe hell was a bit unfair or harsh, then what is this picture teaching you? When you come face to face, you and everyone else will finally only be able to utter one thing …*holy, holy, holy is the Lord God Almighty.* 'Lord, you are right after all. I was wrong. You are right in your judgments and fairness.' That is the picture of heaven.

> Each of the four living creatures had six wings and was covered with eyes all around, even under its wings. Day and night they never stop saying: 'Holy, holy, holy is the Lord God Almighty, <u>who was, and is, and is to come</u>' (4:8).

All of creation is represented giving glory and praise to the Lord. **Holy, holy, holy is the Lord God Almighty, who was, and is, and is to come.** It anticipates the completion of all things with the words, *is to come*, and looks back to his eternal being and control over history as he *who was*. And he *is* reigning now!

Notice the primary activity in heaven is worship. They have seen who God is firsthand. We were created to glorify God, and in heaven we are free to return to what we are created for—worshiping God. But day and night? Is that boring? Do they do it in shifts? Well, it's symbolism, but what do these symbols represent?

What do people do when they look upon beautiful art in a museum or great craftsmanship in a car, or precious stones in jewelry? They admire it. But to others it might be boring. Others might stare at something else or be fixated on someone they admire. A movie star or pop star? Fixated on them for who they are and what they have done. If you are into computer games, you are fixated on them. We might find ourselves fixated staring at the opposite sex, rightly or wrongly depending on whether you happen to be married to that person. People love to watch a favorite TV show. For others, it might be watching their newborn children. Joy. It pleases. For others, it's sport. 'Don't interrupt me now, the game is on!' They love to watch. As long as the game is on, they don't want to interrupt their gaze. Where does the excitement and exhilaration of 'watching' come from? Why do we become fixated on things? Because this is how we were created. We find pleasure in fixing our eyes upon the object that gives us pleasure. That's why living by faith is only a snippet. But seeing face to face? That is another dimension altogether.

However, all the greatest visual thrills of this world combined are nothing … compared to heaven. This is heaven. You will never get enough of being fixated on the Lord—who he is and what he has done, and the precious jewels and diamonds of his being. There is no language to describe the Lord, so we saw in 4:3 he was described as like those precious jewels, jasper, carnelian (ruby), trying to describe in the most beautiful terms the indescribable—the ecstasy of beholding the sight of the Lord himself. This is what we were created for.

And because we were created to be like this, if we don't worship God in this life we will find something else to worship, something else to be fixated on. That's what people are doing in this life. They are fixated on things, worshiping them, but those things never quite live up to the hope. It dies out and we want more. All the greatest exhilaration in this life, be it sexual, visual, emotional, physical, all wrapped up into one, *cannot* compare to when we behold the Lord.

Of course, this scene is symbolic, and in the new heaven and new earth we will not be standing still in one place to worship. It will be rich with fellowship and the activity of the wedding banquet. Just as in Romans 12:1-2, all of life will be an *act of worship*. Here heaven is *symbolized* in John's vision for what it ultimately is, worship! And notice how it's spontaneous.

> Whenever the living creatures give glory, honor and thanks to him who sits on the throne and who lives for ever and ever, the twenty-four elders fall down before him who sits on the throne and worship him who lives for ever and ever … (4:9-10).

Why don't you find the idea of gazing upon the Lord and singing his praises, *holy, holy, holy,* exciting? Why would you rather see sport or a television program? Because you haven't seen the Lord yet! That's Revelation. It's telling us what people who have actually seen him are doing. And they are there to tell you, you are wrong! It's not boring. It's spontaneous joy!

You know what it's like when little kids are told the facts of life and they respond, 'Yuk! I would never want to do that!' And then they grow up and not only do they change their minds, we have to hold them back! When you are a child, you just don't know what you are missing. When you fall in love and get married you will have a whole different perspective. That's what the apostle Paul said about seeing the Lord face to face.

> When I was a child, I talked like a child, I thought like a child, I reasoned like a child. When I became a man, I put the ways of childhood behind me. For now we see only a reflection as in a mirror; then we shall see face to face. Now I know in part; then I shall know fully, even as I am fully known (1 Cor. 13:11-12).

That is what we do in our church meetings. Worship. Unbelievers think the idea of coming to church is either to earn brownie points for heaven or about what you get out of it, to make you feel good. If that is you, you still need to grow in understanding of what church services are about. Primarily they are about worship. They are not to gain points for attending so you can make it to heaven. If you are a believer, you already have been given assurance of heaven. Nor is it a crutch that props you up. 'I need this to make me feel better or cope.' Maybe it does that, but that is not the central point. The reason you come to church primarily is to worship, as it is in heaven—together. It's worshiping God for who he is and what he's done. And no, we can't experience all the joy and exhilaration of what it will be like in heaven here on earth. But we set aside one day a week to come together and worship as a small foretaste, and contemplate the truth of who God is and what he has done to save us. It's a foretaste of our destiny. The presence of the Lord …

> Whenever the <u>living creatures</u> give glory, honor and thanks to him who sits on the throne and who lives <u>for ever and ever</u>, … (4:9).

Notice he is eternal and we are creatures. This is as relevant as ever. It used to be only Eastern religions that believed God is in everyone and everything. Now Westerners say that too. 'We are all part of God.' But where do people get that idea? In fact, how can you know about God unless God comes down and tells us? Well, he did just that in Jesus, who came down to earth and passed on to us this very peek into the throne room of God. And what do we see? God is not part of creation! The creation bows down to God. They are not one and the same thing. If someone says creation and God are the same, we must ask them, whom should I believe? You or Jesus? Jesus came down from heaven and said God and the creation are not the same. So ...

> The twenty-four elders fall down before him who sits on the throne and worship him who lives for ever and ever. They lay their crowns before the throne and say: ... (4:10).

In 4:4 we learned the 24 elders represent God's people from the OT and the NT. They too are on thrones of their own, but they are not worshiped. They **fall down** worshiping the One at the center. All their power and authority comes from the One on the throne and they acknowledge this when they lay their crowns before him. They were given crowns having been victorious. Jesus told us in the letters to the seven churches that *the one who is victorious* would receive a crown. But now it's apparent that everything they achieved came from him, and they even **lay their crowns** before him.

We need to meditate on that. You don't have anything from your own achievement that wasn't given to you by God (Jas. 1:17). Even the discipline and hard work ... it was God all along who gave you that gift, and it will one day be returned to him. The greatest achievements all are laid down before him. Humans try to gain crowns for themselves in this life such as success, power, glory and skills. But all these were given by God and they will be returned to him either in praise, like in 4:10, or in judgment for those who are exposed as thieves and liars who claimed they achieved these things by themselves and didn't give God the glory. Where did the atheist get the brain to even argue the existence of God? Their very arguing becomes self-contradicting. Humans have achieved great things with great gifts in science and technology. They have achieved great things in art and music, exploration, discovery, sport, and architecture. But they actually have the temerity to think these achievements prove they don't need God! Out of all those given gifts, very few give him the glory and dedicate it to him. But one day they all will.

There is nothing that you have, or could have, apart from him who created you. And there is a day when he will call to account all of what you did with what he had given you. It's like the parable of the talents (Matt. 25:14-30) when the master demands an accounting for what his servants did with what he gave them. Even the man with the one talent admitted, 'here take back what is yours!' One day, all will lay them down before him. **They lay their crowns before the throne.** God gave you gifts and talents for his glory, so cast them before him for use in his kingdom because one day you will cast them down whether you like it or not. Everyone will, either in willing submission in this life, or in humiliation broken down in the next.

The crowns of these elders are the reward for being victorious, and now they are acknowledging it was the Lord who enabled them to be victorious. What craziness it is to fall for jealousy or to envy something someone else has or does in their ability or talent, their marriage, job or lifestyle. What craziness. It's God you are against! Despising what God gives to someone else. When we get to heaven we are released from that nonsense. All crowns are laid down and we see it was all of God's grace. All glory to him! That is how it is in heaven now. This is the meaning of life. Glorifying God. And finally, everyone does what he or she was created for.

So all you need to ask yourself now is this: Is everything you do in submission to the glory of God? All your gifts and abilities? What is the difference between the believer and the unbeliever who lives life and enjoys family and has a good job and even achieves worldly crowns? The difference is that the believer acknowledges every single detail has been given by God and is for him and must be used for him, and ultimately will be laid down before him. Everything you have is from God. Life, breath and everything in it. The next breath you take will be your last without God pressing a button in this control room we picture here. Here is the secret. This is a picture of heaven's throne. The secret is that the Lord is on the throne now! He gives the gifts and he is to be worshiped and lived for now. He is worthy.

Some Christians try to divide things and time into 'Christian stuff' and 'stuff for me', but everything we have is from him and for him. Everything you have is given to you on loan and has to be returned and laid down before him.

John is the only one who saw this vision. But wait, that's not entirely true. Jesus gave this revelation to John to give to who? *His servants!* (1:1). *Blessed are those who read it and take it to heart* (1:3). Not everyone will take this to heart, so it's not for everyone. Unbelievers who neither read it nor take it to heart will miss out, but for those who believe, right here is a picture that unbelievers would love to get a look at (if only they knew).

Here is the secret of the universe from the very throne room. Everything you have and achieve will either be used for the world and burned up and turned back to haunt you forever, or will be used for the glory of God and will be laid down before him as a glorious crown. He will ask what you did with the money he gave you, with the talents he gave you, and with the time he gave you. Did you use it in the lampstand to shine for God? He is the one who gave it to you. Will you be like Achan (Josh. 7) who kept for himself those things that were meant to be dedicated to God? Achan was exposed and the earth swallowed him up. One day all who did that will be swallowed up. We need to lay it all down now. What are you holding back? Lay it all down before the throne!

So here is the secret to understanding history! You were looking so closely at the several-headed beasts and multiplying it by 666 and taking away the number you first started with, that you missed the message of Revelation and the real secret to history! The secret to understanding life now and in the future, is this: Jesus wins!

The secret is this sneak peek into heaven. God is on his throne sustaining and controlling all creatures from every possible angle. He gave you all the things you have to be used for his glory. One day you *will* cast all your crowns before him. That is the secret. It's revealed here. It's telling you this is where you are headed.

... the twenty-four elders fall down before him who sits on the throne and worship him who lives for ever and ever. They lay their crowns before the throne and say: 'You are worthy, our Lord and God, to receive glory and honor and power, for you created all things, and by your will they were created and have their being' (4:10-11).

Study Questions

1. What relationship if any do the letters of Rev. 2-3 have to the rest of the letter and why?

2. Why do we find it hard to interpret Revelation?

3. Should we take Revelation literally? When, where and how?

4. What reasons are there to consider taking the imagery symbolically?

5. Is hell a place of cruelty? How does this text speak into that?

6. Is heaven boring with constant worship? If not, why not?

7. What does this text teach us about worship and our motives for worship?

8. How can you respond to the person who says God is one with the creation?

9. How does this text speak to the gifts we have?

10. Have you laid all your crowns before him?

14
Why God Created the World
(Revelation 4:11)

What else can this glimpse into heaven teach us?

> You are worthy, our Lord and God, to <u>receive glory</u> and honor and power, for you <u>created all things</u>, and by <u>your will</u> they were created and have their being (4:11).

Why did God create this world? For his glory. We see that here, **'You are worthy ... to receive glory ...'** But God didn't need anything. He didn't need glory from us. He already had the highest glory. Father, Son and Holy Spirit glorifying one another forever (John 17:5). So why did God create this world for his glory if he didn't need any more glory? Right here we have the answer. It's Revelation, revealing the secrets again. The secrets are known to heaven, but we get a look into heaven here. If God doesn't need any glory from us, why did he create this world? Answer: Because he wanted to! It pleased God ... **by <u>your will</u> you created all things.**

This is amazing. God didn't need to create the world, but he wanted to. It was his *will*. It was in his will before he created. There was never a time when God did not plan this. Wow, did you get that? God did not sit around in all eternity and get lonely. Dark space. God sitting there in nothing. Contemplating. How about I create a world? No! God has always known what his plan would be. There was never a time when God didn't have all this in mind. The three persons of God existing forever, Father, Son and Holy Spirit, deliberately planned it. Why? Because God wanted to! By your *will* they were created. That means there was never a time you were not planned from before the world began in all eternity. Some say, 'I wish I'd never been born.' Some say children were a mistake or born unwanted. Born out of immorality. Born disabled. Born as a result of rape or accident. No. Each individual was born because of the will of God. Why were you born? No purpose? No meaning? No one really wants me? Have you ever felt like you have been left out? Dealt a bad blow? Does it really make any difference if I was born or not? Does God really care? Was it coincidence that one little cell formed me and could have been any number of others? No! Not an accident. God cares, because it was his will that you were created. *By your will they were created*.

Yes, but doesn't God just set reproduction in order? Go forth and multiply. He set the ball rolling. But is God directly involved with our individual creation?

> A prophecy: The word of the LORD concerning Israel. The LORD, who stretches out the heavens, who lays the foundation of the earth, and <u>who forms the human spirit</u> within a person, ... (Zech. 12:1).

He didn't just set and forget and let humanity create itself. God creates every individual. He forms the spirit in you. It was always a plan. Why? Because God wanted to! Wow! Now we can enter into, **'<u>You are worthy</u>, our Lord and God, to receive <u>glory and honor</u> and power, for you created all things, and <u>by your will</u> they were created and <u>have their being</u>.'**

Everything has its life and being in God. Every creature. Every action. Look at 4:6-8 with the eyes in every direction, all at the behest of the Lord. And at the end of 4:11 everything has its *being* in God. All things! That means hypotheticals are out. They are of the devil. What if I made a mistake? What if that person hadn't come into my life? What if I had married someone else? What if I had not stayed single or had not divorced? What if I had children, or no children? Different children? Different job? Hypotheticals all come from a god of our own making. There is no such thing as hypotheticals! The living God created all things according to *his will*. This is so comforting if you are struggling and have hypotheticals thrown up at you. What if I had done this or not done that, as if life is all up to you, or time, or chance? If it was, then of course you should be worried! But this same God has promised to do good and to work all things for good for those who love him. And this is how. He controls it all. Those people in your life are part of the plan. They were created by the *will of God*. No hypotheticals. When you lost loved ones, lost hope, or lost time, it's okay. It was the will of God as the plan of him who has a time and place for people and created everything beautiful in its time (Eccl. 3:11). Everything is as it should be. I often read this text at funerals:

> A person's days are determined; you have decreed the number of his months and have set limits he cannot exceed (Job 14:5).

This tells us there are no 'what ifs'. If only I had done this or if only I had done that. God has a time for everyone, and you couldn't have changed another person's time no matter what. God also knows what you need because he created you according to his will. Why? Because he wanted to. It was his will! And his will is always good, pleasing and perfect (Rom. 12:2). What a comfort to know. It was not up to you. It was all about his will. John is seeing in a picture form what we've seen in words in …

> In him we were also chosen, having been <u>predestined according to the plan of him who works out everything in conformity with the purpose of his will</u>, in order that we, who were the first to put our hope in Christ, might <u>be for the praise of his glory</u> (Eph. 1:11-12).

His will. His plan. Predestined and for the purpose of his glory. That's what is being said with: *'You are worthy, our Lord and God, to receive <u>glory</u> and honor and power, for you created <u>all things</u>, and by your will they were created and <u>have their being</u>.'* All things. All ideas. Every creature and their being. That's why we left off in our previous chapter with the crowns being laid down before him. All we have comes from him. Our gifts and abilities, even our ability to think. He has done it all. Where did we get our will? People have developed great theories to eliminate God from the picture, such as evolution. But where did people even get the ability to come up evolution? If we are not created by God's will and in his image, then where did we get a will?

Buddhists believe suffering is caused by desire. On a deeper level the Buddha taught that imagination causes desire, which causes us to be born, and all birth into this world causes us suffering.[18] Will anyone stand up and say the Emperor has no clothes? The Buddha has no clothes! Where did he get this idea? Imagination causes desire

---

[18] Buddhist Scriptures, translated by Edward Conze, (London: Penguin Books, 1959), p.113

which in turn causes suffering? Who says? Siddhartha, the original Buddha, doesn't even hide the fact he didn't get the idea from God. He didn't get a look into the throne room like John here. Unless God comes down to tell us why things are the way they are, we are just guessing in the wind. We need revelation from God. That's what this book reveals.

In 1:17 Jesus says he is God. *I am the First and the Last.* He is quoting Isaiah 44:6 *I am the First and the Last, apart from me there is no God.* So this is a revelation from God who came down (Jesus). That's what we need. Revelation.

The Buddha didn't even claim to know God and was not even sure if there is a God. There is no supreme creator God in Buddhism. But if the Buddha's ideas are not from God's will, then how does he know it's true? Imagination causes desire, and that is the reason we are born to suffer. Who says imagination causes suffering? Where did you even get the will to make up such an idea if there is no *will* behind your existence? Buddhism says there is no will behind existence. But *revelation* tells us *all things were created by his will, and <u>by his will they were created and have their being</u>.*

Where would this world be if it were not created by the will of God? Atheists, we want to love you and respect you, but can we please stop pretending it is the creationist who has let go of reason? Believing in a world with no *will* behind it is letting go of reason. There was a 'big bang' and the world creates itself without any *will*, proceeds to design itself without any *will* behind it, a piece of slime without any *will* 'decides' to evolve its way up over millions of years to become human beings who eventually get to the point where they have what? Their own *will!* And they even use that *will* to decide to reject that there could be anyone who has a *will* to create them.

'Oh, but the world started with hydrogen and other gas.' Did the gas have a will? Did the hydrogen have a will to become more than hydrogen? Let alone even asking, 'Where did the hydrogen come from?' 'Oh, but where did God come from?' It's right in our text at the end of 4:9. God, the One on the throne is **forever**. God didn't *come from* anywhere! God is *eternal.* Forever. 'Where did God come from?' That is a child's question because children can't accept concepts beyond their own thinking. Eternity is too big a concept. But God is an eternal being. One who has always been there. If God came from anywhere then he would not be God, because God is eternal—always there. The question is not, 'Where did God come from?' The question is, 'Where did *we* come from if there is no eternal One who has always been there and had the *will* to create us?' Where did *we* get a *will*? We are the ones who can't be explained without a God who created us by his will.

Richard Dawkins and Cardinal George Pell debated the existence of God on an ABC Q&A episode.[19] Far more damage was done to the Christian cause by the RC Cardinal than the atheist scientist. To many at that time, the Cardinal supposedly represented Jesus in this country. He told Australians the book of Genesis is a myth. Cardinal Pell also said you don't have to believe in Jesus to get to heaven because anyone, even atheists who sincerely seek after truth are going to heaven. He said hell was basically empty. Hardly anyone going there. It's gonna be a lonely place George!

The funny thing was that when it came to scientific arguments, George Pell trounced Richard Dawkins. Dawkins was quoting his physics professor colleague to bolster a theory of creating 'something out of nothing', but Pell had read this professor's book, whereas it seemed Dawkins had not. Pell was able to quote exact page numbers of this other professor to show that he never said any such thing that Dawkins was claiming. Pell was impressive on science. And yet on the other hand, Dawkins trounced Pell on theology! When Cardinal Pell said Adam and Eve were myth and evolution was true, Richard Dawkins cornered him with, 'Well then what happens to original sin?' Where then is the need for Jesus to die on a cross? And he's right. Richard Dawkins understands Christianity better than the RC Cardinal. Both George Pell and Richard Dawkins were lacking in their own fields but were able to show each other up in their opposite field.

But for our purposes, Cardinal Pell basically gave in to Dawkins, not giving any credence to God as the Creator. He should have read Revelation that says *by your will they were created and have their being*. And Cardinal Pell gave in to Dawkins saying you can't prove God. We shouldn't shy away from this. You *can* prove God's existence. Romans 1:19-20 says we have irrefutable evidence that God exists…

---

[19] https://www.youtube.com/watch?v=tD1QHO_AVZA&t=1749s

> ... since what may be known about God is <u>plain</u> to them, because God has <u>made it plain</u> to them. For since the creation of the world God's invisible qualities — his eternal power and divine nature — have been <u>clearly seen</u>, being understood from what has been made, so that people are without excuse (Rom. 1:19-20).

We look at the things made and know they must have come *from somewhere*. Nothing comes from nothing. That is scientific. Richard Dawkins, we still await any actual *scientific* evidence that something can come out of nothing, that is, repeatable, observable evidence. Great thinkers have applied reason to this issue and concluded there must be a first cause of our existence, even back to ancient Greek philosophy such as Aristotle. He coined the term 'Unmoved Mover'. That is, an eternal first cause with the power of being within, because out of nothing, nothing comes. As R.C. Sproul says, if ever there was a time when there was nothing, there would be nothing here now. If there is anything here now, there must be something or someone who has always been there, with the power of being within.[20] But more than power. A *will!* Unless there is a *will* behind this universe, how can you make sense of any reason or will in this universe because out of nothing, nothing comes. How can you make sense of this existence? A look into the throne room tells us how ... *by your will they were created and have their being.*

An annual atheist convention in Melbourne was called a 'Celebration of Reason'. Can you really claim to have a monopoly on reason when you believe there was a time when there was nothing and suddenly a 'big bang' (Who lit the fuse? Don't ask curly questions!), and poof! A finely tuned universe, springs into being. But wait! It doesn't stop there. Whatever non-intelligent matter appeared out of nothing has enough genius *'will'* in itself to proceed to eventually design itself into intelligent beings without any intelligence driving it! All this originally popped out of nothing! And religious people are supposed to be the ones who have let go of reason? The evidence is before our eyes. There has to be a God. God has made it plain. We do have proof. Every day the atheist walks out the door he or she is confronted by irrefutable evidence. Existence! *Because of the things that have been made so that people are without excuse.*

If I suddenly find a Lego Batman toy in my locked cabinet, do I

---

[20] R.C. Sproul, Nothing Left to Chance, Video series, Ligonier Ministries

conclude a 'big bang' caused it to pop out of nothing? To the contrary, I have *irrefutable evidence* there is a 'someone' who put it there. I may never know *who* it is (even though I have my suspicions). I may never know how they got into my locked cabinet. It may always remain a mystery to me, but just because I can't see that person, it doesn't make them cease to exist. I can't see Richard Dawkins' brain, but does that mean he doesn't have one? There is ample evidence that he has a brain, *and a will*, even if I never see it.

So why don't they admit it? Why go to such lengths to refute the basic evidence before our eyes? We even hear Richard Dawkins saying on the film 'Expelled' that perhaps aliens started our world. That's an old one, but what a cop out for an atheist! That's not true atheism. That is just saying aliens are our god. So Richard Dawkins, the world's most famous atheist, is not an atheist. He said aliens could have sowed life on this planet. That is a direct admission that this universe has all the evidence of a will that created it, only in this case it's the will of aliens. (But who made the aliens?) What he is really saying is, 'I will believe in *anything*, even aliens, rather than the *will* of God.'

When Richard Dawkins was on that Q&A panel and put down religion, Australians cheered. When he puts down people of faith he gets a bigger cheer. He makes fun and calls them child abusers for teaching their children about Jesus. More cheers. The viewing audience participated in a survey and overwhelmingly (about 80%), said religion has done more harm than good. Bigger cheers. Stamp religion out of schools, parliament, off the streets and anywhere else you can. Standing ovation! But with all of that, why is it that if you take that same group of Aussies and remove the religious connotation from the God question, nearly all of them would say they believe in some higher creative force, power, greater being (every which way they can say God without admitting there is a God).

In other words, despite all the fans Dawkins and the evangelical atheists have gained, people still just don't buy it. They don't buy something popping out of nothing. The fact is we have the proof before our eyes, there has to be a *will* behind the universe, and hydrogen and big bangs don't have a will. Even after all the international fame Dawkins has, people don't buy a universe with no will because God has made it plain that he exists by the things that have been made so that men are without excuse. It's interesting the most recent atheist convention in Melbourne in 2018 with Richard Dawkins headlining was cancelled due to lack of interest.

Now wait. If the evidence is so abundant that very few really buy the full atheist argument, and ultimately most people really do believe in a God in some description, why do they remain unbelievers?

The answer is they hate God. We will see Revelation unfold into a divide—those who hate God and those who don't. It's not usually in the outward way like Richard Dawkins, who seems to be on a crusade to attack the God he doesn't believe in. But what about all those nice people who have no antagonism, who basically don't even think about God?

What is the greater contempt someone can have for you? Active opposition, or if they act as though you don't even exist? In some ways, the latter can be even worse. Idolatry is hatred for God. Trying to recast God in our own image as to how we want God to be. 'I think God is like this or that…' 'I believe in God in my own way.' 'God doesn't bother me, so I don't bother him.'

These are all forms of the same thing. Mankind has a hatred for God. Passive hatred by just ignoring the One who we know deep down gave us life and a *will*. In Romans 5:10 it says we are naturally enemies of God. Everyone knows God exists, but they have chosen to set up their own kingdom. They want to tell God what is right and wrong. They will set the limit as to how much God will have a place in their lives. This is why you come across people who call themselves Christian, but they are still at war with God. The kingship battle with God continues, confining God to 'just how much I will let him interfere with my life'.

Unbelievers say, 'I don't hate God. If he is there why doesn't he just show up?' Answer: He did. He showed up in person and we hated him so much we killed him. He proved who he was. He defied the creation, stopped a storm, made dead people come back to life, and walked on top of water in the middle of a storm. He did all that, but we didn't like it, so we killed him. And then he proved even more profoundly he was God by coming back from the dead.

But we hated what he had to say. He proved *who* the *will* behind the universe was, but we didn't like *his will!* He came to pay the penalty of hell and give heaven for free to all who would believe in him. But when we heard that we were sinners in need of saving because we had rebelled against him as Lord, we hated him. We don't want him being king over us. We want to be our own Lord.

Even if you could get a Q&A audience to let their guard down and admit they believe the evidence is before their eyes, that there is a God who must have created this world by *his will*, if you just let it slip to that same audience words like 'they are sinners in need of a Savior', then you will only get anger! And if you get on to how they should live with comments like, 'abortion is murdering helpless little children', or 'not only no gay marriage but no sex outside of marriage', you can feel the blood boil. They don't just disagree anymore, now they want to kill. They hate it. They won't let go of the hatred. It comes up later in Revelation ...

> The rest of mankind that were not killed by these plagues still did not repent of the work of their hands; they did not stop worshiping demons, and idols of gold, silver, bronze, stone and wood—idols that cannot see or hear or walk. Nor did they repent of their murders, their magic arts, their sexual immorality or their thefts (9:20-21).

They wouldn't lay down their crowns. They hate God. But why? If atheists are so intelligent, why can't they see their own ability to argue proves a will behind the universe? It's because they don't want to utter these words... *You are worthy*, our Lord and God, to receive *glory and honor and power* ... They don't want to cast down their crowns and admit he is worthy to receive glory and honor. Who is worthy? "Me! It's mine. I gained it for myself! I don't need God." So this is all a kingdom issue. Rev. 4 is all about who is at the center. Who is king?

Near the beginning of the Bible is the story in Genesis 3 of the fall of man, where man lifts himself up to take over kingship for himself. He will be 'like God' and he will determine right and wrong himself. And now we study the last book of the Bible. It looks into heaven and then looks into the future, and what does it tell us? The true king is God. He reigns, and he will be vindicated and shown to be the true king, and he will be shown to be truly worthy. There are no usurpers there. Jesus wins! The true king is at the center. The truth finally comes out about who is Lord.

'You are worthy, our Lord and God, to receive glory and honor and power, for you created all things, and by your will they were created and have their being' (4:11).

Study Questions

1. Give reasons why God created the world.

2. How could this reason be helpful to someone with no self-worth?

3. Why should we trust the teachings of Christianity over Buddhism?

4. Why hasn't atheism gained more popularity among unbelievers?

5. Panspermia is the belief that aliens created our world. What are arguments for or against that?

6. Is there evidence for God's existence? If so, why don't all people believe?

7. Are people more likely to reject Jesus as Lord *or* Savior? Why?

15
The Sealed Scroll
(Revelation 5:1-4)

Many years ago, when I started work in the entertainment industry, the first television commercial I did was a 15-second advertisement for 'Famous Grouse Whiskey'. If I had known one day I would be a Christian and a minister, it might not have been the best product to endorse, but it stayed in my memory being my first one. To film 15 seconds, it took from 8:00am to 9:00pm. Why so long? Because after 42 takes of me sipping that whiskey I thought I was filming a commercial on a merry-go-round at Luna Park, but I had a good time. And no, they didn't use cold tea. It was the real stuff. But I didn't actually get drunk. The real reason it took so long is because it is standard practice in the film world, especially with TV commercials, to take a long time because of their attention to detail and long camera set-ups. The director wanted every possible camera angle and each shot to be filmed in meticulous detail. There could not be a drop of whiskey on my lips as I sipped it for the close-up on the mouth. There were shots of the sip, the swallow, the reaction and the punchline joke from several angles to get the most out of the humor, so when you saw it on the screen it all came together as one package.

Now long before the modern film industry, the book of Revelation was written. It was given to us by a Master film director, Jesus himself. You the viewer, get the benefit of different camera angles in order to bring out all the detail. If you can remember this little analogy as we go through Revelation, it will help us put the whole film together and do our final editing.

The first camera angle was filming earth. The earthly perspective. The letters to churches in Rev. 2-3 are the earthly perspective. Then the camera angle changes. From 4:1 *after this,* John gets a look into heaven. This time the perspective is heaven. But like any good film, it's telling a story ... going forwards. John is told *what must take place after this* (4:1). So, this film reaches forward into what comes to pass after John's time. We have already seen that the key word mentioned 15 times is 'throne' (Rev. 4-5). The message is God is on the throne. He is sovereign. Those first readers from Ephesus and Smyrna, Pergamum, etc. didn't stop reading at Rev. 3. These chapters are for them too. It's a different camera angle, which they so desperately *needed* to see as they felt all the pressures from the one who claimed *he* was on the throne in their day, the Roman Emperor, Domitian. But it's not just for them. It sweeps across the history of the church up to the end. Blessed are all who read the words of this prophecy and take to heart what is written in it.

In Rev. 4, John was invited to *come up here* to peek into the very throne room of the God of the universe. Now we are into Rev. 5, continuing the same scene, only now the action is developing as we see the camera pan across the throne room and then a close-up. The camera slowly zooms in to the one on the throne ...

> Then I saw in the right hand of him who sat on the throne a scroll with writing on both sides and sealed with seven seals (5:1).

Ancient Roman law required wills to be sealed seven times. Emperors Augustus and Vespasian did that for their successors. But we are using the Bible, not culture, to interpret Revelation. Remember in the Bible the number seven symbolizes completeness. So this scroll has a complete sealing. God himself has sealed it. Did you notice the Master film director zooming in, so you could see the very hand of the one on the throne? **Then I saw in the right hand** ... now that you see the close-up, you see the scroll in all its detail down to the seals on it, and you can even see the writing on it. It's in the very grasp of God's own right hand. The camera zooms in on that scroll. It's sealed all right. The next scene will reveal it's so firmly sealed *no one* can open it.

You can tell a good film director by the way they set up the camera shots and close-ups to get you to focus on a particular part in the scene. This scene has zoomed in on the scroll. It's obvious the scroll is so important. So what is in this scroll? Some say it must be the book of life. But in the following chapters as each of the seals are unlocked, the contents include judgments on unbelievers and all kinds of amazing action, so it must be more than the book of life.

Others say it's the OT. Christ is the only one able to fulfill, to 'unlock' the OT. That sounds good, but how could you know? Many Futurists say it's a deed or land title that Satan has held. Still others say it's a book which details events of the future. It could be. But what future? The immediate future from John's time, as in, *what must take place after this?* In that case it would be past for us. Or will it be future from our time? How could you be sure? Revelation is so complicated. Some of these guesses might be true, but how could you know which is right? Whose opinion should we go with? How about we ask the guy who climbed the ladder to get this sneak peek of the film set when the camera crew was rolling film in heaven?

What was the apostle *John* thinking when he saw a scroll that was sealed? Remember the lens we are trying to use on Revelation? Even Sunday school children could interpret the rainbow around the throne in 4:3 as God's sign of mercy. Things taught at a young age can stay with you for life. When John the apostle was 'little John', the Rabbi's taught him in Saturday school and it was all OT. He knew his OT Scriptures the way our kids know the story of Jesus being born in a manger and dying on a cross. What did *John* think when he receives a vision of a sealed scroll? His favorite book of the OT of course! The one all the kids loved. Daniel and the lion's den! John's favorite as a kid ... well at least we know it just happens to be the favorite of Revelation. Daniel is alluded to constantly in Revelation. In fact, by the time we get to the end of Rev. 5 we will see it's the book of Daniel that is referred to most, especially some of the most profound scenes from Daniel. So here in 5:1 when John saw the scroll that was sealed, what did he think? Sealed scroll? His mind immediately went to the end of the book of ... *Daniel!*

> But you, Daniel, roll up and <u>seal the words of the scroll until the time of the end</u> ... He replied, 'Go your way, Daniel, because the words are <u>closed up and sealed until the time of the end</u> (Dan. 12:4,9).

Daniel's scroll was sealed. And it was sealed until the time of the end. What does John think of as the time of the end? When did John think the last days were? John was standing there beside Peter on the day of Pentecost when God poured out the Holy Spirit and Peter said ...

> These people are not drunk, as you suppose. It's only nine in the morning!

> No, this is what was spoken by the prophet Joel, 'In the last days, God says, I will pour out my Spirit on all people ...' (Acts 2:15-17).

Peter was saying we are in the **last days** *now!* We don't know when the last days finish. But we sure know when they began. When Jesus came the first time ...

> In the past God spoke to our ancestors through the prophets at many times and in various ways, but in these last days he has spoken to us by his Son ... (Heb. 1:1-2).

The **last days** are from the time of Jesus on earth. So, John knows Daniel's scroll was to be sealed up until the last days. But wait a minute, John is thinking. '*I* am living in the last days. It's time to open it!' That is, if anyone is able. But what is in the scroll?

Well, if it's the same scroll that was sealed in Daniel's time, then quick, go back and look up the prophecy given to Daniel *before* it was sealed. John didn't have to look it up. He knew it well. Daniel was told to seal the scroll which was the prophecy given to him in Daniel 10-12. It was apocalyptic, cosmic stuff that sweeps across history and climaxes with the Day of Judgment and the salvation of God's people. God's plan for both *salvation and judgment*. This is the scroll that was sealed up until the *last days*.

But if we are in the last days, is it time for this scroll to be opened? The book of Daniel could only tell us so much. In fact, what about that book of Daniel? It is among the most amazing prophetic books in the Bible. It gives with incredible accuracy the prophecy of the rise and fall of the earthly superpowers in the ancient world. Babylon, Medo/Persians, Greece and then the Romans. Then after that it predicts another king who would set up his kingdom, right in the middle of the last earthly kingdom, the Roman Empire. This king, unlike these other worldly kingdoms, establishes a kingdom that would last forever. Daniel had to seal it up. It was to be sealed until the last days when this king came with a new kingdom. What king came in the time of the Roman Empire saying, 'the kingdom of God is at hand'? In Matthew 12:29 he said, 'If I drive out demons by the Spirit of God, then the kingdom of God is upon you.' It's here!

John was there when Jesus said that! John knew that scroll in Daniel outlined God's plan for salvation and judgment, but it didn't have all the detail and was to be sealed until the last days! But it's the last days now! The scroll is before John's eyes. In the right hand of God on the throne! *Then I saw in the right hand of him who sat on the throne a scroll with writing on both sides and sealed with seven seals.* It's been sealed since Daniel's time. There was no one with the authority to open it in his time. The scroll contains God's plan. Remember what John was told at the end of 4:1? *Come up here, and I will show you what must take place after this.*

Well now John is about to be shown exactly that—*what must take place after this.* It's a panoramic view of God's judgments and saving work in history all the way to the end of history. That's what is inside that scroll!

It's **a scroll with writing on both sides,** just like the Ten Commandments. The old covenant! Now this new covenant scroll is covered front and back. What is that telling us? It's thoroughly comprehensive. Nothing is left out in judgment and salvation, all the way to the end! And we will see the contents of this book. How? If those seals can be broken, we can get a look at what's inside and see this plan of the saving and judging works of God in history. It must take place!

And from the close-up on the scroll, the camera pans across to someone who is making a pronouncement. It's a new camera angle. Shot three. Take one …

> Then I saw a mighty angel proclaiming in a loud voice, 'Who is worthy to break the seals and open the scroll?' (5:2).

This mighty angel has a **loud voice.** How loud? The whole universe is addressed from heaven! As we see from the next verse, heaven and earth is being addressed! This challenge is thrown out to the whole of heaven and earth. Who can open it? The word **proclaiming** is a participle in the present tense in the original Greek language. The angel is proclaiming and proclaiming! Anyone? Anyone worthy?

> But no one in heaven or on earth or under the earth could open the scroll or even look inside it (5:3).

There is no answer in all heaven or on earth! Who can open it? No one! There is no one who can open it. There is no human in history who has the power or authority to be either judge or save themselves, let alone anyone else.

> I wept and wept because no one was found who was worthy to open the scroll or look inside (5:4).

John starts to cry. He must have sensed from his knowledge of the book of Daniel that this was a scroll which needed to be opened if the plan of God's salvation and judgment is to be revealed. But why is he crying? If this scroll is just a matter of predicting things to come, and John is upset that he doesn't get to find out, then get some grit and man-up John, stop crying like a baby! But if John senses this scroll is more than just words about the future, that it represents God's judgment and salvation itself, then if this scroll can't be opened and there is no answer, the very destiny of souls is at stake. If this scroll can't be opened, the eternal destiny of all those John ministered to in his churches are in jeopardy. If this scroll holds the answer and its opening relates to the destiny of all humanity (not to mention the justice and vindication of what is right and fair throughout the history of this world); if this scroll is the one that was sealed in Daniel 12 which spoke about God's final saving work and his putting everything right as judge; if no one is worthy to open this scroll, then weep John! Weep!

If there is no one righteous and worthy to save, no one qualified to judge, no one to bring an end to the suffering and no one mighty enough to fix this mess, no wonder John is weeping! What about all the suffering and evil? Is there no end? What about all the churches to whom John ministered? What about the faithful at Smyrna who were persecuted? When, O Lord, will be your righteous judgment? What of those who are faithful and yet have great pain and toil? Weep Christian. You who persevere and still continue to suffer injustice, pain, isolation and depression—John is depressed. He is crying. Unless this scroll can be opened the bad guys are gonna win! Evil will win. Paradise is lost and so is mankind.

It's not that there is any shortage of people who have *tried* to open that scroll. Many people have tried throughout history and some claim to be worthy to open it. Man's answer to justice. The US Civil rights movement tried to open the scroll! But racism continues. Justice for the workers was a cry, so Karl Marx tried, paving the way for communism, but he couldn't open it. No justice for people there. What is the answer for those who have been abused and suffered injustice and evil? Religions have tried to answer that. The Buddhists and the Hindus have tried to open the scroll of justice. What is their answer to those who have been abused? The evil person will be reincarnated to a worse life. Of course, they won't actually feel a thing themselves, but boy that person who they are reincarnated as, they really cop it. The Buddhist answer to the suffering abused child or woman who is raped is that they are getting what they deserve from what they have done in this life and/or a previous life. It's called karma. In fact, those children being abused were the ones who did something as bad as that to someone else in a previous life because now they get what *they* deserve. That's right, all of you would-be Western Buddhists. Check your Buddhist theology. This is how Siddhartha Gautama, the founder of Buddhism tried to open the scroll of justice. Hindus try to open it in a similar way.

The philosophers who try to eliminate God, attempt to open the scroll to find justice in this world, but they come up against what the great atheist Friedrich Nietzsche highlighted. If there is no God, there can be no ultimate good or evil, and therefore no basis for complaint against evil. Even Richard Dawkins in his more sober moments admitted that without God there is no such thing as good or evil.[21] At least then Dawkins admitted he couldn't open the scroll, but since that time he has become the evangelistic atheist, so he has had a go at opening the scroll with some confused atheist ethics. But Dawkins' own earlier writing testifies what Nietzsche and other great atheist philosophers have come to. If there is no perfect, personal holy God who has revealed, 'You shall not', then who is to say, 'I am right and you are wrong?' Even Hitler thought he was right. Who says he is wrong? If there is no final arbiter, then there is *no such thing as good or evil*. No one can open the scroll. No one has an answer.

But a suffering and hurting world which cries out for justice says to the atheist, 'You lie. There is such a thing as evil. There is right and wrong. We know it.' But who can open the scroll? Who can bring an answer to the evil of this world? Atheist Christopher Hitchens raged against God, but he died a frustrated man. Brilliant, relatively young, but angry because he felt he had so much more he wanted to do. Life is so unfair. There is no justice in this world. Bad people win. The race is not always to the swift or the battle to the strong. Fools

---

[21] Richard Dawkins, *River Out of Eden: A Darwinian View of Life*, (London: Harper Collins Publishers, 1996) p. 96

are put in high positions. Evil men have their way. Meaningless, meaningless, all is meaningless.

Many say let's get rid of religion altogether and educate people. That will open the scroll of justice. But our children are more educated, more technologically advanced and less religious than ever, and there is more suicide than ever. More depression. More hurt.

So we weep if that scroll cannot be opened. The world cries out for an answer! Justice! How can you ever have justice? What is the answer for children who have been abused? What is the answer to a cruel hard life? *Who can open the scroll* and give an answer, a plan, and a solution to this? Humanity has cried out for an answer to: Why does God allow suffering and evil in this world? He can't stop it and he can't reverse what has already happened. There can never be any justice for this world. The great cry of humanity is *no one can open that scroll!* The angel proclaims to the universe, *who* can open it? And no one answers!

Who could bring a plan where every deed is righteously brought to full justice? Not like our limited justice system; a couple of years in jail and back out to do it all again. What about *complete* justice? A full compensation for righteous suffering. Not the world's consolation prize, a million-dollar compensation but you still have to live with the pain and a life of sorrow or loss. Money can't buy back lives! And what about all the times the bad guys are not even caught or brought to account? How could we have a full compensation and reward? We would need a judge who has the power to fully reverse evil. That's what we long for ... but actually we don't! That kind of perfection means every deed will be brought into judgment, including every hidden thing.

> He will bring to light what is hidden in darkness and will expose the motives of the heart (1 Cor. 4:5b).
>
> I tell you the truth men will have to give account on the day of judgment for <u>every careless word</u> they have spoken (Matt. 12:36).

Every careless word! So should it be—weep because no one can open the scroll? Second thoughts—weep if anyone *can* open that scroll to let those judgments out! Leave that scroll alone! You break those seals and it's like smashing the glass at the aquarium and all those massive sharks and stingrays that were swimming on the other side of the glass are now falling on top of you! Keep that thing sealed!

But wait! The scroll is also the salvation secret. Who can open that? Many have also tried to open the scroll of salvation. Siddhartha Gautama, the founder of Buddhism, tried to open that scroll to save as well. Nirvana he said! Okay, so reincarnation and hell were meant to be the justice end, so what would be salvation? Nirvana. Nirvana literally means extinction. Release from desire and the delusion of self. So, you spend many lives trying to detach yourself from all desire, including human relationships, so you can stop suffering, get rid of your desire, get rid of the self, so you can finally achieve what? Nothing. Not heaven. Not a personal ongoing existence that reunites with others and sees a victory over evil with love and triumph. Not a place that sees *anything*, because you are not you anymore, devoid of personality, the self. You have been extinguished. Nirvana. It's the Buddhist annihilation of the self. The Buddha tried to open the scroll by eliminating desire.

But what about all the times you have desired wrong things? The Dalai Lama admits he is a sinner. His own Scriptures say, 'Even a flight into the air cannot free you once the deed is done.'[22] How could anyone really even reach it? Answer: No one can open the scroll. None have even claimed to be sinless. None have an answer to take away the full judgment of our sin. None have even *offered* a way to do that.

Mohammed, the founder of Islam, tried to open the scroll. Pray five times a day, try to do good. But what about the times you have *not* done good? No offer of a solution there. When a young Muslim man read one of my books, he invited me to his home and we had a great discussion. He invited me back the next week and asked if he could invite another friend. Each week he would invite me back to meet more Muslim friends until after some weeks I was meeting a room filled with Muslims. These men were far deeper in their thinking and a lot less self-righteous than the average Aussie. I showed each Muslim the law of God (which they believe to be the word of God), the Ten Commandments and each one of them said, 'Well I must be going to hell. I just hope Allah will let me out some time.' They knew deep down in their hearts no one could open that

---

[22] Buddhist Scriptures, Translated by Edward Conze, (London: Penguin Books 1959), p.83

scroll. Mohammed himself didn't claim he could open that scroll. The Koran says Mohammed is a sinner in need of forgiveness (Surah 47:19), and even Mohammed had no assurance of heaven (Surah 46:9). He didn't say he could take away our sin. Who can open that scroll?

The average Aussie is not like the Muslim. He is totally self-righteous! He thinks he is able to open the scroll. How puffed up he is. 'Yeah I could open it. If there's a heaven I should get there. I'm not as bad as some people. In fact, I'll have a few things to say to God about why he didn't stop all this evil.'

But if you could open that scroll, you still have no idea what you are opening. You won't just open up justice against the 'bad guys'. God doesn't grade on a curve. By the time we get to the end of Revelation, we read that his judgments are each one according to the things they have done as recorded in the books (20:13). No mention of time off for good behavior, because good deeds can't outweigh bad deeds. No one can open the scroll in heaven. I've never met anyone who could even open a police officer's scroll. Ask a police officer what the most popular excuses are when they catch someone speeding. 'I'm not as bad as the real bad drivers. I'm normally a very good driver. You should catch the real criminals.' But how does all that good driving help? You can't even open the police officer's scroll. How much more with a perfect judge who judges every detail?

That's why hell is not a cruel place where the really bad guys go. It's simply perfect justice. People who have gone to hell are not complaining about injustice. Read the parable Jesus told of the rich man in hell (Luke 16:19-30). He does not complain about injustice, only his discomfort. 'Here is what I so richly deserve. I was just too self-righteous to see it before.' Now he can see it! It's all so fair, so right and accounted for, down to individual culpability, not some blanket punishment for all, but each one dealt with individually according to the things they have done.

People think it's all so confusing with lots of religions, but it's not complicated at all. Either there is, or isn't, someone who is worthy to *Judge* and has the power to *take away* our sin. It would need someone who is qualified to bring full, fair and complete justice! But that would mean punishment of all sin (including mine), so justice is fully done to every tiny speck of this universe in every minute detail of history. That's why maybe we don't want that scroll opened. So we don't just need someone worthy to judge, but also worthy to save. One who could pay the full penalty we deserve. One who is eternal, so he can take an eternal judgment. But wait! Only God is eternal. But God never sinned. Only humans sinned. So, it would have to be one who is human, so he can take human penalty, so justice is complete. One who is worthy because he has never sinned, so he has credit, as it were, to pay the debt. (How could anyone pay a debt if they are in debt themselves?)

The only one who has never sinned is God. So, even if someone came up with the idea of giving themselves up as a substitute to be punished for sin, they would have to fit that criteria. God eternal, human, sinless and willing.

Why all the confusion about different religions? There has never been anyone in the history of the world religions who has even *offered to take* the eternal judgment of our sin away. Neither Buddha, nor Mohammed ever dared to claim to open *that* scroll. There is *only one* in the history of the world who has claimed to be the righteous judge who has the authority to judge all evil, to bring about the great reversal of judgment and full reward for righteous suffering. No one else has offered to save. No one else in history has been *able* to open that scroll. And you better not die before you get to the next chapter because we have to wait until then to find out who that someone is.

Study Questions

1. In what way can we liken Revelation to a modern-day film?

2. What is inside the scroll? How can we confirm that?

3. Why was no one able to open the scroll?

4. Why does failure to open the scroll upset John so much?

5. What ways have people in history tried to open the scroll.

6. Why might people not really want the scroll to be opened?

7. What qualifications are needed for one to be 'worthy' to open it?

16
The Lion and the Lamb
(Revelation 5:5-7)

We left John the apostle weeping because no one could open the scroll. But if there was no one to open it, then there is no salvation for anyone and no answer to justice for this world. But as John was weeping in despair ...

> Then one of the elders said to me, 'Do not weep! See, the Lion of the tribe of Judah, the Root of David, has triumphed. He is able to open the scroll and its seven seals' (5:5).

One of the 24 elders around the throne (from 4:4) speaks to John. He comes right out of the scene to explain the vision to John. This is the beauty of Revelation. You have John down below suffering in a cave on the island of Patmos, and then he gets lifted up to heaven and gets a word from a fellow Christian in heaven! The Christian says: 'It's okay John. Stop crying. Don't you know how this story ends?' This is what John needs while suffering in that cave on Patmos, with the worries of his churches throughout Asia Minor on his mind. A word from a Christian who is already in heaven and who has been victorious says, 'You don't have to worry. It's okay. Look here! There is someone who can open the scroll.' **The Lion of the tribe of Judah.**

Of course John recognizes Genesis 49:9, Jacob's prophesy about the tribe of Judah. The scepter (the symbol of royal authority) will not depart from Judah! The promise then was that the royal king, the Messiah, had to come through the line of Judah and more specifically through the line of King David. But did you notice the one who descends from David is in fact the **Root of David?** How can that be? He is before David (the root) and over him, and yet descends *from* David? The Lion is the Root *and* descendant of David. That is what had to take place to reveal God's plan! The scroll sealed in

Daniel's time. This is now unsealed. The plan of God is revealed! Revelation!

One big picture of Revelation is paradise lost and regained. We all know about paradise lost in Genesis 3. Mankind banned from the garden and the tree of life. But from the opening letters, to the church at Ephesus ... *to the one who is victorious, I will give the right to eat from the tree of life, the paradise of God* (2:7), and Philadelphia (3:12), the New Jerusalem coming out of heaven. So where is Revelation headed? In Rev. 21 we see the *New Jerusalem coming out of heaven* and the final picture of restoration with the tree of life (22:1-5).

Adam was to rule but plunged humanity into sin and judgment. No one was found worthy to open that scroll. No man is without sin. This explains what we learnt in our previous chapter. A substitute to take away man's sin has to be a man, and so the last Adam came from the human line, the tribe of Judah. King David's descendant. And yet only God is without sin, so he is also *before* man. He is the **root of David.**

Just as through one man (Adam) all sinned, through this second man (who is worthy to open that scroll), all who are in him follow in that blessing and become a kingdom and priests (5:10). Adam's place to rule is restored in humanity because the Lion *has* been victorious.

Hey, are you guys listening in those local churches in Ephesus and Smyrna (under persecution), Pergamum and Thyatira? Now you know you can be victorious because the Lion has been victorious for you. He is victorious over those enemies who were against you. He is victorious in his resurrection and he is victorious as the Lion in control now.

So now John looks to see just who is this Lion? As soon as the elder in heaven announces to John not to worry because the Lion of the tribe of Judah can open the scroll, the camera cuts to another shot where John looks to *see* this Lion who is able to open the scroll. Remember no one else in heaven or on earth was able to open that scroll. Only this Lion has the power, the authority. So brace yourself John, as the camera pans to this mighty LION. But when John looks at him, instead of his appearance as a powerful lion, what does he see?

> Then I saw <u>a Lamb</u>, looking as if it had been slain, standing at the center of the throne, encircled by the four living creatures and the elders. He

had seven horns and seven eyes, which are the seven spirits of God sent out into all the earth (5:6).

He sees not a lion but a lamb! And a lamb which looks as though it was slain. This is craziness. Anyone in the world can tell you that you don't win without power. Lions have power. But lambs? And a lamb that has been killed? Only one is worthy and has the power and authority to open the scroll and it's—a lamb? A lamb to conquer? Conquering by having died? Giving yourself up? This is foolishness. Isn't that what 1 Corinthians 1:18-27 said? The cross is foolishness to those who are perishing. God chose the foolish to shame the wise, weakness to shame the strong.

That is the way of the Lion who is the Lamb. That is the way of true followers of the Lion who is the Lamb. They conquer with love for their enemies. Because that is how he conquered for us. It's Jesus! He is the Lion and the Lamb. He is the Lord at the center, and yet a man from the tribe of Judah, a descendant of David.

Remember the book of Ruth, how Naomi was in need of a kinsmen redeemer? One who had the right to buy back the land that had been forfeited? But he could only be a redeemer if he was a kinsman (related). For anyone to redeem humanity and open that scroll to purchase people from every tribe, nation and tongue, he has to be a *kinsman* of humanity. He has to be a human. Not an angel or some other created being, but a human. But a kinsman redeemer also had to come up with the cash. He had to bring the full price of payment to redeem. Only Jesus has the qualifications of both, as a man (tribe of Judah), to pay the human price, *and* pay as a sinless sacrifice. Who is sinless except God? The Lion and the Lamb.

What did John think of when he first saw this lamb? We don't think for a moment that Jesus' appearance in heaven is that of a literal lamb with seven horns and seven eyes. No. This is a prophetic vision. People have tried to draw the description here as though it has some literal appearance of Jesus. But drawn on paper, a lamb with seven horns and seven eyes doesn't even look like a lamb, let alone any other reality, especially when you ask, 'How do you depict a lamb that *looks* like it has been dead?'

So this is not what Jesus will literally look like in heaven. We have already established from that defining statement of Jesus at the start of Revelation (1:1), that we should be looking for symbols in this sort of imagery. In fact, Jesus is depicted in various ways in the rest of Revelation, not as a lamb or lion or with a sword coming out of his mouth (1:16), but each time by different symbols depending on what point is being taught.

We are meant to take these images of this vision and glean all the truth that immediately would have registered for John. What does the appearance of a lamb mean to John? And the answer is the same thing as it does to us. John was there the day John the Baptist shouted, 'Behold the Lamb of God who takes away the sin of the world.' But the image of a lamb for John would have taken him back to his upbringing in the OT Scriptures. God's suffering servant was predicted ...

> He was oppressed and afflicted, yet he did not open his mouth; he was <u>led like a lamb to the slaughter</u>, and as a sheep before its shearers is silent, so he did not open his mouth ... he poured out his life unto death, and was numbered with the transgressors. For he <u>bore the sin of many</u>, and made intercession for the transgressors (Isa. 53:7,12).

A substitutionary lamb for our sins. That also would have reminded John about the Passover lamb. What saved God's people from the judgment of death? The Passover lamb, slain.

But look where the lamb is in 5:6, **standing at the center of the throne!** Wait a minute. A slain lamb, standing? He looks as if he was dead, but he is not dead, he is risen! What is all this teaching? The resurrection!

He is at the center and is about to approach the throne. He has seven horns and seven eyes. Remember the number seven is the symbol of completeness. Seven horns equals 'complete strength'. All powerful. We are told at the end of 5:6 that the seven eyes represent the seven spirits of God. Remember it's not now an expansion on the Trinity, but rather seven spirits simply represent the complete, all-glorious Holy Spirit. When was the Spirit of God sent out into all the earth? Jesus told his disciples to look to the day of Pentecost.

> But you will receive power when the Holy Spirit comes on you; and you will be my witnesses in Jerusalem, and in all Judea and Samaria, and to the ends of the earth (Acts 1:8).

From Pentecost to the ends of the earth. What is 5:6 saying? The

Holy Spirit is being **sent out into all the earth,** to every nation and tongue!

How do we sum up all this strange imagery? Have we been looking so closely as to miss the big picture? This is the *gospel!* The good news message of Jesus unfolded in picture form that a child could understand ... as long as that child had been brought up on OT Scriptures like John, the Jewish apostle.

Here is the gospel in pictures—Jesus' death for our sins. The Lamb of God slain, who takes away the sin of the world. The resurrection, the Lamb is alive! Standing! He is risen! Then he ascended to heaven as King, to the very throne of God (he is the Lion). And from there he is sending forth his *Spirit* to the ends of the earth to turn our hearts towards him. By the end, every creature and every knee shall bow, and every tongue confess he is Judge of all, as well as Savior (5:13). It's all here in picture form! He is the only one worthy to take the scroll and open it! He does it all!

What a symbol for a victorious ruling king! A lion that is a slain lamb? It makes no sense. But this is the Christian faith. We worship a king who is worthy, powerful to judge. A Lion who is victorious by being a slain Lamb. But then the camera cuts to a climactic piece of the drama.

> He came and took the scroll from the right hand of him who sat on the throne (5:7).

The camera again zooms in on the action. The close-up. Now the Lamb moves towards the one on the throne. In fact, he moves right up to the very throne and the One seated on it. What is going on here? Does this look familiar to you? No? Of course not! You are not an aging Jew brought up at the feet of the Rabbis from childhood. But to John this is putting together a jigsaw puzzle that every Jewish child had always wondered!

John sees it so clearly with the vision before his eyes. He immediately recognizes the action from his favorite Bible book the Rabbi's taught him. John knew the book of Daniel so well. It's like this vision in Rev. 5 is following the story line of Daniel 7, that great moment when the son of man approaches the Ancient of Days. It's the only time in the OT a Messiah-like figure approaches the throne to be given the very authority of God. While John is seeing this, try and picture what he would be thinking as he recalled Daniel …

> In my vision at night I looked, and there before me was one like a son of man, coming with the clouds of heaven. He approached the Ancient of Days and was led into his presence. He was given authority, glory and sovereign power; all nations and peoples of every language worshiped him. His dominion is an everlasting dominion that will not pass away, and his kingdom is one that will never be destroyed (Dan. 7:13-14).

The son of man comes towards the very throne of God, into the presence of the Ancient of Days, and he is given all authority! Just like in Rev. 5. Notice the seven eyes, which are the Spirit of God being sent forth from heaven. To what? To all the earth! All authority! When we get to 5:9, he is purchasing men from every nation.

In 5:6 he is the Lamb who suffered, but also the triumphant king who approaches the throne. Do you know what we are seeing here in 5:7 when the son of man approaches God, the Ancient of Days? By the end of Rev. 5, we see it is the Lamb who is being worshiped at the throne. What is happening? This is an enthronement scene!

When the new king of England is crowned, the whole world will stop to watch. There are billions of viewers who just love to watch a royal wedding, let alone the enthronement of a new monarch. I am always fascinated how many people watch royal occasions. We haven't seen a royal enthronement in England for six decades, but we have had royal weddings. And billions of people watch. Why is that? I actually don't know. Not a lot of action. Lots of just waiting, waiting. Nobody kicks any goals or tackles anyone. Maybe if that happened it would make me sit up? But what John is seeing is a coronation not of British royalty, but of the Son of God being enthroned as king of the universe!

When is this happening? Now bear with me if you believe this is all taking place in the distant future and the church has been raptured out at the beginning of 4:1. I'm suggesting this is not happening in some distant future. The slain Lamb is alive and is the Lion now! What we are seeing is the enthronement of the triumphant Son of God being installed on the throne with his Father, after his victory at the cross and his resurrection. This then is his ascension into heaven. Right now we are seeing the ultimate, royal coronation! He is the only one worthy because of who he is and what he has accomplished. He is given all authority. Taking his rightful place with the Father when he ascended into heaven. At the very end of the seven letters (Laodicea), it left off with Jesus saying ...

> To the one who is victorious, I will give the right to sit with me on my throne, <u>just as I was victorious and sat down with my Father on his throne</u> (3:21).

When did Jesus sit down? When did he take up his position on the throne as the royal king? He says it happened from the time he was victorious at the cross and resurrection in the first century. (See also Heb. 10:11.) It is not future for us, or even for those first readers in the first century.

The whole point of Rev. 5 for those first readers of the seven letters to the churches is that Jesus is now at the center with his Father, and it is *Jesus* whom they fall down and worship in 5:8. What John believed by faith, now he sees by sight. It's real! It's now! It's not future. It's a look into the actual throne room. The true King has been victorious, and this is his coronation. Jesus is on the throne. This is what those first readers of those seven churches needed to see. It's showing us in pictures what other parts of the NT taught us in words.

> ... [the power] he exerted when he raised Christ from the dead and seated him at his right hand in the heavenly realms, far above all rule and authority, power and dominion, and every name that is invoked, not only in the present age but also in the one to come (Eph. 1:20-21).

He reigns in the *present age as well as the age to come*. So I am going to disagree with those who insist Jesus' reign waits until some future millennium. What the apostle Paul said to the Ephesians we see in Rev. 5. Jesus is installed as king and reigning now!

> For he must reign until he has put all his enemies under his feet. The last enemy to be destroyed is death (1 Cor. 15:25-26).

This is the enthronement that was promised in Psalm 2 *I have installed my king*. Psalm 110 *Sit at my right hand until I make your enemies your footstool*. We get to see in word pictures because John is seeing it all firsthand. He is seeing the coronation of the king!

The letters to the churches are the earthly camera angle. But this is a cut away to a different scene. Heaven! While it seems evil is winning below, don't worry, the king is enthroned above, and all authority is handed over to him. Here is the close-up! No matter how bad things are looking in the scene below, we know something has been revealed. Like those masterful filmmakers and quality television programs like the Batman TV series, when Gotham city was under attack from the villains, we cut away to another shot of Batman and Robin flying overhead in the Batcopter and the inspector would say, 'It's great to know they are up there doing their job.' Then we, the viewer, knew that all would be well. Well look at this, John! While you and your suffering companions below are persecuted, look who is at the throne! The mighty king is reigning above.

Perhaps this is not as exciting news if it's all confined to the future, but if this enthronement took place at Jesus' ascension then this is a crucial teaching, a revelation that Jesus is reigning now! He has dominion over all the nations and is marching forwards sending those seven eyes, his Spirit, into all the earth, conquering souls from every nation, tribe and tongue. This is the king we will see breaking seal after seal, all the way to the ends of the earth until it is all over. It's underway. It's happening from John's time. It's relevant to us. It's happening now!

There is John on that island of Patmos in prison, but thoughts of that dark, dank existence in that cave have been temporarily forgotten. This is glorious. This is magnificent. Look at heaven!

John can't wait to get back down the ladder and pass this 'Revelation' to those struggling churches he ministered to in Asia Minor, the seven churches. This is what they need to see. The king is enthroned. Now! This is also what we need to know. Blessed are all who read the words of this prophecy. Not just those who read the first three chapters, but this is all a blessing to *all* of us!

Take this to heart. The first shot in Rev. 4 had the Lord controlling every creature and every action. Creatures covered with eyes all over. Now the One who is victorious takes up his position at the throne with his Father, that is, Jesus. Now *he* is the one at the control room of the universe and controlling every action, in every direction. Go back and read Rev. 4-5. Firstly, there are all those eyes on those creatures. All actions! All things. The eyes are going everywhere because the Lord is at the controls of every creature and every action.

Is there one of those eyes for each area of your life? Is there an eye for the direction of your future? Is there an eye for your spouse? Your children? Is there an eye for your direction and plan for your life? Is there an eye for when you are sick? Is there an eye for when you are alone? Yes! Now we know who is at the very center of the controls in heaven, working out every eye for his people. It's the one who gave his life for you! It's our Jesus. He is the king! The Lion and the Lamb. And he must reign until he puts all his enemies under his feet.

Then I saw a Lamb, looking as if it had been slain, standing in the center of the throne, encircled by the four living creatures and the elders. He had seven horns and seven eyes, which are the seven spirits of God sent out into all the earth. He came and took the scroll from the right hand of him who sat on the throne (5:6-7).

Study Questions

1. What does Lion of Judah mean?

2. What is significant about the Messiah being both a Root of David and a descendant?

3. What is a kinsman redeemer and how does this relate to the Messiah?

4. Would John have been shocked to see the Lion as a lamb? How would he have interpreted that from the OT?

5. How does this chapter draw heavily on another Bible book?

6. What event is being described in this chapter? Give details.

7. When does Jesus begin his kingly reign? Give Scriptural support.

8. How does our theology of Jesus' kingly reign impact our walk?

17
The Golden Bowls
(Revelation 5:8)

Jesus the Master film director has given the apostle John a super IMAX film. We've just seen the coronation of the King. In this amazing scene the Lamb that was slain and now lives turns out to be none other than the God of the universe, and heaven acknowledges this. Everyone bows down and worships him. Don't miss it, JWs. No one is to be worshiped except God (Matt. 4:10). The spontaneous reaction is like that of doubting Thomas, *My Lord and my God*. They fall down in worship before the Lamb!

> And when he had taken it, the four living creatures and the twenty-four elders <u>fell down</u> before the Lamb. Each one had a harp and they were holding golden bowls full of incense, which are the prayers of God's people (5:8).

This has to be one of my favorite verses in the Bible. We now know Jesus is reigning as king in heaven at the center, but did you notice what was in those golden bowls? Incense! The incense is a symbol of course, and we get the explanation of what it represents. We are told **... the golden bowls full of incense, which are the prayers of God's people.**

There is no qualification as to what type of prayers the incense in these bowls represents. In Rev. 6 the saints in heaven are praying for God to administer his justice, but in Rev. 5 in this scene it is simply the prayers of God's people. We are exhorted to all kinds of prayers in Scripture. Prayers of praise, confession, requests, and petitions. Prayers for spiritual protection. Bring them all. And what happens when you pray? Does God hear? Sometimes?

Have you ever filled out one of those website request forms that register your name? You put in your email address and details and click 'submit' and it goes off into cyberspace and you never hear anything again. It's out there somewhere. They never get back to you unless they want to sell something, right? Is that how we think of prayer? Maybe this one will get through, others not. There is a major Buddhist statue where worshipers go to throw a piece of mud at the statue. The idea is that if your piece of mud sticks, then your prayer is heard and will be answered. If not, your prayer just falls to the ground. Or do we treat prayer a little like SETI? Search for Extra Terrestrial Intelligence. Billions of dollars have been spent sending signals into outer space in the hope they might get 'lucky' and get a response. Firing off messages, hoping one might get through. Is that how you treat prayer to God? Maybe he hears some of my prayers, but I haven't got an answer yet, or not the answer I was expecting, so maybe the Lord didn't bother with those or they slipped into outer space?

Oh, how we need Revelation! How we need this heavenly perspective. This film shot. This peek into heaven itself. Because there they are! The prayers of God's people being held up to Jesus! They weren't forgotten. They are right there in the *golden bowls full of incense, which are the prayers of God's people*. The prayers are there, long after you have forgotten—but the Lord hasn't. I worshiped at a church where much prayer was offered up for the sick. As time passed God healed people, even people who were supposed to die. But because it was months, even years later, we forgot that those prayers had been prayed and to come back and give thanks. It's as though we didn't believe it could happen when we prayed and because it took so long, we forgot. But the Lord didn't forget. All those prayers were in those bowls.

A member of my local congregation, Dennis Tranter, serves as a missionary in outback Australia. Decades ago he and his wife planted a church in Borroloola in the Northern Territory among the indigenous people. Our church in Melbourne is Dennis' home church. When Dennis was in Melbourne about 35 years ago, he went out to an entertainment spot for a family night out. He saw a worldly comedian on stage and enjoyed the performance, but thought to himself, 'What is this guy doing serving the world? He should be a Christian! He should be a Minister! He should be using his life for God!' So he prayed for years for this man. Dennis' wife would ask why he was praying for someone he didn't even know. But when I was first called to minister in the church in Frankston in outer Melbourne, I received a phone call from outback Borroloola. Dennis had seen my appointment published in a magazine and was able to tell me the whole story and say, 'You are the man!' All those years earlier Dennis was just one person sitting in a crowd of 600. It took many years from that night when Dennis began praying before I became a Christian, then many years after that I became a minister, and then I became a minister of his home church! But it took about 20 years for all that to happen. And here I am today, by the grace of the God who heard the prayers of Dennis Tranter. But 20 years? Who is in for the long haul? To fill up those golden bowls! What if it takes another 20 years to see the lost loved ones in your life saved?

Our prayers are in the bowls right before the throne of God. How do you know your prayers are heard? Here is a scene of the very throne room of God and you get a picture that your prayers are actually there, being held up before the God of the universe, before Jesus himself. Did you ever notice this in John's gospel?

> Very truly I tell you, whoever believes in me will do the works I have been doing, and they will do even greater things than these, because I am going to the Father. And I will do whatever you ask in my name, so that the Father may be glorified in the Son. You may ask me for anything in my name, and I will do it (John 14:12-14).

Jesus says, you may ask *me* and I will do it. Doesn't he say the Father will do it? No. *I* will do it. Yes, we pray to the Father. Jesus even told us to pray to *Our Father*. But here also the Son says 'he' will do it! How is that? Only God can control the universe to answer prayer. Well, Jesus is God at the center of the throne with the golden bowls right in front of him! They **fell down before the Lamb.** He is worshiped as Lord!

How can you, a mere creature, let alone a sinful one, have the ear of God? You can't even get in to see your local politician. Have you ever tried writing to the Prime Minister? I have. I just got a form letter back which probably means it never got past the minders. I'll never know. But this is access to the throne room of the universe, and if you are someone who prays, then look closely at that incense in these bowls because your prayers are in there. Now! This is alive!

Why *your* prayers? Because you are a super-saint? Aren't you just a sinner? The answer is in 5:8. It's because the Lamb is at the center of the throne. Look what the apostle Paul said in relation to this ...

> Who then is the one who condemns? No one. Christ Jesus, who died—more than that, who was raised to life—is at the right hand of God and is also interceding for us (Rom. 8:34).

Your prayers are there in the bowls held up before Jesus who is there interceding for us.

> ... but because Jesus lives forever, he has a permanent priesthood. Therefore he is able to save completely those who come to God through him, because he always lives to intercede for them (Heb. 7:24-25).

It's because of the Lamb who is there! Some people say there is power in prayer, but there is no power in prayer itself. The power is in the one who *receives* the prayers! The one who intercedes for you. Those prayers are not wasted or missed. Those prayers are heard because it's not by your name they are received. It's in the name of Jesus who is at the throne!

What did this mean for those first readers of Revelation in the seven churches in Asia Minor, some struggling against persecution, and others struggling against worldliness which surrounded them? The culture pressured them to give in to temptation, sexual immorality, and idolatry. There was also false teaching in the church. They felt it. 'The church is being attacked. I am being attacked.' And then they get this picture. When they thought their prayers weren't being answered as the persecution intensifies, 'The Lord has abandoned us', how they needed to see this picture! What this meant to them was ... keep praying. Fill up those bowls! The Lord has not forgotten your prayers. They are held up before him.

This is a reality we so desperately need! We need Revelation. We need to see this picture of heaven where your prayers are not floating off hoping ET might catch the signal. There they are in heaven! In Jesus' presence! If you are not praying, you are not walking with the Lord. You are simply not living out reality. Look at this reality. This is the scene above of heaven itself. If all you can manage is five minutes in prayer or none, you need this view of reality. This is the camera angle of the scene of heaven above, while we are down here struggling away in our daily life and you are wondering why you are not growing in the Lord. You are wondering why an evangelism opportunity doesn't happen. If you are wondering why you seem to be under attack from the evil one and have seemingly no strength to combat it, I can tell you why. Your bowl is half empty! Those guys holding the bowls in heaven have run out of space in the dishwasher. 'Yeah, here is another bowl from down there, nothin' but crumbs in that one. Put that one straight in the dishwasher too, it's empty!'

Do you see what Revelation is doing? Revealing! The earthly perspective that your prayers are not always heard or cared about is wrong. Has prayer become like a duty that gets in the road of your busy life? You do a bit of praying here and there. But heaven rebukes you. The picture of heaven that we need to see is that the bowls are there ... but if your bowl is nearly empty, what do you expect? You have not, because you ask not!

If you don't have time with the Lord, what kind of relationship do you really have with Jesus? Is the world really winning in your life? Smartphones, computers, Facebook, and TV? Which god wins in your life? We don't want to be legalists, right? We should only pray when we feel moved to get into prayer, right? Really? Is that a relationship with Jesus? Try and picture any other relationship like that. I can just see how that works with your spouse. 'Alright I haven't spoken to you this week honey, but I didn't want to be legalistic, so I only spoke to you when I felt moved ...' You'll be feeling something that moves you alright. Ouch! The discipline of prayer isn't about legalism. It's about love and faith. We often do acts of love for those we love when we don't *feel* like it. The Christian definition of love is one that is unconditional. It's not dependent on how I feel. It's about faith. And this picture in 5:8 tells us Jesus is intimately aware of all the prayers of his people. All we need to do is take up that grace. Why? He checks his messages and emails!

Do you like to check your messages and emails? It's good to get communication from friends. Picture Jesus viewing those bowls. 'Let's see what we got from the saints down there today.' Another dishwashing load, more crumbs? Are you really in a relationship with Jesus? Isn't that what sets us apart from people who just say they believe in God. We are actually in a relationship with him! If you really believe in him, look at this wonderful thought. All those prayers you prayed for people and situations, all of them are there. Even where the answer is 'not yet', or 'something else', or 'something better'. Even the 'no' is a caring response because God knows best. This verse is teaching us that much. Doesn't it make you want to fill up those bowls?

If you are not praying, you need to seriously question your relationship with Jesus. Where is it at? If your prayers are relegated to the last seconds before you fall asleep at night, where do you start? The first thing is to pray and ask for forgiveness for not speaking to your spouse for so long. I mean your heavenly spouse, the Lord.

If you don't know what to pray, follow the pattern of the Lord's Prayer. Our Father. It's a relationship! You are praying to a heavenly parent! Father God. Then Praise! Hallowed be your name. How much can you praise God for? All that he has done! What about the cross? Then pray for his kingdom to come. In your life. In your heart. To change you. You will need more of the Holy Spirit. Ask and you shall receive! Pray 'your kingdom come' into the lives of others in your life. There is your call to pray for other people! Fill those bowls. What souls will he save? Whose prayers will he hear? Not the ones with empty bowls, but those who fill them up! Pray for his kingdom to come into the wider church and world. Pray for your own church. Pray you can reach the lost. If you have needs, bring them before him every day. Give us this day our daily bread. The implication is that you would be praying daily for your needs. Bring all your requests to him.

If you are a sinner, you need to confess. Forgive us our sins, as we forgive others. There is half an hour alone on that prayer. If you are struggling in temptation, *lead us*—not into temptation! Deliver us from the evil one. Do you pray that? For spiritual protection? Or are you heading into the great spiritual battle each day unarmed and you are confused as to why things are so tough? Pray! Your bowl is empty!

What have you gained from this world by skipping prayer time? How has life been going? All that extra time you have because you don't pray so much. Has all that time on Facebook, TV, or the computer enriched your life so much you can say, 'I am glad I don't pray too much. Serious prayer time would encroach on my life and I will miss out on my things. I won't have time in my day.' Wrong! Look at this scene. The golden bowls are before the control panel of the one who controls the universe! Remember every action, every direction, every moment! You can't outsmart God! You can't gain any extra time or enrichment in this life without the Lord who is in control of all things. He has your time in his control as well as your fulfillment too.

If you put aside your priorities for those you love, will you do it for the Lord? And what might the Lord do if you filled up those bowls? Do you need to be challenged as to where you are at in your priorities? What would you do if I told you that if you set aside time to pray each day, and instead of incense you would fill up bowls with stacks of $100 bills? Every day you can get a stack of $100 bills, whatever money you can pray into those bowls, you will receive in an envelope the next day. Would you be a millionaire by the end of the week? But when would you have time to do all that praying? You would have to slash time on your phone, TV, computer, or whatever else you needed to, that's how. You would go to bed earlier to get up and pray! You'd do it for love of money. How about for love of Jesus?

It will not happen if you treat Jesus like the spouse you only speak to when you feel moved. This would have to be a genuine unconditional love 'whether I feel like it or not'. If you can say right now your bowls are nigh on empty, that you are not on talking terms with Jesus and so you are not in a healthy relationship with Jesus, then you need to repent.

But this is not meant to be bad news. It should be the most exciting news ever. The bowls are there and Jesus is waiting to hear and answer prayer. *You do not have because you do not ask God!* What are we waiting for? Slash things where the world is encroaching.

Jesus is there. He hears and answers our prayers. And this scene tells us it's all because of the coronation of the king. Didn't Jesus say to his disciples, 'It is to your advantage that I go away' (John 16:7). Why? Here is the answer. He is sending his Holy Spirit from the very throne of God. While he was on earth, he was one man walking around Palestine, so his ministry was limited. Now he hears and answers prayer from the power room of the universe.

And when he had taken it, the four living creatures and the twenty-four elders fell down before the Lamb. Each one had a harp and they were holding golden bowls full of incense, which are the prayers of the saints (5:8).

Study Questions

1. How might this text speak to Jehovah's Witnesses?

2. How does this text shape our theology of prayer?

3. What are some of the different answers the Lord might give to our prayers?

4. Why would this text be encouraging to be like the persistent widow (Luke 18:1-8) over a long period of time?

5. Why would this text have been important to the seven churches?

6. Why don't we pray more?

7. How does a prayer life relate to the health of a relationship with Jesus?

8. What are the key elements to include in our prayers based on the Lord's prayer?

9. Why would Jesus have said to his disciples it was to their advantage that he goes away?

10. What should motive us to pray?

18
God's Personal Love
(Revelation 5:9-14)

Through the apostle John's vision, we have been getting a peek into the very throne room of God. John was weeping because there was no one worthy to open the scroll. But then there he is! The Lion and the Lamb, Jesus! Heaven is rejoicing, so John can stop crying. There *is* someone worthy to open the scroll, so heaven bursts into song …

> And they sang a new song, saying: You are worthy to take the scroll and to open its seals, because you were slain, and with your blood you purchased for God persons from every tribe and language and people and nation (5:9).

Remember the reason John was weeping was not because he was worried he couldn't get to see what was inside the scroll, but because the scroll represents the very judgments and salvation of God. If no one can open the scroll, there will be no justice and salvation. So we learn Jesus isn't just opening it so John can get a look inside, but he is the one who is worthy to carry it out! Judgment and salvation! We will see as we progress that he opens the seals through Rev. 6-7.

Jesus is worthy, so they rejoice. **They sang a new song.** It's imperative a new song be sung because this is a new work. The Christ has come. The old songs of Moses in Exodus 15 and the Psalms are good for God's people to sing, but they are sung in the framework of the old covenant deliverance. 'I am the Lord your God who brought you out of the land of Egypt, out of the land of slavery.' The old songs could only at best look forward in shadows to the hope of the new and full salvation. But now the new has happened, so there must be a new song. There is one found worthy, who was slain, who purchased humans by his blood. This is fulfillment. A new song!

This is one reason why I disagree with our brothers and sisters who insist we sing only Psalms in worship. Why did they sing a new song? Because we must sing of Christ! Worthy is the Lamb! This new covenant must be expressed in praise to the Lamb. To sing a new song is not referring to new in the sense of, 'Hey, we made up a great new song!' The important thing is that it is new in the sense of all the riches of the new covenant. The news revealed about God's salvation has to be included in our praise in this 'new' song. The death, resurrection and ascension of Christ on the throne! It's a new song because of these new things that have happened in salvation history. It is new because it is sung to the Christ! **You are worthy to take the scroll and to open its seals, because you were slain, and with your blood you purchased for God persons from every tribe and language and people and nation.** The Messiah has come. Look at the new things he has done. This is why we must sing a new song. Restricting this wonderful good news to the old covenant is limiting worship this side of the cross. We have greater knowledge than John the Baptist. We know of the worthy Lamb who was slain for our sins and was raised.

The Psalms looked forward to this when they told us to 'sing a new song' (Ps. 33:3). We live now to see he has *done* new things. So our new song must include those wonderful new truths unfolded in salvation history that speak of Jesus' death, saving work and by implication the risen Lord. Old songs (Psalms) are not to be *excluded*, but here is the NT evidence we must also sing a new song!

We noted that Rev. 5 is the gospel explained in picture form. The Lamb who is standing, *looking* like it had been slain. So with this arrival of the gospel comes a new song.

This *new song* is what those first readers in those seven churches needed to hear and sing. It's what we need to hear and sing. We need to praise our Lord for the victory plan he has already accomplished. It's new. It's glorious. Sing of Jesus, the name above all names!

What's more, we see in this passage that we use musical instruments to accompany our singing of Christ. They were using harps (5:8). The OT commands the use of a variety of instruments and this is a NT picture of what is going on in heaven now and a model for us. So we seek to do on earth as it is in heaven. And what are they doing in heaven? Playing music and singing a new song to Jesus! The Lamb who was slain and is standing!

In this song, we also get a picture of the personal love of God. I know a lot of people struggle with the concept known as 'limited atonement', but I think it is an unfortunate term, as it doesn't do justice to the wonder of the love of God. Definite atonement is better. It refers to Jesus' death on the cross and its benefits as being definite and effective for those who will believe. In fact, what this passage is teaching is very positive. It demonstrates the very personal love of God in Jesus at the cross for believers. The beauty of the cross fully and completely atones for our sin. It is an *effective* atonement. That is, Jesus really paid the price for the sin of believers from the entire world. It was not some token death for everyone, (including those who would *never* believe), but a specific price paid for a specific number of people. This verse is telling us that when Jesus hung on the cross it was not to purchase every tribe and language and people and nation, but rather **with your blood you purchased for God persons <u>from</u> every tribe and language and people and nation.**

We have seen in Rev. 4 God's wonderful sovereignty in controlling the universe—every creature, every eye, so that every action in every direction is controlled from the throne. That is how he is able to work all things together for good and we can know there is this personal love he has for us. Then in 5:8 we have the symbol of the Lord personally hearing our prayers. Again, it is *personal.* The bowls of incense of our very own prayers are held up before the Lord. How he cares personally for us. Now this verse is telling us that when he hung on the cross, Jesus actually pays the purchase price personally for his people who would believe … *and with your blood you <u>purchased</u> for God persons <u>from</u> every tribe and language and people and nation.*

He did not purchase every tribe; he purchased people *from* every tribe. It's specific. It's definite. He *purchased.* You were bought. It's strong language. An exact price for an exact debt. It's the same Greek word used in the NT every time someone pays a price in exchange for something. 'They *purchased* the Potter's field.' They paid a specific price, 30 pieces of silver, for a specific amount of land. What does all this tell us? The cross was a personal love. A plan of love. When 1Peter 2:24 says he took our sins in his body, it is real. What do I mean? Some say Jesus died for every single person, even those who will never believe. But if that was the case then Jesus didn't effectively die for anyone. If Jesus' death on the cross was for all people, including those who would never believe, then the cross would not be saving you believer, at best it would only be opening up the *possibility* of saving you. If Jesus died for everyone, the only thing that really separates you from the unbeliever is not the work of the cross! The only thing that separates you from the unbeliever is your faith in and of itself. Salvation is no longer about the object of your faith, the cross. It's about your faith on its own. Faith in your faith.

It gets even more complicated. If Jesus died for every single person, then it challenges God's justice system and the fairness of hell, because there would be people who would spend an eternity in hell for sins that have been paid for. A just God cannot punish twice for the same crime. That goes against the gospel. If Jesus died for people who would never believe, the unbeliever could say to God on the Day of Judgment, 'You pervert your own justice if you don't let me into heaven, because Jesus died for my sins too. The price is already paid!' But you say, 'Well not if they don't believe.' But isn't unbelief also a sin? If Jesus died for all the sin of all people, then God would be unjust to keep unbelievers out of heaven because even their sin of unbelief is paid for.

I know this is a difficult area, but what I want to highlight is not a glass half empty and the negative thoughts people conjure up of an atonement that is limited to believers (as though that somehow negates the offer of the gospel), but rather the glorious personal love of God and the complete salvation he gives. It's a powerful effective saving atonement. He *purchased*. And he purchased for *whoever* will believe. We can get caught up with our proof texts and miss how much this is about God's personal love. We say Jesus gave his life as a ransom for many, not all (Mark 10:45). But the other side argues that Jesus is the Savior of the world.

> He is the atoning sacrifice for our sins, and not only for ours but also for the sins of the whole world (1 John 2:2).

Then we counter that with texts like the one before us. Rev. 5:9 says that the *world* is indeed represented, as Jesus purchased men *from* every part of the world, including every tribe, nation and tongue. Then others will say God so loved the world (John 3:16). Then I will say the word 'world' is qualified in all kinds of ways in Scripture; from how bad the world is, to the Roman Empire, to an evil system. Besides, Christ loved the *church* and gave himself up for *her* (Eph. 5:25), not those who will never believe. Both sides have their explanations of these proof texts. But proof texts will never convince either side and never the twain shall meet.

What we need is a meta-narrative; the big picture of salvation that should drive our interpretation of the 'proof texts'. Salvation is a whole package. It's like the golden chain in Romans 8:30 that can't be broken. Those he predestined he also called, justified and glorified. It's a planned package from God. The most complete description of that package is found in Ephesians 1:3-14.

> Praise be to the God and Father of our Lord Jesus Christ, who has blessed us in the heavenly realms with every spiritual <u>blessing in Christ</u>. For <u>he chose us in him</u> before the creation of the world to be holy and blameless in his sight. In love <u>he predestined us</u> for <u>adoption to sonship</u> through Jesus Christ, in accordance with his pleasure and will, ... In him we have <u>redemption through his blood</u>, the <u>forgiveness of sins</u>, in accordance with the riches of God's grace ... (Eph. 1:3-5,7).

Ephesians 1:3-14 goes on to speak of the Holy Spirit given to believers guaranteeing their inheritance all the way to glory. You have all these things *in Christ*. That is the phrase repeated ten times through the passage, 'in Christ' or 'in him' etc. It begins with God choosing us 'in him' all the way through to glory. Salvation is a *package* of *all the things* a believer has 'in Christ'.

It's a plan of love. The cross is part of that package. Who are those he chose? Believers of course. What else do believers have *in Christ* (listed in Eph. 1:3-14) that those who will never believe do not have? Believers are *predestined. Adopted.* They have *forgiveness of sins* and *redemption through his blood.* The gift of the *Holy Spirit.* An *inheritance* waiting in glory. These are things given to believers *in Christ.* And one of the things we have in Christ is the cross. Did you see it in there? *Redemption through his blood.* You can't yank the cross out of the chain and say it was for unbelievers as well. You wouldn't say that about anything else on that list of things we have *in Christ.* You wouldn't say those who will never believe are also *chosen* or *adopted* or *forgiven their sins* or have the *Holy Spirit.* So clearly neither can those who will never believe have *redemption through his blood*, the cross. Why? Because he PURCHASED believers with his blood. He paid the price in full. The cross is part of the whole package of all the spiritual blessings we have 'in Christ'. Come back to that *personal love.* How much pain did Jesus endure on the cross? Did he literally go through it to purchase the price of you, believer, or was it some generic death that has no personal relationship to you and your sin? This is what you need to know if you are struggling with assurance of salvation. Here is where this sometimes-fierce debate swaps over from one which theologians theorize over, to a deep pastoral issue of the heart. How do you know you are saved? Answer: Jesus died and rose again. He really did *die* for you. It is a completed work. You don't find your assurance in yourself or in the level of your faith. It's not about you!

Where do you look to know if you are really saved? If the only difference between you and the unbeliever is not the cross but your faith, what if your faith has not been what it should be? You need to repent of course. But when do you know you have enough faith to repent sincerely enough? Will God accept you if you have been unfaithful and it's dependent on your level of faith? Is that where you are saved? By the strength of your faith? If your only hope is in you and your level of faith, then maybe you have every right to doubt. But if your assurance is in the *object* of that faith, if your assurance is in the cross where you were *purchased*, if Jesus really died for you, then even if you have been struggling, you can repent and what? *Believe in the cross!* Be assured. Believe in him, not in yourself and your faith.

What is your plea on the Day of Judgment? I hope it's not 'I've lived a good life'. I hope it's not even 'I believed'. Many unbelievers will cry that saying, 'Lord, Lord'. But I hope your only plea and cry is the *one thing* the unbeliever can never say—Jesus died for me! Even me. He died for me personally. *Purchased!* It is finished! He took away everything that could rightfully keep me out of heaven. What ultimately made me right with God is the cross!

It is a *definite* atonement! The cross is real. He really died for me. As Peter said, he took our sins in his body. He did not die some generic death that makes it only *possible* for salvation. In other words, he hung there on that cross for specific people for a specific amount of sin and did not give in, until every careless word, every evil thought, every selfish motive of those he was purchasing was fully paid for, until he could say, *It – is – finished!* If you believe, then he did this for you.

For some strange reason, some people think that believing this takes away from our motive for evangelism, but it's quite the opposite. In fact, this is our hope for our lost friends and family. Do they seem hardened? No sign of believing? What hope is there? Only this. God is *determined* to save. He has paid a price. He *purchased!* Whom did he purchase? Well funnily enough the ones who get saved are those who are evangelized and prayed for! It's his plan! This is our hope to keep praying and evangelizing! The Lord has those bowls of prayers before him (5:8). We know he is determined to save those dead in sin, and he hears our prayers. It's not hit and miss, dependent on whether they might be willing to change their minds. This God is determined to save because he already paid the price. He purchased!

God's love goes throughout the world. He does not discriminate between peoples. He purchased people *from every tribe and language and people and nation*. What was the promise made to Abraham? '...All peoples on earth will be blessed through you' (Gen. 12:1-3). 'How?' says Abraham? Are you joking? A converted idolater from Ur of the Chaldeans in 2000 BC is told he will become so great that he will be a blessing to every nation on earth? Sounds a bit far-fetched back then. But it was always a plan. It's fulfilled right here in 5:9. This is how Abraham, the father of the Jews, would be a blessing to all nations. The most famous Jew ever, Jesus, purchased men from every tribe, language, people and nation. For God so loved the *world* that he gave his one and only Son that whoever believes in him will not perish. *Whoever* believes is purchased!

> From one man he made all the nations, that they should inhabit the whole earth; and he <u>marked out</u> their appointed times in history and the boundaries of their lands. God did this so that they would seek him and perhaps reach out for him and find him, though he is not far from any one of us (Acts 17:26-27).

God has *marked out* where people live and the time they live. He has determined their exact time and place as the old NIV puts it. Of course this is speaking of where nations dwell and at what point in history, but it also relates to individuals who make up those nations. So why has God determined where and when people would live? He says it's for salvation! He did it so people *would seek him!* What about those people the missionaries never reached that might have believed? No such thing! God has determined to track down *all* those who will believe. He marked out their *exact time and place*. Do you see the underlying personal love of God in Rev. 5? We have seen his sovereignty over all things, every creature with every eye, from every angle in Rev. 4. There is no small thing in your life that is not controlled personally by the one who is at the center of the throne. And then we saw those prayers in 5:8. Jesus personally sees the bowls with our prayers and intercedes for us personally. And now you see the personal love of Jesus on that cross. What is Jesus hanging on that cross for? Just some general token death? No, he *purchased!* Personally! People from every tribe, language, people and nation. And this personal plan goes on to become a longer-term plan …

> You have made them to be a kingdom and priests to serve our God, and they will reign on the earth (5:10).

This personal love goes on into eternity. God has an eternal plan for you. You thought heaven was just holding a palm branch and learning to play the harp. But there is a greater plan, immeasurably more than we asked or imagined. We are to be a kingdom and priests, and we will reign on the earth. This is too big. But it is the plan of the personal love of God with his very own people. It's a plan that goes all the way to the new heaven and the new earth … **and they will reign on the earth.** It *all* culminates where all history will end. Every knee will bow and every tongue will confess. This is where Rev. 5 reaches forwards to this time …

> Then I looked and heard the voice of many angels, numbering thousands upon thousands, and ten thousand times ten thousand. They encircled the throne and the living creatures and the elders. In a loud voice they were saying: 'Worthy is the Lamb, who was slain, to receive power and wealth and wisdom and strength and honor and glory and praise!' Then I heard every creature in heaven and on earth and under the earth and on the sea, and all that is in them, saying: 'To him who sits on the throne and to the Lamb be praise and honor and glory and power, for ever and ever!' The four living creatures said, 'Amen,' and the elders fell down and worshiped (5:11-14).

It will all end in worship and glory, but we are not there yet. We need this vision John sees so we know how it will end. If you are a believer, it's all part of a plan. The cross. Your prayers. All the way through until you are a kingdom and priests forever. We are not in the new heaven and earth yet. Until we get there, we will need this scene as we face the tribulations ahead. We need to know there is a future plan. That it's all under the control of the One whose love for you is personal. Nothing is wasted. None of your suffering. None of your prayers. None of your perseverance. Fighting the good fight. Because Jesus, who has this personal love for you, is on the throne! And Jesus wins!

We needed to see this before we head into tribulation. The churches needed to see this. Ephesus, Smyrna, Pergamum, and all the other churches. He purchased you. He reigns. Fill those bowls in heaven now with your prayers! Brace yourself through your tribulation and hold fast because you will be a kingdom and priests and you will reign on the earth.

Study Questions

1. In what way is the 'new' song new?

2. What elements of the new song should shape our worship?

3. What does limited atonement mean?

4. How does this text speak into the topic of limited atonement?

5. How does that relate to the personal love of the cross?

6. What are the elements of the salvation package we have 'in Christ' (see Eph. 1:3-14)?

7. Where do you look to find assurance of salvation?

8. How does Abraham's promise relate to this text?

9. What does it mean to be a kingdom and priests that reign?

10. Why is this text so important to struggling Christians?

19
The Four Horsemen
(Revelation 6:1-8)

The book of Revelation is a revelation of Jesus Christ to John in vision form. These visions are sort of the forerunner of modern tele-*vision*, only better because it's real history and real future. The Lord is the Master film director and John is on the film set and has seen the shot of heaven where he sees the one found worthy to open the scroll. It's Jesus. He is worthy! But now we come to an even greater dramatic part of the movie!

It's one thing that the Lamb is worthy of opening the scroll. But what is actually in that scroll? What happens when those seals are opened? Before, John was worried no one could open those seals. But should he now be worried they *can* be opened? Once those seals are opened, nothing can stop it. The drama of watching this movie is that it's not fiction but a picture of history, and John is watching it unfold. He will see *what must soon take* place from his time *after this*.

So break out your popcorn and enter in the next exciting scene of the opening of the seals. We see it through the camera lens of what John saw, awestruck as he looked on and says ...

> I watched as the Lamb opened the first of the seven seals. Then I heard one of the four living creatures say in a voice like thunder, 'Come!' (6:1).

Thunder comes from the throne as the Lamb opens the seals. You need to remember you are not the only one in this movie theatre. There were many interested viewers watching with great anticipation before you even got here. Remember this book of Revelation was addressed to the seven churches in Asia Minor in the first century. They know this letter is not only from John, but Jesus (1:5). So this movie was brought to you by John, but is also brought to you from the producer/director, Jesus, who is *ruler of the kings of the earth* (1:5).

But how is it that Jesus is the ruler of the kings of the earth when we are going through such a horrible time here on earth at the hands of these earthly kings?

Cut to this shot of heaven and this great dramatic moment tells us how. Who is opening the seals? Yes, evil is going forth, but Jesus is the one in control of even that. He is sovereign over these evil forces against you. They can't win! Jesus wins!

Jesus' opening address in this book in 1:5 is not just lip service. He said he *is* ruler of the kings of the earth. Not he *is going to be*. We don't have to wait for a future 1000-year reign. He rules now! *He* is the one opening the seals. He will bring about salvation and judgment and bring his people through trials, persecution and even death. What about famine or nakedness or the sword? What about sickness? What about earthquakes and disaster? Even death is not able to separate us from the love of God in Christ. He is sovereign even over those things. Let's look at what's inside those seals? Tune in your TV set.

> I looked, and there before me was a white horse! Its rider held a bow, and he was given a crown, and he rode out as a conqueror bent on conquest (6:2).

Jesus opens the first seal and out comes a rider on a white horse. Who is it? That's a hard question. I changed my mind a couple of times with this horseman, so I have to be wrong one of those times. Scholars are evenly divided. Some say this white horse rider is one of the evil forces because the other three riders certainly are—war, famine, and death. This is a fair argument because I will be proposing that the seals, trumpets, bowls are parallel pictures of history (though not meant to be identical), so it would be consistent with that view if all the four horsemen were malevolent.

But unlike the other four, there is no mention of this white horse rider conducting any disaster/evil such as violence, famine or death, as is mentioned with the others. And white is always associated with good. Scholars have noted Jesus is on a white horse in Rev. 19, so is this rider also Jesus? The trouble with this is that Jesus is opening the seal which let this horse and rider out. Even allowing for the cinematic license of a vision, it seems strange if Jesus is letting himself out (though not impossible in this film industry).

So if it's not Jesus, then who? Well perhaps we shouldn't be looking for a 'who' but a 'what'. In fact, none of the other three riders personified represent people but concepts of what the seals execute. So what does the white horse and its rider represent? John certainly would remember a parallel to all this. John was standing right there when Jesus gave his great speech on the Mount of Olives. The events in Rev. 6 with the breaking of the seals just happen to follow a parallel with Jesus' end time speech on the Mount of Olives. All the things he spoke about are found with these horses. War, famine and death. And right in the middle of Jesus telling those things to come in the judgment, wars, rumors of wars and famines Jesus says ...

> And this gospel of the kingdom will be <u>preached in the whole world</u> as a testimony to all nations, and then the end will come (Matt. 24:14).

By the time we get to the end of these seals, the end will indeed come. And along the way there will be war, famine and death. But what else must happen? The gospel is to be preached to the ends of the earth. That is exactly what we saw from the time *after this*, when Jesus ascended from the apostles. Earthly scene: Jesus leaves the disciples and ascends. Cut shot to John's movie in heaven and the scene changes. In Rev. 4-5 we see Jesus' ascension and coronation, then what? The Holy Spirit (represented by the seven spirits of God), going forth to all <u>the earth</u>! Just as Jesus said ...

> But you will receive power when the Holy Spirit comes on you; and you will be my witnesses in Jerusalem, and in all Judea and Samaria, and to the <u>ends of the earth</u> (Acts 1:8).

This gospel conquers to the ends of the earth! And here we see ... **a white horse! Its rider held a bow, and he was given a crown, and he rode out as a conqueror bent on conquest.** So we could think of this first rider not as Jesus personally, but the *gospel* going forth to the ends of the earth to conquer. In the ancient world, the white horse is not only a sign of good, but also the victor in war rode a white horse. Jesus wins! Souls!

The word *conquer* in 6:2 is used in a strange repetition in the original Greek language. It literally says, 'he rode out conquering and in order to conquer'. Repetition is used for emphasis, but conquering is only used in the Scriptures for good, not evil. And that rider in 6:2 is given a *crown*. A *crown* is used in Scripture as a symbol of those on the side of God. We have already seen the crowns given to the Christians who overcome in the seven churches. The saints. The Lord has a crown, but never an evil force.

Of course, all those same arguments could all be reasonably used to say this one is a counterfeit, thus anti-Christ, and I am open to that possibility (I have changed my mind before). But another hint is that by the time we get to 6:9-11 we are told there are still souls on earth who will die for Jesus, and this is holding back final judgment. In other words, *not* until that gospel witness gets to the last one will the work of the gospel be finished. Not until that rider reaches the ends of the earth.

Another point is the context before these seals were opened. Remember John was weeping because no one was worthy to open the seals. Hence there was no one to judge, and also no one to save. But the reason why Jesus was worthy to open them was because his blood purchased men from every tribe, language, people and nation (5:9). The gospel is the reason Jesus was worthy to open the scroll as well as his authority to judge. He is the Savior! In 5:6 God sends out his Spirit into the earth. When did all this happen? When Jesus ascended to heaven and sat down at the throne with his Father and opened those seals, the gospel goes forth!

Having looked at all of this, it seems strange to me that anyone would want to be dogmatic on the identity of this first horse and rider, because unlike the other horses we are not told exactly what it represents. Most importantly, the identity of the first horse doesn't affect the overall scene because ultimately, it's about Jesus being in control of these actions anyway.

But while the identity of the white horse is disputable, the other horses and riders are clear. The next horse is fiery red, and its rider brings judgment ...

> Then another horse came out, a fiery red one. Its rider was given power to take peace from the earth and to make people kill each other. To him was given a large sword (6:4).

Violence comes on the earth. *People killing each other.* (We will have to look more closely at this second seal after this.) Then the third seal is opened and out comes a black horse with scales, which are associated with famine in the Scriptures. Food has become expensive and scarce. But we will notice later in 6:6 the luxuries of oil and wine are still available, so food is only scarce for those who can't afford it.

But when are these things going to happen? Remember our four main views. The Preterist says it happened before the destruction of the temple in AD 70. The Historicist generally has each of these seals happening in some kind of sequence throughout history, beginning in the first century. Unfortunately, history doesn't pan out that way, where we have periods exclusively of war, followed by periods exclusively of famine, etc. The most popular view, the Futurist, has all this happening during a seven-year tribulation at some time in the future. And the Idealist says it's happening repeatedly throughout history from the time John was given this Revelation. That's the view I'm taking because I want to ask ... 'What about those churches who received all this? What were they thinking when they read all of this? When did *they* think this was going to happen?' John has been told at the beginning of this scene at 4:1 that he will be shown what must take place *after this* ...

What was going on in those seven churches receiving this message in their day? Remember, they were under persecution from the Roman Emperor Domitian in the AD 90s. (I am yet to explain why I prefer the later date, along with most scholars, rather than the Preterist date of pre-AD 70.) What were Christians experiencing when those churches received the letters and the whole book of Revelation? During Emperor Domitian's reign, there was bloodshed. Persecution of Christians. Violence. The red horse and rider. There was a severe grain famine in AD 92 ... the black horse and rider. And we also saw many of the churches suffered poverty, especially in Smyrna. With all the poverty, persecution, and death going on a Christian could lose heart.

But this scene in Rev. 6 tells God's people that even though evil forces have their intent, it is Jesus who is sovereign over all things. Jesus is the one opening the seals. He is in control. As evil goes forwards, so too does the gospel. These evil messengers bring judgment on the world, but there is also persecution and suffering for God's people on the earth as well, as we will see in 6:9-11. This is not to say the Lord is the author of that evil. The Lord has often used the hands of evil men in the OT to punish, such as Babylon and Assyria. Yet the Lord still holds those nations accountable for their own willful choice to do evil. It's the Lord who sets the agenda and limits. Even though the evil is committed by evil forces, the Lord is sovereignly over it, using it to carry out his purposes. It's like the cross itself ...

> Indeed Herod and Pontius Pilate met together with the Gentiles and the people of Israel in this city to conspire against your holy servant Jesus, whom you anointed. They did what your power and will had decided beforehand should happen (Acts 4:27-28).

The greatest evil act ever committed was *conspired* by those who will be held to account for it, but the Lord sovereignly ordains the plan to bring about his greater purposes for good. Jesus wins.

This is why John needed this revelation. This is why the first century readers needed Revelation. This is why *we* need Revelation. When evil strikes, when evil people do evil things, Jesus is still sovereignly over it. Jesus is the one who unlocks the seals. Evil perpetrators are putty in his hands. They never did anything apart from him *breaking the seals*. It's all Jesus. Yes, evil is evil, but it can never outsmart Jesus or his purposes. We need this book of Revelation when trouble or evil strikes. This book is a blessing to everyone who reads it through the church age and takes to heart what is written in it. (1:3). Evil can't beat Jesus. So be victorious, saints! Jesus wins!

This is how he can make all things work together for good for those who love God. Jesus is the one opening the seals! It's Jesus' plan that these horses and riders are bringing partial judgments on the earth, but they are also used for good to refine and grow the true believers and bring salvation.

But we didn't get to the fourth seal. And surely this fourth seal gives the Futurist the best argument. So if you are convinced of the Futurist rapture view and you are cheering for the *Left Behind* series to not be left behind, this next verse looks good. When could this happen?

> When the Lamb opened the fourth seal, I heard the voice of the fourth

> living creature say, 'Come!' I looked, and there before me was a pale horse! Its rider was named Death, and Hades was following close behind him. They were given power over a fourth of the earth to kill by sword, famine and plague, and by the wild beasts of the earth (6:7-8).

This fourth rider summarizes and adds to the previous two horses. Violence (the sword), famine, plagues and wild beasts ... in other words, all kinds of death. The apostle John who wrote this down would have recognized the wording of 6:8 from Ezekiel 14:21. It's not the final judgment. It's limited to a fourth of the earth.

But we look at this description here in 6:8 and go, 'Wow, look at these terrible things. People killing each other. Famine. People short of food. A lack of peace on the earth. Plagues! What about those beasts of the earth? And death sweeping across a quarter of people on the earth. This is awful!' The official death rate in Australia is only about 1% per year. So when could all this happen? A quarter of the earth! What kind of world would it be when this took place? I've been suggesting this has happened throughout history. But how? A fourth of the earth?

John is receiving a vision. This is big picture stuff. Will it be exactly one-quarter down to the last number? Is that the point being made? But even allowing for the big picture teaching of a vision with all its symbolism etc., how could this be speaking into our day or through history when currently only about 1% of people die per year in Australia. Surely there is a good argument for the Futurist view? It would be easier to imagine all of what is being described as happening sometime in the future. Violence, famine, plagues and wild beasts killing people.

Okay, so we better get those *Left Behind* books back out of the trash, back on the shelf. Even if I argue we are not compelled to take one-quarter of the earth literally down to the last number, don't we fall so far short of this and have to concede it must happen sometime in the future? When could there be such a time? People killing each other, death, war and rumors of wars going on in so many parts of the world? When could millions be starving?

Or are we so conditioned to this world that we are desensitized to what goes on around us? Previously I encouraged you to check the Global Rich List, and on the minimum Australian wage you are in the top 1½% richest people on earth. So what are the other 98½%

of people doing? Much of the world is starving or living in poverty now and has been throughout history. But not the rich (6:6). They still have their **oil and wine**. And people are killed. Diseases ravage millions. How could we have missed the fact that we cry out against these very things? Oh Lord, what is going on in the world? And now we know. The seals! The powers of those evil riders harnessed.

This world is under judgment. It is a cursed world. On one hand, we reel at the atrocities, we are given more global awareness of starvation, and yet we still try to bury our heads in the sand. We shake our heads at nations and peoples bringing war and violence, and peace never seems to be on the earth, and you still want to wait for some future world to come when there will be war, bloodshed, famine, and peace taken from the earth? Try telling that to the millions who have felt the pain of war, death, and violence in the Middle East and Africa in recent times. It's here!

Where do we see people killed **by sword, famine and plague, and by the wild beasts of the earth?** What about the plagues? Disease. Viruses. Now if you want to take those *beasts of the earth* literally, it has to include every creature of the earth. The word in the original Greek that translates 'wild beasts' includes every kind of creature. It's the same word that is translated 'viper' that latched itself to Paul in Acts, so this must include not only the obvious beasts which have caused death, such as large predators, but every creature of the earth would have to include everything down to snakes, spiders and all of the bugs and germs that take millions of lives. Also, remember the text is not saying the wild beasts of the earth take a fourth of the deaths. The end of 6:8 tells us they are only one part of the *many* ways that death comes to the earth. Animals kill other animals as well as human beings. Mosquitoes are widely regarded as the deadliest creature on the planet, killing anywhere between 750,000 to one million people per year, but the mosquito is not the real killer. Malaria is a parasite carried by mosquitos. But these creatures are just part of life, aren't they? It's normal, isn't it? Have we gotten so used to a world under judgment we don't even notice? It's *not* normal. This is *not* the world God created as very good.

And the death rider rides on into history to do what Jesus said in 4:1, what *must* take place *after this*. From the time of John, as each generation reads Revelation, experiencing the violence, famine and plagues that occur throughout history, each one who takes to heart what was written in this book is blessed. And the intensity continues to progress from the time of the opening of the seals.

By around AD 300, Emperor Diocletian delivered the worst persecution in Roman times. Here we can borrow from the Historicist interpretation. They look for a strict chronological unfolding of these horses, so they highlight the period AD 248-296, when nearly half the population was killed from war, pestilence, famine, invasions and tyrants. Eusebius records that some became food for dogs (beasts of the earth). But we can go further than the Historicist and see that rather than these evils being restricted to particular periods unfolding throughout history, they are repeated through to our day. This is the world we live in. This is history before our eyes being described in overview. Human sin caused this world to be cursed and under judgment! The intensity of this is more apparent from the time the seals have been opened.

Rev. 6:8 says plagues! What about the plagues throughout history? What about the Bubonic plague and others? In the 14th century the Black Death killed about 50 million people, with some reports having the figure as high as 75-200 million people. At least a fourth of the world's population at the time, if not more. It swept across from Asia into Europe and North Africa. In Europe, it killed between 30-60% of the population! And that was the second outbreak. The Spanish flu (1918-1920), infected up to 500 million people and killed between 50-100 million people over two years. This is just straight after World War 1 (1914-1918), with about 40 million military and civilian casualties. What about plagues in our day? AIDS; Sars; Ebola; Covid 19? Today 38% of people end up with some sort of cancer.[23] The second and third seals have been opened!

In the last century, we saw two devastating wars, World War 1 and World War 2 (about 60 million dead). **Violence. Famines.** People killing each other. No one knows for sure, but it is estimated between 40-80 million people died in China at the hands of Mao Tse Tung. Many were deliberately starved to death. Not long before Mao, a famine in Henan province in China killed between two to three million people in 1942-43. People die. Some say most of those are

---

[23] https://seer.cancer.gov/statfacts/html/all.html

natural deaths. No, they're not! Death is *not* natural. It's evil! It's an intrusion into God's good world. It's the rider of death. It's this world under judgment. 'The wages of sin is death'. For much of history that death rider has taken great numbers through plagues (diseases). Until modern medicine, the life expectancy for children in infancy for much of history could easily be said to be what? About one in four expected to die! This is still the case in much of the third world today! What world are you living in? At our local church, our Sudanese guest preacher tells us his name is a common name for children in Sudan because it means 'instead of', because they are so used to losing a child. So we can account for one in four not surviving in much of the world. But one in four is so unrealistic in our modern society, so this horse rider of death must be sometime in the future for us.

Really? Today we have another means of killing off the children, don't we? In the US, babies are aborted at a rate of what? About 22%. If you want to look for a fourth of the population being killed, there it is. (The creatures and diseases don't have much ground to make up the rest of the one in four deaths. We are taking care of most of it ourselves.) One fourth of people don't even get to grow up to be killed. How do you think the one billion people in China managed to keep their one-child policy through those decades? India is notorious for its infanticide. The figures are horrendous. We can easily account literally for a quarter of the earth without even taking license for this being a vision in sweeping symbols.

Life begins in our mother's womb (Psalm 139:13), so what we have more than ever is human beings killing each other. Look at the end of 6:8 again. *Killed by the sword?* In John's day, it was a long sword. Today it's a scalpel as millions of unborn babies are killed.

What about of the **plagues?** Just when modern medicine overcomes one virus, another one pops up and the pale horse charges forth again. Today we are hearing more and more about superbugs, that is, viruses that don't respond to any medication.

We look at these terrible things and say, 'Wow, what would it be like if those things happened sometime in the future?' In the future? What world are we living in now! Take a look around you, snoozing in cozy Western-world Hobbiton. If this is not a time of tribulation, how much more death do you want? Don't you feel it? This world is filled with evil. Perhaps we *don't* feel it because we have been sheltered. But this world is filled with conflict, violence, and disease which brings many of us down. Pain. Loss. Heartache. There is no peace. Some of us even live in turmoil and conflict in the home. Peace is taken from the earth.

Some of the well-known Futurist scholars see the third horseman with famine as relating to economic upheavals. So they say, one day in the distant future there will be great economic upheavals and woes, inflation, recession and economic panic. Perhaps like some sort of global financial crisis? People losing homes which are sold for a song? When might something like that ever take place? Didn't we just live through it? In the US in 2007-2008 people were selling their homes for $300! Kevin Rudd was Prime Minister of Australia during that time and he said the greatest difficulty in guiding Australia through the GFC was that Australia was almost entirely unaffected by it. Australians were still complaining about their everyday problems, unaware and unable to relate to the rest of the world (even other Western countries), desperate to survive a true crisis.[24] That may be one of the difficulties for us trying to understand Revelation. We are so insulated from how the world really lives today and throughout history that we can't see the world through the lens of the seals being opened.

But even without this perspective we still know about death and suffering, we still know about violence, and we still know disparity between the poor and rich … how the poor can't afford basics while the rich enjoy their oil and wine. The 'haves' and 'have nots'. We still know about the germs, viruses, cancers and deaths that strike us all eventually.

Tribulation? Anyone suffering? With all the benefits of a modern Western society, there will still be some reading this who know what it is to go through pain, loss, and have even been ready to give up. Are we so desensitized as to not notice the very world we are living in? Is this your idea of normal?

And it gets worse. Have a look what follows the pale horse and rider of death … right behind him like a shadow. Did you see that? Hiding right there behind death so most people on the earth didn't

---

[24] Kevin Rudd, *Not for the Faint-hearted* (Australia: MacMillan, 2017) p. 564

even know he was there ... **Its rider was named Death, and <u>Hades was following close behind him</u>.** Hades. The realm of the living dead. Pain and torment. What is the unbeliever's great hope? 'When you die you die, you go to nothing.' Well, hope all you like, but here is Jesus opening the seal and his message is that right behind death's door follows Hades. The death horse rider is sweeping across the earth and this *tribulation* the world is going through is a partial judgment to say wake up. This is just a warning. It gets worse. Death is coming, but so is Hades!

How are you gonna get out of Hades? There is no getting out. Once you are there, that is it! But you who read this book of Revelation, if you are taking it to heart, remember what we read at the start ...

> I am the Living One; I was dead, and behold I am alive for ever and ever! And I hold the <u>keys of death and Hades</u> (1:18).

The keys! It was right there at the opening of this book in that vision Jesus gave John. If you put your trust in Jesus—he has the keys!

This book was written for you! It's for you now! It's written to tell you to hold on to Jesus in the midst of the tribulation of this world. How will you be able to hold on? Because it's Jesus who is opening the seals! This is the kingdom that Jesus is reigning over now. He is risen! He has ascended. He is King and must reign until all enemies are brought under his feet. The horses are going forwards. This is a dying world. The death rider has been released. Hades is following right behind as each one goes through that door of death. One after another. Shoomp! Into Hades. What hope have we got in this world under judgment with the evil riders of death and destruction?

When we get to Rev. 19, we find another rider will come. This one is the King of kings. The one who opens those seals to release God's righteous judgment is also the one who comes into this dark evil world and *defeated the death rider!* He took on death! He went to the cross to take away the sin of all who throw themselves under his mercy wings. All who have him as their king. That is, not to merely pay lip service, but follow him as the true king.

It all comes down to this: he alone has the keys of death and Hades. And the message is: *wake up!* Now is the time to take refuge in him! Repent and believe in him.

Study Questions

1. What are some of the arguments for the identity of the white horse and rider?

2. Why should we be less concerned about different views of the white horse than the others?

3. When would John and his readers have expected these events to take place? Give reasons as to why they might have that expectation?

4. Why would Jesus release evil on the earth and how does that work when he is not the author of evil?

5. In what ways can we see these seals released up to our own day?

6. Why might we miss that?

7. How does 1:5 speak into this text?

8. What elements of this text speak into your own life personally?

9. Why would Hades be a greater concern than any of the other judgments?

10. Do you think the Futurist view has a strong argument on this text? Why?

20
A World Under Judgment
(Revelation 6:8)

We started off on earth with John on the island of Patmos. In Rev. 4 the film changed scenes and we looked into heaven. Then in Rev. 5 we saw the coronation of the King. He was slain, is alive and has risen. He has ascended to heaven and takes up the center of heaven as the only one found worthy to open the scroll. Then he opens the seals. The four horses and riders go forth over the earth. There is so much to learn about our life in this world from these seals being opened that I thought it would be good to explore these four horsemen more fully. It means we might spend so much time in Revelation that Jesus might come back before we finish, but wouldn't that be a good place to be when he blazes across the sky? The cheer goes up. 'We're only up to Rev. 6 Lord!' And he could tell me where I'm going wrong with all this.

The number four is typically used in relation to creation and encompassing the whole world, as in four corners of the earth. So we expect the whole earth to be under the effect of the four horses and riders in some measure. We also looked at the fact that the Lord sovereignly uses the works of evil men, even Satan, for his own use for good. We cited the greatest example of this concurrence in the cross, where Pilate and Herod conspired to do the most evil act of all, but it was God's plan to do good. The point is that Satan and the forces of evil hate believers, but they also hate unbelievers. None are exempt from the attacks—including death. But for the believer, we have Revelation. It tells us Jesus rules over all of history. He is actually the one who opens the seals. So he can still work good for his people even while the horses bring judgment on this world.

If you don't believe in original sin, then Rev. 6 makes no sense. But God's word says:

> Therefore, just as sin entered the world through one man, and death through sin, and in this way death came to all people, because all sinned ... (Rom. 5:12).

In Adam you were there and you believed the lie, 'you will not surely die' (Gen. 3:4). This world is cursed and is under judgment and is headed towards a full and final judgment. But humans continue to deny what happens before their eyes. The wages of sin is death. You will surely die. And the message is that this life is fleeting. You are burying your head in the sand if you haven't noticed. This world is cursed and now is the time to flee to the Savior before it's too late! The seals are highlighting the intensity building since the time Jesus ascended.

Yet people deny it. They still cling to the lie, 'You will not surely die.' They cling to this life as the only true meaning. Even people who say they believe in God continue in rebellion against God and ridicule heaven as just a pie in the sky when you die.

We are so desensitized to this world under judgment that we think this is normal. Mankind resists the truth effectively saying, 'We are not dying, we are evolving, and things will get better.' Well, they do in one sense. We invent technologies to relieve people. Global help for the poor and technology enables help in ways we never imagined. But then we turn around and use that technology to kill or abuse more people in ways never imagined before, and the pale horse rider rides on to the ends of the earth. The fourth seal.

The seals are broken but man buries his head further. We try to invent ways to avoid death. Deny! The wages of sin is *not* death. I am not a sinner in need of saving. 'You will *not* surely die.' Advances in medicine enables us to put it off. We are living longer and think we can avoid death. But then someone we know dies and we are shocked at death as though it's something strange. But then we get back to our lives and it's as though nothing has changed. The call goes out: *Wake up!* But people still don't listen.

We pretend God isn't there so we don't have to listen. Now how would you do that? If a builder builds you a house and you move in and don't pay the builder, he says, 'Who do you think built this house?' And you say, 'No one!' But that is plain ludicrous. The house that built itself? Intellectual absurdity. But is it only intellectual? Or is it because you have every reason why you don't want to give the builder credit? Otherwise you will have to pay the price! Man invents ways and theories to try and eliminate the builder. People pretend this world popped out of nothing. Anything but admit there is a God whom I have rebelled against and to whom I am indebted. But here is the amazing thing. Instead of the builder who has the power to just send the wrecking ball through the whole thing and take back his house right away, instead, warnings come. Warning after warning.

That is what these horses are. Judgment, but also warnings. And still we ignore it. We think of people only as dying when tragedy strikes. Thousands of people lined the streets of Melbourne to mourn the horror of the rape and murder of a young woman. One mourner said, 'Her death must not come to define us. That is not what it is like to live in the Melbourne we know.' But that is exactly who we are. We are eminently capable of anything. We are a city that has rejected God. Look again at the evil rider of violence.

> Then another horse came out, a fiery red one. Its rider was given power to take peace from the earth and to make people kill each other. To him was given a large sword (6:4).

It was understandable there was great grieving over the tragic death of that young woman. But another 200,000 Australians died the same year. It's also understandable the great anguish caused when 3000 people died at 9/11. But that same year about another two million people died in the US. We act as though death only happens in a tragedy. But speak to the loved ones of those two million and for many of them, the loss is just as big a tragedy. The more extraordinary the deaths, the greater the warning, but they are not necessarily a judgment on the people involved any more than other deaths. In fact, it may be more of a judgment and warning for us who are left behind. If the person who dies is right with God, then it is far from a judgment on them, but deliverance from tribulation. But for those of us who are left behind, it's God's way of warning us. You are gonna die too! Wake up! Get right with the Savior now! This was Jesus' response to a terrorist act as well as a tragic accident in Luke 13:1-6. He said it was not a judgment on the victims, but he used their deaths to highlight his listeners' mortality too. *Unless you repent you too will perish.*

I acknowledge this book of Revelation is difficult and that I'm going against the most popular interpretation that this is all going to happen in the future. That the seals of judgment being released upon the world from Jesus' time throughout history to now is not my own isolated interpretation. It seems the apostle Paul was of the same view.

> The wrath of God is being revealed from heaven against all the godlessness and wickedness of people, who suppress the truth by their wickedness, ... (Rom. 1:18).

When? When does this anger, this wrath, this judgment of God occur? Paul says it is being revealed from his day. That is, after Jesus ascended and opened those seals! It's happening in the world around us. Look at this world! Why is God so angry? Paul continues ...

> ... since what may be known about God is plain to them, because God has made it plain to them. For since the creation of the world God's invisible qualities—his eternal power and divine nature—have been clearly seen, being understood from what has been made, so that people are without excuse (Rom. 1:19-20).

God has proven his existence. He built the house! Houses don't pop out of nothing! You have to come up with the most fanciful nonsense imaginable to deny the existence of God. The world popped out of nothing and designed itself! No wonder the wrath of God *is being revealed*. And no wonder it intensifies since God sent his Son whom we killed! The seals have been opened. God is revealing his wrath from heaven. And what is the primary way the Lord does this? Simply by giving man up to himself, as Paul says further along in the same text.

> Therefore God gave them over in the sinful desires of their hearts, to sexual impurity for the degrading of their bodies with one another. They exchanged the truth of God for a lie, and worshiped and served created things rather than the Creator—who is forever praised. Amen. Because of this, God gave them over to shameful lusts. Even their women exchanged natural relations for unnatural ones. In the same way the men also abandoned natural relations with women and were inflamed with lust for one another. Men committed shameful acts with other men, and received in themselves the due penalty for their error. Furthermore, just as they did not think it worthwhile to retain the knowledge of God, so God gave them over to a depraved mind, to do what ought not to be done. They have become filled with every kind of wickedness, evil, greed and depravity. They are full of envy, murder,

strife, deceit and malice. They are gossips, slanderers, God-haters, insolent, arrogant and boastful; they invent ways of doing evil; they disobey their parents; they have no understanding, no fidelity, no love, no mercy. Although they know God's righteous decree that those who do such things deserve death, they not only continue to do these very things but also approve of those who practice them (Rom. 1:24-32).

The seals and the release of the horsemen! Do you see it all in there? Violence, greed, famine, starvation, plagues and death. Here is something so politically incorrect you can come and visit me in jail. This Romans passage highlights sexual promiscuity, including homosexuality, as being a judgment upon men and women who are given up to themselves and receive the consequences.

I am always the first to chastise Christians who pick on gays and lesbians as though they are the only sinners out there. If you are straight, you can still find yourself in that Romans list of sinners as much as any gay or lesbian. As I always say, there will be more heterosexual people who end up in hell than homosexual. And the gift of God, eternal life in Jesus, does not discriminate and is available to all. We are all 'bent' and in need of repentance and trusting in the Savior no matter what our sexual orientation. But if I had said to you before 1980 (before AIDS) that God would send a plague (pale horse 6:8) on the world, and its initial victims would be 99% homosexual men and intravenous drug users, you would have laughed it off as some kind of religious fanatical craziness. How could a plague target those people? Romans 1 says God gave them up to themselves. Australians were outraged when Jim Wallace of the Australian Christian Lobby mentioned the statistical fact that the expected lifespan of gay men is much shorter than the norm. But he was simply stating a fact.

Ah, but then the plague spread to the heterosexually promiscuous. AIDS became more encompassing. And as we have noted with these seals being opened, death and plagues do not exclude Christians. Now the incidence of HIV and other STDs has dramatically increased way beyond the gay community. Others get caught in the crossfire just as with the other horses of violence, famine, and death. Babies and innocent women become infected though they have not committed those sins. Yet the message still is loud and clear. We are *all* dying. This is world under judgment. Eternity counts. Flee to the Savior and death will not harm you. But still they won't listen.

Throughout history the warnings, wake-up calls and partial judgments have been doing one of two things—either saving you, or deepening your judgment. There were two thieves crucified either side of Jesus. Both were going through the most horrible deaths. They were under judgment. For one, it was the wake-up call to salvation ... 'Don't you fear God? Remember me Jesus'. For the other, it was hardening, shaking his fist at God. 'If you are God why don't you help me now?' Even in the face of the judgments and warning some will be saved through the exact same means that will harden others. God will work out his purposes.

While many will shake their fist at God because of a plague like AIDS, at the same time God is drawing in those in the gay community who are his, even through this. I saw a moving video years ago of a young man dying of AIDS. With only days to live, he had come to faith and said he wouldn't want to change places with anyone now that he came to know Jesus. He died just after that. *Now* he knows it's worth it.

After the vote on same-sex marriage in Australia a woman who had been in a long-term lesbian relationship wrote to me saying she had walked into a bookstore and read my little book on the subject and felt as if it was written just for her. She came to repentance and faith and wondered if God let the same-sex marriage vote happen to save people like her? Answer: Yes! God will still do his saving work despite man's rebellion. The white horse also goes forth.

This is a world that was given by God as good and we have rebelled against God and we reap what we sow. The natural disasters are *not* natural. They are unnatural to the world that God originally gave. But we were represented by Adam. How were we represented? Perfectly. Perfectly, because God chose Adam as the perfect representative. We show how well Adam represented us when we sin every day and confirm that no decision was made on our behalf that we would not have made. We are collectively responsible for sin, but continue to prove it individually when we sin against God. We have declared war on God in his world he graciously gave us, saying we don't want God ruling over us. What do you think he is going to do about that? Especially given the West's Christian heritage, forged by many of God's people over centuries of sacrifice, war, and persecution? Answer: The wrath of God is being revealed from heaven! The seals have been opened. The horses and riders go forth.

So, if God sovereignly overrides evil to bring about his purposes and partial judgments on the world, where does good begin and evil end? How does God do that without being the author of evil, and how can evil people still be held fully responsible? And when bad things happen, how can you tell what is a judgment and what is just a general result of the fallen world? We can't always answer that and need to be careful presuming his judgments. His judgments are unsearchable (Rom. 11:33). What about believers and innocent parties who suffer in this world? When a tsunami hits, when a 9/11 strikes, when innocent people are infected with AIDS, or evil men commit evil acts. The evil riders with evil intent. What about that?

Well, that is what the book of Revelation, in particular Rev. 6, is answering. This is exactly what those people in those seven churches who first read Revelation needed to hear. It is what we need to hear. It is still Jesus who is opening the seals. It is still Jesus who is in control of all this. It is still Jesus who is with his people even in and through death itself. How many times did those seven churches get told Satan is attacking you? Satan will put you to death. Jesus' answer was be faithful even to death. I am with you. The plan is bigger than just this life. Much bigger! There is an eternal plan, and if you don't get that you will never make sense of this life. This life is not it! This life is short. Death is real. Revelation screams out ... life is over quickly. Where are you going to spend eternity? *That* is what you need to be thinking about! Even when you are confronted by tragedy and evil, think about who is in control ...

> The righteous perish, and no one takes it to heart; the devout are taken away, and no one understands that the righteous are taken away to be spared from evil. Those who walk uprightly enter into peace; they find rest as they lie in death (Isa. 57:1-2).

Isaiah says we don't ponder it. Sometimes people are taken early or unexpectedly and all we think about is *our* loss or pain rather than the point of view of the person who has died. But Isaiah says the Lord knows this evil-filled world and often spares those who are his from having to go through some evil that he knew was up ahead for them. So he takes them early rather than have them go through more and says, 'I want this one to come home early and be with me.' There is no understanding of this life without an eternal perspective. For example, if someone is right with God but dies tragically at age 18, and I live until I'm 99, we say it's not fair. But after 50 billion years in heaven, I will turn to that one who died at 18 and start complaining. 'This isn't fair. How come you only had to put up with that bad place for only 18 years and I had to put up with it for 99!' Of course I won't really say that, but that is how ludicrous the earthly differences will appear in light of eternity.

So it's important for us to see these seals being opened as not just random death, disease and so on, but part of the plan of the coming King to come in *final* judgment. They are warnings! Death is real. Flee now to the one who can take away your sin and present you clean when the final judgment comes. There is forgiveness which came at the great cost of the cross, where Judgment Day came early and was dealt with for those who trust in him. In the meantime, the warnings and judgments go on.

The terrorist attack in 9/11 was way back in 2001, but people still talk about the aftershock and effect and how it changed the world. There was another aftershock that went unnoticed after 9/11. Immediately following, the attendance in churches went through the roof, as much as a 25% increase in the US. No doubt some of that was just worldly fear and for some of them it would soon be back to business as usual, but just as the fiery red horse and pale horse of death were released, so too was the white horse with the gospel released. Jesus, the Lord of the harvest would save many through that act by evil men and that rider of death.

Bear with me if you say this is all happening at some point in the future. How did Revelation start? What does Revelation say about Revelation? *The revelation of Jesus Christ, which God gave him to <u>show his servants</u> what must <u>soon take place</u>* (1:1).

Something must *soon take place*. Is it more natural this kind of language refers to something that happens thousands of years in some distant future which has no relevance to those readers or any Christians for at least another 2000 years plus? Or does it come alive with richness from the first verse saying it's for all his servants. Blessed are all who read it and take it to heart, as this is going to reveal events and warnings that are happening *now!* And heading into the future *warning us* of what will happen. It is speaking to us! And through this, when we sing 'Jesus reigns', it's real, not just some lip service. He is the one who has opened the seals. He is reigning, from the throne in heaven. But when he returns every eye will see him (1:7) and every knee will bow, and there won't be any second chances, no extra seven years, or three-and-a-half years, or 1000 years to change your mind. That will be it! Today is the day to turn to Jesus!

How many warnings do you want? You know people who just don't heed warnings no matter how many they get. Revelation is a warning! The story of the Titanic has been a well-used analogy to explain Revelation.

> During 14 April 1912, Titanic's radio operators received six messages (warnings!) from other ships warning of drifting ice. The first warning came at 9:00am, 'Bergs, growlers and field ice'. At 1:42pm the Greek ship Athenia messaged that she had been 'Passing icebergs and large quantities of field ice'. At 1:45pm, the German ship SS Amerika, reported she had 'passed two large icebergs'. At 7:30pm and at 9:40pm SS Californian reported 'three large bergs', and the steamer Mesaba reported: 'Saw much heavy pack ice and great number large icebergs.' The radio operator, Jack Phillips, may have failed to grasp the significance of the warnings because he was preoccupied with transmitting messages for passengers. A final warning was received at 10:30pm from operator Cyril Evans of the Californian, which had halted for the night in an ice field some miles away, but the radio operator cut it off and signaled back: 'Shut up! Shut up! I'm working Cape Race.' Although the crew were aware of ice in the vicinity, the ship's speed was not reduced, and she continued to steam at 22 knots, only 2 knots short of her maximum speed of 24 knots. Sticking rigidly to a schedule that would guarantee their arrival at an advertised time. [25]

Warning. Warnings. Warnings. This is the world we live in. You see it all around you. This is a dying world and it is screaming out to you as a warning of what is to come. The seals have been released and we are not listening. But there will come a day when he will no longer hold back his full wrath. What happened? You were warned. Jesus will release the final seal. All these seals opened, lead to the final judgment—the eruption when Jesus explodes across the sky. Heed the warnings. Two things are happening at the same time. Partial judgment, but warning. The warning is love. What are you living for right now? If you are not walking with Jesus as you ought, don't go down with the Titanic. Heed the warnings of the horses! Jesus saves.

---

[25] Sean Coughlan, Titanic: the final messages from a stricken ship, April 10, 2012, http://www.bbc.com/news/magazine-17631595

Study Questions

1. How does original sin come into focus in Rev. 6?

2. In what ways do people deny that our world is cursed?

3. How does the NT (outside Revelation) speak of judgment already begun in this age?

4. What are some of the ways being 'given up to ourselves' becomes a judgment?

5. What are the two responses that partial judgment brings?

6. How are we represented by Adam? Is that fair?

7. Why is it unwise to speculate on whether an individual is receiving judgment from God in this life?

8. How can we easily misunderstand the meaning of someone's death? (See Isa. 57:1-2)

9. From when does Jesus reign?

10. Why don't people heed the warnings?

21
The Saints Above
(Revelation 6:9-11)

Picture being a Christian in the late first century. You have been under persecution from the Roman Emperor Domitian who demands that you call him lord and god. You battle daily with the temptations to compromise. You know you have to stand up for the Lord. But the persecution has been intensifying from both the Jews and the Romans. You are nervous about what might happen every time you meet for worship. And it has come to the point where to stand up for Jesus, you might be executed as some of your own church members have been.

At this time, you receive this book of Revelation. It's written by Jesus himself, dictated to John. You are there in the church at Smyrna. Jesus told you to hold fast, even to death (2:9-11). Or you are at the church at Pergamum where one of your church members, Antipas, was already executed for the faith (2:13). Or you are in the church at Philadelphia, where there is an 'hour' of testing coming upon you, indeed even the whole known world. Jesus has said it would happen and now it's here. Some of your people who have stood up for Jesus have paid the highest price. The cost of their own lives.

As a Christian, you are familiar with the teaching about the heavenly hope for those who die in the faith, but it's all so theoretical when you face the reality of the death of one of your brothers or sisters. It's one thing to know about heaven. It's one thing to believe in theory that your late loved ones have gone there. But then comes this new camera angle. A new scene of what? There they are! While you are still going through this tribulation below, you get a glimpse of heaven through this word picture, and now you can see them! Your friends who have died in the Lord. Look at this picture!

> When he opened the fifth seal, I saw under the altar the souls of those who had been slain because of the word of God and the testimony they had maintained. They called out in a loud voice, 'How long, Sovereign Lord, holy and true, until you judge the inhabitants of the earth and avenge our blood?' Then each of them was given a white robe, and they were told to wait a little longer ... (6:9-11a).

They have made it! They are there! They are dressed in a **white robe!** Isn't that what Jesus told us in the church in Sardis (3:5)? The one who is victorious will be dressed in white. Well, look at what they are wearing! There is Antipas in his white robe! Can you see your loved ones who have died and gone on? They are resting in peace. Isn't that what we said at their funeral? Rest in peace. But what did that really mean? At their funeral, it was said through tears, putting on a brave face, but now we see them. It's real. This is what we in the church on earth needed to see. They made it. They fought the good fight. They finished the race. And they long for us to join them. They are even told to wait for us ... to **wait a little longer.**

So if you are a Christian in the first century you are reading this saying, 'Yes! There! Dressed in white. Purity. Blessed!' White also represents the glorified state. White is victory. Waiting for us to join them. But it's not just any 'waiting', like a boring wait in a waiting room when it says *wait a little longer*. The word *wait* in the original Greek language is a waiting as in *rest*. It's the same word used in Luke 12:19 when the rich man says he will sit back and *take life easy*. That is effectively what those in heaven are told. The joy of heaven is to take life easy. That's how you wait. When Jesus said, 'Come all who are weary and I will give you *rest*', it's again the same word as translated *wait*. It's a comfort. Paul used the same word to say *refreshed ... For they <u>refreshed</u> my spirit ...* (1 Cor. 16:18). So those in heaven can wait with rest, refreshed, taking life easy.

So here we are at the opening of the fifth seal. Let's not forget who is opening it. He is the One who is showing his servants what is happening now and what must soon take place.

But these in heaven are **under the altar.** What is that? The ultimate altar is the cross. These ones are under the heavenly protection of the cross of Christ. And the white robes mean they are robed in Christ. There is no condemnation for those who are in Christ Jesus. They have the right wedding clothes (Matt. 22). They are safe now. Obviously, this is at least referring to those Christians who have died for the faith. Martyrs. Some scholars say they represent all Christians who have been victorious. Remember Jesus said: *Anyone who loves their life will lose it, while anyone who hates their life in this world will keep it for eternal life* (John 12:25). So, in a real sense, all Christians must lose their life in this world. Remember Revelation is a vision John is receiving which is meant to convey truth through these images. So this could be more than just martyrs. We don't need to get hung up on that or insist we understand every detail, but how many times did Jesus call on Christians to die to this world? Take up your cross and follow me (Matt. 16:24). Or as the apostle Paul said, offer your bodies as living sacrifices (Rom. 12:1).

If you are there in the first century, you know what you have to go through. You also remember all those who were victorious among your brethren (mentioned in the churches in Rev. 2-3). They were promised they would wear white. They were victorious over all kinds of persecution. They did not give in to the compromises of the world. They were not giving in to pressure to bow down to the Emperor to get work. They were not giving in to sexual immorality. They testified to Jesus even to the point of death. They were victorious and now they enjoy heaven. But now you wonder how long before the final end. Evil still seems to be reigning below. God's people are still suffering. Has the Lord overlooked the evil committed against us? Then you get a glimpse of those in heaven for **the testimony they had maintained. They called out in a loud voice, 'How long, Sovereign Lord, holy and true, until you judge the inhabitants of the earth and avenge our blood?'**

Those in heaven want to see an end to bloodshed and want final judgment for sin against *them*. This is not quite what we might have expected from people in heaven. We will have to look at that later. The cry in 6:9-10 is that there is much injustice. We feel it too. We have seen in 6:1-8 that the Lord is bringing about partial judgments through the horsemen. But how long until the full and complete vindication of good over evil? Those going through death and famine and plagues include the Christians as well. This was alive and happening in John's day for those people in those seven churches who first read this. Jesus predicted these things were going to happen right there from the first century ...

> They will put you out of the synagogue; in fact, a time is coming when anyone who <u>kills you</u> will think they are offering a service to God (John 16:2).
> Brother will betray brother to death, and a father his child. Children will rebel against their parents and have them put to death. Everyone will hate you because of me, but the one who stands firm to the end will be saved (Mark 13:12-13).

Many *were killed* and now we see them. They stood firm and we see them in heaven waiting the final day.

> Then each of them was given a white robe, and they were told to wait a little longer, until the number of their fellow servants, their brothers and sisters, were killed just as they had been (6:11).

This is the answer to their question, 'How long do we have to wait?' Answer: **A little longer, until the number of their fellow servants, their brothers and sisters, were killed just as they had been.** So rapture Futurists, you will have to indulge me, but can you see why I don't think these chapters are talking *exclusively* about some future time *after* the rapture of the saints, because there are saints still on the earth going through this tribulation. This is what the saints in heaven are told to wait for.

The other Futurist view says Christians *do* go through the tribulation, but it's still all yet to happen in the future. This would mean this text is saying that at some time in the future a great many Christians will die for the faith. The voice of the martyrs says differently. People were being slain for their testimony of Jesus in John's day when he wrote to those churches, and it has been going on throughout history. It would seem to me extraordinary to think this text is only referring to Christians who die for the faith at some future time. What are we to think of the millions of Christians who have given their lives for Jesus? There were more martyrs killed for their Christian faith in the last 100 years than the previous 1900. There have been nearly one million Christian martyrs in just the first 10 years of the 21st century.[26] Was their testimony unto death of no consequence? Are we meant to say to those who have seen multitudes killed for the faith, even their own loved ones, 'Just wait until you see it really get bad!' Or rather is this text alive now, speaking to the faithful followers of Jesus in John's day as well as

---

[26]www.ordonconwell.edu/ockenga/research/documents/1martyrdomsituations.pdf

those Christians throughout history and speaking to us now!

I concede these are disputable things which Christians are allowed to disagree over, and we don't claim infallibility on difficult texts like this, but one thing these verses most certainly debunk are the cults which say that when you die, you do not go into heaven or hell but into unconsciousness. The JWs and Seventh Day Adventists (SDA) say there is no hell, and when you die, you go into a soul sleep and know nothing until you get woken up on the Day of Judgment. I have always found that curious. If there was no hell, why would you even get woken up? The ungodly get woken up to learn they missed out on heaven and then? 'Now you just go right back to sleep.' This would come as a great relief to Adolf Hitler and evildoers who suddenly face God only to find that there is no judgment for their sin. You just get put back to sleep (or in some theologies a short intense burst of punishment but then off to beddy-byes). But this flies in face of the cry in 6:10. It is a cry for justice and for evil persecutors to be judged. People in unconscious sleep don't talk! Well, some might. But as opposed to unconscious soul sleep when you die, what do we notice about these verses?

They are in heaven and they speak! The souls who have gone on in the Lord are very much awake after they have died, waiting in that rest while still waiting for Judgment Day. Notice the richness of the soul. It's not some non-descript piece of cloud floating around. We wouldn't rely on these verses alone to build our theology of heavenly existence, since it is a vision conveying a central truth, but it does speak basic truth from a heavenly perspective so it's worth examining.

They called out in a loud voice, 'How long, Sovereign Lord, holy and true, until you judge the inhabitants of the earth and avenge our blood?' This verse suggests when you are in heaven in your soul, you are fully recognizable, fully communicating and able to have two-way conversations. They speak, they sing, they feel, and they think. They have a heavenly appearance. They have on robes! Clouds don't wear robes. They can enjoy resting. Take life easy. All the joys of heaven. Yet they still do not have their resurrection bodies. In fact, it's that resurrection they wait for. Until then it's what we call the 'intermediate state' before Judgment Day.

So when people have died, they are not sleeping unconsciously. For those in heaven, resting and able to enjoy the presence of the

Lord, they are able to speak to the Lord face to face. What did Jesus say to the thief on the cross? *Today* you will be with *me* in paradise. Not, 'Go to sleep for a few thousand years and I will wake you up later.' Rather, immediately in paradise! And those in hell are separated from God but fully conscious, held for the Day of Judgment. But neither of these situations are the full and final destiny which is the resurrection of our bodies to join our souls. That is where Revelation is headed. A new heaven and new earth. That's what these saints in heaven are calling for (6:10).

So they are there now. What are they doing? What are they thinking? I don't want to stretch this vision beyond what it's teaching, but it's tantalizing to look at what it might suggest. This is not the only place in Scripture where we are given an example of people who have gone on to the afterlife in their souls. In Luke 16, the rich man is in torment while Lazarus was 'comforted'. Yes, it's also only a parable, but it's still interesting to note the rich man in hell was worried about his loved ones. Suddenly he wants to be an evangelist. 'Can Lazarus go and tell them, so they won't come to this horrible place.' The point is he has a real interest in what is going on with those still alive on earth.

In 6:9-11 we are told there is conversation going on, suggesting heaven is taking an interest in what is also going on with the saints below. What about Luke 15? The parables of the lost sheep and the lost coin both finish by saying rejoicing is going on in heaven over one sinner who repents. This basic thought occurs in a few places in Scripture as well as in 6:9-11. It's an amazing thought. Does heaven really take an interest in what is going on down below? In Luke 15 there is the roar of the crowd in heaven that goes up over that one sinner who repents. Does heaven get a daily update or something? If you are a believer, those in heaven are aware they have to wait until you go through the suffering to join them. Or if you are unsaved, the people in heaven rest, waiting for that great cheer to go up when one sinner repents. Cheering and waiting in rest. Do you know anyone who has gone on in the Lord before you? Are they right now cheering you on, waiting to be re-united with you? Or are they still waiting for you to repent?

The primary call they have in 6:10 is: **How long before you judge the earth *and* avenge our blood?** They are appealing to the Lord in his character as **holy and true.** They are calling on God to be wrathful. Wouldn't it be more appropriate to have a cry of forgiveness? Isn't that the cry of Jesus from the cross? Luke 23:24, *Father forgive them.* Or Stephen (Acts 7:60), *do not hold it against them.* We below are meant to emulate that mercy cry, not judgment. What happened to forgiving? That is the message of the cross. But the cross proves God is wrathful as well as forgiving. God doesn't forgive without avenging full justice. The cross is the most powerful evidence that God is wrathful because he is pouring out the wrath we deserve on his Son who was fully willing to take it in our place. Justice and mercy kiss at the cross. Both are fully met. It goes against God's character to overlook evil. God does not deal in cheap forgiveness. God is not indifferent to injustice. He is *holy and true* (6:10). If God forgave but didn't care about justice, then why would he bother with the cross? God is wrathful. God is angry at evil. But aren't you? Aren't we all angry at evil? When you hear of child abusers do you say, 'Gotta love them. Let them alone, gotta forgive?'

God is *holy and true* and is angry at sin and those who commit it! The trouble for us is God is angry at all sin, down to the smallest detail. This is the amazing insight we are given in these verses. The heavenly perspective. When you are in heaven and you no longer have sin, you will see things more purely. You will see things more from the Lord's point of view. The Lord is *holy and true*, and the people who have gone on can see that, in a way we can't below. We have snippets ... now they see and cry, *how long before you judge?* We might know it in lip service, or when we see horrific evil we long for justice, but only those on the other side can really see it. Only they can see how right and good it is that the Lord would judge. They can see the beauty of holiness. They love justice. They are free from their own pain and sorrow, but they want to see full justice done.

How long O Lord? The OT cries for justice for God's people. In Psalm 79:5 the Psalmist cries 'how long', and also wants God to uphold his name (79:9). This can help us understand the imprecatory Psalms more. These are the Psalms calling on God to smite his enemies. Some of those Psalms I still can't get my head around—the cries for punishment. But C.S. Lewis said the reason we have trouble with the imprecatory Psalms is because we don't understand how wicked sin is.[27]

---

[27] C.S. Lewis, Reflections on the Psalms (New York: Harcourt, Brace and Company, 1958), pp.20-33

But these guys in heaven don't have any trouble with that anymore. They can see evil for what it is in God's sight and the rightness of judgment for the wicked. In fact, this is a major issue of Revelation. The people in those churches like Smyrna and Philadelphia are being persecuted. *How long O Lord before those persecutors are brought to justice for what they have done to us?* But it's more than persecution, because we have just seen in the four horsemen what is happening to the world, and Christians are not exempt from famine, plagues, and death itself. Why are Christians, the innocent, caught in the crossfire? How long O Lord will you let the innocent be hurt and killed? Christians are not exempt from pain. They are not exempt from losing a loved one tragically or unjustly. How long before you vindicate your name Lord, how long before you judge?

Have you ever wondered how you could possibly enjoy heaven while there were people whom you knew were in hell? Well, here is the answer in Rev. 6. When you see how evil sin is and how right and fair and just is God's *holy and true* justice, you will not want it any other way. The only question you will have is, 'What am I doing here instead of receiving justice?' The answer: Grace. But for the grace of God go I.

As the apostle Paul said: *Now I know in part; then I shall know fully, even as I am fully known* (1 Cor. 13:12). I will fully know. On the other side, they now fully know what sin really is and they love justice. They love the richness and rightness of justice. This is why the unbeliever cannot comprehend hell from a loving God. They have no concept of what is *holy and true* and how right and good and just it is that God punishes sinners in hell forever. In Ezekiel, God speaks of how his people will be consoled when they see how right his judgment was.

> 'Yet there will be some survivors—sons and daughters who will be brought out of it. They will come to you, and when you see their conduct and their actions, you will be consoled regarding the disaster I have brought on Jerusalem—every disaster I have brought on it. You will be consoled when you see their conduct and their actions, for you will know that I have done nothing in it without cause, declares the Sovereign Lord' (Ezek. 14:22-23).

Heaven strips back the veil of sin which clouds our minds and sees sin for what it is, and heaven knows, even longs for the right thing to be done. Why do Christians debate over whether we need God to make us spiritually alive when we were dead in sin (Eph. 2:1)? Some want to turn 'he chose us' into 'we chose him'. Why? Because down here we think sin is not that bad; we don't grasp that it makes us dead and even an enemy of God (Rom. 5:10). Somewhere deep down in our hearts, we think we are on neutral ground and that we are capable of choosing good and that God is somewhat obligated to offer salvation. It's not really grace. It's what God *should* do. Deep down in the sinful heart we also think hell is the bad side of God, instead of what is good about God. Hell is where God richly manifests what is *holy and true*. His holy justice finally wins! And instead of finding hell a difficult thing, the people in heaven are able to rejoice that justice is done. They long for it. No one in hell is treated unfairly, no one in heaven will say there is anyone in hell we should feel sorry for. There is only rejoicing that what is *holy and true* is being done.

An unbelieving relative of mine asked, 'What if I were to die and end up in hell? How would you feel about your God then, knowing that he put your loved one in hell?' I said, 'I wouldn't be happy about it. But if you killed someone and ended up in prison, I wouldn't be happy about that, but I wouldn't be asking for you to be let out, because jail would be right and fair.' It's just a matter of whether you can see God's jail in that light. In heaven, they can.

Yes, the Lord is wrathful towards evil, but he also holds off! He *waits* for this reason …

> But do not forget this one thing, dear friends: With the Lord a day is like a thousand years, and a thousand years are like a day. The Lord is not slow in keeping his promise, as some understand slowness. Instead he is patient with you, not wanting anyone to perish, but everyone to come to repentance (2 Pet. 3:8-9).

The reason for the delay of allowing suffering and evil in this world is that they must wait until those who are his below, have come to faith. God's plan of mercy and grace must be completed. If he wrapped up judgment sooner, some who are yet to come to repentance would miss out on heaven for eternity. And God is not willing that any of his perish. That is effectively what 6:11 is saying *… until the last one comes in.*

So how do you feel now if you are a Christian in the first century reading this for the first time, while you suffer and see loved ones die for the faith? All this time you thought the Lord had forgotten you.

Then you read Revelation and you realize it's the exact opposite! It's *because* of his love for you and others that he delays the Judgment.

How long? *Until the last one comes in.* Later in Revelation it talks several times about the book of life. There are a number of names in that book. Each name is accounted for (ticked) as they make it home into heaven. When the last one is in, that is the day it will be all over. When is that? We don't know. It could be one of your loved ones you are praying for right now. If you are unsaved, it could be you, the moment you repent and turn to Jesus. Until then…

… wait a little longer, until the number of their fellow servants, their brothers and sisters, were killed just as they had been (6:11).

Study Questions

1. How would this text be a relief to those in the seven churches?

2. Does this picture of saints suggest heaven is not all it's cracked up to be?

3. What NT teaching might suggest this text is speaking beyond those who have been physically martyred?

4. What is of interest in this text for the Futurist, both pre-tribulation and post-tribulation rapture?

5. What might this text say to JWs and SDAs?

6. Is heaven aware of what goes on in the earth? What Scriptures might suggest this?

7. In what ways does this text speak about how holy God is?

8. How could people in heaven rejoice knowing people are in hell?

9. What is the attribute of God that the heavenly saints have overlooked in this text?

22
The Wrath of the Lamb
(Revelation 6:12-17)

In our previous chapter, we left the saints in heaven crying out, 'How long before the Judgment?' The answer was that Judgment will come, but not until the last of God's people have completed their destiny on earth. Now following that cry, Judgment has finally arrived ...

> I watched as he opened the sixth seal. There was a great earthquake. The sun turned black like sackcloth made of goat hair, the whole moon turned blood red, and the stars in the sky fell to earth, as figs drop from a fig tree when shaken by a strong wind. The heavens receded like a scroll being rolled up, and every mountain and island was removed from its place. Then the kings of the earth, the princes, the generals, the rich, the mighty, and everyone else, both slave and free, hid in caves and among the rocks of the mountains. They called to the mountains and the rocks, 'Fall on us and hide us from the face of him who sits on the throne and from the wrath of the Lamb! For the great day of their wrath has come, and who can withstand it?' (6:12-17).

At least it looks like Judgment Day to me, but the Futurist sees this text as not describing the Day of Judgment. In fairness to the Futurist, they point out that people here are hiding. If it's Judgment Day, why do people get a chance to **hide** in the **mountains?**

However, I suggest we can read these verses together and simply take this as one cosmic event of Judgment as it unfolds. There is no need to insert any delay in between when people try to hide and then their confrontation with the Judge. This is how it all happens. Cosmic upheaval, signs in the sky, people in terror, people trying to hide and wanting to die because there is nowhere to hide. And they face the Judge! Literally see his **face** (6:16)! If they only want to hide, why do they want to die? Because the Day is here and there's no escape! There is no more time, no second chances. No extra seven years to change their minds. No extra 1000 years to re-think it all. No more opportunity. They would rather die than face this. **The wrath of the Lamb!** In fact, we might ask how could this be an invisible return of Jesus (to rapture his people), when the unbelievers can actually see his face? And perhaps the clincher is that he is seated on the judgment **throne** (6:16).

In fact, these verses seem to be giving us, in the most graphic terms, the final judgment and the answer to the question in the previous text, 'How long before you *judge?*' Immediately after, here he is effectively responding with, 'I haven't forgotten.' This is how Judgment Day will look!

The only trouble with my view is that if Judgment Day is being described here at the end of Rev. 6, what am I going to write about for the rest of the book of Revelation? After all, why would Judgment Day be happening this early in the book? Well, that's a fair question we will have to delve into later, but does it get any more final looking than this? Some of the things mentioned are …**The sun turned black … the moon turned blood red … the sky receded like a scroll … Then the kings of the earth, the princes, the generals, the rich, the mighty, and <u>everyone else</u>, both slave and free, hid.** Why are they hiding? **For the great day of their wrath has come.**

So are we to take this passage at the end of Rev. 6 literally? Possibly, because it's the fulfillment of many OT judgments. But even if it's symbolic, it's meant to be symbolic *of* something, and when the thing being described is so terrifying beyond description, only metaphor can try and grapple with it. It doesn't mean the reality will be less, but worse! What is being described is so horrific and final that it can only be described with these great cosmic phrases.

There are hints that some of it could be symbolic, for instance, the **stars in the sky fell to earth, as figs drop from a fig tree.** Stars have been used in Scripture to refer to powers. Jesus holds the seven stars in his hand in Rev. 1, referring there to angels of the churches. But if even one literal star fell to earth what would happen? The sun is one of a billion stars and is 333,000 times bigger than the earth, so if even one star fell to earth it would be like an insect splatting on your windscreen when you are on the freeway. Nothing left to speak of. Others have suggested the stars could be meteors, and that would be more realistic, if this is literal. But we don't need to get hung up on this. The point is that it is a cosmic shaking of the universe. Let's not forget where Revelation is headed. A literal new heaven and new earth. The Day of Judgment will bring cosmic wonders in some shape or form. This kind of language in Rev. 6 also fits with the Day of Judgment described elsewhere in the NT ...

> But the day of the Lord will come like a thief. The heavens will disappear with a roar; the elements will be destroyed by fire, and the earth and everything in it will be laid bare (2 Pet. 3:10).

It is clear what is portrayed here is Judgment Day. It's big. Cosmic. Final. Universal. Terrifying. And just like Rev. 6 when the sixth seal is opened, we know it is the final Day of Judgment because it is called the Day of the Lord, or in the case of 6:17, *the great day of wrath*. Read carefully over these words again in 6:12-17 with the great earthquake, sun turned black, moon turned blood red, sky receded like a scroll, every mountain and island removed and all kinds of people running for their lives to hide from the wrath of the Lamb, asking to die rather than see his face. If this isn't the Day of Judgment, then I would hate to see how much worse Judgment would look.

Let me give some reasons why I think this is the final judgment, and why it is not as the Futurist says just the ongoing tribulation or a secret rapture of God's people. Firstly, we've already noted, the immediate context is that this is an answer to the question in 6:10, *when is the final judgment?* These following verses describe what final judgment will look like and who can withstand it. In fact, the literal words in the original Greek language translated **who can withstand it** are literally *who can stand* (or, who is able to stand). So it is really asking the question *who can stand* in themselves before a holy judging God or *withstand* his holy wrath? The ESV and the old NIV translate it in that way, *for the great day of their wrath has come, and who can stand?* The Judgment Day, the great day of wrath is here! It *has come*. And *who can stand* in that judgment? The sun, moon and stars are destroyed. How much more final could this be? Along with the Futurist, we all agree that 20:11 is final Judgment, and these verses replicate the final judgment described there ... *heaven and earth flee from his presence*. Isn't that what is happening here? Heaven and earth flee? This is the sixth seal. The unleashing of Judgment Day ... *The heavens receded like a scroll being rolled up, and every mountain and island was removed from its place*. It's a judgment which affects everyone. Political leaders, financial powerbrokers, the bankers, the rich, the leaders of countries, military leaders, the powerful, but also every lowly servant and slave. *Then the kings of the earth, the princes, the generals, the rich, the mighty, <u>and everyone else, both slave and free</u>, hid in caves and among the rocks of the mountains.* And they are praying to the mountains to hide them from his face and his wrath. If we look at the OT texts drawn on to paint this picture of judgment, one particular sin is highlighted. Notice the similarity ...

> Go into the rocks, hide in the ground from the fearful presence of the LORD and the splendor of his majesty! The eyes of the arrogant will be humbled and human pride brought low; the LORD alone will be exalted in that day. The LORD Almighty has a day in store for all the proud and lofty, for all that is exalted (and they will be humbled), ... for all the <u>towering mountains</u> and all the high hills, ...and the <u>idols</u> will totally disappear. People will flee to caves in the rocks and to holes in the ground from the fearful presence of the LORD and the splendor of his majesty, when he rises to shake the earth. In that day people will throw away to the moles and bats their <u>idols</u> of silver and <u>idols</u> of gold, which they made to worship. They will flee to caverns in the rocks and to the overhanging crags from the fearful presence of the LORD and the splendor of his majesty, when he rises to shake the earth (Isa. 2:10-12,14,18-21).

The OT judgment context was to do with idolatry and fleeing from the presence of the LORD. Idols are more common than the idolater realizes. To worship an idol is to replace God with some other exalted created thing. And every area of idolatry is represented here in Rev. 6. Economic (monetary), social, political and material. *The mighty.* People we idolize. We can take any good thing given by God and turn it into an idol. Relationships, sex, 'save the turtles', 'save the trees'. Even ourselves. Especially ourselves! 'I will be my own Lord!' 'The human heart is a factory of idols' said John Calvin. But now we see exalted man is humbled ... *then the kings of the earth, the princes, the generals, the rich, the mighty* ... Kings. Princes. Generals. The rich and the mighty. All the people whom we thought were 'up there'. All the coveting we did. 'I wouldn't mind having some of their money.' 'I wish I could have achieved more like that person.' *The mighty.* Think about your favorites, like mighty athletes. The mighty actors. Your favorite rock stars. The very people you admired so much and put up on a pedestal and thought, 'I wish I could be like them.' But now look at them! *They are hiding!* Now they would rather die. *They called to the mountains and the rocks, 'Fall on us and hide us from the face of him who sits on the throne and from the wrath of the Lamb!'* What did all their achievements add up to?

But it is not just the rich and famous, but also ... <u>everyone else, both slave and free</u>, *hid in caves and among the rocks of the mountains.* It doesn't matter if you are poor, even a slave. You are there too! It's all the people who lived for this world and its desires. And now where are those desires? As the apostle John had written in his first epistle ...

> The world and its desires pass away ... (1 John 2:17).

Now John can see firsthand in this vision what this verse means. This verse is for all those living for this world who knew about God, but did nothing about it and said, 'I've always believed in God.' 'I knew there was something out there.' But if you knew, why didn't you let that belief enter your life? You didn't want to let him get too close, but now he is a whole lot closer than you want and there is nowhere to run, nowhere to hide. And it's scary. It says you can even see his face (6:16)! And all the excuses you had ... 'But I was busy with things. I was under pressure.' But the things of this world don't last. You knew the things of this world were not everything. You said it yourself. Oh, but they said it *would* last. Rock and Roll is never gonna die! Well maybe, because there will be loud music in heaven, but every part of that music which dishonors God will definitely die. As will all self-centered pleasures of this world! Most people will tell you those things are not everything. They never fully satisfy. But the same people still wouldn't let them go. And now they want to hide, they would rather die with rocks falling on them than see his face.

All the idols that promised so much are now cast down. And it's all over so quickly. Have you ever seen someone speeding past you on the freeway? They really think they are getting somewhere fast, but further up the road you see them again. The police officer has pulled them over and as you drive past you go 'ha' and give them a raspberry (in a kind of gentle Christian way). All that good time they were making added up to nothing.

Rush, rush. Gotta rush. 'Life is highway. I'm gonna ride it all night long.' Too busy for this life. No time for the Creator. But then you look up and see! No escape! You even call on the mountains *'Fall on us and <u>hide us from the face</u> of him who sits on the throne...!'* The Police officer has pulled you over. Now you try to hide us from his face!

God gave us this place to live and everything in it. He gave it to us, but we worshiped and served created things rather than the Creator (Rom. 1:25), so even the old earth has to go. The earth itself will be burned up. Now it all seems so foolish if you put your life and efforts into loving created things. 'Save the planet.' Save the planet? Too late! Now even the sun, moon, sky and stars have to be removed. 'I checked my horoscope to get the stars to help me direct my way.' What an insult to the one who created those stars. But even those stars are not there anymore. They can't direct you anywhere. There will only be God left. The living and true God. And now everyone has to face this living God. Who is he? Who is the Judge and who is the true God? Who is this wrathful God? It's the *wrath of the Lamb!*

The wrath of who? The Lamb. It's Jesus who is the Lamb of God. Gentle Jesus, meek and mild? Remember the humbled one…

> … Christ Jesus: Who, being in very nature God, did not consider equality with God something to be used to his own advantage; rather, he <u>made himself nothing</u> by taking the very nature of a servant, being made in human likeness. And being found in appearance as a man, <u>he humbled himself</u> by becoming obedient to death — <u>even death on a cross</u>! Therefore God exalted him to the highest place and gave him the name that is above every name, that at the name of Jesus every knee should bow, in heaven and on earth and under the earth, and every tongue confess that Jesus Christ is Lord, to the glory of God the Father (Phil. 2:5-11).

Now we see it pictured in the future. The Lamb who was slain is shown to be the true king. The true Judge. And he is the one whose wrath is displayed. Jesus wins! *The wrath of the Lamb!*

Why so wrathful? We looked at this before. Every time you see something evil that makes you angry, God is infinitely angrier in a righteous way. We learned in our previous chapter he holds back his anger waiting for the last one destined to come into his kingdom. But there comes a time when the last one appointed to eternal life comes in, and all the wrath he has stored up is unleashed. *Who can stand?* It doesn't matter how rich you are, or how mighty you are. Your status or achievements don't matter. All of that is irrelevant. If anything, the more you have, the more accountable you are, as in the parable of the talents. All your money, gifts and opportunities. Did you use them for the glory of the Lord? And how appropriate that the gentle

Lamb is the one whose wrath we face. A judge who gave himself up for a world that said 'no thanks'. Who can complain about that kind of judge? And they see how right and fitting and worthy he is to judge them. That is why they want to hide in terror … *They called to the mountains and the rocks, 'Fall on us and <u>hide us from the face of him</u> who sits on the throne'* … Again, this is borrowing from OT prophecy, Hosea and Jeremiah, when they hide from the judge. But there is another text in the OT from which this is drawn. There is another time when humanity hid from the Lord …

> Then the man and his wife heard the sound of the LORD God as he was walking in the garden in the cool of the day, and <u>they hid</u> from the LORD God among the trees of the garden (Gen. 3:8).

The Lord brings things full circle. Humanity's last day of getting away with sin will end the same way sin began — humans pathetically trying to hide from the presence of the Lord. In the beginning, they are hiding behind a tree. Hiding behind a tree from God? Couldn't God find them to judge them then? Of course they couldn't hide from him any more than they can hide in 6:16, when they call on mountains to fall on them to hide them from his face. But this is the final judgment.

Why didn't God crush humanity in the beginning? Why didn't he bring that judgment when Adam and Eve first sinned? He found them behind the tree. Instead he promised one who would crush the head of the serpent and defeat death. One who would be crushed in our place. And he delayed throughout history this judgment out of love for those he foreknew, waiting for them to be born into this world and come to faith. Here we are again with the question from 6:10. *How long O Lord?* Why wait through all these ages of humanity rebelling against you? The answer is the amazing patience of God. But even God's patience runs out. He hasn't forgotten justice … *the great day of their wrath has come, and who can stand?*

Didn't Jesus warn us about the same thing when he was on earth?

> 'There will be signs in the sun, moon and stars. On the earth, nations will be in anguish and perplexity at the roaring and tossing of the sea. People will <u>faint from terror</u>, apprehensive of what is coming on the world, for the heavenly bodies will be shaken. At that time they will see the Son of Man coming in a cloud with power and great glory. <u>When</u>

> these things begin to take place, stand up and lift up your heads, because your redemption is drawing near' (Luke 21:25-28).

Look up! The day is here. And now here it has arrived... *hide us from the face of him who sits on the throne and from the wrath of the Lamb!* They can actually see his face. They see the judgment throne. It's so terrifying to look at the Lamb. This reminds us of the opening of this book, written by Jesus, dictated to John.

> 'Look, he is coming with the clouds,' and 'every eye will see him, even those who pierced him'; and all peoples on the earth 'will mourn because of him.' So shall it be! Amen (1:7).

Think about those great people looking up and now trying to hide, even wanting to die. Those who mocked. Those who received adulation. Rich, famous, 'I don't need God.' The God who gave them every gift they had. And those who were weak and lowly but still wouldn't humble themselves. They had nothing and wouldn't even let that go. Those who were too busy. Who can stand?

The people are hiding. What are they hiding from? It's not the falling rocks or earthquakes they are so afraid of because they want the rocks to land on them. That would be scary enough, but 6:16 says it's his *face* they are hiding from! All those pathetic excuses seem so embarrassing now when they see his face. All that bravado about how you would have a few things to say to God if you had to face him. But now there is no bravado. There is no hiding behind silly arguments, pseudo intellectual philosophies, or even rocks! There is only his face with the eyes like blazing fire and with a Judge's sword. 'How could we have been so arrogant as to think God didn't have an answer to those questions, as if we could actually face God and say, you can't answer why you let me go through this life of pain. You can't answer why a loving God could have a hell.' As if God will respond on that Day, 'Wow, I didn't think of that. You really got me on that one. Come on into heaven!' But one look into that face on that Day will tell people they know there is an answer to all those things. In fact, he had answers in his word all along.

But now you are looking at the very one whom you passed off as a mere 'man', whose name you took on your lips as a swear word. Try blaspheming the name of Jesus Christ now! Try saying 'OMG'. Jesus said men will give account on the Day of Judgment for *every* careless word they have spoken, and all the consequences of those words are now staring at you. His eyes are like blazing fire. All those times he sent his messengers and proclaimed the day of grace and forgiveness and you mocked them. Or copped out by blaming hypocrites, as if that was really an excuse to reject Jesus and his church. Because on that Day, the hypocrites are beside you trying to hide too! Instead of taking up the message of forgiveness, you used that very message as another excuse. 'People only become Christians because they grew up in a Christian country. If I grew up in a Hindu country or Buddhist country, they would be telling me to be a Hindu or Buddhist.' But Jesus came by your door! He *put you* in the country and exact place where you should live so that you would seek him (Acts 17:26-27). It was your opportunity. And now the day has come, and every eye sees the wrath of the Lamb. The day of grace has left. The Buddhists and Hindus who *did* hear and received the Son of God got in ahead of you!

Those who mocked the loudest now scream the loudest in terror. Looking to hide. Now you can see God was not wrong. YOU WERE WRONG! *For the great day of their wrath has come, and who can stand?*

Only those who know the Lamb slain for them can stand. Only those who repented of trusting in themselves. That's right. They didn't trust in themselves, unlike the self-idolaters, who thought they could stand before a holy and true judge and still say, 'I've done enough good. I'm good enough to be worthy of forgiveness on that day.' Those who didn't repent trusted in themselves as to what was right ... as to how they would find meaning in life. They trusted in themselves. No, they didn't stand.

Only those who trust in the Lamb can stand. Only those who emptied themselves of self-righteousness and threw themselves on the mercy of the Lamb slain for forgiveness of sins. Only those who believed they were just passing through this world. Not earthly citizens. Those who forsook the pleasures of this world. Those who chose to forsake things because they remained faithful to the Lamb. They didn't have all the luxuries. They used worldly wealth to think of others. Some might have lived a single life because they wouldn't disobey the Lamb and marry a non-Christian. They rejected sexual immorality. Some persevered in unhappy marriages or families because they wouldn't forsake the one who was slain for them, the Lamb. *They* could stand. But others ... who could stand?

A massive hurricane hit the East Coast of the US in October 2012, but unlike other parts of the world, the technology was such that they were prepared to evacuate days before to save their lives. What was fascinating and tragic was that some lives were still lost. How could that happen with all the warnings? Some people just wouldn't move. They wouldn't listen. Revelation is warning of a hurricane coming. You are told in advance this hurricane is going to hit. Today is the day to put your emergency plan into action. Today Jesus is still the Savior. Tomorrow you will see his face as Judge.

Look at the sun! It's gone completely black. The moon is red like blood of judgment. So how are we going to see anything? In fact, there is a far greater light than you ever want. It's like those police helicopters that come through the night and shine their big spotlights down on the criminal who has nowhere to run and nowhere to hide. He pathetically tries to run but can't escape the light in the sky. But this is not a helicopter. What is it? It's the Lord and you can see his face! It's a face of wrath (6:16-17)! Can you picture it? A face of wrath! Anger! All those complaints about why God was allowing evil to continue, and now we see firsthand his anger. He is letting it go! Holy burning anger. If you don't know him as Savior today, tomorrow this is whom you will face.

Study Questions

1. Is this text describing the rapture, the tribulation or the Day of Judgment? Give reasons and Scriptural confirmation for your answer.

2. Should we take this scene as literal or symbolic? Why?

3. Give at least two reasons why it's appropriate for Jesus to Judge.

4. What OT history reminds us of people hiding from God?

5. How would your life change if you knew you had only one month?

6. What makes you think you will be able to stand?

23

The Seal on the Forehead
(Revelation 7:1-3)

Six of the seven seals of judgment have been opened and the Day of Judgment has come. We looked at that terrifying time. Heaven and earth rolled up. The Lord is on his judgment throne and you can see his face (6:16)! There is only one more seal to be opened. But before it can be opened we were left with this great question: *Who can stand* (6:17)?

After seeing everyone fleeing and hiding, who *can* stand? Who of us have no idols? Who of us have never sinned or succumbed to temptation? We are all in that list in 6:15. The rich and poor, the weak and strong, the slave and free. And the shock and terror of that day leaves us with this one question, 'Who can stand before the throne and wrath of the holy Lamb?'

Well those who believe, right? But if you are there in one of the churches in the first century and have just read in Rev. 2-3 how your church is lukewarm, or compromising with sexual immorality, or you think you are alive but are dead, all that stuff came from the same Lamb whose wrath is on display now! He is the one who gave the warnings. How do you really know you can stand?

Have you ever wondered that? How can I stand? When you look at the words of Jesus, 'Not everyone who calls me Lord, Lord will enter, but only he who does the will of my Father' (Matt. 7:21). Who can stand now and say they have always done the will of the Father? Who *can stand?*

We need to take a deep breath. John is seeing these visions. He has seen the people crying out in heaven, 'How long must this evil go on before you judge' (6:10)? And then 6:12-17 shows the Lord keeps his promise to judge the earth. But how are *we* going to survive and stand in that judgment?

This new scene has the Master film director, Jesus, giving another camera angle. We have had a shot of heaven. We have been brought in this film all the way up to the climactic ending of the movie. The great and terrible ending when the whole world is brought to this … now we await the seventh seal, the climax of that judgment scene which began at 6:12-17.

But then as judgment is raining down, we think of all the people who have been bit players in the movie. We got to know and love them. We related to those people in the seven churches from Ephesus with their lost love through to Laodicea with the lukewarmers. How will they survive the climax of the movie? Who can stand? We are not ready for the opening of the seventh seal. We need to be prepared to be able to answer the question: *Who can stand?*

We need what many a good film director gives at this point. A flashback. A recap of the story so far, to be able to answer that question. Those still suffering or fighting temptation, how can they stand? Take a closer look at that previous scene in 6:12-17. There are people fleeing, terrified. It's the last day. Everyone was there, rich and poor, high and low. John is seeing the future judgment. You were there. Did you see yourself there? Were you standing? We will all be there in that final judgment scene, when the last seal is opened. So this is just as much a question for us. *Who can stand?*

We will see later in 7:9 that there are those who are standing. Literally! Standing before the throne and the Lamb. So some must be standing! But we still want the answer to the question: Who of us can stand? So here our movie goes into an interlude …

> <u>After this</u> I saw four angels standing at the four corners of the earth, holding back the four winds of the earth to prevent any wind from blowing on the land or on the sea or on any tree (7:1).

These are John's words. He begins with **after this.** So after John saw the vision of the final judgment, then he sees this. Remember John is seeing visions one after another, so it's 'after this, I saw that'. This is not a continuation of the sixth seal, but a new scene altogether. We don't get the last (seventh) seal until 8:1. Rather, this is Master film directing. This is the interlude in the film. This is the much-needed recap to answer the question of John, his first readers, and us, which is: *Who can stand?* In 6:12-17 Judgment Day came about as powerfully as it could be described with the sun darkened, the moon the color of blood and people running in terror. What hope have we got?

Now in this next scene, John sees **four angels standing at the four corners of the earth holding back the four winds of the earth** ... We've noted before that four is the number regularly used to signify the complete creation, such as, *the four quarters of the earth* (Isa. 11:12). And this number four gives us the same idea of completion when it comes to the *four winds*, also drawing on the OT (Jer. 49:36). This is laying the foundation of the sovereignty of God over all things in heaven and earth.

Some scholars have related these four winds to the four horses we encountered in Rev. 6. All went forth into the world. And some scholars connect those horses with the horses in Zechariah.

> I looked up again—and there before me were four chariots coming out from between two mountains—mountains of bronze! The first chariot had red horses, the second black, the third white, and the fourth dappled—all of them powerful. I asked the angel who was speaking to me, 'What are these, my lord?' The angel answered me, 'These are the four spirits of heaven, going out from standing in the presence of the Lord of the whole world. The one with the black horses is going toward the north country, the one with the white horses toward the west, and the one with the dappled horses toward the south.' When the powerful horses went out, they were straining to go throughout the earth. And he said, 'Go throughout the earth!' So they went throughout the earth (Zech. 6:1-7).

These are the four spirits. In Hebrew (OT) as well as in Greek (NT), the word *spirit* is the same word translated as *wind*, so it's only the context that determines which is which. The four winds are going forth. So many think the horses of 6:2-8 and winds of 7:1 are the horses of Zechariah 6. All things are possible; however, I would suggest that John didn't think of these *winds* as the *spirits* and *horses* in Zechariah because there are some serious differences.

In Zechariah, the spirits come from heaven. In 7:1 the spirits or winds are coming from earth. The four horses in Zechariah aren't all the same colors as in Revelation. Dappled horses don't appear in 6:2-8. The horses in Zechariah are plural. Instead of a red horse it is a chariot carried by *several* red horses and so on with the black horses, etc. Also the winds in 7:1 have somewhat different goals from the horsemen of 6:2-8. So, does this mean the Zechariah text has no relevance at all? I would rather think that for John brought up on the OT and familiar with Zechariah, the horses would call to mind the concept of *judgment*, without necessarily drawing directly on the details.

So what is going on in 7:1? We are seeing the judgments going forth into the world through these four winds, but they are being held back at first. Why? Well that gives us the answer to the terrifying question: *Who can stand?*

Remember we argued in 6:1-8 that while there are agents of evil going forth in the world, the Lord uses them to bring about his partial judgments, yet he sets the limits and holds them back just as he did with Job while Satan was doing his evil (Job 1:10). So too these winds have evil intent, but they are under the control of the one who is on the throne who directs his angels, so they are *holding back the four winds of the earth*.

The number gets repeated, four, four, four. It's land, sea, and trees. In other words, there is no area of the whole creation or its inhabitants that these winds will not seek out if they are given the opportunity. Why are the four angels of God holding them back? Now we learn why ...

> Then I saw another angel coming up from the east, having the seal of the living God. He called out in a loud voice to the four angels who had been given power to harm the land and the sea: 'Do not harm the land or the sea or the trees until we put a seal on the foreheads of the servants of our God' (7:2-3).

The word to look at here is **until**. The full judgment will not come upon the earth *until* all of those who are God's are **sealed**. Believers don't need a protective seal *after* the tribulation; that would be too late! No, this seal is put on believers before they go through the tribulation to enable them to stand at the final judgment! Who can stand? Who can even survive these judgments of the four winds? Well as it turns out, there was a plan. It wasn't hit and miss, as to who or how the people of God could survive. The movie is recapping and telling us that before God unleashed the four winds, he sent out another angel for this purpose. *To apply the seal!*

In the ancient world, slaves were marked to identify who they belonged to. Ownership was indicated that way. The *Lord* owns these who are sealed. John's OT background knowledge helps him understand how those who were the Lord's were sealed. Two examples would come to John's mind ...

> Now the glory of the God of Israel went up from above the cherubim, where it had been, and moved to the threshold of the temple. Then the LORD called to the man clothed in linen who had the writing kit at his side and said to him, 'Go throughout the city of Jerusalem and put a mark on the foreheads of those who grieve and lament over all the detestable things that are done in it.' As I listened, he said to the others, 'Follow him through the city and kill, without showing pity or compassion. Slaughter old men, the young men and women, the mothers and children, but do not touch anyone who has the <u>mark</u>. Begin at my sanctuary' (Ezek. 9:3-6).

John would have recognized this when he hears of the sealing of the people in his Revelation vision. But perhaps as a first century Jew, an even greater event in Scripture would come to mind for John where judgment would pass over those who had a mark. The Passover itself.

> Take a bunch of hyssop, dip it into the blood in the basin and put some of the blood on the top and on both sides of the doorframe. None of you shall go out the door of your house until morning. When the LORD goes through the land to strike down the Egyptians, he will see the blood on the top and sides of the doorframe and will pass over that doorway, and he will not permit the destroyer to enter your houses and strike you down (Exod. 12:22-23).

It is a mark in blood on their homes which saves them. With the Passover, as here in Revelation, they are not taken out of the violent scene with enemies abounding, but rather they are marked so they could survive 'through the tribulation'. So I am disagreeing with the idea that Christians are raptured out *before* the tribulation, but rather they are sealed to survive going through it! The seal is a protective measure as highlighted later in …

> They were told not to harm the grass of the earth or any plant or tree, but only those people who did not have the <u>seal</u> of God on their foreheads (9:4).

Those with the **seal** were still going through the tribulation and can suffer the evils of those horses and riders. The believer is not immune to suffering at the hands of violence, famine, plagues, disease, and death. But those who are sealed cannot be taken out of the Father's hand. The same thing that hardens and judges unbelievers will work for believers good and refinement. Instead of shaking their fist at God in trial, they will never give up. Why? They have been sealed. They will not be hurt by the second death. They will not lose their salvation or their faith.

> ... he who began a good work in you will carry it on to completion until the day of Christ Jesus (Phil. 1:6).

This is spelt out a little more clearly later ...

> Then I looked, and there before me was the Lamb, standing on Mount Zion, and with him 144,000 who had his name and his Father's name written on their foreheads ... These are those who did not defile themselves with women, for they remained virgins. They follow the Lamb wherever he goes. They were purchased from among mankind and offered as firstfruits to God and the Lamb (14:1,4).

They kept the faith, they didn't compromise in purity, but notice they were those who were bought with the precious blood of the Lamb. In Rev. 14 we will examine why there are only 144,000 Jehovah's Witnesses in heaven (not really), and where the Jews fit in with these 12 tribes. But for now, what exactly is the **seal on the foreheads of the servants of our God?**

I don't think this seal is a visible tattoo on believers, Jewish or otherwise. If it were, we wouldn't have any wheat growing up with the tares. It would expose who were the real believers immediately. We would not have to wait until the Day of Judgment to find out to whom Jesus would say, 'Away from me, I never knew you.' We would all know by the visible tattoo. 'Hey, there goes one of the true believers, fish sign on the back of the car and sign on the forehead.' The saying would go around, 'It doesn't matter if you got the fish sign on the car, it's the sign on your forehead that counts.' We would have no need to question who should come into membership at church or take the Lord's Supper. 'Sorry, no mark on the forehead.' 'But I'm a believer.' 'Nope, I can tell you are lying, no mark.'

In contrast, Judas was right there among the believers. We are warned constantly of those whose outward appearance is that of sheep, but who are actually wolves in sheep's clothing. There is no visible seal. So I am suggesting the seal is not a visible seal, at least not visible to us, but a protecting seal which God sees. It's also a guarantee from God that he sets apart his true people and keeps them through the tribulation and from falling away. Where would we see such a guaranteed seal for believers elsewhere in the NT?

Try and picture sitting there in one of those seven churches in the first century. You were among the first readers of this book of Revelation, penned by John. The first letter was to the church in Ephesus. What would you Ephesians think? You were given some pretty harsh rebukes. *You have forsaken your first love, so repent and go back to your first love* (2:1-7). What might you have done if you were in that congregation? You know the apostle Paul had written to the churches in your area many years earlier, and his letter (to the Ephesians) had become widespread throughout the Christian church. But this letter to the church at Ephesus was written to your particular church. And now Jesus says through John, 'Go back to your first love.'

So what do you do? You just might go back and re-read Paul's letter sent to your church, written a few decades earlier. Now you can see the height from which you have fallen as you go back to where you were. From the first chapter of Ephesians all those wonderful things we have in Christ … chosen, predestined, adopted, redemption through his blood, forgiveness of sins, and that section climaxed with a mark, a seal …

> And you also were included in Christ when you heard the message of truth, the gospel of your salvation. When you believed, you were marked in him with a seal, the promised Holy Spirit, who is a deposit guaranteeing our inheritance until the redemption of those who are God's possession—to the praise of his glory (Eph. 1:13-14).

You already know what the *seal* is. It is the *Holy Spirit!* You knew this Ephesians letter well. It was written to your church! But let's be frank, any Christian in the first century, indeed, any Christian today can and should know the letter to the Ephesians including this …

> And do not grieve the Holy Spirit of God, with whom you were sealed for the day of redemption! (Eph. 4:30).

So if you were *any* Christian in the first century, what would you think when you read in Revelation about the seal? What would the seal mean to you? In fact, it's not just the letters to the Ephesians you are familiar with, all the NT letters were read in all the churches …

> Now it is God who makes both us and you stand firm in Christ. He anointed us, set his <u>seal of ownership</u> on us, and put his <u>Spirit</u> in our hearts as a deposit, <u>guaranteeing</u> what is to come (2 Cor. 1:21-22).

There it is again. If you were there in the first century and the Bible was driving your interpretation of Revelation, you are not looking for tattoos on foreheads for God's seal when you read in Revelation about *a seal on the foreheads of the servants of our God*. You think of the *seal of the Holy Spirit*. Through the trials he will keep us. Not one of his sheep will be lost. You are in the Father's hand. He who began a good work in you will complete it. You have a guarantee, a deposit, and a seal. The Holy Spirit. There is no tribulation that can take the seal away. No power of hell, no scheme of man can ever pluck me from his hand, if you have the seal. In 7:2-3 it's the same sentiment as from the apostle Paul ...

> For I am convinced that neither death nor life, neither angels nor demons, neither the present nor the future, nor any powers, neither height nor depth, nor <u>anything else</u> in all creation, will be able to separate us from the love of God that is in Christ Jesus our Lord (Rom. 8:38-39).

If you have been saved, you will always be saved. But what if I backslide? Well, if you are one of his, the Holy Spirit in you will grieve and will call you back to repentance. If you have the seal, you can't stay comfortably in sin. I know people who have claimed to be Christians for years but never really committed to church life, purity, love and forgiveness. But if you have the seal, the Holy Spirit, even if you backslide and sin, the Spirit will convict you and you will be troubled. You will hear the rebuke of God. You will listen to what the Spirit is saying to the churches.

Who can stand? Only those who have been cleansed by the blood of the Lamb. They believe in Jesus. But how does that happen? Because of the seal!

> ... he saved us, not because of righteous things we had done, but because of his mercy. He saved us through the washing of rebirth and renewal by the Holy Spirit, ... (Titus 3:5).

You believed in Jesus because you received the seal. The Holy Spirit pointed you to Jesus. Even when you are weak and your prayers are weak, he will even keep your prayers going ...

> In the same way, <u>the Spirit</u> helps us in our weakness. We do not know what we ought to pray for, but the Spirit himself intercedes for us with wordless groans (Rom. 8:26).

Even through your weakest times the Holy Spirit takes those prayers and turns them into something. You have the seal to get you through.

If you are there in the first century in one of those seven churches and going through persecution, this is what you need to hear. It's obvious the servants of God are not protected from physical travail on earth, so how can I be assured I will make it spiritually? The seal of God. This is the strengthening we need. We are eternally protected—spiritually protected. He will keep you through the tribulation. Even when these four winds are released and wreak havoc on earth. *Who can stand?* Only *those who have the seal!*

So, do you have the seal? Do you bear the mark of the seal on your forehead? (In what you believe in your mind.) Do you have the Holy Spirit? Do you believe in Jesus? Do you show evidence of the mark of the seal of God? It's not a tattoo. Here is how the mark of the Spirit shows ...

> But the <u>fruit</u> of the Spirit is love, joy, peace, forebearance, kindness, goodness, faithfulness, gentleness and self-control. Against such things there is no law. Those who belong to Christ Jesus have crucified the flesh with its passions and desires. Since we live by the Spirit, let us keep in step with the Spirit (Gal. 5:22-25).

If you have the seal of the Holy Spirit you will show his mark (his fruit), and if you are not showing the fruit, it will grieve you. You will rush back to the cross for forgiveness and cleansing. You will repent and put to death old sins and start again. And if you have the seal of God you can't be touched by the tribulation, even in death. Who can stand? Answer: Those who have the seal. Those who put their trust in Christ, the Lamb, and followed him as Lord and Savior, because he first put his seal upon them.

'Do not harm the land or the sea or the trees until we put a seal on the foreheads of the servants of our God' (7:3).

Study Questions

1. Why might Christians in those first seven churches need an interlude to answer; who can stand?

2. If the Day of Judgment occurs at 6:12-17, why are the four winds of judgment coming afterwards?

3. Many have connected the horses of Zechariah to the horses of Rev. 6. Give reasons for or against that view.

4. Give OT examples of believers receiving a 'mark'.

5. How would John and his first readers have interpreted the 'seal'?

6. How does the 'seal' work in giving us assurance?

7. What evidence can we see of having received the 'mark' or 'seal'?

24
The 144,000
(Revelation 7:4-8)

The Jehovah's Witnesses are surely right after all! There are only 144,000 people in heaven! It's here in the Bible in Rev. 7. Well, actually these 144,000 are not in heaven. When we get to Rev. 14 the 144,000 are in heaven, but the context of this 144,000 is that they are on *earth*. In our previous chapter the angels were holding back the winds of judgment from coming on the whole earth until the seals were put on them.

> 'Do not harm the land or the sea or the trees until we put a seal on the foreheads of the servants of our God.' Then I heard the number of those who were sealed: 144,000 from all the tribes of Israel (7:3-4).

They are on earth. The first thing we notice is that this 144,000 are from *all the tribes of Israel*. They must surely be Jews. So when is this happening and who are these Jews? And why are there only 144,000? Are there only 144,000 Jews saved? And if so, is it exactly 12,000 Jews per tribe and no more? Is this number literal or symbolic? Symbolic numbers fit with the genre and use of numbers in this apocalyptic book. And if we acknowledge the number is *symbolic*, does that mean the tribes of Israel are symbolic?

One popular theory is that the 144,000 are all the Jews saved near the end. In fact, there are a few different theories, and I think we have to admit this is not easy. Even the way the tribes are recorded makes it difficult.

Of all the OT tribes of Israel, Judah is rarely listed first, but now we have the hindsight knowledge that Jesus the Messiah came from that tribe. He is the Lion of the tribe of Judah (5:5), so Judah takes priority. Genesis 49:10 foretold the promise that the scepter (the royal line), would not depart from Judah.

The most popular interpretation is that Christians are all raptured at the beginning of Rev. 4, so there aren't any Christians left on earth at this point. Therefore these 144,000 must be ethnic Israelites of the literal 12 tribes. These Jewish converts are left behind and are going through the tribulation but are sealed (protected physically). We might wonder why the Jewish believers have to go through the tribulation and not the Gentile believers?

But in fairness to that view, our text clearly states 12 tribes of Israel. Wouldn't it seem a bit odd for 12 tribes of Israel to be Gentiles? But I wonder what the Jews from the first century thought when they first read this book of Revelation. They would have immediately noticed this text is not speaking of the true and literal 12 tribes of Israel. First, they have would noticed the tribe of Dan is omitted. They would say, 'We are down to only 11 of our true tribes.' Then they would have noticed Ephraim is also omitted! 'Now we are down to 10.' How does that make up 12?

The Levites were the priests. They were never apportioned a lot or counted among those inheriting the land. But in 7:7 ... *from the tribe of Levi 12,000,* ... And Joseph never formed a tribe, but there is his tribe in 7:8 ... *from the tribe of Joseph 12,000...*

We can surmise Dan and Ephraim are omitted because of their history associated with idolatry. But you can't literally remove them as ethnic tribes of Israel. They existed as a literal tribe, so are they figuratively removed here? Are they spiritually removed and replaced by names that were never literal tribes? If they are, look at the implication! If you omit any literal tribe, you automatically exclude a literal restoration of all the tribes of Israel. What happened to God's promises? If you are a first century Jew reading this, you see there's a lot of literal Israel missing. Something is terribly wrong! There is too much missing and unexplained.

Another difficulty is if we think these are literally Israel's tribes at some time in the future, then how could the people be identified as belonging to their tribes? Ten of the tribes virtually lost their identity when they were exiled by Assyria from 722BC, and from the most ancient times the faithful ones of other tribes joined the more faithful tribe of Judah (2 Chron. 11:13-17). Then the genealogical records were destroyed with the temple in AD 70. Add to that, mixed marriages between the Israelite tribes and the spreading of peoples have made it more than difficult for there to be an ethnic delineation of the tribes in John's time, which makes it virtually impossible by our time, much less if we were to think of all this happening sometime in the future.

If you are a Jewish Christian in one of the seven churches having just received Revelation from John, then there are some serious difficulties with this representing your true heritage. You have just been told by Jesus in these seven letters that one of the main temptations to compromise in your day is idolatry, so that might explain the figurative omission of the tribes of Dan and Ephraim. Pergamum and Thyatira were both warned against idolatry. Jesus told the church they had to be purer than Israel of old!

And these tribes of 12,000 are sealed. What are they sealed with? All believers in Christ, both Jew and Gentile, are sealed with the Holy Spirit (Eph. 1:13-14; 4:30, 2 Cor. 1:21-22). But what would you make of the 12 tribes and 12,000 of each?

If you are one of those first readers and have read this far through Rev. 1-7, you have seen from the beginning that nearly all the numbers in the book have some figurative, symbolic significance. You have read in this chapter of the four corners of the earth, yet you know the earth doesn't have any corners. You were told of the seven spirits of God, and you know seven is God's general number of completion, hence God's complete Holy Spirit. Then there is the number 12. You have seen 12 before relating to the people of God. The elders representing people of God from the 12 OT tribes and the 12 NT apostles adds up to 24, which is the number of elders surrounding the throne of heaven (4:4). Here we are dealing with 144,000, which is 12 x 12, but in the 1000s. The number 1000 is a basic military division in the camp of Israel in Numbers 31:4-5, but 1000 is also a common OT designation of a great indefinite number. So this 144,000 conveys a larger version of the 12 x 12. It's 12 x 12 in the 1000s! A great, indefinite number. And how are the people of God represented in the heavenly building in Rev. 21? The foundation is made up of the 12 tribes and the 12 apostles.

> It had a great, high wall with twelve gates, and with twelve angels at the gates. On the gates were written the names of the <u>twelve tribes of Israel</u>. ... The wall of the city had twelve foundations, and on them were the names of the <u>twelve apostles of the Lamb</u> (21:12,14).

Israel's tribes and Jesus' apostles combine to make up the heavenly city. This was the promise to the Gentile Christians at Philadelphia (3:12). *Him who overcomes I will make a pillar in the temple of my God.* In fact, these measurements 144 and 12,000 appear again in that heavenly building. Right there in that passage in Rev. 21 after we see the foundations of 12 tribes and 12 apostles.

> The city was laid out like a square, as long as it was wide. He measured the city with the rod and found it to be 12,000 stadia in length, and as wide and high as it is long. The angel measured the wall using human measurement, and it was 144 cubits thick (21:16-17).

The wall is 144 cubits. Why? It's a complete number of 12 x 12, Israelite and Gentile believers. The city of God is made up of Jews *and* Gentiles, including Israelite believers of old. And what is the name given to Gentiles and Jews combined? Jesus told the Gentiles as well as Jewish Christians in the church at Philadelphia, they all have the *name of the city of my God, the New Jerusalem* (3:12). The first Christian readers of the book of Revelation are told they are the New Jerusalem. This is where Revelation is headed. The bride, the people of God. What are they called?

> I saw the Holy City, the New Jerusalem, coming down out of heaven from God, prepared as a bride beautifully dressed for her husband (21:2).

The bride, the church of Jew and Gentile believers in the Messiah, is given the most 'Israelite' of all city names, the New *Jerusalem*. So these first Christian readers were already introduced to the idea of the church, made up of Jew and Gentile, as being the New Jerusalem. Furthermore, the promise to Israel of old was that Israel would become a kingdom of priests, and now these Christians (Jews and Gentile believers) are told ...

> ... To him who loves us and has freed us from our sins by his blood, and has made us to be a kingdom and priests to serve his God and Father—to him be glory and power for ever and ever! Amen (1:5-6).

This **kingdom and priests** is repeated in 5:10, and that would have struck a chord, as it's so similar to that famous statement God made to Israel in Exodus 19:6. *You, Israel will be for me a kingdom of priests.* So here is the church (Jew and Gentile together), being told they fulfil that designation given to Israel. The *kingdom and priests*.

What is the gospel to Jews and Gentiles? The gospel makes the two one. The gospel is not Israel being *replaced* by Gentiles. 'Replacement theology' is such an unfortunate and even misleading term. The apostle Paul never said anything about replacement. He says through Christ Gentile believers were grafted *into* Israel. He said they were *added* to Israel and given all the privileges including 'citizenship in Israel' ...

> Therefore, remember that formerly you who are Gentiles by birth and called 'uncircumcised' by those who call themselves 'the circumcision' (which is done in the body by human hands)—remember that at that time you were separate from Christ, excluded from <u>citizenship in Israel</u> and foreigners to the covenants of <u>the promise</u>, without hope and without God in the world. But now in Christ Jesus you who once were far away have been brought near by the blood of Christ. For he himself is our peace, who has made the <u>two one</u> and has destroyed the barrier, the dividing wall of hostility ... [Now through the church in the gospel, Jew and Gentile are one.] Consequently, you are no longer foreigners and strangers, but <u>fellow citizens</u> with God's people and members of his household ... (Eph. 2:11-14,19).

Fellow citizens! Gentile believers now joined with Israel as God's holy people in the church of Jesus. It's through Jesus, the Jewish Messiah, that Gentiles are included as God's holy people. All the promises of God are 'Yes and Amen' in Jesus (2 Cor. 1:20).

The New Jerusalem is made up of ethnic Jews who believe in the Messiah, *and* Gentiles joined to Jews in the church. The gospel is not saying 'out with the Jews and in with the Gentile believers'. Rather, Paul's letter to the Romans tells prideful Gentiles to not be arrogant. You were formerly out, now you have been grafted in (Rom. 11:17), and are *included* with Israel, the people of God. Israel was the foundation, the natural branches, so Gentiles, don't be conceited, you are not replacing them, you are now included in *Israel's* citizenship and Israel's promises through Jesus.

Jesus said it. Salvation is of the Jews! (John 4:22). Paul said they have been entrusted with the very word of God (Rom. 3:2). Theirs are the promises. Theirs are the covenants (Rom. 9:4). And Ephesians 2:11-22 tells us the gospel is all about joining the Jew and Gentile together under the same promises.

Israel is the foundation, the natural branches, so rather than excluding or replacing the Jews in the gospel the two are joined together.

The 144,000 can't exclusively be literal ethnic Israel since literal tribes are missing. And it's unrealistic that only 144,000 Jews are saved (sealed) and only exactly 12,000 from each tribe. So if it can't be literal, then we have a symbolic number on our hands. Remember how Revelation started out? Expect symbols and signs. This was flagged in the very first verse of Revelation (1:1, see explanation in ch.13, p.143-144). And this is what we have seen so far with the book's imagery and numbers. Jesus is depicted with a sword coming out of his mouth, then as a lamb that was slain, then as a lion. Symbols. Symbols. Symbols. And here is Israel, God's people. Jews along with Gentiles added through the Jewish Messiah, believers together, 12 x 12 in the 1000s makes 144,000, the complete people of God.

Does that mean God failed in his promise to the Jews? By no means! What was the original promise of salvation from the beginning of the Jews? God says to the father of the Jews, Abraham.

> I will make you into a great nation and I will bless you; I will make your name great, and you will be a blessing. I will bless those who bless you, and whoever curses you I will curse; and <u>all peoples</u> on earth will be blessed through you' (Gen. 12:2-3).

All nations are blessed *through* Abraham. Through the Jews! How are **all peoples** (Gentiles) blessed? They can inherit the promises given to Abraham in Genesis 12 by becoming children and co-heirs with the Jews through the faith of Abraham, through believing in the Jewish Messiah (John 8:56). The 144,000 are God's answer to his promise to Abraham that all the nations would be blessed through Israel (not apart from Israel).

In fact, we didn't need to make it so hard for ourselves. We were already told in 7:3 who are the 144,000. They are the **servants of our God.** The seal is on the *servants of our God* who are then described as the 12 tribes of Israel. Only these 144,000 are designated servants of God. Aren't all believers servants of God? Aren't all believers sealed? The term *servants of God* is *never* used in Revelation of exclusively Jewish believers, but always includes all believers. The Bible makes no distinction between Jew and Gentile when it uses the term 'servants of God'. In fact, we need to remember to whom this book of Revelation was written. Go back to the start ...

> The revelation of Jesus Christ, which God gave him to show <u>his servants</u> what must soon take place (1:1).

The servants, both Jew and Gentile, are those who have trusted in the Jewish Messiah, Jesus. We learned in our previous chapter that the servants of the Lord were desperate to know where they stood. We had left the end of Rev. 6 with Judgment Day and the terrible cry: *Who can stand?* Those first readers going through trials in those seven churches wanted to know: *Who can stand?* Every servant of the Lord throughout church history who has read this and looked at the judgment at the end of Rev. 6 asks the question: *Who can stand?* Then we received the answer at the beginning of Rev. 7. Those servants who are sealed with the Holy Spirit, they *will* make it. They will persevere. They will stand! It speaks to all God's servants. If you are a believer you are sealed with the Holy Spirit. *You* have been included in the commonwealth of Israel. As the apostle Paul calls believers both Jews and Gentiles added, you are ...

> ...the Israel of God (Gal. 6:16).

You are among the servants of God. This is for *you!* Hold fast in tribulation, he will keep you! The idea that Gentiles would join the Jews to make up Israel was not foreign to the OT.

> ... Foreigners will join them and unite with the descendants of Jacob. <u>Nations</u> will take them and bring them to their own place. And Israel will take <u>possession of the nations</u> ... (Isa. 14:1-2).

Rev. 7 prophecy fulfilled!

> 'Shout and be glad, Daughter Zion. For I am coming, and I will live among you,' declares the LORD. '<u>Many nations</u> will be joined with the LORD in that day and will become <u>my people</u>. I will live among you and you will know that the LORD Almighty has sent me to you. The LORD will inherit Judah as his portion in the holy land and will again choose <u>Jerusalem</u>' (Zech. 2:10-12).

So Jerusalem is again favored, but this time it's the nations (Gentiles)

joined as part of Jerusalem, the New Jerusalem. Hear the apostle Paul.
> So in Christ Jesus you are all children of God through faith, for all of you who were baptized into Christ have clothed yourselves with Christ. There is neither Jew nor Gentile, neither slave nor free, nor is there male and female, for you are all one in Christ Jesus. <u>If you belong to Christ, then you are Abraham's seed</u>, and heirs according to the promise (Gal. 3:26-29).

You are Abraham's seed! Did God reject his people? Did his promises to Israel fail? The classic unbeliever's question is, 'Why didn't all the Jews believe when Jesus came?' For the same reason most Jews didn't believe through the OT history! The promise of God was only ever for a remnant.

It's not for me to say how many ethnic Jews will be saved from now on. I hope it's many, but not all Israel are Israel (Rom. 9:6). People who read the OT for the first time are shocked. How many of God's people were faithful? How many wanted to worship the golden calf? And throughout OT history how many of the Israelites really believed at *any time?* What about during the times of the kings? King after king led Israel into idolatry. Only a remnant was faithful. This was Paul's great argument in Romans. God's promise to the Jews never failed, because the Lord only promised a remnant would be saved (Isa. 1:9). Elijah was so despondent he thought he was the only believer left in all Israel. The Lord had to rebuke him and say that he still had faithful people in Israel. *I still have my 7000 who have not bowed the knee to Baal.* Paul also argues in Romans there is a remnant of faithful. And the Lord used that faithful remnant of Jews to carry salvation to the world!

In fact, stop picking on the Jews. Can't you see that Israel is like a microcosm of the whole of humanity? It's a narrow road that leads to life and only a few find it. Most people will reject the Messiah. Today we see Israel's history replicated in the population of 'Christian' countries, people who have had all the privileges of hearing the gospel of Christ but reject the good news of Jesus.

What we have here in 7:4-8 is ethnic Israel who trusted in their Messiah, joined by the grafted-in Gentiles. Just as the temple wall in Rev. 21 is 144 cubits, with Jew and Gentile as the complete people of God, the 144,000 (in the 1000s shows a great multitude) here are God's people, still going through tribulation on earth.

What was the answer to the question at the end of Rev. 6: *Who can stand?* Who is the true Israel? For those first reading this Revelation from John in those churches, both Jew and Gentile believers, seeing these 12 tribes without the idolaters Dan and Ephraim is massive. Obviously, this can't be a literal 12 tribes, but maybe instead it's preaching to me? What was the big issue at stake in those seven churches? Idolatry! The trade guilds, worldly pressure and false teaching! Idolatry in worship at Pergamum. The sexual immorality. Who can stand? Or more to the point. Can we stand?

The answer is this. You can stand if you have the seal, the Holy Spirit who moved you to trust in Christ. If you have the Messiah of Israel, then you are joined to the people of God. Then you will put down your idols because the Holy Spirit in you will move you to repentance and to find your all in Jesus. You who were foreigners are now what? Part of the commonwealth of Israel (Eph. 2:12). We are sealed with the same Holy Spirit. How can the two be one with Israel? By believing in the one Messiah of Israel. Jesus the Christ!

Study Questions

1. Where are the 144,000?

2. What arguments for and against could you make for the 144,000 being exclusively *ethnic* Jews?

3. What arguments are there for the 12 tribes being literal or symbolic?

4. Does the promise of God point to a separate future for Jew and Gentile? If not, how would you argue that from Scripture?

5. How do God's promises to Abraham figure in this text?

6. Who are the servants of God in 7:3?

7. If the church is the New Jerusalem, did God's promise to Israel fail?

25
The Great Tribulation
(Revelation 7:9-14)

When the JWs knock on your door next time, what will you tell them about the 144,000? I took a stab at trying to understand who those 144,000 were, and I disagreed with the JWs and said the 144,000 was a symbolic number representing all who trusted in the Jewish Messiah.

So why didn't Rev. 7 just say believers, Jew and Gentile, instead of 144,000 with 12 tribes? In one sense, it did, when it said *servants of our God*. But the main reason is so that even Gentile believers, as well as Jews, can be assured. That is, if you trust in the Messiah, even you Gentile believers are grafted into Israel, and are heirs of all the promises of Israel along with your Jewish brothers and sisters. Hold fast, you *can* stand because you have the Holy Spirit and you are joined to God's people. *You will make it through the tribulation!*

So if the 144,000 symbolize the complete number of God's people on earth, then they are what we call the church militant. They are still fighting the good fight, going through the tribulation. We noted last time that 12 x 12 in the 1000s would be familiar to John in that the number 1000 is a basic military division in the camp of Israel (Num. 31:4-5). These 1000s are in a military battle of a spiritual nature. They are not in heaven yet. Several scholars have even noted the similarity of the structure of numbering the tribes in divisions of 12,000, replicating the armies of Israel. That would help build our case that this is the church militant. God's people, Jew and Gentile who believe in the Messiah, are still battling it out down below. They are not the church triumphant; that's the church in heaven.

After the terrible scene in 6:12-17 with the Day of Judgment and people fleeing in terror, the question was asked, *Who can stand?* And after reading about the struggles in the seven churches which included a lack of love, lukewarmness, immorality, and compromise, we might think that hardly anyone can stand. It's a narrow road that leads to life. Maybe the JWs are right. Will there be only 144,000 in heaven? Or less? How many people are really going to make it? John might well have asked that question ... until he saw this next shot.

> After this I looked and there before me was a great multitude that <u>no one could count</u>, from every nation, tribe, people and language, <u>standing before the throne</u> and before the Lamb. They were wearing white robes and were holding palm branches in their hands (7:9).

Where is this multitude? Standing before the throne in heaven! So much for only 144,000 in heaven! The JWs should have looked at this verse ... **a great multitude that no one could count** ... Beyond counting!

Also note these believers are from *every* nation, which must include the Jewish believers in Jesus as well, because they are *from every nation, tribe, people and language*. And where are they all together? **Standing before the throne and in front of the Lamb. They were wearing white robes and were holding palm branches in their hands.**

You know how some people like to wave flags on the side of the road as the Pope's cavalcade passes? Or are you the person behind the Pope-mobile honking and yelling, 'Will you move that heap of junk so I can get past!'? But many love to be at the roadside of a famous person passing. Well, they did in the first century too. And it wasn't flags or banners they were waving. Remember this scene?

> The next day the great crowd that had come for the festival heard that Jesus was on his way to Jerusalem. They took <u>palm branches</u> and went out to meet him, shouting, 'Hosanna!' 'Blessed is he who comes in the name of the Lord!' 'Blessed is the king of Israel!' (John 12:12-13).

They were waving **palm branches**! Palm branches are the sign of victory, which was Jesus' triumphal march then. Well, now in heaven you get palm branches supplied. Everyone gets one, because this is the great victory over death, sin and hell by the one on the throne and the Lamb, thus 7:9 says they wear *white robes of purity*. They are washed clean. Try and picture yourself as a member of one of those seven churches that first received this book of Revelation. You've just read the letters where Jesus rebuked you (Rev. 2-3). You are there in Sardis and you see this scene of people in heaven wearing white robes and you recall: *the one who is victorious will, like them, be dressed in white* (3:5).

So here you are, struggling away, wondering if you are going to make it through the tribulation of persecution, and then you come to this scene, and you see those you knew from Sardis who have died in the Lord. They are dressed in white! Look at this! All of God's people are in white. They made it! Victorious! The message is that if we hold fast to the Lord we'll be dressed in white too.

> And they cried out in a loud voice: 'Salvation belongs to our God, who sits on the throne, and to the Lamb' (7:10).

All nations and tongues are there. So how can they all sing together if they speak different languages? Did they all learn English because we know this song and it's in English, *Salvation Belongs to our God*? But this text was originally in Greek, so do we all have to learn Greek by the time we get to heaven? Maybe that's why there will only be 144,000? No, the reason they all know the language is because what we have here is a picture of the great reversal of the judgment at the Tower of Babel. What happened there? God brings judgment on the earth and divides the people for their rebellion by separating them by languages. What we have here is the joining together again of the people with one language to praise God. And the angels respond…

> All the angels were standing around the throne and around the elders and the four living creatures. They fell down on their faces before the throne and worshiped God, saying: 'Amen! Praise and glory and wisdom and thanks and honor and power and strength be to our God for ever and ever. Amen!' (7:11-12).

There is that symbolic number seven again, meaning *completion* in relation to God. Where is it? Count the number of ways God is praised. It's sevenfold: **praise, glory, wisdom, thanks, honor, power, and strength.** Complete praise and glory …

Rev. 7:9 told us the Lamb is at the center, again a symbol to describe Jesus. Jesus won't literally look like a slain lamb in heaven. But this symbol reminds us that in his resurrection body, the only visible marks of the old life are those wounds of the cross, just as he bore in his risen glorified body. 'Look at my hands and feet' (Luke

24:39). Surely that contributes as to why you and everyone else in heaven will spontaneously exclaim **salvation belongs to our God.** When you see the one with those marks that were for you, then you will fully know, and you will be fully known. It was all of him and his glory and mercy at the *cross!* Who sent his Son? Who took away your sin at the cross? Who put you in your exact time and place? How did you just happen to grow up where you heard the gospel? How was it that the trials you went through brought you to where you are now before the throne? It was him all along. It was all a plan. *Salvation belongs to our God and unto the Lamb! All praise, glory, wisdom, thanks, honor, power and strength.*

In 7:10 the angels also join in. What are they so excited about? Well they have been personally involved in this salvation and have also seen it was all of God ...

> Are not all angels ministering spirits sent to serve those who will inherit salvation? (Heb. 1:14).

Angels have a personal interest in salvation and have had since the beginning of creation. Since the beginning at the fall and through the ages, they have been waiting for this time. How long do angels live? Answer: Forever. They don't die. They are not like human beings who have sinned and will die. So think about that in relation to them being ministering spirits, serving those who will inherit salvation. They have been doing that since the fall. They were there when Adam fell! Devastating. Adam dies, but the angels don't. They were there when the first murder is committed, when Cain kills his brother. Then in the flood of Noah's time the whole world gets judged. It's not looking good, there are only a few people saved. And then on throughout history with the calling of Abraham, there is hope. But then Abraham lied and compromised. But God keeps on working his plan of salvation. And the angels are there through all this, throughout Israel's time and all their failures. Throughout all the kings and the apostasy of Israel. They were there during the exile. Remember how they ministered to Jesus in his struggles? (Matt. 4:11, Luke 22:43). And then they were there at the cross.

It hasn't been smooth sailing for the angels. Remember one third of the angels fell with Satan. There are fallen angels who have literally demonized the world, who are trying to cut off this salvation. So they have been warring against each other for thousands of years. *A war over the souls of those who would be saved* has been going on for century after century as the gospel goes forth throughout the world. And just when Satan and his demons were trying to stop *you* from coming to know Jesus and leading you into such turmoil or temptation or the wrong path, God directed his angels to spare you, to minister to you.

So after all this, now the angels explode in praise as well saying … Amen! Salvation is all of God. All wisdom, power and strength. The wisdom of God. He knew what he was doing, and he had the power and strength to carry it out. So when the final victory happens, Christians in heaven can finally see it. They are no longer living by faith but by sight. Sometimes you come to church or you pray and it's hard to connect to the joy of the Lord because you are battling this world each day with all the stress and strain. But when you get to heaven and see that Lamb who was slain, that is reality. Then you see without distraction. That is why Rev. 7 is written for you. It's not irrelevant for Christians, relating only to some future time. It's written for the church age to say, "Hold fast in tribulation". Look up to where you are going. Here is a picture of that reality! Praising God, free from all the worries of this life that drag us down. Those things are not reality. The reality is praising God.

Salvation belongs to our God. Those words are an offence to every other religion and human system, including the cults of Christianity. They all say salvation is of man. Do enough good stuff to be saved. Roman Catholics say, 'Believe in Jesus', but you also have to measure up and be a 'good Catholic'. The Mormons say in the Book of Mormon: *'It is by grace that we are saved, after all we can do'* (2 Nephi 25:23). The human heart does not want to be humbled enough to express that salvation is *fully* of God. Eat of the fruit and you will be like God. You will not surely die. You can save yourself. It's the great cry of humanity. How do you expect to get to heaven? 'I've been a good person.' 'I'm not as bad as some.' 'I've been a good Christian.' I! I! I! Salvation belongs to *me!* It's about me, not God's mercy. That is a sure-fire recipe for hell. The human heart refuses to acknowledge the simple fact that salvation belongs to our God.

You were the helpless sinner at the precipice, ready to be cast down into the pit. Now in heaven you can see the past. The shaky old footbridge of life you had been stumbling along, like in those movies with those old footbridges across the great canyon, slats broken, rotting, and you are ready to fall through into the everlasting fire. You had to walk across that bridge of life and could have slipped through. But God saved you! He sent his Son to take away your sin and we just read in 7:3 that he gave us his Holy Spirit so we could believe. Sealed! It is all of God! Sing it! Salvation belongs to our God!

In heaven, no one is arguing with that. Angels and humans alike sing: Salvation belongs to our God. The apostle John is watching all of this on film and then …

> Then one of the elders asked me, 'These in white robes—who are they, and where did they come from?' I answered, 'Sir, you know.' And he said, 'These are they who have come out of the great tribulation; they have washed their robes and made them white in the blood of the Lamb' (7:13-14).

… they have washed their robes and made them white in the blood of the Lamb. How do you get something white from washing it in blood? Remember with these images in Revelation we are dealing with symbols of an apocalyptic vision. We understand that the representation of the blood of the Lamb symbolizes Jesus' cross. What can wash away my sin? Nothing but the blood of Jesus!

If Christians are raptured out *before* the tribulation and only unbelievers are *left behind* to go through the tribulation, then this text gives us a bit of a problem. Did you notice it says **these are they who have <u>come out</u> of the great tribulation?** In other words, Christians must have gone *through* the great tribulation!

In fairness to those with the rapture view, they would say these people in heaven are not all Christians in general, but only those who have come to faith *after* the Christians were raptured out. So out of those who got left behind, some come to faith. They didn't respond to the gospel during the church age, but after the Christians got raptured out they rethought their position. You could understand why, if suddenly all the Christians in the world disappeared. 'Where did all the Christians go?' All the lukewarm 'Christians' left behind would be saying, 'That rapture theology must be right after all. Better get right with Jesus.' Who wouldn't? I think that would be extremely convincing evidence to unbelievers, a great sign indeed. No faith required. How could you miss it!

So it's understandable why in this view John MacArthur says of this text that this seven-year tribulation would be a time when more people come to faith than ever before.[28] Why wouldn't they with such an obvious sign? But doesn't this give people a reason to mock the urgency of Jesus' words in the parables about coming to faith *before* he returns (Matt. 25)? And his words to *be ready* (Matt. 24:44)? Be ready for what? To change my mind if it turns out the rapture idea was right. Quite frankly, when skeptics hear this (including myself before I came to faith) they can mock any need to come to faith and just say, 'No worries, I'll just wait for my second chance at the seven-year tribulation and if it turns out you are right, then I'll be one of the unprecedented number coming to faith.'

But as we look at this picture in Rev. 7, does it really look like it is trying to convey a select group who were left behind who came to faith separate from the Christian church (that has been raptured out)? The language seems to be clearly a picture of heaven filled with all the fullness of believers from everywhere, every tribe, nation and tongue. It's **beyond counting!** It doesn't read like a limited group of people who come to faith *after* the church age.

Other Futurist scholars say this scene in 7:9-17 is not heaven. These worshipers and angels are not before the heavenly throne, but the throne on earth during the earthly millennial reign. However, it seems that by the time Rev. 7 finishes it has all the clear hallmarks of the heavenly scene which are repeated in Rev. 21, with God wiping away every tear. And with those heavenly angels, isn't this is a picture of heaven? Look at 7:11 which describes the **elders** and **living creatures.** This scene is a wider angle of the same scene we saw in Rev. 4 when we were told John got a look into heaven!

So if this is heaven, then what is the massive implication? Christians go through the great tribulation! *'These are they who have <u>come out</u> of the great tribulation...'*

Some Futurists point out that 7:14 adds the adjective *great*. So it's a *great* tribulation, as though this adjective distinguishes it from the tribulation John speaks of in 1:9. This kind of distinction sounds a little suspicious, almost reminiscent of the JWs trying to distinguish between 'Mighty God' and 'Almighty God', as though they are two different Gods. But Jesus settles this difference for us anyway, when in his speech on the end times he uses both *tribulation* and *great*

---

[28] John MacArthur, *The MacArthur Study Bible*, (Nashville: Word Publishing, 1997) p. 2002

tribulation interchangeably to mean the same thing (Matt. 24:9, 21, 29). The implication is that there is no rapture *before* the tribulation, and importantly, no getting left behind for a second chance! Believers caught up to be with the Lord? Absolutely! But that will be it! No second chance for those left behind. The very text that is used to justify the rapture in 1 Thessalonians, seems to be saying it is anything but a secret or invisible return of Jesus and a secret rapture of saints (with those left behind for another opportunity). Rather, it is the Day of Judgment.

> For the Lord himself will come down from heaven, with a loud command, with the voice of the archangel and with the trumpet call of God, and the dead in Christ will rise first. After that, we who are still alive and are left will be caught up together with them in the clouds to meet the Lord in the air. And so we will be with the Lord <u>forever</u>. ... for you know very well that the day of the Lord will come like a thief in the night. While people are saying, 'Peace and safety,' <u>destruction</u> will come on them <u>suddenly</u>, as labor pains on a pregnant woman, and they will <u>not escape</u> (1 Thess. 4:16-5:3).

This is it! For those left behind it's judgment! *Destruction!* No escape! If Rev. 7 is a picture of all of God's people in heaven (not a select few), what does that say about second chances? The time to come to know Christ is now! There *are no* second chances, nor are there signs and wonders such as Christians suddenly floating up or disappearing and you get left behind with time to change your mind. We are in tribulation and *today is the day of salvation!* When the Lord takes us up to meet him in the air, the only thing for those left behind is judgment! When he returns he will cut them to pieces (Luke 12:46).

So the tribulation is what we are experiencing now. Yes, the Western world is shielded from what goes on in most of the world and through history (for now). Yes, the tribulation may well yet increase in intensity. But how much does it escalate? I don't know. We could be in the middle or near the end of it right now. Jesus said his return will be unexpected.

But all Christians must go through the tribulation in different degrees and in different ways. *Through many hardships we must enter the kingdom* (Acts 14:22). In the original Greek language, the word translated as *hardships* is the same word translated in 7:14 as *tribulation*. It's also the same word when John says at the beginning of this letter in 1:9. *I am your brother and companion in the <u>tribulation</u>* (suffering). In fact, Jesus told us all to expect this tribulation.

> 'I have told you these things, so that in me you may have peace. In this world <u>you will have trouble</u> …' (John 16:33).

Again, the word translated *trouble* is the same Greek word translated *tribulation* at 7:14. And what do you think Paul meant when he used the same word for *tribulation* in …

> Who shall separate us from the love of Christ? Shall trouble or <u>hardship</u> [tribulation] or persecution or famine or nakedness or danger or sword? (Rom. 8:35).

Look at Paul's list of tribulations in that full passage and he might well have been describing the four horsemen of Rev. 6. We have all faced at least some of the trials described in those seven churches: persecution, temptation to compromise, idols, false teachers, Satan's attacks from without and within, and conflict. This is the tribulation described in those seven churches. But what we see in these verses is the victory *after* the tribulation. That's why there are palm branches. It harkens back to the OT Feast of Booths/Tabernacles, with its palms celebrating God's provision *through* the wilderness. Through the great tribulation! Well, we are in the wilderness right now. And we have to go through it.

This means that this picture of heaven in Rev. 7 has immediate pastoral relevance to Christians. If we push the tribulation to some future time which has no relevance to Christians, then this would not speak pastorally to Christians throughout the ages. But if 7:14 is a picture of Christians who have come through the tribulation in the church age, try to think what it would mean to believers, from the time of those first readers in those seven churches going through such tribulations, such as having to bow down to Caesar at the threat of your life. Indeed, picture Christians in every century going through tribulation and seeing this victory, white-robe wearing, palm-waving victory, singing praises to God. Standing! Jesus wins! Picture it yourself. This is meant to convey a great source of encouragement. Blessed are *all* who read this and take it to heart, all who have been wrestling in tribulation, wondering: *Who can stand?*

And *who can stand?* Do you sometimes wonder if heaven will be a lonely place? Look around you? How many people in society are really clinging to Jesus? Jesus said himself *narrow is the road and only a few find it*. And then we look to the church and it's in a mess! How many people in church are going to make it? I wonder if the people in the seven churches thought the same thing. When they read Jesus' words that they were backsliding, lukewarm, even dead, and Satan was attacking. They might wonder if only the super-saints will make it. What about the idolatry of Israel in the OT? How many of them made it? But when John sees this picture, what an encouragement, what a strengthening of the church on earth, the limited but symbolic number (144,000), the church militant. When he sees the whole church triumphant in heaven, there are so many people you can't even count them!

Also notice that in 7:9 John sees all the nations represented in this picture of heaven. We will not all be clones void of any individual appearance that we had in this life. Did you notice John recognized different ethnic backgrounds? Who you are as a person is not lost, including all of your individual nuances. The heaven John sees is so rich! Not negative.

So you'll have ethnic identity without racism. Memories of the past, but without the sorrow or regret. All that is good will remain. All that is wrong and evil will not come to mind. The NT speaks of relationships reunited in heaven and of recognizing one another. We are not to grieve like those who have no hope. We will be together again (1 Thess. 4:13-17). There is also the promise of sitting down with Abraham, Isaac and Jacob (Matt. 8:11). We remember and recognize who they are. We will recognize people we haven't even met before, as the apostle Paul says *we come to know fully, as we are fully known*. So heaven is more and better, not less! Remember what the apostle Paul said to the Philippians? *For to me, to live is Christ and to die is gain* (Phil. 1:21).

So heaven is more of what is good in this life and a release from the bad things of the past. Perhaps it's a little like when you were a child and you had fears that greatly troubled you, like the bogie man, or you had a fear of the sound that water made going down the plug hole after a bath. It was once such an issue, but now it doesn't even come to mind (I hope).

The point is that everything good will have continuity and

everything bad will not. By the time we get to the end of Rev. 7 we will see everything that hurts, or causes pain and trauma is forgotten and every tear is wiped away. And talk about rejoicing! No wonder they are waving those palm branches around. Look again at what John saw ...

> After this I looked and there before me was a great multitude that no one could count, from every nation, tribe, people and language, standing before the throne and before the Lamb. They were wearing white robes and were holding palm branches in their hands (7:9).

John could see the future of all who believed and persevered through tribulation, pain, and struggle against the world, flesh and devil. The only question we need to ask is, did John see you there? This is a picture of that heavenly victory. Were you in that multitude, as John's eyes panned across the crowd? Maybe you didn't get a front row spot or maybe someone's palm branch covered your face as he looked. But if you are really saved, then you were in that future crowd that John saw. You are there, aren't you? Have you trusted in the Lamb fully? What reality are you living right now? Are you caught up in the things of this world, or are you living for your destiny, holding fast through tribulation? Remember, Jesus wins.

Study Questions

1. What is the church militant and how is that portrayed in Rev. 7?

2. What is the church triumphant and where does it appear in Rev. 7?

3. Give reasons for the significance of being dressed in white for the seven churches.

4. In what way could this text be an encouragement to Christians?

5. What would motivate the angels to be in praise with the saints?

6. Give several examples of why the phrase 'salvation belongs to our God' is disputed.

7. What are the implications of 7:14 for the tribulation?
8. Will we recognize each other in heaven?

9. If you can picture John seeing you in that multitude, what effect would that have on your life now?

26
The Great Reversal
(Revelation 7:15-17)

If you are going through the great tribulation and are fighting temptation, isolation, persecution and stress, then what is in store for you? Immeasurably more than you could have asked or imagined.

Those who washed their robes in the blood of the Lamb, who did not shrink from their testimony in Jesus, who rejected the world and held fast to Jesus and him alone, they come through the great tribulation. But what becomes of them then?

> <u>Therefore</u>, 'they are before the throne of God and serve him day and night in his temple; and he who sits on the throne will shelter them with his presence' (7:15).

What will heaven be like? Boring? Just standing in one place waving your palm branch? No! Look. They **serve him.** Here we see heaven both in its activity and bliss. We couldn't have one without the other. We see the people before the throne of God and *serving* him **day and night.** That not only indicates activity, but the joy that it is to be in his presence. God is what makes heaven, heaven. It's a return to the Garden of Eden where man and woman literally walked with God in the cool of the day ... after a day of gardening. It's that closeness again, returning to Eden.

We see this in the following verses. The beauty of Eden was interrupted by Satan and man's sin which hurtled us into a history of suffering and turmoil. What can we do about it? It's too late for us to do anything. Our sin history unfolded in its evil. How can even God reverse that? This is what people have been saying throughout history. If God is there, he can't be good because he allows evil and suffering and he can't possibly undo what's already been done. But look at this! **... he who sits on the throne will spread his tent over them.** The original Greek word literally says that he *tabernacled* over them. A fascinating choice of words. The tabernacle was the tent used by Israel as the forerunner to the temple. Now the temple itself is mentioned, but it's the heavenly temple. No longer the earthly shadows and copies.

> But when Christ came as high priest of the good things that are already here, he went through the <u>greater and more perfect tabernacle</u> that is <u>not made with human hands</u>, that is to say, not a part of this creation ... For Christ did not enter a sanctuary made with human hands that was <u>only a copy of the true one</u>; he entered heaven itself, now to appear for us in God's presence (Heb. 9:11,24).

Revelation reveals this in fullness. The true temple (not the copy) is spelt out as the Lord and his presence with his people later ...

> I did not see a temple in the city, because the Lord God Almighty and the Lamb are its temple (21:22).

So again, bear with me if you have the view that the Lord is going to set up an earthly tabernacle or temple in the future. Revelation (and Hebrews) is saying the temple fulfillment is not another physical temple, but Jesus and all his people in his presence. The temple was the way into the presence of God. Now in heaven the fulfillment is the true temple, Jesus and his people ...

What would 7:15 have meant to John as a devout Jew who hoped for the fulfillment of the promises to Israel? He knew the earthly temple had been destroyed in AD 70. So if John is writing this in the AD 90s and the great temple has been destroyed, does John think we can no longer go into the presence of our Lord? What does this scene mean to John when it says, 'the Lord tabernacled over them'? John knows the curtain of the temple tore in two when Jesus died on the cross, opening access for all into God's presence. The temple was the place to enter into the presence of the Lord. But now here it is. Jesus is the temple! He is the way into God. John knew it from his own observation in his gospel ...

> The Jews replied, 'It has taken forty-six years to build this temple, and you are going to raise it in three days?' But the temple he had spoken of was his body (John 2:20-21).

Jesus is the true temple! The Lamb *is* the temple. *He* is the way into

God's presence. It was not coincidence the temple was destroyed in AD 70, because there was no more need for an earthly temple once Jesus completed his work.

So how powerful is this statement? They *serve him day and night in his temple; and he who sits on the throne will spread his tent over them.* How personal is this? It's like a hen with her wings over her chicks (Luke 13:34). But this is the One on the throne. God himself! *He* will spread his tent over them. *He* will tabernacle over them. But for John it's more. It's the climax of what Israel looked for in the future. What is the fulfillment of the tabernacle? The temple. The presence of God. Now it's reached its goal. God himself tabernacling over his people.

Look how rich 7:15 is if you are the apostle John, a Jew in the first century brought up with the temple and priests serving in the temple day and night. And what does John see in 7:15? This is surely an allusion to the OT priesthood ... *and serve him day and night in his temple*. That is the priesthood of Israel. But now it's the priesthood of all believers with all the people of God, Jew and Gentile, from every nation! We've already been introduced in Revelation to Christians now being a kingdom and priests in 1:6 and 5:10, which pointed us back to Israel 'you will be for me a kingdom and priests' (Exodus 19:6), but now applied to the church in heaven.

See also Exodus 19:10,14 with the people 'washing their garments'. And in Leviticus 8:30, the garments were sprinkled in blood to serve God in the tabernacle. Moses consecrated the priests of Israel by sprinkling the blood of sacrifices on them and the altar (Exod. 29:10-21). Now what is happening here in this heavenly temple? They have washed their robes in blood (7:14). It's all so rich for John. Israel, your temple rituals were not irrelevant! They are found in the Lamb! All the promises of God are 'yes' and 'Amen' in Jesus (2 Cor. 1:20). And the complete redeemed people of God, Jew and Gentile are together! A kingdom and priests and God tabernacles over them. Here is the promise fulfilled ...

> I will make a covenant of peace with them; it will be an everlasting covenant. I will establish them and increase their numbers, and I will put my sanctuary among them forever. My dwelling place will be with them; I will be their God, and they will be my people. Then the nations will know that I the LORD make Israel holy, when my sanctuary is among them forever (Ezek. 37:26-28).

How long is forever? Not just 1000 years! God tabernacles over them *forever*. The nations and Israel are joined. This prophecy for Israel is fulfilled in 7:15. What was John thinking when he comes to this next verse?

> Never again will they hunger; never again will they thirst. The sun will not beat upon them, nor any scorching heat (7:16).

Can you imagine how John's mind went back to his childhood Scripture memorizing classes? ...

> They will neither <u>hunger nor thirst</u>, nor will the desert heat or the <u>sun beat upon them</u>. He who has compassion on them will guide them and lead them beside springs of water (Isa. 49:10).

And then in Revelation ...

> For the Lamb at the center of the throne will <u>be their shepherd</u>; 'he will <u>lead them to springs of living water</u>.' 'And God will wipe away every tear from their eyes' (7:17).

The Lord is my **shepherd**. He leads me beside **springs of living water.** This fulfillment picture draws all of Israel's hopes together. All human desires are brought together. All our wants ... *The Lord is my shepherd; I shall not be in want.* No more hunger or thirst. Can you picture this? Our life in tribulation is characterized by 'want'. Restlessness, or lack of rest, but always 'want'. We are never filled. Some of us have different hungers, passions, and longings, but we all have this in common—we want. Do you hunger? Thirst? That is what it is like being part of the 144,000, the church militant. Fighting it out below. Hungering. Wanting. This is why we need the sealing of the Holy Spirit as a deposit, a down payment on what is to come, because sometimes in this time of tribulation our wanting and suffering can nearly overwhelm us. But this picture is extraordinary. It's beyond comprehension for us that in the countless number in victory, in glory, you will no longer want. What is it like, to no longer be in want? Why all this bliss? **For the Lamb at the center of the throne will be their shepherd.**

The Lamb is at the center. It's Jesus! Jesus didn't just come to save us like those old westerns where the hero rides into the poor Mexican village and the Cisco Kid rescues the oppressed and rides out again. Jesus came to save us, but also to stay *with us*. He came to tabernacle among us. *The word became flesh and made his dwelling* [literally 'tabernacled'] *among us* (John 1:14). He became a man and remains a man forever in relationship with us. He is our spouse. It is the perfect relationship that no mere earthly human relationship could ever replicate in this life. God became a man, and yes, he is still Lord, but also a man we can relate to and yet serve as our God. It's an extraordinary thing.

He is also the one who meets our every desire. No more hunger or thirst. Why? Because of the *springs of living water* and being face to face with the Lord, having him spread his tent over you and **wiping away every tear from their eyes.** Can you see the personal touch of these words? It's not just 'no more tears', but *God will personally wipe away every tear from their eyes.*

And those *springs of living water?* The Lord is my shepherd. I shall not be in want. He leads me beside quiet waters. Spiritually and physically satisfied to the point that we want for nothing. Springs! Of *living* water! It's a return to Eden where the rivers flowed out of Eden. He meets our every need. John could remember these words of Jesus.

> Then Jesus declared, 'I am the bread of life. He who comes to me will never go hungry, and he who believes in me will never be thirsty' (John 6:35).

John would have also remembered ...

> He will swallow up death forever. The Sovereign LORD will <u>wipe away the tears from all faces</u>; ... (Isa. 25:8).

There was the promise in the OT and now in 7:17 *God will wipe away every tear from their eyes.* Have you experienced tears? Brought on by the evil horsemen, the riders of death, disease and conflict? The trials of this fallen world touch each one of us in some way. But this is the beautiful picture. What a personal touch. All the trial and tribulation you went through is finished. It's over. You wondered how you could keep going when the pain is so great. Some suffer depression so badly they just want to give up. How can you keep going? Some suffer tears in their own private times. How can you endure? You are

going through the tribulation ... and you need a glimpse of this ...
And God will wipe away every tear from your eyes.

Every tear. What about all the past that still hurts? Answer: Every tear. What about regrets? Every tear! Some ask, 'Will there be anything that can be brought up to shame me?' Every tear means every possible thing that could cause you sorrow he will banish as he wipes away every tear. But look at those words. How incredible. Who will wipe away every tear from their eyes? It's God himself! Your heavenly Father. The Father from whom all fatherhood derives its name (Eph. 3:14). The perfect Father. Everything our earthly fathers could not live up to. Picture God the Father, like the perfect loving dad when you were young. He kneels in front of you to wipe away the tears. Or maybe your dad didn't do that? Well this one does! If you don't know what it is to be loved and comforted — you *will* if you are one of his.

What is the point of this part of Revelation? We have seen the 144,000 who in battle formation in divisions of 12,000 are the church militant. And this part in 7:9-17 is every bit as necessary for going through the battle ... to see the finish line ... to see this beauty. What is it saying? Why was this written? To whom was it written, for what purpose? It's from Jesus, to his servants, for Christians to see the final picture that Jesus wins! And the message? Hang in there through the tribulation! Don't give up. This will be yours as well. Finish the race! Tempted to give up? You need to see this. Can you see it by faith?

Can you see the Lord himself wiping away the tears from your own eyes? If you are a parent you've done that when your kids were little. What a picture. But this also tells us there *will* be tears while you are among the 144,000, the believers going through the battle below. But when you are in the midst of that uncountable number of people throughout history ... no more tears! What did Paul say?

> I consider that our present sufferings are not worth comparing with the glory that will be revealed in us (Rom. 8:18).

Not worth comparing. You ain't seen nothing yet! Once those tears are wiped away. In this tent, we groan until we are fully clothed (2 Cor. 5:1) ... More and more I see the answer to getting through this life and this tribulation is to get a picture of the end. The vindication. We look for vindication in this life. We have to let that go. Jesus is the only one who wins! You need to let go of those people who have troubled you, hurt you and criticized you. Our own failures. If you want justice and vindication now, or you are tempted to envy and rivalry, then repent! 1 Cor. 4:5 says all motives will be exposed, and yours will be too unless you repent. And when you trust in the Lord, then even the times you failed with wrong motives will be washed away like your tears.

It's strange how we are always looking forward, even from a young age. 'When I finish school, that's when I will start living.' Then you grow up and it's, 'When I find my life partner and get married.' Then, 'When I can have kids.' Then, 'When I can get rid of the kids!' Always looking forward. 'When I finish the week's work. The weekend!' 'When I get my holidays.' 'When I have made enough money to be comfortable.' 'When I can retire.' We are always waiting, waiting, waiting, always restless looking for the future. There is something in us that makes us never at rest. But all we have to do is wait just a little longer, because just up ahead is the rest that lasts forever.

It might seem weird to fix your eyes on the joy set before you or to set your hope fully on the grace to be given when Jesus Christ is revealed (1 Peter 1:13). But it's closer than you think. Life seems to drag, but then it's gone. Pray to see this picture in 7:17 by faith. The end that is the beginning. The more heavenly-minded you are, the more earthly-use you are! You are released from the worries of now. Just make sure you are walking with him now. Those who have done you wrong; let them go! Let people have their day. Jesus is the only victory that counts. Jesus wins and his people share the spoils of victory.

Now here is the picture of the Garden. The fall is reversed. Earlier in 7:10 we saw the tower of Babel reversed with all the people of the different languages able to sing the same song in one language. But what about the reversal of the greater catastrophe—the Garden of Eden itself? The complaint that has echoed down through history is: 'God can't do it. Maybe he can bring every deed into judgment (hell takes care of sin and sinners), but how can he bring a complete reversal for pain, sorrow, depression, anguish and torment that people have experienced? He can't really wipe away EVERY tear.' But that is exactly what Revelation is teaching us. In the end that is exactly what God will do. Every tear!

Study Questions

1. What are some of the ways the NT (apart from the book of Revelation) suggests the church has always been in tribulation?

2. Will heaven be boring? Explain.

3. Give reasons for the significance of being dressed in white for the seven churches.

4. How does this text speak of temple fulfillment?

5. What are the arguments for and against a physical temple rebuilding in this text and wider Revelation?

6. What OT texts does 7:16-17 draw on and what do they point to?

7. Is God wiping away every tear literal or figurative? What are the implications?

8. How could this text encourage Christians?

9. Does this text rebuke your Christian walk?

27
The Silence in Heaven
(Revelation 8:1-5)

The Master film director, Jesus, brought us along in this film all the way to the climax in the movie—the great and terrible end where we saw the whole world come under judgment raining down (6:12-17). We think of all the people who have been players in the movie. Remember how we got to know them and related to those people in the churches at Ephesus, Smyrna, Pergamum, Thyatira, Sardis, Philadelphia and Laodicea. How could they have survived the climax of the movie? Who can stand? Then we got that brilliant film director's interlude in the movie to retrace our steps, so we can be prepared for the end of the movie. The flashback over history. Until then we were not ready for the opening of the seventh seal. We needed to be prepared to be able to answer the question from the end of 6:17: *Who can stand?*

That is what Rev. 7 gave us. The flashback. The interlude. How could anyone, even the people of God stand, if judgment is so complete? The answer is the seal on the forehead. The seal of the Holy Spirit, who enabled you to believe in your mind (the forehead). These were the ones who inherited the promises of Israel, both Jew and Gentile, the 144,000. In fact, we were then given a beautiful picture of *their* future in heaven, after they had made it through the tribulation, and there they were, *standing!*

So now we are ready for the end of the movie, the opening of the seventh seal. We know who can stand. Those who have the seal of the Holy Spirit of God. Those who have the eternal armor. They are ready for Judgment Day. So after the interlude of Rev. 7, we begin Rev. 8 as a continuation from the opening of the sixth seal (at the end of Rev. 6), and Judgment Day! Now we come to the opening of the seventh and final seal.

> When he opened the seventh seal, there was silence in heaven for about half an hour (8:1).

Why silence? Some say it's silence because the seventh seal is empty and there is nothing in it. Others say the silence is God's rest. Still others say it's God's silence on Revelation as between the OT and NT. But if we think of this as a continuation, picking it up from the end of Rev. 6 with Judgment Day arriving, the Master film director (having given us that interlude in Rev. 7), now returns to the dramatic pause, unfolding the very judgment itself. The finality of it. Everyone is silent before God on that day. Certainly, this section climaxes with typical judgment language...

> Then the angel took the censer, filled it with fire from the altar, and hurled it on the earth; and there came peals of thunder, rumblings, flashes of lightning and an earthquake (8:5).

There is that familiar idea of God's judgment we see in OT texts. But before we get to the crescendo, it starts with silence ... **when he opened the seventh seal, there was silence in heaven for about half an hour.** Then the camera pans across and the apostle John follows the filming ...

> And I saw the seven angels who stand before God, and seven trumpets were given to them (8:2).

We are not told who these particular seven angels are (seven is the number of completion). Are these the seven angels of the seven churches? Remember those seven letters were addressed individually to seven angels of the respective churches. At the time, we asked who those angels were. Were they Pastors of the churches? Were they heavenly representatives of those churches? We are not told the details about these angels, so we won't try and fill in the blanks, but we do know God uses angels to execute his judgments (Exod. 12:23). At this stage, we are not told why they are to hold the seven trumpets. So we will hold that thought. Then the apostle John follows the movie as the camera pans across to ...

> Another angel, who had a golden censer, came and stood at the altar. He was given much incense to offer, with the prayers of all God's people, on the golden altar in front of the throne (8:3).

Some have said this angel is Jesus. But Jesus makes intercession for the saints, whereas this angel was 'given' incense, so it's not likely this is Jesus. But it's fascinating to follow the imagery in 8:3 in light of our prayers. Here we are in the very throne room of God in Revelation, and we see the prayers of God's people being taken up with incense to the throne of God. Think about what happens with those prayers of yours. You thought it was all about you and how well you pray, if you just feel that real connection or pray with the right words your prayers will reach heaven. But here the incense is sanctifying our prayers. What did the apostle Paul tell the church at Rome? ...

> In the same way, the Spirit helps us in our weakness. We do not know what we ought to pray for, but the Spirit himself intercedes for us through wordless groans (Rom. 8:26).

In fact, these prayers not only go to the throne room, but the angel takes the prayers and then takes them to God. We got into the wonder of this back in 5:8, but here is the close-up camera angle. Look at the detail of the imagery. The angel actually hands your prayer over to God. How is this for the personal touch of God handling your prayers ...

> The smoke of the incense, together with the prayers of God's people, went up before God from the <u>angel's hand</u> (8:4).

You can even see his hand! Your prayers are being handed over from the angel's hand to God. Those prayers weren't wasted! Sanctified, mixed with incense, and then personally handed on with a hand stretched out to God himself. If we could see this scene by faith, we would be kicking ourselves for not praying more. Prayer wasn't about how good we are, but simply about setting aside the time to pray. Here is an amazing look behind the curtain of God's personal room. It's a 'Behind the Scenes', 'The Making of...' This is an amazing scene. We see God personally handling our prayers! *If we are praying.* If not, we are tossing aside a gift from God. Do you want a gift from God? Well here it is: you are able to pray to the God of the universe and know that those prayers have been handed on personally.

But unlike the prayers back in 5:8, these prayers are a specific answer to a specific prayer. Remember the cries of the saints back in

6:9-11 ... I saw under the altar the souls of those who had been slain because of the word of God... 'How long, Sovereign Lord, holy and true, until you judge the inhabitants of the earth and avenge our blood? Where were they? Under the altar. Where are we now when these prayers are being presented and answered? **Another angel, who had a golden censer, came and stood at the altar** ...

God heard those prayers and cries for justice. 'How long O Lord?' Well, here is his answer. Their prayers were not forgotten. Here is your answer saint! What is the answer? The seventh seal! Judgment. Vindication. Truth has the victory. The persecuted are rewarded. Evil is punished. Judgment Day has arrived. Yes, the Lord heard those prayers and the **smoke of the incense, together with the prayers of God's people, went up before God from the angel's hand.**

Those prayers have now officially been taken before the Lord. The angel delivers them personally to God. They are accepted and sanctified by God. The people who prayed had offered their bodies as living sacrifices to follow the Lord and have prayed, 'how long?' Those who have remained faithful, in some cases even to death, see the final victory. They cried out from under the altar (6:9) their prayer reaches God, handed on personally at the altar (8:3). But now brace yourself, be careful what you pray for, you who prayed for an end to the evil of this world, because here is the terrifying answer to those very prayers. **Then the angel took the censer, filled it with fire from the altar, and hurled it on the earth; and there came peals of thunder, rumblings, flashes of lightning and an earthquake.**

Here is the final judgment. John recognizes the four terrors of thunder, rumblings, lightning and earthquake. A bit of Exodus 19:16,18, a bit of Psalm 77:18-19, Isaiah 29:6, Psalm 18:7-13 and Matthew 24:7-8. It's earthquakes that usher in the final judgment of God.

What an amazing thought. The sovereign Lord who determines all things, controls all things in his power, actually brings about the end of the world in response to the prayers of his lowly people. You could see the hand holding those prayers, and then what? Kaboom! ... *peals of thunder, rumblings, flashes of lightning and an earthquake*. How incredible to think God uses the prayers of his people to set off the very judgment of the universe. We think, 'What difference does my little prayer make anyway?' But it's all part of God's plan, and as soon as those prayers fill up the bowls, God is ready. God takes them from the angel's hand and boom! So speed his coming (2 Pet. 3:12)! Every time any Christian has ever prayed, 'Your kingdom come...' it's filled up closer to the full measure until the prayer bowl is full. The answer is here! God planned it all around the prayers of his people. Not one prayer has ever been lost. Never wasted. God uses this to bring about his purposes. God saves souls. But he has this eternal plan to use the prayers of his people. Does that make you want to pray for revival or lost loved ones? Pray and don't give up! This is how God plans the universe. It's all his doing, not ours, but he actually chooses to use us! Incredible! And now the picture here is of the end. The very Judgment of God.

Remember the final judgment commenced with the sixth seal back in 6:12-17. The sky rolled up. People were running but they couldn't hide, so terrified they wanted to die under falling rocks because of the wrath of the Lamb. So leave aside our movie interlude for a moment (Rev. 7: the flashback). What happens after the great day of wrath has come and there is nowhere to hide? Silence (8:1). Everyone is silent before God. The seventh seal is opened, the Judgment itself, and we realize this is what happens to those who do *not* have the seal on their foreheads.

What would the apostle John have been thinking when he saw these things, as someone brought up on the OT Scriptures? Silence is mentioned many times in the OT, and it's often in the context of the LORD as the holy judge of the nations.

> Be silent before me, you islands! Let the nations renew their strength! Let them come forward and speak; let us meet together at the place of judgment (Isa. 41:1).

> Be still before the Lord, all mankind, because he has roused himself from his holy dwelling (Zech. 2:13).

No more running. Be still. Be silent. The seventh seal is not empty, as some would have it. This is the finality of Judgment. Of course 6:12-17 was the final Judgment. What could have been more final than that? The destruction of the sun, moon and stars. Did you see those people at the end of 6:12-17 running, trying to hide, wanting the rocks to fall on them? But there is nowhere to hide.

So now they appear before Almighty God! The wrath of the Lamb! Be silent! The ruler and true king you rejected is seen to be what he claimed all along. Jesus is Lord. Jesus wins. And no one is talking back. How we heard it a thousand times, that chat show interviewer's line. 'And what do you think you will say to God when you meet him?' 'I would have a few questions for him. I would ask him why he allowed all this evil in the world.' But now the day arrives. And there is *silence*. You are not asking that question because you have the answer before your eyes. He *doesn't* allow evil. Here he is, bringing it all to judgment. And then you are next to step up to give account.

It's like being in the crowd when they ask for volunteers. That is not the time to raise your hand and object. You go silent. You even sink into your seat. But you can't sink far enough. And then your name gets called out anyway. You can't run anywhere! How much worse when you are in a courtroom? You are silent in the courtroom waiting for your name to be called — to face the Judge! Have you ever been in court? Even in a human court those guys who think they are so tough are like jelly in front of a human judge. And what about all those people who were going to tell God a thing or two when they meet him? What do they want to say now? Nothing. There is nothing but silence.

Bertrand Russell (1872-1970) was a famous atheist and one of the founders of analytical philosophy. Richard Dawkins and other famous atheists (and not so famous, like Philip Adams), love to quote Bertrand Russell, especially this one when someone once apparently asked Russell at a meeting:

> 'Lord Russell, what will you say when you die and are brought face to face with your Maker?' He replied without hesitation: 'God,' I shall say, 'God, why did you make the evidence for your existence so insufficient?'

That sounded so clever back then, but now the Day has arrived and look! In the crowd. It's Bert! Bertrand is there! But in silence. He is not speaking. He doesn't ask God why God hid himself because by now Bertrand already knows the answer to his question. Because Bertrand has been waiting in the holding cell in hell since 1970 when he died, and in his cell, they have been replaying on the loud speaker…

> … people, who suppress the truth by their wickedness, since what may be known about God is plain to them, because God has made it plain to them. For since the creation of the world God's invisible qualities—

his eternal power and divine nature—have been <u>clearly seen</u>, being understood <u>from what has been made</u>, so that people are <u>without excuse</u> ... [<u>without excuse</u> ... <u>without excuse</u>] (Rom. 1:18-20).

Over and over again. All the evidence was there. They suppressed the truth by their wickedness. God proved his existence from the things that were made so that man is without excuse. Without excuse. Without excuse. Without excuse.

So what does Bertrand Russell say to God when he gets to that Judgment seat? Nothing. He is silent. Anyone else got a question for God? The world is silent.

It's silent for half-an-hour. That's not necessarily a literal time any more than other numbers in Revelation that are used to teach us wider truth. So what might this be teaching us? Half-an-hour tells us lots. In one way, it's a short span of time, but standing before the Judge in silence, it's also an incredibly *long* time.

Remember the apostle John is seeing this movie unfold. Now the pictures are there on the screen but the dialogue in the movie has gone completely silent. John is watching the movie and there is silence ... seconds. Minutes. Half-an-hour! The dread. How long is this tension! The Judgment. All those who ran but couldn't hide, they are all there. All those who were confident that they would be able to justify themselves. Now it's just dark silence.

Does dark silence remind you of anything? Think of the grim, dark silence when Jesus was on the cross. Jesus went through that silence of judgment. Darkness fell on the land. Silence. The wrath of God poured out in that silence.

> He was oppressed and afflicted, yet he did not open his mouth; he was led like a lamb to the slaughter, and as a sheep before her shearers is <u>silent</u>, so he did not open his mouth (Isa. 53:7).

Now in 8:1, the people are silent before the wrath of who? The same one who was silent and went into darkness soaking in the wrath of God. This is the One they rejected. They are silent before the wrath of the Lamb!

What have we seen going on in heaven up until now? Songs. Praises. Day and night, they never stop singing 'holy, holy, holy is the Lord God Almighty'. But even the praises stop in heaven. There is only one thing that can interrupt the singing of God's praise in heaven. His judgment. Even heaven's praises are silent to hear the answer to prayers (6:9-11), and to wait on and hear God's judgments.

This is where it all ends. This silence is our destiny. The judgment seat of Christ when the wrath of the Lamb is exposed. Your destiny is not your achievements or retirement, or the time when you can take life easy, or your marriage, or your children or grandchildren. Your destiny is that silence. We must all stand before the judgment seat of Christ (2 Cor. 5:10). Silence. Undone.

Half-an-hour. You feel every second as the perspiration pours from your brow as you wait. Your life all comes down to this silence. Have you ever been nervous about appearing in public? You don't know quite how you will speak? Waiting for your turn. Waiting. Seconds. Minutes. Half-an-hour! How long will it seem standing before the Judgment seat waiting for your turn before the judge to bring down the gavel ... upon you! It's silence alright. Half-an-hour is agonizing when every second your heart wants to faint. Half-an-hour would seem like an eternity. Waiting. Waiting. Just you and the sight of the holy Judge of the universe. Can you hear that silence?

The only thing that finally breaks that long silence is the word GUILTY! That's the verdict ... unless you have the seal. The seal of the Holy Spirit. In that case you will rejoice to meet that judge who went through the dark silence for you at the cross! A glorious day! The Holy Spirit who convicted you of sin and moved you to throw yourself on the mercy of the cross and cry, 'Wash me Savior or I die!' The Holy Spirit who changed your heart so you couldn't go on in that sin any more without hating it and wanting to put it to death. The Holy Spirit who moved you to repent. Do you have him? Do you bear the mark upon you? The fruit of the Holy Spirit? Love joy, peace, patience, kindness, goodness, faithfulness, gentleness and self-control. Are you right with God now? 'Later I'll get it right.' But later it's too late. Only silence.

When he opened the seventh seal, there was silence in heaven for about half an hour (8:1).

Study Questions

1. Why is there silence in heaven and how would John have deduced what it meant?

2. How can this text be a continuation of 6:12-17 when we are up to 8:1-5?

3. What does this text tell us about prayer?

4. What might be the prayer in 8:4, that is coming before God?

5. Why would silence be a good description of the Judgment?

6. What might be the significance of the time of duration of half-an-hour?

7. Where else in Scripture can we find 'silence' as being significant?

8. Can you picture what that time of silence will be like for you?

28
The Seven Trumpets
(Revelation 8:6)

I have a confession to make. I've been dreading getting to these trumpets. Anyone who gets dogmatic about understanding all the book of Revelation has to be kidding. I've been so worried about these trumpets that I've been hoping Jesus would come back before I got to Rev. 8 so I could find out how this is supposed to end. Then at least I could say, 'Oh, there you are Lord, I'm having a little difficulty with Rev. 8, if you could tell me what happens next ...'

Last time we looked at 8:1-5 with the seventh seal being opened ... Judgment Day. But now the question is, 'What are we going to do with the rest of the chapter?' Because right within those first five verses were trumpets ...

> And I saw the seven angels who stand before God, and to them were given seven trumpets (8:2).

What are we going to do with these trumpets? Well, it's simple, isn't it? You have seven seals and straight after they are opened we have seven trumpets that follow the seals. Notice the trumpet judgments haven't even been sounded. They are preparing to sound them.

> Then the seven angels who had the seven trumpets prepared to sound them (8:6).

But how can that be, if the trumpets are simply following on *after* the seals? We've already had the final judgment (6:12-17). That was about as final as it can get with the sun, moon and stars going completely dark. We had the people running everywhere from the *wrath of the Lamb*. And then after the interlude there is silence. It's Judgment Day culminating with the peals of thunder, lightning and fire hurled to the earth (8:5). Surely this has to be the final judgment?

How can the trumpet judgments be happening *after* Judgment Day? If you read Rev. 8 you will see that only one third of things are affected by the trumpet judgments. What does that mean? It means the trumpets are only partial judgments. But how can you have a partial judgment after the final judgment is completed? How could you have all these partial judgments and warnings after the finality of the sixth and seventh seals?

For instance, if the sun, moon and stars are extinguished back in 6:12-17, then how can the trumpets introduce the darkening of *one third* of their light in 8:12? They have already been completely darkened (three-thirds) at the final judgment in the sixth and seventh seal. And trumpets are for warning! Warning means you still have a chance, not the end.

> ... then if anyone hears the trumpet but does not take warning and the sword comes and takes their life, their blood will be on their own head. Since they heard the sound of the trumpet but did not take warning, their blood will be on their own head. If they had heeded warning, they would have saved themselves (Ezek. 33:4-5).

How does this all fit? How can you have a warning *after* a final judgment? It's complex! But could this be the work of a Master film director—Jesus himself? Have you ever seen one of those clever films that start at the end? They start with a scene such as a funeral, and then the film goes back over all the events that lead to that finality.

I know this is not the only understanding of these trumpets, but bear with me and see if you can see the pattern of a great filmmaker. This series of trumpets will take us over the same period of history and fill out more of what happens, leading us all the way back to the end. The seven seals led to the end. And then we have a recap and the seventh seal leads into the trumpets. And we are going to see the same thing with the trumpets and bowls. Look at the end of the seventh trumpet ...

> Then God's temple in heaven was opened, and within his temple was seen the ark of his covenant. And there came flashes of lightning, rumblings, peals of thunder, an earthquake and a great hailstorm (11:19).

Sound familiar? Déjà vu? We have been here before ...

> Then the angel took the censer, filled it with fire from the altar, and hurled it on the earth; and there came <u>peals of thunder, rumblings, flashes of lightning and an earthquake</u> (8:5).

But 8:5 was the final judgment! How can you have more than one final judgment? You can't. It's just clever film directing. In fact, Jesus does it again! First seals, trumpets and then what happens after the seven bowls? The same thing that happens after the seven seals and the seven trumpets.

> The seventh angel poured out his bowl into the air, and out of the temple came a loud voice from the throne, saying, 'It is done!' Then there came <u>flashes of lightning, rumblings, peals of thunder and a severe earthquake</u> ... (16:17-18).

Wait a minute! Didn't we already do the full lightning, rumblings and judgment thing two times before? Yes, but the trumpets, as with the seals before and as the bowls after, lead us to the end, but fill out more of the detail and show us more of what happens leading to the end. They all lead up to that final judgment with the lightning and peals of thunder, etc.

Many see the trumpets as simply continuing chronologically from the seventh seal. But apart from the problem we examined (trumpets come after there has already been a complete black out judgment), the trumpets are also repeating much of what has happened in the opening of the seals and again leading to the same end. The partial judgments of the trumpets increase the *intensity* of judgment. This time it's thirds rather than quarters. But how could the trumpets give partial judgments after the final judgment? The answer is that this is a movie flashback. These seals, trumpets and bowls are parallel all through the book of Revelation, leading to the final judgment.

> SEALS   1, 2, 3, 4, 5, 6 (interlude) 7th (final judgment, thunder, rumblings, lightning, earthquake).
>
> TRUMPETS   1, 2, 3, 4, 5, 6 (interlude) 7th (final judgment, thunder, rumblings, lightning, earthquake).
>
> BOWLS   1, 2, 3, 4, 5, 6 (interlude) 7th (final judgment, thunder, rumblings, lightning, earthquake).

It's just like a Master film director to give us different close-up camera angles of the same period of time. Just as after the sixth seal we had an interlude before the seventh seal (final judgment, lightning thunder, earthquake), so now we will see the same after the sixth trumpet, with an interlude before the seventh trumpet, the final judgment of lightning, thunder and earthquakes. And what do you think happens after the sixth bowl? There is another interlude before the seventh bowl. Final Judgment with peals of thunder, etc. (see 16:17-20). It's called recapitulation. I'm calling it movie flashback. Going over it again with different camera angles. Still leading up to the end.

We have reached the end at the seventh seal (judgment) and now the trumpets recap. How do we explain this? It's the Master film director. The key is to notice that 8:1 is the opening of the seventh seal and in the very next verse we see what is *inside* the seventh seal and it's the preparation for blasting the trumpets. The trumpets are actually *inside* the seventh seal.

When my youngest son was little he played a prank on me. He gave me a present. A large present all wrapped up. I got all excited at such a large present, but when I opened the present there was another package wrapped up inside. So I opened that package and guess what was inside? Another present. And I kept opening and opening until I got down to a little tiny package and it was all so frustrating I can't even remember if there was actually anything inside the last one.

The point is these packages were not separate presents given to me one after another chronologically. They were given at the same time, and each unwrapping showed more and more of what is within, what is within, what is within. Packages within packages. That is what is going on in Revelation. The seventh seal is opened and what is inside? The trumpets! The trumpets are not coming later than the seals but are inside them. They are given at the same time, revealing more of what was inside the seals. The bowls are *inside* the trumpets, *not after*, but giving even more detail. Revelation is not confined to some future time, irrelevant to Christians now. It is revealing more detail — to us!

We have to also note the seven seals starting in Rev. 6 are not necessarily being opened in chronological order either. What do I mean? Think about those seals. The four horsemen. The first white horse rider is debated, but the next three are not up for debate. They are judgments. The red horse of violence, the black horse of famine and the pale horse of death. These have all unfolded in history, but not necessarily chronologically, but all at the same time. There are no points in history where there is exclusively violence, exclusively famine or exclusively death. (Nor would we expect there to be in the future!) Death, violence and famine occur concurrently in history, but all lead to the final judgment itself. Yes, there is a progression to final judgment, giving us more detail leading up to that final judgment. Different camera angles. That is what the trumpets and bowls do.

So the seventh seal opens to reveal final judgment, but what do we find inside? Another package! Seven more trumpets within that seal. So we go back over that lead up again. The more you open Revelation, the more you see inside another package unveiling more and more inside. The seals open the scroll, but inside that scroll are seven trumpets. And they reveal the bowls. But it all leads to ... Kaboom! Judgment!

The opening of the seven seals revealed judgments on the earth, but inside those seals the trumpets tell us more about that judgment, specifically on *unbelievers*. The seals and trumpets are not exact replicas of each other but different camera angles. The horsemen are different from the trumpets in several ways. The first four trumpets affect the natural world and the following two affect the inhabitants of the earth. But they cover the same time-frame leading to the last trumpet, which takes us back to the final judgment again, as did the seventh seal. And yet at each successive opening, the seals, trumpets and bowls reveal a little more each time of the same things leading up to the judgment. So when you open each package there is another package inside. That is vastly different from opening separate packages at different times. These packages are delivered at the same time, within each other. Just when you thought you knew what the lead up to judgment was, you find more than you bargained for.

By way of analogy, one of the reasons I don't believe in evolution from a scientific point of view is the progressive discovery of what is involved in DNA. In Charles Darwin's day, DNA was understood as just a simple cell. So Darwin said natural forces could account for DNA. But the more discoveries in science, the more it seems preposterous that DNA could have formed by itself. And just when it seems preposterous, they discover more complexity about DNA. The package looked the same from the outside! But the more they study DNA, the more they find inside.

Peter Line is a scientist who lectured in anatomy and physiology at a university in Melbourne. He explained it to me this way. 'DNA was not identified until about a decade after Darwin published his *On the Origin of Species* in 1859. However, its significance was not recognized until the mid-20th century, when DNA was recognized as the molecule that mediates heredity. The findings of the so-called *Encode* project, where it is now coming to light that probably all of the supposed Junk DNA (which was said to be discarded as evolutionary leftovers from our ancestors in our genome), appears to have a function after all. Currently 80% is estimated as functional, but this figure will probably approach 100% when all the cells are eventually analyzed. Of course, this makes the genome orders of magnitude more complex than even thought of a decade or so ago, let alone in Darwin's day, when they didn't even know what its role was in the cell.'

The more DNA is analyzed, the more complexity they discover inside. What seemed like a good idea in Darwin's day, DNA as a simple cell, now seems quite silly. That is the same problem as having a simplistic attitude to God's work in the world and to the book of Revelation. We look at the world and we see it all looks rotten. What is God doing? If you are an unbeliever, you shake your fist at God and claim there is no rhyme or reason as to what goes on. If you are a believer you know there is judgment coming and you leave the confusion to God, but you are still confused. But when we looked inside the seals we discovered God is actually at work even bringing judgment before our eyes. Well, the trumpets are going to reveal this in even more detail.

The seals are partial judgments on the whole world, while the trumpets are the close-up camera angle, zooming in, because they are specifically judgments on unbelievers. These unbelievers die and shoomp. It's too late to go back. They will face the judgment they have been storing up for themselves. They have been through trials, like believers, but for them it all adds to nothing. Whereas for the believer, the trial works out for their good, both in this life and the life to come.

If you are reading Revelation and you pick up on this pattern, you might wonder what all the repetition and extra detail is teaching us? How do we explain what is going on in history? We saw it when we looked at the seals. It was all summed up in one sentence from the apostle Paul ...

> The wrath of God is <u>being</u> revealed from heaven against all the godlessness and wickedness of people, who suppress the truth by their wickedness, ... (Rom. 1:18).

Remember his wrath is being revealed, in history. That is the explanation of the seals and the trumpets. We know from the seals that Christians get caught in the crossfire of the judgments on this world. The innocent along with the guilty are harmed by the evil going on in this world. But what is judgment for one, is refining for another — a preparing for and transforming into the likeness of Christ (2 Cor. 3:18). It's working for the believer's good.

It might appear as though God has left us, but the seals and now these trumpets are telling us, 'No! The Lord is at work bringing about answers to your prayers for justice and righteousness, even leading up to the end!' He is doing more than you could imagine because he is also working it all together for the good of the saints and judgment of the unrepentant. But it is also a demonstration of God's great patience and mercy in providing warning ...

The wrath of God is being revealed from heaven first in the seven seals: 1, 2, 3, 4, 5, 6, 7.
You didn't fully get that? Let's try a different angle.
The wrath of God is being revealed from heaven in the seven trumpets: 1, 2, 3, 4, 5, 6, 7.
You still didn't get that? Let's try another camera angle.
The wrath of God is being revealed from heaven in the seven bowls: 1, 2, 3, 4, 5, 6, 7.

All are leading to the final judgment of lightning, thunder and earthquakes. Do you think the book of Revelation is trying to tell you something? Picture yourself in one of the seven churches that first received this book of Revelation (although if you are a Christian, in one sense you are there, because remember seven represents the complete church, so you are one to whom John has written). You are either the Christian who has lost your first love (Ephesus), the Christian who is being persecuted and in poverty (Smyrna), the Christian who is falling for false teaching and sexual immorality (like Pergamum and Thyatira), the Christian who is soiling their clothes and is dead (Sardis), the Christian who is standing up for Jesus and getting attacked for it (Philadelphia), or the rich Christian who thinks he is rich but is about to be spat out of Jesus' mouth (Laodicea). All this repetition is for you. Why?

Warning. Warning. Warning. Seals, trumpets, and bowls. Warnings out of love because *we are not listening*. That is what trumpets do. They sound a warning!

I shudder at the opening of the seventh seal. I shudder at the seventh trumpet blast! And I shudder at the seventh bowl! No more warnings. *Wake up O sleeper!* Why is he repeating and recapping everything that leads to the Day of Judgment? Didn't we get enough of it the first time? No! We didn't!

It concerns me how few heed the warnings, even amongst professing Christians—like those who put their faith in a nice little compartment. 'I'm happy to live my faith out on my own terms. I don't want to let my faith interfere too much with my life.' But I'm not the only one who is concerned that some are not hearing. So is Jesus! That's why he gave the book of Revelation and wrote specifically to local churches.

Not everyone will agree with this idea of the replay of the seals, trumpets and bowls. But I am not introducing some innovative concept, foreign to the Bible.

The idea of repeating the same warning using different symbols like these seals, trumpets and bowls is the same literary technique used in Revelation's favorite OT book!

In Daniel, there is a threefold warning/prophecy of four kingdoms that would rise and fall. The four kingdoms: Babylon, Medo/Persians, Greece and Rome would come. But this history of their rising and falling was *repeated* through the book of Daniel using different symbols. So he was not given new eras of history, but given more detail of the same period of history of the four kingdoms with these three different images ...

STATUE
1. Babylon (gold) 2. Medo/Persians (silver) 3. Greece (bronze) 4. Rome (iron)

BEASTS
1. Babylon (gold) 2. Medo/Persians (silver) 3. Greece (bronze) 4. Rome (iron)

RAM, GOAT, HORNS
1. Babylon   2. Medo/Persians   3. Greece   4. Rome

The first was in Daniel 2, with the statue of different metals that represented the four kingdoms. Then in Daniel 7 the same kingdoms were represented by the four beasts. It was a repeat of the first prophecy but with different symbols. Then in Daniel 8 the ram, goat and horns were used to symbolize the four kingdoms again. And Daniel 11 repeats the prophecy, but it's all about the same warning of what would happen to those same four kingdoms with different detail.

So there is a precedent in Scripture with these cycles where the same thing is being described with different symbols. The book of Daniel does what Revelation is doing. But notice another significant parallel between Daniel and Revelation. Daniel repeats the warnings of what would happen to the four kingdoms, but also prophesies the coming of a new king during the fourth kingdom (Roman Empire). Daniel was predicting the first time Jesus came into the world.

Revelation seems to be using the same sort of cycles as Daniel, leading up to Jesus' second coming into the world. Instead of statues, beasts and horns of Daniel, Revelation uses seals, trumpets and bowls as the warnings. Both books are apocalyptic literature but repeat the warning of things to come with different symbols. *But the point of this prophecy is a warning ...*

The Futurist sees these terrible things happening at some time in the future with the trumpets following chronologically after the seals. I'm suggesting it's worse than that. It's upon us! The warnings are here in this world now!

It was the same thing Jesus said in Matthew 24. What was his point in describing wars, rumors of wars, violence and famines? They go on in the world through history. They are a warning, then a warning, and then another warning that these would continue in history as a *wake-up call* to the world we live in. A passing world. A dying world. A world under judgment. The wrath of God is being revealed to this world. And with all these warnings in the seals, trumpets and bowls, there is an intensifying leading to that final judgment. So the same thing is repeated! Yes! But the warnings are getting louder and louder. And the seven trumpets are building on the seals because they are the warning. And the warning is not listened to, so we open that package again and inside are the seven bowls of wrath. The repetition comes with an increasing intensity until it all explodes, or more to the point, Jesus will explode across the sky and come to judge the world.

The time to flee to Jesus to be saved from the wrath of God is now! Repent and be saved. Don't trust in yourself. Don't trust in finding satisfaction in the things of this world. Live for Jesus now. Believe in the cross and his resurrection to take away your sin. Get right with God now. Because if you don't, you miss out forever. But whatever you do, don't say you weren't warned.

Then the seven angels who had the seven trumpets prepared to sound them (8:6).

Study Questions

1. What logical difficulties are there with having the trumpets chronologically following the seals?

2. How can we explain the trumpets being inside the seventh seal?

3. What arguments can be made for seeing the seals, trumpets and bowls as parallel?

4. What factor might suggest the seals were not chronologically opened?

5. If the seals and trumpets are parallel does that mean they are identical? If not, why not?

6. Name one thing the trumpets reveal giving more insight than the seals?

7. Can you name a significant NT text outside Revelation that

summarizes the thrust of the seals and trumpets? Explore that passage.
8. What is the OT parallel to Revelation and how does it follow the pattern of the seals, trumpets and bowls?

9. What significant difference does that OT book unfold compared to Revelation in regard to the Messiah?

10. What is the significance of the symbol of trumpets? How does that affect you?

29
Hail and Fire
(Revelation 8:7)

This is the work of a Master film director. So far in Revelation we have had several scene changes. First, we got a picture of earth in Rev. 2-3. Then in the following chapters we've had scenes of heaven and earth again, this time under judgment when the seals were broken. Now we have close-up scenes zooming in on more detail. But most importantly, they take us forward in intensity towards the end of all things.

Here is the close-up. The seals announced what the horses and riders would do, but the close-up of the trumpets gives more description of the actual calamities themselves, and it's hotting up. Did you notice the big difference from the seals? With the seals *one-fourth* of things were destroyed or in calamity. Now with the trumpets it's *one-third*. By the time we get to the bowls there are no fractions. It's 100%! Total devastation. The book of Revelation is intensifying, revealing more and more until it all explodes in final judgment.

What is going on here? The world is under judgment. It has been happening right before our eyes, but we are so used to the pain we are beginning to think it's normal. So the screws are tightened to give us no excuse but to acknowledge something is wrong in this world.

The first four trumpets unleash a kind of un-creation. What did God create first? In the beginning God created the heavens and the earth. What next? Then he created light, then dry land, water, sky, the trees and vegetation. It was all very good, but now it's slowly unravelling. What we have here in the trumpets is a *reversal of creation*. We've got everything going backwards. We've got hail, fire, trees, land and sea now being destroyed. We've got the beautiful rivers, the water of creation, now turning bitter. And last of all in the creation order we have the total reversal of, 'Let there be light', because it ends with darkness. It's the great reversal of the 'very good' creation through these trumpets. The natural world is under stress. Where have we read that before?

> We know that the whole <u>creation</u> has been groaning as in the pains of childbirth right up to the present time (Rom. 8:22).

When does the creation groan? It's happening *now* says Paul. This reversal of creation is not foreign to Scripture. In the book of Exodus, the partial judgment plagues brought on Egypt *also followed* a reversal of the creation pattern, ending in darkness. Look at where we start with our trumpets.

> The first angel sounded his trumpet, and there came hail and fire mixed with blood, and it was hurled down on the earth. A third of the earth was burned up, a third of the trees were burned up, and all the green grass was burned up (8:7).

The plague in Exodus 9:22-25 started the same way as our first trumpet. Hail and lightning. Here it's referred to as fire. The second and third trumpets have waters turning to blood and the fish dying (8:8-11), which were also plagues in Egypt (Exodus 7:20-25). The fourth trumpet (8:12) fits the darkness in Exodus 10:21-23. The fifth trumpet (9:1-11) are the locusts as in Exodus 10:12-15.

Exodus 9:22-25 Hail, lightning	Revelation 8:7 (1st trumpet) Hail, fire (lightning)
Exodus 7:20-25 Water to blood	Revelation 8:8-9 (2nd & 3rd) Water to blood
Exodus 10:21-23 Darkness	Revelation 8:12 (4th trumpet) Darkness
Exodus 10:12-15 Locusts	Revelation 9:1-11 Locusts

The trumpets are bringing the judgments in Exodus to our world now. And just as the plagues in Egypt served as a warning and hardened Egypt and Pharaoh's heart, leading to final judgment, so too these trumpets warn us, harden some and lead to a final judgment.

The similarity with Exodus also says something about the world we live in now. It's a world where people are hardening their hearts against God. They are not listening to God. In fact, like Pharaoh and his people, they are not only defiant against God, but are committed to their idols. Idolatry was the big issue of ancient Egypt and it's the same problem today. People are committed to their idols, not necessarily something like a statue, but putting God in second place, *anything but God.* And today God's people are persecuted. That was happening in ancient Egypt.

In Exodus 3:7 God heard the cries of his people. Then came the plagues. In 6:9-11 we saw the people of God crying out for justice. *'How long before you judge the inhabitants of the earth?'* And we have seen that God's response is these trumpets (inside the seals).

In the Exodus plagues, God destroyed the idols of ancient Egypt, their gods of the sun, the river Nile and livestock. So too the trumpets take away the things people put their trust in for their security, such as food and water supplies.

The most popular view is that this is all happening in some unspecified future time when Christians have been raptured from the earth. But I am suggesting Christians are still on the earth when this happens because this book is written *to* Christians *for* Christians. The seals and trumpets are real and alive for us and have been building from when John was told back in 4:1 *what must take place soon 'after this'.* It's been happening throughout history since the time John heard those words 'after this'. But the very nature of these judgments being a third of this and a third of that, as opposed to a fourth in the seals, highlights the intensity.

I am the first to admit this is difficult and the different views can have good things going for them. It's hard to be too dogmatic about these trumpets. But I've noticed even some Futurists who demand we take Revelation literally, also take some license with a far from literal interpretation. For instance, Hal Lindsey says in this verse that when the grass is burned up it is the result of nuclear disaster.[29] Well that could be true, but where does it literally say anything like that in the text? I'm taking the words given to John in 4:1 *what must take place after this*, literally, because in its most natural meaning these words contain no imagery or OT connection that could be naturally taken as a symbol. So in plain language, *after this* started from John's time and has been building up ever since into our day, and will continue all the way to the end. So here we are in the trumpets, and the intensity is increasing with hail, fire and a burning up of vegetation.

Some Historicists see the hail as false teaching and the trees and the earth as the Roman Empire. The trees are those that are hurt by

---

[29] Hal Lindsey cited in Revelation, Four views ed. Steve Gregg, (Nashville: Thomas Nelson Publishers, 1997), p. 153

them. But how can you tell this from the text? Yes, Revelation told us to look for symbolic language from the very first verse, but the context should usually make it clear when to look for a symbolic meaning of a word through imagery or OT connection. For example, the obvious OT parallel with this first trumpet judgment seems to be straight out of the plagues in Exodus 9:22, but in Exodus hail is not a symbol for anything. It's just hail ...

> Then the Lord said to Moses, 'Stretch out your hand toward the sky so that hail will fall all over Egypt—on people and animals and on everything growing in the fields of Egypt.' When Moses stretched out his staff toward the sky, the Lord sent thunder and hail, and lightning flashed down to the ground. So the Lord rained hail on the land of Egypt; hail fell and lightning flashed back and forth. It was the worst storm in all the land of Egypt since it had become a nation. Throughout Egypt hail struck everything in the fields—both people and animals; it beat down everything growing in the fields and stripped every tree (Exod. 9:22-25).

So how is 8:7 to be fulfilled? Maybe we have been looking so close at the hail we missed the rain! *The first angel sounded his trumpet, and there came hail* ... I could be wrong, but what if instead of the hail being a nuclear fallout or false prophets, what if the hail is ... hail (unlike the many symbols in the book of Revelation, there is nothing inherent in the word 'hail' or connected to the OT that demands it must be symbolic). Hail and other storms occur all the time, as does bushfire and lightning that can cause death. But what does **mixed with blood** mean? What does the Bible mean, or for that matter, what does anyone mean when they talk of shedding blood? When we say the blood of Jesus cleanses us, it's not some ugly idea of having a bath in blood. No, we know blood means death. Hail and storms can cause death. The blood represents death. When hail and fire or lightning do cause death, they can even literally be *mixed with blood*. But the common use of the term 'blood' is an equation with death, or at the very least serious injury.

But notice in 8:7 it is not the death of humans where the most damage is done. Hail, storms and fire cause widespread damage to the trees! The greater destruction on earth in 8:7 is the vegetation. A third of the trees. All the green grass is presumably all the green grass within that third. I always feel for the farmers when we hear on the news about the destruction of crops, fruit trees and all kinds of vegetation. How often do they hear good news? Sometimes it seems like every second or third year we hear how hail has wiped out the year's crop. Often farmers lose a whole lot more than a third of their produce from their trees to hail or storm devastation. There are lightning storms that cause fire. Burning up! How many times farmers would wish it was *only* a third! It often seems much more.

But one-third is still some big fire to affect one-third of the earth. Yes, lightning could be the fire referred to, but fire is a metaphor used in the OT for both judgment and specifically famine. The land is burned of its food supply in extreme heat. The opposite of hail and extreme rain is no rain, just the burning sun scorching the land. John might have thought of the very similar words in Ezekiel 5:2,12, where there was a similar threat of judgment by fire that ends up meaning famine.

> A third of your people will die of the plague or perish by famine inside you; a third will fall by the sword outside your walls; and a third I will scatter to the winds and pursue with drawn sword (Ezek. 5:12).

This *third* of the land and trees burned up in Revelation seems to be drawing on the judgment by *thirds* in Ezekiel 5. The very beginning of Ezekiel 5:1 is about 'scales', which is an OT metaphor for famine. But there is another reason the fire might represent famine. Remember the trumpets are inside the seals covering more detail. They are different camera angles with more of the same judgments but showing the increased intensity. Remember when the seals were opened, one of the great judgments, the black horse in 6:5-6 represented famine and was represented by scales! Just as in Ezekiel 5:1 ... famine.

Ezekiel 5 finishes with the final judgment emphasizing famine in 5:16-17. So picture John as he sees this vision. The idea of judgment in thirds would bring to mind Ezekiel, where these strange *third* judgments occurred against Israel. And in Ezekiel the judgments were symbolized as fire (burning fire at the center of the city), but fire was metaphor for famine. So when John sees the land, trees and grass burned in 8:7, he sees the food produced by that fire (famine) taken away by a third. Rev. 18:8 has the same kind of metaphor using fire to represent the plagues, pestilence and famine.

So in 8:7 we don't have to rule out or exclude literal lightning and fires that so often devastate vast amounts of land and trees, but it could include extreme *heat* that burns much of the earth. Burning drought that causes widespread famine. Either way it affects the land and trees and burns up the food supply ... **trees were burned up, and all the green grass was burned up.**

When is this going to happen? Hail, fire, famine, drought and all this intensity? It's right before our eyes! What world are you living in? Extreme weather conditions. Heat that 'burns up'. Hail, storms, bushfires and drought that cause death. And people think this is normal!

No one seems to think too much about where the hail is coming from. What does 8:7 say? *The hail is hurled from heaven!* God's judgment! What is going on in this world? The same thing that was happening with the seals. And so we come back to the same quote of the apostle Paul because he said the same thing ... *The wrath of God is being revealed from heaven* (Rom. 1:18)! It *is* being *revealed!* What is being revealed? The wrath of God is being revealed from *heaven*. Where is God showing us his wrath? Take a look next time there is hail (if you dare).

But the hard heart of man puts it down to 'bad luck' and will not acknowledge the God of heaven, similar to Pharaoh in Egypt. It's like someone living with a skin cancer, leaving it alone, then it festers and develops pus, but it all happens so gradually they just live with it, until someone else discovers it in shock and horror. 'How did it get to this stage?' 'I've had it for ages.' They lived with pain and discomfort because it became 'normal'.

The whole creation is groaning! But it's *not* normal! Hail is *not* normal. That is not how God created this world. 'Oh, but it happens every so often, so it's natural.' It's *not* natural! There is no such thing as a *natural* disaster. There was no hail in the Garden of Eden. It's not natural! It's part of a fallen world. Sometimes we hear people say a storm is an *act of God*. Now that is much closer to the truth. *Hurled from heaven.*

Are we meant to count the devastation to see if it is exactly one-third? Is that the point? Or is the point that the intensity has gone from one-fourth with the seals to one-third with the trumpets. Yes, the world has been like this since the fall, but the seals and trumpets show an increasing intensity during the church age. Sometimes the devastation on a particular area at a particular time will be *more* than a third. The real issue is that we are supposed to have an increasing awareness of judgment. Something is wrong. Much of the world is in food shortage and crops are destroyed by drought or hail. But we are so used to the devastation we look at it on the news and say, 'It must be bad luck to live there.'

When we look at creation and the fall of man, we see the natural world was affected by human sin. God says in Adam we sinned. Of course, we don't like the idea of our solidarity with our first parents, but God says in our sin we were there. And we confirm that every day in our own sin. What is the big result of the fall of man? It's that the world is under judgment. Something is wrong. We learn that even thorns and thistles come about. The natural world is not natural. These things were not part of the good creation. Storms, earthquakes, famines, hail …

But here in Revelation we are learning that in the church age, since the coming of the Messiah, there is a new intensity to the judgment that is already ripe and happening … and it's increasing all the way to final judgment. And just as the grace of God is more fully on display since the coming of the Messiah, so too is the warning intensifying and judgment intensifying. So we are without excuse because we can *see* something is wrong. You've got to have blinkers on your eyes to say there is nothing wrong with this world.

And this trumpet now is blasting from God to warn the world. The hail and fire are hurled to earth from heaven. We are being warned this life is fragile. You can't put your hopes in this world or this life because you could be dead before the day is out.

And just like Pharaoh, these trumpet blasts will only harden and judge some people further. It's like the parable of the talents. Each one is given so much, but the guy with the one talent buries it. Instead of taking hold of the opportunity he has, he hardens his heart and shakes his fist at God calling him harsh. But if you really think God is harsh, you have even less excuse. How much pride do you have if you dig your heels in—if you believe God judges and *still do nothing about it!*

But God is not harsh. Even these judgments tell us that. The judgment is only one-third. There may well be droughts, heat waves or hail that affect a third or more of the world, but then there is relief. We are back to 'normal'. And then it happens again, but in some other part of the world. The grass is gone—but then it grows back again. Or the hail destroys the crops one year, but in the next two years they have a good harvest. It is partial. It is not full judgment. There is mercy mixed in with judgment. Full judgment is held back though he promises it will come. Why the delay? God is warning. He has put it right before our eyes that this is a world under judgment. Hail is not normal. Burning up heat is not normal.

Those climate change experts won't dare explore this explanation, but there is something far bigger going on, so don't put your head in the sand regarding the real issue! There is something, someone, far greater *behind* the upheaval of this world. Man wants to save himself even with climate change, and he still refuses to acknowledge the God who controls the climate. As of 2020, Australia has experienced its most damaging year of drought, followed by a record summer of heat and the most devastating bushfires in many years. Much of the country was darkened. Satellites showed the fires spread smoke haze to other parts of the world. NASA reported the smoke would circuit the whole earth. The ABC news reported on the horrific fires on the last day of 2019, interviewing a man in the midst of it. He at least got the message as he described his moment of terror. "At that point, I was praying. I was an atheist mate. I was praying to God. I was praying to Jesus." But for most, the warning falls on deaf ears.

But, it is still *only* a warning. It doesn't increase so quickly. It only goes from one-fourth to one-third. That is a small enough increase that speaks of mercy. It has been increasing in the time of the trumpets blasting, but God is holding back full judgment. But it's also a small enough increase for people to ignore it if they want to say 'life goes on'. It's not doubling. It's just enough to make you think, or to wake you up if you have ears to hear. But who is listening? Look at the patience of God who warns this world in no uncertain terms it is not a safe place. You cannot put your hope in the things of this world. They can and will be destroyed.

So you will do one of two things with these partial judgments. You will either see the glass half full or the glass half empty. You will either see God's mercy holding back two-thirds (full judgment) and see a day of grace to live for Jesus, or you will harden your heart and shake your fist at God who is taking away your hopes of this world. You will say God is harsh ...

But the world is not under judgment because God is harsh. It's because of us! *We* rebelled against God. All of us in our own way. Compare the Exodus parallel. We look at Pharaoh and see he and his people deserved what they got. They acted cruelly to the Israelites and their hearts were hard. Doesn't that tell us something about these partial judgments through church history? They are deserved! Before we get to the last trumpet, there is still an opportunity to repent. But when we get to the second last trumpet (9:20-21), they still refuse to repent. How does Revelation finish? If anyone *adds* to these words ... God will *add* the plagues described in this book. What plagues? Well if you think you got 'lucky' and escaped in this life and can outsmart God with your 'luck', these are the very things that will be upon you in the next life. Fire burning. Eternally. Thirst and hunger.

Have we forgotten how we got to this point? Who opened the seals out of which came the trumpets? The One who is worthy and has every right to judge is the same one who gave himself up for this world under judgment. He came into this world before Judgment Day and took the judgment in advance on the cross and offered himself in love for all who will believe. It's Jesus! Jesus wins in judgment, and Jesus wins in saving those who are his. The glass is not half full. It is overflowing. It's still the day of opportunity to repent and find the Savior.

Study Questions

1. How do the trumpets relate to Genesis?

2. How do they relate to the Exodus?

3. Is there a general rule as to how we can tell when something is meant to be symbolic?

4. How might John have interpreted *fire* and what OT text might he have drawn on? How might the seals also contribute to interpreting this?

5. How does Romans 1:18 speak into explaining the trumpets?

6. If this world is clearly under judgment in contrast to Genesis 1-2, why don't more people see it?

7. Are we meant to see an exact third of devastation based on the trumpets? What else could it be teaching?

8. How do the trumpets relate to the final text of Revelation?

9. The trumpets will elicit one of two responses. What are they and which one are you prone to?

30
A Third of Blood and Water
(Revelation 8:8-12)

We are up to the second trumpet blast now. The second angel blows his trumpet and an atomic bomb is seen exploding in the ocean. And you can clearly see this in the text ...

> The second angel sounded his trumpet, and something like a huge mountain, all ablaze, was thrown into the sea. A third of the sea turned into blood, ... (8:8).

At least it's clear to some who interpret this verse in the book of Revelation. Hal Lindsey says it's a meteor or more likely an H-bomb exploding in the ocean.[30] John MacArthur suggests it's a huge meteor or asteroid surrounded by gases that will ignite as it enters earth's atmosphere.[31] It could be, but how can we be sure from this text since those are not literal interpretations?

How are we to interpret this passage so we can understand it? We must not forget John is seeing a vision. He is not seeing things that are literally taking place at that moment. So far we have seen literal truth conveyed with symbols. And we are told right here in 8:8 it is not a mountain that is thrown into the sea. What did John see?
...something like a huge mountain.

So right up front we are told it is not a literal mountain. Another hint that we are dealing with figurative language is the fact that a third of the sea turns to blood. That doesn't make literal sense. Once blood enters water it permeates the whole thing. Another hint of figurative language is at the end of Rev. 8, we have a talking eagle and a star that falls on a third of the world's fresh water. So, God is teaching us

---

[30] Cited in Revelation four views Ed. Steve Gregg, (Nashville: Thomas Nelson publishers: 1997) p.161
[31] John MacArthur, The MacArthur Study Bible, (Nashville: Word Publishing, 1997) p.2003

through signs and symbols. The question is, 'How do we understand what these things are telling us?' Of course, all things are possible. God can make an eagle talk. But is that what God is teaching us, that he can make eagles talk or blood can go into one-third of the sea?

We need to consider the apostle John, who as a student of the OT from a young age, would use the Bible to interpret the Bible. Otherwise we are just guessing. Another question we must consider is, 'When is this happening? When is *something like a huge mountain going to be thrown into the sea?*'

Of the four main views, many scholars including some Futurists, accept that *something like a mountain* refers to a kingdom or earthly power, because the word *mountain* is often used as a biblical term to refer to a *kingdom*. The Preterist says the *mountain* is Jerusalem, burned by the Romans. That could be supported through Jesus' words cursing the fig tree, in reference to Israel's failure. There Jesus says, '*If anyone says to this <u>mountain</u> go throw yourself in the sea ...*' The Preterist says Jesus is alluding to the fall of Jerusalem.

The Historicist says this *mountain* refers to the Vandals under King Genseric, AD 428-468. All these interpretations have some merit. But if Revelation is a blessing and encouragement to the suffering church reading this book throughout the ages, shouldn't it speak beyond just the first century and before some distant future? We don't need to discount these historical examples, but we should see them recurring as a warning, a *trumpet* throughout history building towards the end, signaling we are a world under judgment. But who is listening and who is being hardened?

There is something similar to *something <u>like</u> a huge mountain, all ablaze, being thrown into the* sea, later in 18:21, with a great stone is hurled into the sea. In that passage, the stone is interpreted for us as the great evil kingdom of Babylon. In Jeremiah, Babylon is also referred to as a mountain ...

> Before your eyes I will repay Babylon and all who live in Babylonia for all the wrong they have done in Zion,' declares the LORD. 'I am against you, you destroying <u>mountain</u>, you who destroy the whole earth,' declares the LORD. 'I will stretch out my hand against you, roll you off the cliffs, and make you a <u>burned-out mountain</u> (Jer. 51:24-25).

By the time you read to the end of this chapter in Jeremiah, this mountain (that is Babylon) is being thrown into the Euphrates river!

> ... When you finish reading this scroll, tie a stone to it and throw it into the Euphrates. Then say, 'So will Babylon sink to rise no more because of the disaster I will bring on her. And her people will fall' (Jer. 51:63-64).

This evil kingdom in Rev. 18, referred to as Babylon, holds power over the world's evil system and is coming under judgment. There are various other times where mountains (symbolizing nations), come under God's judgment, e.g., in Isaiah 41:15; 42:15; Ezekiel 35:2-7 and Zechariah 4:7. Massive worldly kingdoms are brought down. The idea of something *like a mountain* referring to a worldly kingdom is familiar to John who knows his Bible. Remember these trumpets have a great parallel to the Exodus, Pharaoh, and the judgments on Egypt. Pharaoh was a powerful king of a great kingdom (*mountain*), but God brought him down.

Now in what period of the church age can we see an evil *mountain* (kingdom) being brought down? How about all of them! Godless kingdoms rise and fall. Mountains are built. Impregnable mountains. In John's day, it was unthinkable that the Roman Empire could be touched, let alone toppled. They were so powerful they controlled the whole known world. Anyone who tried to stand up against Rome would be put down, as Jerusalem certainly experienced in AD 70.

In the last generation of our time, the Soviet Union and communism lifted itself up against God, like Pharaoh. It did exactly what Pharaoh did. The communist state suppressed God's people and demanded the atheist state was the highest power. And for those of us living before 1989, the idea that one of the two great superpowers of the world (Soviet Russia) could be brought down was unthinkable. What could they possibly do to stop it? It's not as though they could just knock the wall down! But the trumpet blasted and just like in Jericho, the wall came tumbling down!

The second trumpet also has its impact as **a third of the sea became blood.** John remembers this from Saturday school. The Exodus was taught as much as any other book of the Bible to young Jewish boys. What does the water turning to blood recall for John? Exodus 7:20, when Moses turns the water to blood in the Nile and the fish died. The trouble is that in Revelation it's only a third of the sea. But how does only a third of the sea turn to blood? What is that trying to teach? Blood is the biblical metaphor for death. In 8:9 there is blood in the water and **a third of the creatures in the sea died.**

It's possible it simply means just that. Again, we are so used to living with death we think it's normal. When we opened the seals (parallel to the trumpets), we saw the *pale horse of death*. There has always been a massive number of fish and creatures of the sea dying. A lot of them survive by eating each other! There is blood in the sea. Death! It happens in massive numbers. A third? But isn't that normal? That's our problem! We are so used to living in a cursed world of death, we think it's normal. Death and bloodshed are not normal. It's judgment on this world.

God did not give us a world with death and bloodshed in it. That is *not* normal. The trumpets are sounding, and you are not listening! The point of *the third* is that it is increasing during the church age. Remember in the seven seals it was one-fourth of everything. Now it is up to one-third. The difference is a relatively small increase. So what is this trying to tell us? It's increasing gradually enough that we can still say, 'Well that's normal. One-third of the fish in the sea dying. That's just life.' No, that's death!

We are like the people who have a tray of kitty litter in their house. When you visit them you say, 'What's that horrible smell?' And your host says, 'It's okay, you get used to it after a while.' And you think to yourself, 'If you can get used to this, that's when you really know you've got a problem.' So for those of us who are not used to it, we are turning purple gasping for air, but others are 'used to it'. In the same way, we get used to a world of sin and death, a world under judgment. So much so that we think death is normal. But it's not normal. It's God blasting these trumpets to scream at us *there is something wrong!* This is a world under judgment.

The point is not to count how many fish are dying. The point is to see it as increasing from the seven seals, where only a fourth of the earth was affected by judgment.

But it doesn't stop there, because **a third of the ships were destroyed.** There are all types of upheavals in the sea including storms and tsunamis that disturb shipping. But by the time we get to Rev. 18 we see the great mountain Babylon cast into the sea, and it specifically refers to the trade and commerce of shipping.

> Woe! Woe to you, great city, where all who had ships on the sea became rich through her wealth! (18:19).

So some sort of great financial crisis or the like can bring down the economy by at least a third, so the shipping grinds not to a halt, but is cut back by a third. We've seen global financial crises happen. As recent as 2007 one of the great superpowers, the U.S., one of these great *mountains,* was brought down low in terms of its economic power. It got a shock. Since then we have seen other *mountains* coming down, like Greece and other European nations being cast down economically. In some of those countries, they wish it was only a third of their trade, commerce and shipping destroyed.

But this upheaval on the sea does not have to exclude the natural world. Surely tsunamis were always around. But to be honest with you, I had hardly heard of the word 'tsunami' until the big one in 2004 along the coasts of most landmasses bordering the Indian Ocean, killing over 230,000 people across 14 countries, with waves up to 100ft (33m) high. It is said to be one of the deadliest natural disasters in recorded history. And the level of devastation of the sea from hurricanes like Katrina was unknown to the US until recently.

But the hope is in the *third*. Where a devastating tsunami caused people to die and their blood mixed in the destructive water, then there is calm. And yes, the US goes through economic downturn, yet there is rebuilding, and trade recovers. And shipping disasters happen, but most of us travel safely. The message is that it is not the full and final judgment. It's a warning. John sees the Exodus happening again with the third trumpet. Rivers with undrinkable water. The Psalmist gives a commentary on the Exodus.

> 'He turned their river into blood; they could not drink from their streams' (Psalm 78:44).

> The third angel sounded his trumpet, and a great star, blazing like a torch, fell from the sky on a third of the rivers and on the springs of water— the name of the star is Wormwood. A third of the waters turned bitter, and many people died from the waters that had become bitter (8:10-11).

Even some leading Futurist writers argue the *star* is symbolic of a person, either an apostate, the final Anti-Christ, or the Pope. Others argue for a literal star. But we noted back with 6:13 that if a star literally fell to earth (the sun is a star and is 333,000 times bigger than the earth), then you can be assured it would not be only one-third affected. There would be no one left to tell about it. So if it's not literally a star, is it a meteor? It's possible. Meteors hit the earth from time to time. But even if it was a meteor, how do we account for the recurring theme of *a third of the rivers and springs turning bitter* from the impact of a meteor?

If we let Revelation do its own interpreting, in Revelation a star usually refers to angelic beings. Right at the start Jesus said the seven stars are the seven angels of the churches (1:20). We will see it repeated in Rev. 12. A third of the stars fell with Satan, but the stars are fallen angels. The star in 8:10 could be an unseen spiritual power unleashing judgment on the earth. That would make sense of how a third of the waters can be struck by a star.

Perhaps there is a hint in how this star falls as a blazing fire and causes those waters to turn bitter. Remember in the first trumpet we noted how John, seeing the vision, is looking at great images that were familiar to him from the OT. We said with the first trumpet that 'fire' was an OT metaphor for famine. And what have we got here? Familiar to John as a metaphor for famine is *Wormwood* (Jer. 9:15; 23:15 KJV). In Jeremiah *wormwood* is used as a metaphor for *judgment* and *bitterness*. This burning star in Rev. 8 is called *bitter*, that is *Wormwood*, the kind of burning heat that causes famine and the drying up of the earth, which so often causes the *waters to become contaminated* (See also Jer. 8:13-14).

But when could such things happen? A third of the water in the world contaminated and many sick from bitter waters? Again, we are so sheltered from the reality of how a great portion of the world lives. What about the rest of the world? The third world? Where do we get that term? Is it a 'third' of the world starving or lacking clean, safe drinking water and regularly suffering drought? It would be convenient if the term 'third world' meant a third of the people in the world, but that's not what 'third world' means. It means third in order of economic class, which accounts for *more* than a third of the world. It's a majority of countries. What are you told when you go to India, Africa, Asia, or other third world countries? Don't drink the water!

One of the ways our local church has supported Orbus (a work for needy children) in Malawi is to build wells, because one of the primary dangers and concerns in the third world is people having access to clean water. A lack of clean drinking water is one of the main causes of disease and death. It's a major world issue, **and many**

people died from the waters that had become bitter.

So, if *many people died*, does that mean we give up on foreign aid because it's going to happen anyway? No! It's a trumpet call. *Many people died!* It's meant to wake us all up to a world under judgment. It doesn't mean those specific people are under judgment any more than others. Indeed, they are often the very people where the gospel is going forwards, where people are taking hold of eternal life, even with their contaminated water. All the while those who are rich and have clean water and food are not hearing the trumpet call, even though it's blasting in their ears. The world around them is dying, and Jesus will say to you one day, "Whatever you didn't do for these you didn't do for me ..."

So do the trumpets make you wake up or harden you against God? 'I knew you were harsh, so I buried what you gave me.' I buried my cash so no one could touch it, while the poor starved and lacked for clean water.

> Now listen, you rich people, weep and wail because of the misery that is coming upon you. Your wealth has rotted, and moths have eaten your clothes. Your gold and silver are corroded. Their corrosion will testify against you and eat your flesh like fire. You have hoarded wealth in the last days (Jas. 5:1-3).

The key to the one-third is to notice not everyone is affected. It is just a portion that serves as a warning. It's only a third of the water that is affected. But is it only third world countries?

In recent memory, floods in Australia covered about a third of Queensland and then headed through NSW and into Victoria. It was thought the floods would at least break the drought, but all the water was so contaminated that instead of watering the land, the floods poisoned it with all the waste it brought. Bitter. Now the question we need to ask is, 'How many people recognize this as the trumpet call of God?' How many people think, 'Why did God do this?' Well, lots of people do think that! But they think it in the negative. Instead of saying, 'If God is this angry, I should repent,' they think, 'Now I have an excuse to hate God.' Parents and school teachers see that in some of their children, the more you discipline them, the more they dig in their heels. Do they think they are going to win? They only make it worse. Instead of cutting their loss and getting on with things, they stay defiant right to the very end.

But here is the grown-up version. The Lord is judge and he has every right to judge this world for what we have done in defying him. But humans say, 'I am Lord of my own life. I will not turn my Lordship over to God.' They won't heed the trumpet warning. So there is another...

> The fourth angel sounded his trumpet, and a third of the sun was struck, a third of the moon, and a third of the stars, so that a third of them turned dark. A third of the day was without light, and also a third of the night (8:12).

Futurists Henry Morris and Hal Lindsey see this as days and light shortened by one-third.[32] This seems more plausible than one-third of the sun literally going dark while the other two-thirds still shine. But could it be again simply referring to things we take for granted about life because we are not hearing the trumpets! Every time there is a severe storm darkness covers the earth, and the light of the sun, moon and stars is shut out. And we have the audacity to say, 'But that is just natural!' Are we getting this yet? It's not natural! It's unnatural. There *was* no darkness caused by storms in this world before it came under judgment. God gave us a good world. Now the intensity builds in the church age. But the climate change experts haven't counted on this. He sends out the trumpet warning that our world is under judgment. And we have the audacity to say, 'Oh well, it's just mother nature.' Mother who? Not listening to the trumpets!

I do concede this is still a difficult passage with different possible ways of interpreting the darkening of those heavenly bodies. Rev. 12 gives us a direct reference to stars, even the moon and the sun, but there it is referring not to physical heavenly bodies but spiritual beings. We already noted with the previous trumpet that stars in Revelation refer to angels. And we have a direct reference to *one-third of the stars* as angels just ahead in Rev. 12. The sun and moon get a mention as well and none of them are referring to literal sun, moon and stars.

> A great sign appeared in heaven: a woman clothed with the sun, with the moon under her feet and a crown of twelve stars on her head. She was pregnant and cried out in pain as she was about to give birth. Then

---

[32] Cited in Revelation four views Ed. Steve Gregg, (Nashville: Thomas Nelson publishers, 1997), p.171

another sign appeared in heaven: an enormous red dragon with seven heads and ten horns and seven crowns on its heads. Its tail swept a third of the stars out of the sky and flung them to the earth ... The great dragon was hurled down—that ancient serpent called the devil, or Satan, who leads the whole world astray. He was hurled to the earth, and his angels with him (12:1-4, 9).

We won't delve into Rev. 12 here now, but suffice it to say scholars from all different views of Revelation agree the images of the sun, moon and stars are not literal there. The sun and moon are the clothing of the woman. And the dragon sweeps away a third of the stars. We know the stars are the angels who fell, deceived by Satan. So Satan's deception of people and angels is in mind and could be part of all of what happens back with the trumpets. In Jude 13 *wandering stars* refers to false teachers. We will see the fifth trumpet also connects the darkening of the sun with demonic deception of unbelievers. So this darkening in 8:12 could be an intensifying of the spiritual powers of darkness, principalities and powers. I mention all this only to concede there is more than one possible way of looking at this text. But the point that is clear is that these trumpets are unleashing judgments! Judgment that is partial. Warnings!

A *third* is repeated 12 times. What is the big deal? Do we have to measure how much hail falls, how many fish die or how many storms darken the sun? Does it add up to exactly one-third? Or is the idea of a third highlighting that these judgments of God are firstly partial, and secondly increasing! What did we see in the seals? The judgments came upon a fourth. Now it's thirds. The intensity is increasing. Death, hail and floods, etc. have always affected the earth. Fish and sea creatures have always died at a great rate every year. Waters have always been contaminated at a large rate. But the point here is that there is an increase ... a judgment just like Egypt of old with the plagues. It builds. It's a judgment against a world that persecutes God's people.

The real question is: Have you heard the trumpets or are you clinging to idols? For now, mostly, we drink clean water. Ships sail safely. We survive floods; many survive on the roads without accidents every day. This world is constantly given mercy, full judgment is held back. Today is the day to repent and find Christ and live for him. Today is the day to throw out those idols that are standing in the way of you committing yourself to him, including every area of your secret life. This text is an exhortation to wake up!

Study Questions

1. What indications do we have that this text is not necessarily to be taken literally?

2. What OT texts would help us interpret that which is like a mountain?

3. Give examples of 'mountains' being brought down in history.

4. Why is the blood in the sea not literal and what might it refer to?

5. How does Rev. 18 help us understand how a third of ships could be destroyed?

6. How does Rev. 12 offer another possibility of interpreting the stars?

7. When could a third of the world be struggling to have clean water?

8. What disasters in nature could be used to understand this text?

9. What does the repetition of 'a third' teach us?

10. If this is a judgment against idolatry as in the days of Egypt, which area of your life do you need to examine?

31
Out of the Abyss
(Revelation 8:13-9:12)

If you thought the first four trumpet blasts were fearful, which included hail upon a third of the earth, trees burned up, something like a mountain tossed into the sea, a third of the waters turning bitter, and a third of the light of the sun, moon and stars being darkened ... just when you thought it was safe to go back into the world, a talking eagle tells John that was just a warm-up! 'You ain't seen nothin' yet!'

> As I watched, I heard an eagle that was flying in midair call out in a loud voice: 'Woe! Woe! Woe to the inhabitants of the earth, because of the trumpet blasts about to be sounded by the other three angels!' (8:13).

In fact, the eagle is talking to everyone on the earth. Even those who insist this apocalyptic literature is to be taken literally might make allowances here. This is not a literal talking eagle but a metaphor of warning. A warning of what is about to happen. And how are we to understand the sight of an eagle? We have to stand in the old apostle John's shoes. What does an eagle mean to him? To him it was a familiar OT metaphor indicating that judgment is about to or has started to happen. (See Deut. 28:49; Jer. 4:13; 48:40; 49:22; Lam. 4:19; Ezek. 17:3; Hos. 8:1; and Hab. 1:8.)

So it's familiar to John, although the idea of an eagle making an announcement might seem strange to us. And what is this eagle announcing? Just like in the Exodus, where the intensity kept increasing with each plague, this eagle is announcing intensifying woes. These are the last trumpets.

One of the things about these last trumpets, as opposed to the seals (that wrought terrible things upon the earth with all people affected), is that the camera angle is zooming in and we see these last trumpets are specifically targeted towards unbelievers — those who don't have the seal of God. These trumpets are exposing their hearts and it's showing how deserved their judgments are. Another distinctive aspect of these last trumpets is that they reveal a spiritual warfare which is going on.

> The fifth angel sounded his trumpet, and I saw a star that <u>had fallen</u> from the sky to the earth. The star was given the key to the shaft of the Abyss (9:1).

We've already noted stars falling to the earth can't possibly be literal stars but could represent angelic beings. Literal stars also don't have keys and get to open shafts. It's a star that *had fallen*. How can John know that it *had fallen*? Does it look like Uluru in the ground? Even some of those who insist we take these symbols literally see this star symbolizing an individual being and the Abyss as hell, although we need to correct that. The Abyss is the realm of Satan and his demons. It can't be hell because no one can get out of hell. The Abyss must be some sort of confinement that one could be released from, depending on whether you have the 'key'. Remember the demons who begged Jesus not to send them into the Abyss! They didn't want to go into that holding cell. And yet it's a demonic realm where one could be let out. On this occasion, a star is given the key. By the time we get to 12:4, 9 we see Satan and one third of the angels, referred to as stars, being cast out of heaven. Remember what Jesus said …

> The seventy-two returned with joy and said, 'Lord, even the demons submit to us in your name.' He replied, 'I saw <u>Satan fall</u> like lightning from heaven. I have given you authority to trample on snakes <u>and scorpions</u> and to overcome all the power of the enemy; nothing will harm you. However, do not rejoice that <u>the spirits submit to you</u>, but rejoice that your names are written in heaven' (Luke 10:17-20).

Notice a couple of things about this. Satan falls like a star from heaven. And Jesus gives his disciples authority to trample on serpents and scorpions, which in the same breath he associates with demonic spirits. Rev. 9:11 is where we see the angel of the Abyss is king over the demonic locusts that have the sting of scorpions. So hold that thought, as we will need it when this star opens up the Abyss with a key and we see what comes out stinging like a scorpion.

If this star (9:1) is either Satan or one of his chiefs, one who *had fallen*, it makes you wonder just how much Satan hates humanity. We know Satan and his demons hate believers. But what we often overlook is that Satan hates unbelievers too. He is not on their side. He seduces them, only to torture them and lead them to their destruction. All the Lord had to do was let Satan release more of his forces, like a ferocious animal out of a cage, looking to tear its prey apart.

> When he opened the Abyss, smoke rose from it like the smoke from a gigantic furnace. The sun and sky were darkened by the smoke from the Abyss (9:2).

For the apostle John, this is now familiar judgment language, with the darkening of sun and sky and so on. And *smoke rising* becomes a common metaphor for judgment in 14:11; 18:9 and 19:3. But now, out of this smoke, comes the ugliest locusts you have ever seen. A literal locust plague can block the light from the sun and sky. But just as the star is not a literal star but a symbol for something far worse, so too this darkness could be a metaphor of something far more sinister.

What a scary image John saw. Imagine the shivers in his spine as he saw an image of smoke rising from a gigantic furnace in the Abyss, like coming out of the pit of burning hell itself. The key to the Abyss has been turned. The pit that has been locked for so long, holding in all the ugliness, has been opened, and what comes out? First the smoke rises. Then...

> And out of the smoke locusts came down on the earth and were given power like that of scorpions of the earth (9:3).

If Jesus equated scorpions with demons, what is this passage trying to tell us? We know that a myriad of angels, one third, fell with Satan. Where are they? *On the earth!* They attack people. Their deception causes pain and disillusionment. Powers of darkness in the heavenly realms. This is where our real struggle is, said the apostle Paul in Ephesians 6:12. There are principalities and powers of evil. In Ephesians 2:2 Satan is the *prince of the air,* the devil.

But this is a curly one because some demons are held in the Abyss until this time, and that is where these locusts are coming up from. Jude 6 and 2 Peter tell us there are demons that are already there, held in chains. Now it's open and they are coming out! The more humanity plunges into sin, the more God gives the world up to itself. It gets exactly what it wants — more evil. Only this time, the experts are called in. The full number of troops. Demonic power from the Abyss. And their king is given the key to unlock them. But it's delegated power … they **were <u>given power</u> like that of scorpions of the earth.**

It is the Lord who is sovereignly over this judgment, even while the perpetrators have their own evil intent. We noted the trumpets are similar to the plagues of Exodus that fell on Egypt. However, in the book of Revelation, these plagues are used more than once to refer metaphorically to demonic power. So when we get to the frogs (one of the plagues of Egypt) in 16:13, we are told the frogs refer to demons. And in 9:3 there is also a hint of demonic power with these locusts, which represent some sort of spiritual power. We know they are not real locusts because they don't get to eat any vegetation. In Exodus, the locusts devoured the vegetation and all the fruit of the trees (Exod. 10:15). But here we read …

> They were <u>told not</u> to harm the grass of the earth or any plant or tree, but only those <u>people</u> who did not have the seal of God on their foreheads (9:4).

What kind of locusts are these? They come up out of the Abyss, the realm of demons, they come down on the earth and they don't eat any grass, plants or tree. Instead they go for people. Are they carnivorous locusts? Notice also how these locusts are able to follow instructions. They are *told* what to destroy. The powers coming out of the Abyss are demonic powers. They have intelligence beyond normal locusts. They have power from the Abyss to harm **only those people who did <u>not have the seal of God</u> on their foreheads.**

When the horses went forth, there was violence, famine and death in all forms, affecting all people (Rev. 6). But here we have trumpets specifically targeting unbelievers. We saw in 7:1-3 the true believers have the seal of the Holy Spirit. While this demonic attack is raging and the locusts are ravaging people, those with the seal will be kept. These locusts cannot harm their faith. They will survive. They will be kept *through* the tribulation!

The protection of believers might explain the darkness that comes in

9:2 as a spiritual darkness. It's not normal darkness, but a darkness that comes up out of the Abyss. It is the very thing spoken of again and again in the NT, including from the lips of Jesus himself. In John's gospel, there is a theme of *darkness* being a *moral darkness*.

> This is the verdict: Light has come into the world, but people loved <u>darkness</u> instead of light because their deeds were evil (John 3:19).

That's what is going on here in Rev. 9, only there is a new intensity due to the release of new powers of darkness from the Abyss. And those on earth in darkness are given a strong delusion. They are given up to themselves. There is a new level of dark power coming up out of the Abyss.

> They were not allowed to kill them but only to torture them for five months. And the agony they suffered was like that of the sting of a scorpion when it strikes (9:5).

So these locusts cause great pain, **agony** and despair to unbelievers, who endure the hopelessness of life without God. Life is running out. Meaningless, meaningless, all is meaningless. And yet they lust for more, but it never satisfies. Like the Egyptian plagues, these demonic powers don't kill unbelievers. They just torture them. But why **five months?** Is it a literal five months of intense attack towards the end? Apparently the maximum time of a locust season is five months. Normally a locust plague will swarm for a few days during that five-month season. But this locust attack lasts the full, devastating, five months. Locusts don't literally sting like scorpions, but these do. So just as these aren't literal locusts, we may not be looking at a literal five months. Perhaps the main issue here is the parallel to Exodus where there is a limitation to the plague. It doesn't last forever. It's just a season. The days are cut short for the sake of the elect. But five months is a long time to be tortured. It's limited but sustained for what seems like a long time. There is warning and mercy mixed with the judgment.

Remember, Revelation uses numbers symbolically as we have seen with the seven spirits of God symbolizing the complete Holy Spirit. The four corners of the earth symbolize the complete creation (the earth doesn't have corners). Twelve represents the people of God. As with numbers elsewhere in Revelation, John is seeing a vision. So how could he know it was five months from this vision? Did he have to wait for the vision to last for five months? That would be one long movie. Or is it like the numbers elsewhere in Revelation, it teaches us an important truth using signs and symbols? So, if it's not literal, what truth is it trying to teach us? Sharp and sustained, limited torment, but the 'full locust season' worth.

The word *torture* (or torment) in 9:5 is used elsewhere in Revelation in 11:10; 14:10-11; 18:7,10,15; and 20:10, where it describes emotional pain in judgment. Deuteronomy 28 talks about Israel suffering the plagues of Egypt (Deut. 28:27, 60). Because of their idolatry, they would suffer in ways like a blind man groping in darkness (Deut. 28:28-29), despair of soul (Deut. 28:65), and life will hang in doubt and dread of heart (Deut. 28:66-67). So it's torture of the heart as much as physical torture. This is possibly the same kind of psychological torment and despair that is spoken of here in 9:5, when it says they will be tortured for five months.

What happens when people indulge the darkness of this world, in the lusts of this world? Often their indulgence ends in *despair*. The more they think this world is going to satisfy, the more they are let down and sink into *despair*. We find it even among rich and famous people. They have as much *despair* and trouble as anyone. They too have drug addictions and broken marriages. The more they indulge, the more they become enslaved, addicted and tormented. The promises of this world come up empty. They think it is going to satisfy, but it ends up torturing them in their souls. It would be interesting if we could survey the rate of depression among those who supposedly 'have it all'. We might find that the rich and famous, the hedonistic, those who supposedly have all the freedom to do what they want, are the most enslaved and addicted of all. The devil is such a cruel master. He gets you to sign up for a long-term course of giving yourself to a pursuit of this world and at the end, you meet him face to face, not as a friend but with this big taunting grin on his face and he says ... 'Gotcha!'

The great example often used to show the despair that self-indulgence brings is the Roman Empire, which burnt itself out in luxury and self-indulgence. It ended with despair and gloom in the end.

> During those days people will seek death but will not find it; they will long to die, but death will elude them (9:6).

People have tied themselves in all kinds of knots trying to apply this verse literally, imagining a time when people will try to kill themselves unsuccessfully (the rope keeps breaking, jumping off buildings but landing safely, slashing themselves with a knife but missing). But I think there is something more sinister and closer to reality than that. For every person who commits suicide, there are many more who **long to die,** who despair of life, but are too afraid of death and wouldn't go through with taking their own life. How many people have thought about suicide but instead have continued in their torment and despair and depression? They can't live with life, but they can't die.

Those who have the seal, the Holy Spirit, can also go through times of trial, depression and despair (2 Cor. 1:8). However, they also have the peace that surpasses all understanding (Phil. 4:7). They won't seek death, but strangely, amazingly, they look forward to the time they will be with the Lord, which is better by far (Phil. 1:23). They do not cling to this life as their only hope. They believe and know that the sufferings of this world are working an eternal weight of glory for them. They know 'all things work together for good for those who love God', though they go through trials. But the forces of evil are ferocious, and they are gaining in intensity ...

> The locusts looked like horses prepared for battle. On their heads they wore something like crowns of gold, and their faces resembled human faces (9:7).

So the locusts (demons) have human faces, but are powerful like horses. They have power like a battle horse, but intelligence and mental capacity like humans. Surely we are a long way from thinking of these images as literal locusts, which also cautions us against saying the five months is literal.

In the original language, the Greek word for **crowns** in 9:7 is the same word used for *crown* on the rider on the white horse in Rev. 6. It's normally only used in the NT in a context for good, which was one argument for the white horse being a force for good. There is another Greek word for *crown* that is used for either evil *or* good. But the word for *crown* in 9:7 is the one used in a good context. And note that in 9:7 these evil locusts are not said to have a *crown* but something *like a crown*, perhaps suggesting some sort of counterfeit. Not a crown, but something that looks *like a crown*. Like a crown that Christ might wear? Rev. 14:14 says it's Jesus who wears that very crown of gold. These have something *like a crown of gold*, which could suggest false teaching becoming rampant or an antichrist. Deception! Counterfeit! The whole point of 9:7-10 is that this demonic power is vicious and ferocious.

> Their hair was like women's hair, and their teeth were like lions' teeth (9:8).

We've been told in 9:7 the locusts (demons) have faces like humans, which suggests intelligence, though demonic. Now we read they have hair like women. In other words, attractive. Seductive. 'Beautiful hair, shame about the teeth.' Lion's teeth! The roaring lion, savage. Behind the seduction are the cruel, vicious teeth of Satan.

> They had breastplates like breastplates of iron, and the sound of their wings was like the thundering of many horses and chariots rushing into battle (9:9).

Are we still talking about locusts? The Historicists have one of their most impressive interpretations here, citing this as the rise of Islam and the turbans the Muslims wore as the crowns. But the Muslims also attacked God's people (not just unbelievers), and we read earlier the people of God (those with the seal) are spared. Also, Islam didn't hold back on killing, but as these locusts were told to in 9:5, *They were not allowed to kill them*. So that can't work.

According to some who fought in the Vietnam War, the description in 9:9 is strikingly like a Cobra helicopter, which tortured people with nerve gas sprayed from its tail. Ken Raggio connects this trumpet with the first Gulf War, with Saddam Hussein versus the allies and their helicopters.[33] It sounds impressive, but that still leaves us with a few problems with the helicopters looking like horses with women's hair, etc. Rather, it's meant to be a grotesque vision of demonic power with all its seduction and evil all wrapped up. It's coming. The locusts are coming out of the Abyss, the realm of demons. Helicopters are not usually as versatile as this.

---

[33] http://kenraggio.com/KRPN-SevenTrumpets.htm

> They had tails with stingers, like scorpions, and in their tails they had power to torment people for five months (9:10).

Helicopters tormenting people? Apparently, the sting of a scorpion doesn't normally kill, so the torment is not fatal but limited, hence again the limited time (five months).

> They had as king over them the angel of the Abyss, whose name in Hebrew is Abaddon and in Greek is Apollyon (that is, Destroyer) (9:11).

The king's name means *destruction* in both Hebrew and Greek. Destruction in the OT often refers to Sheol, the grave or death, or the realm of the dead (Job 26:6). The NT develops the idea as Hades, where there is weeping and gnashing of teeth. So this king over the Abyss, at the very least, is some satanic figure, if not Satan himself, which would fit with our star as Satan, the *angel of light* (2 Cor. 11:14). He rules over those who are his, i.e. demons and those who do not have the seal. *You carry out the desires of your father the devil,* Jesus said in John 8:44.

The Satanic tormentors are tying people up with darkness. Darkness covers the land with deceptive teaching that promises to deliver people from their despair, but only ends up leaving them emptier. But of course Satan's goal is to destroy. His name is destroyer. He wants to take people all the way to destruction, hell. He hates believers, but he also hates unbelievers. He wants to destroy both body and soul in hell.

But when does all this happen? Demons are already on the earth and have been for a long time, but there seems to have been an increase in their activity from the time the Messiah began his ministry in the world (note an important part of Jesus' ministry, driving out demons). We are told *our struggle is not against flesh and blood but against principalities and powers, spiritual forces of evil.* They are already here. But this is something new. That smoke rising out of the pit, as though it's rising out of the burning sulfur of hell itself, is a new release of demonic power on the earth. Remember how it came about ...

> When he opened the Abyss, smoke rose from it like the smoke from a gigantic furnace ... And out of the smoke locusts came down on the earth and were given power like that of scorpions of the earth (9:2-3).

These are additional demons being let out. Admittedly for a limited period of time, but they are now being let out! Unleashed onto the world. In other words, whenever this happens it would be a time where there is increased demonic activity in the world. A time when the ways of Jesus are ridiculed more than ever. Even a time when his name was used more as a swear word than it is revered. Can you imagine a time when the Lord of glory's name is more common as a swear word than as Lord? A time when Christian ethics and values are not merely passé, but even attacked, even in so-called Christian countries, even in the church! A time when God-given institutions like marriage would be under attack, even denying our biology as men and women. A time when murder, such as the murdering of children in the womb would be demanded as a choice, even commended. A time when idolatry would creep into professing Christian's lives, even a simple thing like setting aside worship with God's people would be outdone by the idols in people's lives. A time when people who want freedom to defy God in whatever way they want say, 'Just Do It'!

But instead of achieving their satisfaction, people find that doing what they want to themselves (and others) causes great pain and harm. Their indulgence becomes enslaving. Violence increases. If a fresh load of demons were freed from the pit, it would be a time when the occult and demonic would be increasing, it might even become accepted as popular, as another mainstream spirituality. A time when the occult, which was once considered the realm of extremists or at least the dark side, would become so popular they would have a cute character as a wizard and give him a cute name like Harry Potter or something, then celebrate it worldwide.

It would be a time when in Christian countries, unbelievers would no longer be indifferent and agnostic with 'believe whatever you like' but would begin to aggressively oppose the teaching of Christ in public, even in the school system. Atheism would no longer simply be a personally held belief, but a value to proactively stand for with the goal of eliminating faith.

It would be a time when violence and sexual promiscuity would be so accepted, it would be part of everyday entertainment and it would be called an infringement on freedom of speech if you don't allow that entertainment.

It would have to be a time when even the church wouldn't believe in the Bible. Could you ever imagine a time when the church does not even believe the Bible is God's word? Or churches that *do* say they believe it is God's word would no longer primarily use it when they speak in their worship services? A time when the traditional preaching through a book of the Bible in churches would be considered a novelty?

But all these things would torture people. It would be a time when unbelievers who rail against God in these ways would never be satisfied. They would be tortured in their souls. They would rail against that which is good and godly, and let out their anger, thinking that would get rid of it, but they would just get angrier. It would be a time when suicide would increase, but for many more they can't even take their own life. Too depressed. Can't live with this life, can't live without it. A time when there is more depression diagnosed, because they can never find the peace that surpasses all understanding. A time when more time and money is spent in counseling than ever in history, when there is more torment and frustration from those who supposedly have freedom to do what they want, but it just seems to lead to more frustration. A continual lust for more.

When is all this going to happen? I don't know. Have we entered the time when the locusts have been released? Good is called evil and evil is called good and we are reaping the consequences. I have said all along these trumpet judgments are warnings that have an intensifying effect. They increase all the way to the end, so it's impossible for us to judge when 'intense' is intense enough to say 'this is it'. Are we in the 'five months' or is it still coming? Is this partially or wholly happening before our eyes? Or is it still to intensify sometime in the future? Is this the time towards the end? I don't know that. All I know is this: we can never say we weren't warned.

Study Questions

1. What would a talking eagle mean to John?

2. What are two things the trumpets reveal that were not apparent with the seals?

3. Who or what is the star that had fallen? Give reasons for your answer.

4. Is the Abyss hell? If not, why not?

5. Are these real locusts? Give reasons for your answer.

6. Where does the idea of five months come from? What might it be teaching?

7. In what way are people being tortured? Give Scriptural support for your answer.

8. How could people seek to die and yet be unable?

9. The locusts wear crowns of gold, which is what Jesus wears. What might that indicate?

10. What is the overall warning of the text?

32
The 200 Million troops
(Revelation 9:12-21)

Seven trumpets blasted to the world. We have had five already. Can it get any worse?

> The first woe is past; two other woes are yet to come (9:12).

In the fifth trumpet (first woe), we had ugly locusts coming out from the Abyss. Well, in fact, it *is* getting worse. The sixth trumpet is about to be blasted. But before we find out what that entails, we need to recall what we learnt back in 6:9-11. The people who had given their lives for Jesus are now in heaven and are under an altar, the symbol of the ultimate altar, the cross of Christ. And they called out, *'How long, Sovereign Lord, holy and true, until you judge the inhabitants of the earth and avenge our blood?'* What we have here in Rev. 9 is in part an answer to that prayer as we continue.

> The sixth angel sounded his trumpet, and I heard a voice coming from the four horns of the golden altar that is before God (9:13).

This **golden altar** reminds us of those who had prayed (6:9-11). God hadn't forgotten them. This is the answer, the continuing judgment and warnings that come upon the earth. There is a voice coming from that altar and it may well be Jesus. He is the one ultimately in control, opening the seals and now directing the trumpet players.

> It said to the sixth angel who had the trumpet, 'Release the four angels who are bound at the great river Euphrates' (9:14).

These **four angels who are bound** are now released. We are told they are bound at the **great river Euphrates.** This would immediately be familiar to the apostle John. A common sign in the

OT was of God's judgment coming from the 'north' and from the Euphrates River. So John recognizes what is going on here. Judgment is coming. (See Isa. 7:20; 8:7-8; 14:29-31; Jer. 1:14-15; 4:6-13; 6:1,22; 10:22; 13:20; 25:9; 46:6, 20-24; 50:41-42; Ezek. 26:7-11; 38:6, 15; 39:2; Joel 2:1-11, 20-25.)

> And the four angels who had been kept ready for this very hour and day and month and year were released to kill a third of mankind (9:15).

Notice the repeated emphasis, **this very hour and day and month and year,** pinpointing a specific time. In other words, it's a plan! It's God's plan. This is one of the great truths that Revelation teaches us. Even the release of these angels is timed down to the hour. Even though evil rages and is coming upon the earth, the Lord has a plan. Even though things might seem out of control in your life right now, they are part of this plan. It comes right down to the very hour! God is in control, down to the very hour when he releases them.

It's like the book of Job where Satan brought evil upon Job, but it was the Lord who set the limit of what he could do (Job 1:10). Here we have an example of that, down to the very hour, day, month and year. So although things might seem chaotic, don't be thrown by evil. God has control even over evil and works it according to *his* plans.

> The number of the mounted troops was twice ten thousand times ten thousand. I heard their number (9:16).

Two times 10,000 x 10,000 is 200 million! In the original Greek language ten thousand is a myriad.

> The horses and riders I saw in my vision looked like this: Their breastplates were fiery red, dark blue, and yellow as sulfur. The heads of the horses resembled the heads of lions, and out of their mouths came fire, smoke and sulfur (9:17).

Earlier in Rev. 9 we read about the locusts which had similar breastplates and were described in a similar way. The horses and riders are of the same terrifying ilk as those demonic locusts. These have fiery red, dark blue and sulfur-like yellow colored breastplates. And their heads look like lions. Really? Horses, but with heads like lions? How does John even know they are horses then? It's like the locusts that didn't look like locusts. All these symbols are becoming more recognizable to us because they are things related to *the Abyss* which we looked at earlier. Just as those locusts no longer looked anything like real locusts by the time you add their heads, their helicopter bodies and everything else. John is aghast as he says 'take a look at this!' They look like the most unattractive demons you've ever seen! They have the power of horses and the ferocity of lions. And whatever you do, don't smell their breath! Because **out of their mouths comes fire, smoke and sulfur.**

> A third of mankind was killed by the three plagues of fire, smoke and sulfur that came out of their mouths (9:18).

Apart from in hell, where have we heard of fire, smoke and sulfur in that particular order before? In Genesis 19:24, 28 the same words are in that order. The judgment of Sodom. So this would be familiar to the apostle John. But in 9:18 the fire, smoke and sulfur are actually referred to as plagues. So we are getting the idea of things symbolizing other things. Fire, smoke and sulfur referring to plagues.

Some scholars have wondered if the death of a third of mankind is a kind of spiritual death. It could be. When Revelation speaks of death it can be referring to a physical death or a spiritual death (the second death). How can we tell whether this verse refers to a spiritual or physical death? Or if it refers to both? When people die physically, if they die in unbelief (and it is particularly unbelievers whom this judgment is coming upon), they then experience spiritual death, the second death. The door is shut. This is what Revelation is heading towards. In the full and final judgment, we are going to see *fire, smoke and sulfur* on the Day of Judgment. And of course when unbelievers physically die, their fate is sealed spiritually. There is never any escape from it.

One-third of mankind is killed. The death plagues brought on by these spiritual forces of darkness could include all kinds of death. All kinds of wars, disease and disasters. We went through it in Rev. 6 with the horsemen and riders. Humanity is dying from famine, violence and war. But remember we also looked at some of the ways people kill each other. Unwanted children being aborted account for a massive percentage of humanity *killed*, not to mention the overall death rates in third world countries. The point here is that it is increasing.

Also note that the horses do the killing, not the riders, further suggesting these creatures are symbolic. So whether it is war, tsunamis, starvation, or genocide, the kind of things we take for granted that happen in the world ... we ignore it, but it occurs all the time.

> The power of the horses was in their mouths and in their tails; for their tails were like snakes, having heads with which they inflict injury (9:19).

It's not just death, but also **injury.** We see the similarity to the locusts which spiritually tormented people. The fear of death and the despair of this life. But the horses' **tails were like snakes.** Satan is the only one in the Bible who is personified in terms of a snake or serpent. This is a further hint that we are talking about demonic power here. Also, their power is in their **mouths** and tails. Biting at one end (tails), but what about their mouths at the other end? Elsewhere in Revelation, the *mouth* refers to words that come out of the mouth, that is, *deception*. That would fit with the primary focus of the demonic to deceive and lie. We get some more hints that *mouth* indicates deception when we realize there seems to be a parallel between the six trumpets and the six bowls. This sixth trumpet seems to be the same event as the sixth bowl, only from a different camera angle. The sixth bowl (16:12-14) also mentions the Euphrates River and deception. Unclean spirits like frogs coming out of the *mouth* of the Dragon, the Beast and the False Prophet. Demonic lying *mouths* all over the place! It's a typical metaphor for deception. In Rev. 12:15, Satan casts from his *mouth* water like a river. And all these references about Satan in relation to use of the *mouth* strongly suggest deception. It's always a *mouth* speaking blasphemies.

So why aren't the saints harmed by these plagues and death? Why is the focus of these woes on unbelievers? What plague, disease or death targets unbelievers but not believers? Answer: Deception. Deception all the way to the second death. Yes, the believer experiences horrible things like plagues, disease, war and physical death. But for them it's a gateway to glory! How can a plague, disease, or death, affect an unbeliever negatively and not a believer? *Deception!* The serpent (Satan), the horses with tails like snakes and mouths of deception that kills. Yes, physical death. The wages of sin is death, but without Jesus it leads to eternal death. As long as Satan keeps them deceived until death, he has them forever to enter the eternal plague.

> The god of this age has blinded the minds of unbelievers, so that they cannot see the light of the gospel that displays the glory of Christ, who is the image of God (2 Cor. 4:4).

Deceived by demonic power. Jesus rebuked some of the seven churches about deception in those letters. Watch out for false teachers! Those seven letters are not just an interesting introduction to Revelation with no relevance to the rest of the book. What was going on in their churches ties it all together and makes sense of all the warnings. Furthermore, because seven is God's number of completion, it's a warning to the church throughout the ages. Jesus warned and rebuked his people to watch out for deception through false teachers, specifically the churches in Ephesus (2:6), Pergamum (2:14-15) and Thyatira (2:20-21). Those churches had false teachers who taught that compromise, idolatry and sexual immorality were compatible with being a Christian. These demonic deceivers get inside the church! It's a plague and it kills people spiritually. Even a third! How many people who attend church are born again?

So Jesus' warning to *watch out for false teaching* (Rev. 2-3) is revisited now, which tells us false teaching could be coming upon the world, even through this sixth trumpet! The demonic deceivers are out there, and the message to the seven churches was: *Whoever has ears let them hear what the Spirit says to the churches.*

Rev. 9:4 told us believers have the seal of the Spirit. They will listen to what the Spirit says. They might have fallen for false teaching, sexual immorality and idolatry, but they will repent! Did you get that? Those who have the seal will not go on in the deception of idolatry or sexual immorality or false teaching. They will hear what the Spirit is saying to the churches. They will *wake up!* This trumpet blast is a wake-up call. So there is great opposition. Look how great:

The number of the mounted troops was twice ten thousand times ten thousand. I heard their number (9:16). There have been all kinds of attempts to interpret this 200 million. One popular idea is that this 200 million represents the number of invading Chinese troops. But 200 million is a problem even for the Chinese. The largest army in history was the former Soviet Union with 3 million troops. The next largest is the Chinese with 2.3 million. Ironically, those who come up with 200 million Chinese troops are often the very ones who insist we are supposed to be taking Revelation literally. But we might ask where do we literally see in the text any reference to the Chinese military?

One of the great advantages the Futurist view has with difficult texts like this is that because this is happening in the future (no matter how unrealistic it might sound to turn a 2.3 million strong military into 200 million), it can't be argued against, because it's in the future! And we have to admit that anything is possible in the future.

But what if this text is saying something meaningful to those people in the seven churches and to us in our own lives now? What if rather than drawing the Chinese into this, we use the context of Scripture to interpret it. Based on the context earlier in Rev. 9, the creatures are coming out of the Abyss, which Scripture tells us is the realm of demons. And these creatures here have snakes for tails. As we noted, only Satan is mentioned in relation to a snake in the Bible. We have been introduced to Apollyon the destroyer in 9:11. And now we have warfare against an army of 200 million. That might seem fanciful for a human army, but it is not hard to imagine if we think about the warfare which the Bible and particularly Revelation speaks. What warfare would that be?

> For our struggle is not against flesh and blood, but against the rulers, against the authorities, against the powers of this dark world and against the spiritual forces of evil in the heavenly realms (Eph. 6:12).

This is where the deception is coming from. There is deception in the church according to the letters to the seven churches. There is also deception in the world. But here we are told it comes with greater force. What Rev. 9 is referring to is a massive increase at a particular time. This does not limit us from seeing fulfillment through history with the effect of these demonic horses, all 200 million of them working their woe on society. Literal wars and armies can be included in all these things, such as the evil of man stirred up by demonic forces. For example, is it possible you have a demon-driven Hitler causing a world war with more than 40 million deaths in World War 2? This is no less demonic than Stalin killing at least 20 million of his own people and Mao Tse Tung killing between 40-

80 million of *his* own people. Demon-driven deception. And now we are seeing new ways of death. There are suicide bombings and terrorist attacks. What drives people to do such things?

Remember we were told in Rev. 6 that one-fourth of the people were dying. If nothing else, we are meant to note there is this increase of deaths to one-third. It's not astronomically different, but it's a clear increase. And it's all brought about by this warfare of 200 million demonic spirits raging throughout the world. I have been arguing this tribulation rages from the time of John the apostle, when Jesus said he would show John *what must soon take place after this* (1:19). Jesus ascended to heaven and released the seals and inside the seals were the trumpets. They are sweeping through the church age from the time of Jesus and increasing in intensity up to the end and the final judgment. It might be only coincidence, but it has been said about 75% of all people who ever lived are alive today. We have experienced a massive spike in population in the last century. There were only one billion people on earth in the 1800s, now we have seven billion. It would not be a wild estimate to say that since the time of Jesus, one-third of all the people have now died. But we dismiss that as applying to this text, because we think of death as 'normal'. We would rather leave that idea for some time in the future, because we don't want to accept that the world we live in now is under judgment and the trumpets are blasting. But death is not normal. It is the result of a cursed world. We are so used to evil, suicide bombers, super bugs, AIDS and other plagues and death in all its forms that we have grown to think it's all *normal*. We kill our children at a higher rate, higher than ever before in history through abortion.

While demonic spirits rage, what are the trumpets doing? Trumpets warn. There is still hope. The increase from one-fourth to one-third still leaves most people with time to hear the warning. They can see this is a dying world. They can see the deceitfulness of this world. It's a trumpet warning. They can see the futility of putting their hopes in the things of this world. They can see and experience the pain of this world. C.S. Lewis says in his book *The Problem of Pain*, 'God whispers to us in our pleasures, speaks in our conscience, but shouts in our pain: it is his megaphone to rouse a deaf world.'[34]

---

[34] C.S. Lewis, The Problem of Pain (1940; repr., San Francisco: Harper, 2001), p.91

The people of the world can see their own mortality, and some are even tormented by the thought of dying and fear what they might face on the other side. So, what will they do about that?

> The rest of mankind who were not killed by these plagues still did not repent of the work of their hands; they did not stop worshiping demons, and idols of gold, silver, bronze, stone and wood—idols that cannot see or hear or walk (9:20).

Like the plagues of Egypt, instead of people repenting, most will harden their hearts even more. Have you ever looked at how hard people's hearts are and thought, 'What is wrong with this picture?' Answer: Nothing is wrong. It's the great spiritual deception. This text is telling us to expect opposition to the gospel, which will increase all the way to the end. Why? People love their sin. Specifically, they love their **idols.**

Have you ever been fascinated by the audacity of man? The very people who sin against God have the audacity to turn around and blame God for evil, even though it was our sin that caused the evil of this world. So how amazingly gracious is our God? If someone blamed us for the very things they were doing themselves, would we rush to forgive them? Let alone give up our son for them? No. We would give them 'what for!' Boom! No warnings.

How gracious is God that he would send trumpet after trumpet? Warning after warning! The wrath of God is being revealed from heaven, but in a limited way so there is still time to be saved. But humanity wants to rule itself! God says, 'You want to rule yourselves and indulge evil, then here is what it looks like ... but I'm still giving you a day to repent ...' But they would not! Even with the warnings and time to repent, still hardly anyone is listening. Like Jezebel in the church at Thyatira, *I gave her time to repent but she is not willing* (2:12). It is not as though God has not held out long enough. But they would not stop worshiping their idols. People love their idols. They are passionate about them. In fact, whatever your passions are, that is where your heart is. *For where your treasure is, there your heart will be also* (Luke 12:34).

Idols come in all shapes and sizes. Who worships idols? Many cultures. What about one billion Indians? Or the 400 million Buddhists, many of whom even go against what the original Buddha

(Sidhartha Gautama) taught, by worshiping statues of the Buddha himself. Idols of silver, stone, gold, wood and so on. But what about the worship of **gold** and **silver** in the West? Bricks and mortar, **stone** and **wood,** clothing, toys, cars, gadgets and so on. The idolatry of materialism is now unprecedented in the Western world, even in the church! The apostle Paul says ...

> For we brought nothing into the world, and we can take nothing out of it. But if we have food and clothing, we will be content with that (1 Tim. 6:7-8).

Not anymore Paul! Not anymore are we contented with food and clothing! Even in the church we must have more! Bigger and better. More comfort, more stuff! And the idols are taking the place of God. But behind the idols are what?

> Do I mean then that food sacrificed to an idol is anything, or that an idol is anything? No, but the sacrifices of pagans are offered to demons, not to God, and I do not want you to be participants with demons (1 Cor. 10:19-20).

Behind idols are the 200,000,000 troops that are going out! There are plenty of them to cover each of those idols in our lives. That's what is behind our idolatry. Demonic power. The idol worshipers would not stop. The intensity of idolatry today is at fever pitch! In generations past, people were content with a simpler lifestyle when it came to the homes they lived in, their entertainment etc. Today it's consumer crazy. The church no longer considers the needy but makes itself comfortable. The church has become like the world. Why? The demons have been released! They are deceiving millions into the second death as they suffer physical death and think that's the end. Shoomp! 'Got another one.' As long as you are worshiping idols your focus will keep you in the darkness of demons so you can't see the light of the glory of the gospel.

> Nor did they repent of their <u>murders</u>, their <u>magic arts</u>, their <u>sexual immorality</u> or their <u>thefts</u> (9:21).

Murders – abortion. They don't even call it murder. **Magic arts** – psychics. The occult is more popular than ever and even celebrated now. There is even a hint in the original language in the Greek word for *magic arts* that it might include the use of illicit drugs. The words 'magic arts' are translated from the Greek word *pharmakei*, which is where we get our word *pharmacy*. So should we watch out for those chemists? No. But the effects of illicit drugs can sometimes replicate occult experiences. Then we have **sexual immorality.** Like no other time in Western history. The sexual revolution of the 1960s turned the world upside down. But 'free love' turned out to be neither free, nor love. It brought a new idolatry to sexual immorality. Lust in pornography with the advent of the Internet has made it the biggest business in the world. Sex outside of marriage is 'normal'. The last one is the **thefts.** That can include everything from small-time stealing to corporate fraud to copyright theft. Theft is so rampant, most 'law-abiding citizens' are not fazed by illegally copying or downloading games, computer programs, music or movies. It has become 'normal'. It's normal to steal! Everybody is doing it, aren't they? How could it be? Demonic deception released upon the world.

When could there be such a terrible time when these things would go on and the people would be unrepentant? The apostle Paul describes it ...

> But mark this: There will be terrible times in the last days. People will be lovers of themselves, lovers of money, boastful, proud, abusive, disobedient to their parents, ungrateful, unholy, without love, unforgiving, slanderous, without self-control, brutal, not lovers of the good, treacherous, rash, conceited, lovers of pleasure rather than lovers of God ... (2 Tim. 3:1-4).

True believers will heed the warnings. But the majority become hardened. Some will say, 'I will believe if only I had a message from heaven.' Well, Jesus sends Revelation from heaven. If you think this world is normal and you can't see what is happening right before your eyes, you wouldn't believe even if someone came back from the dead! It's not that there is no time left to repent, but people don't want to repent. They don't want to give up their idols. And the time draws near to when God says there is nothing left to do. Man will not repent, so what now? There is no other choice. The Final Judgment. The seventh trumpet will blast.

Study Questions

1. How is this text related to 6:9-11, and what is the evidence for that?

2. What would the Euphrates River indicate to John? Provide Scriptural support.

3. How do the words 'very hour' relate to the story of Job and how might this reflect on our lives?

4. Explain how John could recognize these as horses when their appearance is so distorted?

5. How can physical and spiritual death be related?

6. How could we account for one third of mankind dying?

7. How can you explain a 200 million strong army?

8. In what ways does this explain what we see in the world?

9. If the trumpets bring judgment how can they be seen as gracious?

10. Is there anything in this warning to repent that challenges you?

33
The Colossus
(Revelation 10:1-6)

Remember the great lead up in the seven seals? Jesus the Master film director took us up to an interlude and flashback before the final end of the seventh seal. The movie had all the excitement and dramatic build-up as the Lamb who was worthy opened the seals, one after another. Partial judgments were released. It was a terrifying progression through the first six seals, leading to the end with the climactic statement: *Who can stand?*

Indeed, who *can* stand with that cosmic judgment about to happen? We sat on the edge of our seats expecting the finale of the movie, the seventh seal to be opened! But instead, there was a great piece of cinematic direction. An interlude. There was this pause before the final scene. A preparation to the climax which answered the question of who could stand. The interlude in Rev. 7 did just that. It told us those who were sealed with God's seal, the Holy Spirit, will be able to stand on that great and terrible day.

Then in Rev. 8 the seventh seal was opened. The climax arrived. The Day of Judgment. But it turns out like one of those movies where just when you think you know how it finishes, the plot thickens, and it turns out Arnold Schwarzenegger's brain has been implanted with another memory and you are inside another deeper reality. Just when you get to the final seal and open it up, we opened the package and inside … another package! Inside the seventh seal were seven trumpets.

The trumpets didn't come *after* the seals, they were *inside*, and they repeated the time of the seven seals with increasing intensity and more detail, the progress towards the final end. So we started the judgments again with seven trumpets. First trumpet, second trumpet, third etc., all the way until it brought us up to the big finale again! The sixth trumpet has blasted. Now we are waiting for the seventh and final trumpet, waiting for the final explosion, and the Master film director does it again. Another interlude! The suspense is killing me. After the sixth trumpet, we read in Rev. 10-11 of another interlude before the blasting of the seventh trumpet. The final trumpet will not be sounded now until 11:15. So we can see this parallel pattern again.

SEALS	1, 2, 3, 4, 5, 6 (interlude)	7th (final judgment)
TRUMPETS	1, 2, 3, 4, 5, 6 (interlude)	7th (final judgment)
BOWLS	1, 2, 3, 4, 5, 6 (interlude)	7th (final judgment)

The scene is changing for this interlude. In fact, we have been so caught up in the movie and what John has been watching that we didn't even notice John himself has moved back to earth. It's a new vision. Remember at the start of Rev. 4 John was caught up to heaven. Now we notice his perspective is from earth because he is looking *up to heaven* and seeing something come *down to earth*.

> Then I saw another mighty angel <u>coming down from heaven</u>. He was robed in a cloud, with a rainbow above his head; his face was like the sun, and his legs were like fiery pillars (10:1).

These are visions and it's all so apocalyptic, so it's no big deal that John has now shifted in perspective, seeing things from heaven before and now from earth below, seeing what is **coming down from heaven.** It's no big deal, unless you are of the opinion John going up into heaven at the start of Rev. 4 is a 'type' or 'representation' of the church being raptured up to heaven. Because now he is back on earth and that would mean the church has also been unraptured and returned to earth for a while before the final trumpet. Well no one would agree with that. So I am suggesting that John is simply John (not the church), and there is no mention in Rev. 4 (or anywhere else) of the church being raptured *before* the tribulation. Rather the church goes through the tribulation and desperately needs this book of Revelation, not least of all, Rev. 10 with this very interlude, to assure God's people and enable them to keep persevering through the tribulation.

But who is this **mighty angel** John sees? The best biblical scholars can't agree on this. Some say it is Jesus; others say Jesus can't be an angel. I share that caution. Jesus should not be reduced to an angel.

> For to which of the angels did God ever say, 'You are my Son; today I have become your Father'?... And again, when God brings his firstborn into the world, he says, 'Let all God's angels worship him' (Heb. 1:5-6).

Yet John sees this amazing sight. A *mighty angel*. *Angel* can also be translated *messenger*. But this messenger or angel is like no other mentioned in Scripture. There are attributes of this angel that elsewhere in the Bible are only attributed to God. **He was robed in a cloud,** which is typical OT language referring to the LORD in judgment. But it's not confined to the OT. In Rev. 1 we see Jesus coming on the clouds of heaven! Every eye will see him. And in Rev. 10 John sees this amazing sight of this angel coming down out of heaven surrounded by a cloud! But also **with a rainbow above his head.** Again John, who grew up as a devout Jew, would recall the OT, specifically when Ezekiel saw the glory of the Lord.

> Like the appearance of a rainbow in the clouds on a rainy day, so was the radiance around him ... (Ezek. 1:28).

But we don't need to go outside Revelation to see the Lord encircled with that great sign of his covenantal love, the rainbow. We've seen how it is connected with the presence of God before ...

> And the one who sat there had the appearance of jasper and ruby. A rainbow that shone like an emerald encircled the throne (4:3).

There is the Lord on his throne encircled by a rainbow, showing his covenantal love as the God of mercy. A rainbow also encircles the angel in Rev. 10. In fact, this angel not only has characteristics normally attributed to deity, but specific similarities to Jesus. What does Rev. 1 say of John's first vision of Jesus?

> ... His face was like the sun shining in all its brilliance (1:16).

And so too this angel in 10:1, **his face was like the sun.** In 1:15 Jesus had feet like burnished bronze, and in 10:1 is a similar picture with **his legs were like fiery pillars,** which is even closer to the LORD in the OT who appeared to Israel as a pillar of cloud and a pillar of fire. So there are hints this might be Jesus. Jesus is the Lion of the tribe of Judah (5:5), and this angel has a shout like the roar of a what?

> ... and he gave a loud shout like the roar of a lion ... (10:3).

At the very least this is no ordinary angel. There are these hints all over. He is *coming in clouds, encircled in a rainbow, his face shines like the sun, and he has a roar like a lion*. And we are about to encounter the sheer enormity of this angel in its power, size and sovereignty.

> He was holding a little scroll, which lay open in his hand. <u>He planted his right foot on the sea and his left foot on the land,</u> ... (10:2).

Say what? He places his feet on land and the sea at the same time! How awesome is this scene to John? Picture someone, *anyone*, who is greater than the whole earth and sea. One foot on the land, one on the sea, like the Judge of all the earth, because putting your feet upon something is the great symbol of having it in subjection to you. All under his feet. Like a footstool. *Heaven is my throne, and the earth is my footstool* ... (Acts 7:49). What kind of being spans the earth and sea with one foot on each? John sees a vision of this angel. Just who is this angel? Jesus is not an angel. Yet there were divine messengers in the OT that carried the same enigma. One moment they are referred to as angels, the next as the Lord himself ...

> But the angel of the LORD called out to him from heaven, 'Abraham! Abraham!' 'Here I am,' he replied. 'Do not lay a hand on the boy,' he said. 'Do not do anything to him. Now I know that you fear God, because you have not withheld from me your son, your only son' (Gen. 22:11-12).

This is mysterious stuff. One minute it is an angel of the LORD (messenger), yet the next minute it is clearly the Lord speaking. The scholars debate, 'Is this a pre-incarnate Jesus, or just a messenger of the Lord?' We are left with that weird sense of enigma. So mysterious. And what do we have here in Rev. 10? At the very least, if this is an angel, it's one so powerful that it is meant to represent Jesus because it has his traits. Michael the archangel represents Jesus in 12:7-9. But in Rev. 10 this being is so colossal, with one foot on land and one foot on sea, it seems bigger than any angel. Who is it? There is no consensus among scholars. I would be in good company if I say this is an angel and good company if I say it must be Jesus.

On one hand, you can't have Jesus as an angel, and on the other, you can't have an angel with attributes of deity. And these traits are so awe-inspiring, the very features of Jesus, and maybe that's exactly what it's meant to be. An awe-inspiring enigma. We know at the least this *represents* Jesus, but is it Jesus or a colossal angelic messenger? Try and picture John seeing this vision. It's like when you see someone famous, and it almost seems like you know him or her, but you are just too afraid to ask. Maybe that's what is going on here. We are not told outright, so maybe we are meant to be left in awe and bewilderment. When I picture John looking up at one like this, it sends shivers down my spine. A being that places his feet on land and sea as one who is in control of all the whole earth. Picture standing before this one! His voice is like a lion and it reverberates throughout the world. Who is this? What is the point being made here?

It might help to recap on what we have seen in Revelation so far, particularly what has just gone on before in Rev. 9. And remember, that is exactly what Rev. 10 is doing. It is giving us a recap, a reminder. It is the movie interlude! When we had the first interlude between the sixth and seventh seals, before we headed into the final judgment, the question was asked: *Who can stand?* The interlude answered that question.

What is going on in this interlude in Rev. 10? We've had six trumpets blast. In Rev. 9 we've had partial judgments, chaos and evil. We had strange looking locusts coming out of the Abyss, the realm of the demons. And 200 million troops were released on the earth. All kinds of demonic power going forth. The evil is going crazy! There is a new intensity of evil coming upon the earth through the sixth trumpet. Who can stand against that? And remember the power in the mouths of the horses? Deceiving mouths. Falsehood becomes the norm, so the church is bombarded with false teaching as well as the world. Even some churches no longer believe the Bible and many that do don't preach it.

Are you sure Jesus wins? How can you know? The world is going nuts. Evil is celebrated as good. Remember the last part of Rev. 9 how the people in the midst of the pain of this world *still* would *not* repent. Those demonic forces have been released on a world that is becoming more hostile. Try speaking out against sexual immorality and you will find the most venomous attacks. The response is almost demonic if you voice your opinion that sex should only be within the confines of heterosexual marriage. If you have an opinion that abortion is taking the life of an unborn child, you don't just get an opposing opinion, you get a vicious attack. The locusts have been let out! And the persecution is illogical. You are ridiculed. 'What kind of fruitcake are you to dare to believe that God created the world? That is so naïve. It's like believing in Santa Claus.' You don't merely have another opinion, you are ridiculed as anti-intellectual. But if you believe the world popped out of nothing and designed/evolved itself, now that is intellectual! Then you are educated, reasonable. Is there any question this world is under demonic attack? Where is it coming from? Could it be that the 200 million troops have been released upon the earth? How do you know Jesus is winning? Look at this tribulation right before your eyes. Do you feel it? Pain, opposition, conflict, even in the home! The world has gone nuts. Are you sure evil is not finally going to do you in? Are you sure Jesus wins?

Then you look up ... and this is what you see. An unnamed giant colossus that is for you, bigger than the world itself, comes and plonks his feet on both land and sea. He has it all under his feet. It's under his control. Like big feet that can just squash ants that dare to get in the way. He comes in a cloud surrounded by a rainbow. He has not forgotten his covenant, as the rainbow encircles him. He will not delay his judgment. He has a time and won't go beyond it. We stand looking into the unknown time in the future. To us it has gone on and on and will go on and on. Tribulation, violence, famine, war, disease and death, with evil intensifying. It goes on and we can't see the end. For us life is a struggle. And we get anxious and worried as we go through our conflicts, our tribulations. And we look at the world and the state of the church. Are you sure Jesus wins? But this one stands at the end, beckoning the tribulation to finish its work. Bring it on. He is standing there waiting at the finish line, where there is **no more delay!**

We can't see the end, so for us it's like the story of the marathon swimmer swimming in a cage between Miami, Florida and Cuba, attempting a landmark, marathon swim. After hours in shocking stormy weather with no visibility and with weather so bad the support boat could not see even a few meters in front, and after being several hours over schedule, the swimmer finally abandoned her swim and got into the support boat. She gave up. The tribulation was too great. When she got into the boat, it chugged forward only a short distance through the fog to discover they were only about 100m short of the coast of Cuba! It was only a little further through that storm!

That's what this message of Revelation is telling us, in particular in Rev. 10. You can't see clearly because you are in a storm, but Jesus stands at the other side, waiting at the other end. He can see. Right behind the storm he stands and controls the whole world and is waiting to judge. He knows how close you are to the finish. But he also knows how his people need to see this Revelation. But more than this!

He has all things under his feet now! That's why we have this break in the trumpets, before we go to the big climax. Hang in there! The end is closer than you think. And there is one who stands the other side of it. **He was holding a little scroll, which lay open in his hand. He planted his right foot on the sea and his left foot on the land.** How we need this interlude as we head into the final part of the storm, as the tribulation intensifies. The mighty one was *holding a little scroll* that is going to be heard across the world. We will look at the scroll next. But now we see this mighty one who *gave a loud shout like the roar of a lion. When he shouted, the voices of the seven thunders spoke.* The *roar of a lion* is telling us it's either Jesus, the Lion of the tribe of Judah, or his great representative. It would also be familiar to John with his OT understanding. Who is the lion? He would think of Amos.

> The lion has roared — who will not fear? The Sovereign Lord has spoken — who can but prophesy? (Amos 3:8).

But there is more than John can even prophesy ...

> And when the seven thunders spoke, I was about to write; but I heard a voice from heaven say, 'Seal up what the seven thunders have said and <u>do not write it down</u>' (10:4).

Picture John with a quill in his hand ready to write. But wait John. Don't write this one down. It seems from the way this verse reads that John has been like the secretary of the Board who takes the minutes. He has been furiously writing down everything Jesus has given him in these visions, and he was about to write down what the seven thunders said, but instead this time John is instructed by the voice from heaven saying, 'Don't write this one down'.

Why can't he write this one? The very judgments of God are unfolding to the end, and we don't get to know? Is this part of the unsearchable judgments of God that we don't get to find out? Is this like …

> The secret things belong to the LORD our God, but the things revealed belong to us and to our children forever, that we may follow all the words of this law (Deut. 29:29).

We know what we need to know for now so we can follow the Lord, but maybe it's too much for us to know more. Is this like when Paul the apostle was swept up to heaven and was told …

> [I] was caught up to paradise and heard inexpressible things, things that no one is permitted to tell (2 Cor. 12:4).

These seven thunders of judgment are also things John is not permitted to tell. Do we have to wait until the new heaven and new earth to learn it all? Revelation is revealing new things, but there are still things that belong to the Lord and the future. No one can fully grasp all the Lord has in store for his people. It's like the great mystery about how God could do good out of the greatest tragedy of the Son of God being tortured and nailed to a cross. God brought the greatest good and love for us, saving our souls through that great tragedy. *That has* been revealed to us. So for now we know what we need to know.

The point here with these seven thunders is that however much you think you know, you ain't seen nothing yet! No mind has conceived all that God has planned for those who love him. It's like all the times when you skeptically said, 'How can God be working good amidst all this pain?' Well one day he will show you how wrong you were. You know what you missed? You missed that great colossal being with one foot on the land and one foot on the sea. The one who has everything under his feet, everything under his control until the end. You missed faith! Faith is about trusting when we *can't* see. It's the opposite of sight. You were called to trust and believe God, who gave up his own Son for you, and promised that along with his Son he will give you all things. You were called on to trust that God. Look at those colossal feet and believe!

You who are going through the tribulation, under attack from the 200 million troops, even the pounding you get just from living and working in a secular environment where there seems to be no thought of God. What about the judgments that come upon the earth which Christians get caught up in? Christians get cancer and lose loved ones. Christians have relationship breakdowns. Christians experience the disasters of this world. Christians are lonely and on their own. Christians have marriages that are so painful they are ready to give up. Christians are so stressed from their lives they feel like they are in a prison. Christians experience pain, famine, violence, plague and death. And these trumpets we have been seeing are judgments on an *unbelieving world*. How does that all work for good for God's people? Did you hear those seven thunders? No, you didn't! Because John didn't write them down. You don't know everything. You are going to have to trust. You are going to have to have faith. But on what basis are you going to believe? On the basis of this sovereign colossus who has both earth and sea under his feet. On the basis of God, who gave his own Son for you. What more proof do you need of both his sovereignty and love for you? But in the meantime, there is revelation that we are meant to know. It's given to us here …

> Then the angel I had seen <u>standing on the sea and on the land</u> raised his right hand to heaven. And he swore by him who lives for ever and ever, who created the heavens and all that is in them, the earth and all that is in it, and the sea and all that is in it, and said, 'There will be no more delay!' (10:5-6).

The Lord has set a day when there is *no more delay,* and when that time comes, it's all over. The whole of history is hurtling towards this climax. And once he has accomplished his plan to the ends of the earth, there will be no more delay. Think about how we make plans and set goals. Always thinking about the day when we will be more comfortable and get to where we want to be in life. We are always looking ahead for a day. But the goal of life is the day that the Lord has set. When that day comes, there will be no more delay. The Day of the Lord. *Then* the seven secret thunders will be revealed.

This should at least stir us to contemplate the real goal of our existence. Is the day you are looking forward to the same day the Lord is planning as *the* Day? 'Oh, but it's all going on too long. How do we know it's not just going to keep going? Evil seems to triumph.' This is how. We have a sworn statement from the very one whose feet are stamped on both land and sea, who gives a solemn oath and swore by God the Father himself that the time is coming. *'There will be no more delay.'*

In the meantime, you who think you can't make it through the tribulation ... Don't give up. Keep fighting. Why? Look at this picture that John saw with his own eyes and passed on to you ...

Then the angel I had seen <u>standing on the sea and on the land</u> raised his right hand to heaven. And he swore by him who lives for ever and ever, who created the heavens and all that is in them, the earth and all that is in it, and the sea and all that is in it, and said, 'There will be no more delay!' (10:5-6).

Study Questions

1. Where does Rev. 10 fit with the parallels of seals and trumpets?

2. What is the purpose of Rev. 10?

3. How does this text bring into question the idea that John taken up to heaven in 4:1 represents the church being raptured?

4. Give reasons for and against this figure being Jesus.

5. Are we meant to identify this figure with certainty? If not, why not?

6. In what ways does he give assurance to those going through tribulation?

7. Does the mystery behind the seven thunders give you food for thought about your life?

34

The Sweet and Bitter Scroll
(Revelation 10:7-11)

The apostle John has been stuck in a prison-cave on the island of Patmos, like the modern-day Alcatraz, but he is a prisoner for the Lord. While he is imprisoned and suffering, he gets a vision of the sovereign power of God who has the world under his feet. The Lord is sovereign! That alone is message enough to encourage John. This is what he needed to see whilst stuck in that prison-cave. And this is what we need to see as we brace ourselves through tribulation before we encounter the seventh and final trumpet. We are now in the interlude before the final trumpet. We need this pause to prepare ourselves for the end. And the message of the interlude from the one who stands on land and sea is … nothing is out of his sovereign control. The world is his footstool.

We also read in 10:2 this angel held a *little scroll in his hand*. Small enough to eat, if you are into eating scrolls. What is in the scroll? Do we use our imagination? Do we get some ideas from blogs or websites? Or shall we use the book of Revelation to tell us, because it's not like we haven't encountered scrolls before.

In Rev. 5 we encountered the scroll that no one could open except the Lamb. What did it contain? The judgments and salvation of God. But those things have been unfolding in the seals and trumpets. That scroll was opened and much of the contents have been emptied. Perhaps that is why this is only a *little* scroll. Could this be the remainder of the scroll of Rev. 5? If that's the case, this scroll is continuing to reveal things occurring through Rev. 11-16 and possibly even up to Rev. 22. And here, at the end of Rev. 10 John is re-commissioned as a prophet to proclaim these things …

> Then I was told, 'You must prophesy again about many peoples, nations, languages and kings' (10:11).

This little scroll contains John's marching orders. His commissioning as a prophet to proclaim all that is to follow. There are important similarities with the scroll in the book of Ezekiel, where Ezekiel is told to eat a scroll that is also related to judgment and salvation of peoples, nations, languages that he had to proclaim. So we begin with this text at …

> But in the days when the seventh angel is about to sound his trumpet, the <u>mystery</u> of God will be accomplished, just as he <u>announced</u> to his servants the prophets (10:7).

He **announced** this **mystery.** It was not any old announcing. Here is the key to what is going on with this scroll. The word *announced* in the original Greek language is the same word used many times through the NT that simply means *preaching the gospel.* Jesus used this word when he sent word to John the Baptist. Tell John the 'good news is preached'. All through the gospels, Acts and NT letters, when you read that the *gospel was preached*, or *preaching the good news*, it's translating a single Greek word that is translated here as *announcing.* So it is a specific type of announcing. It's the good news of Jesus! The gospel.

It is announced to **his servants the prophets,** meaning OT prophets and NT prophets. John is the last prophet before the wrapping up of the word of God. So this verse says in announcing the gospel, the mystery of God is accomplished. What mystery? At least one of the seven churches to whom John was writing would immediately think of the mystery of the gospel explained to them in another letter written to them years earlier by the apostle Paul. The church at Ephesus.

> …that is, <u>the mystery</u> made known to me by revelation, as I have already written briefly. In reading this, then, you will be able to understand my insight into <u>the mystery</u> of Christ, which was not made known to people in other generations as it has <u>now been revealed</u> by the Spirit to God's holy apostles <u>and prophets</u>. <u>This mystery is</u> that through the gospel the <u>Gentiles</u> are heirs together with Israel, members together of one body, and sharers together in the promise in Christ Jesus (Eph. 3:3-6).

The mystery is that Jew and Gentile are joined together as one church. It is the mystery only revealed in the church age. We know

Israel is God's people, so how can the world be saved without everyone becoming Jews? How can the world be joined to Israel? Here is the mystery revealed. For God so loved the *world* that he gave his one and only Son. By believing in Jesus the nations of the world can be joined to Israel as God's people. What is John told here? **'You must prophesy again about many peoples, nations, languages and kings.'** The world! Mystery revealed. Paul talked about this same mystery in his letter to the church at Rome.

> Now to him who is able to establish you in accordance with my gospel, the message I proclaim about Jesus Christ, in keeping with the revelation of the mystery hidden for long ages past, but now revealed and made known through the prophetic writings by the command of the eternal God, so that all the Gentiles might come to the obedience that comes from faith, ... (Rom. 16:25-26).

The trouble is that we take this mystery for granted. For centuries the mystery of God was kept hidden. Israel was God's chosen nation. But what about the rest of the world? Destined to hell? What is the answer to that? It's in the gospel. The good news of Jesus. The mystery is that the Jewish Messiah is for all. Salvation comes from the Jews and through them a plan for the world. And John is told in 10:11 to prophesy to the *world*. To *peoples, nations, languages and kings*.

What was sealed up in Daniel's time is now an open book! A *little scroll* (10:2), but this little scroll is revealing far more of the mystery than just the gospel joining Jew and Gentile. As the mystery of this little scroll is opened in the following chapters, we see the wonder that while it looks like Satan is winning by bringing persecution to God's people, God is actually outsmarting Satan. Jesus wins. How does Jesus do that? By laying down his life. And what we see in the mystery unfolded and what follows in Revelation is that those who follow Jesus and follow in his footsteps will also lay down *their* lives for him. That is part of what is going to follow from here as we see the people of God persecuted. What is being revealed in Revelation and in this little scroll is the final end that will come about, but that it will come through great tribulation.

Good will be fiercely opposed by evil. That is also what this little scroll is going to uncover. Praise God he gives us Revelation. We might otherwise go nuts, because as we see the world going crazy, we could doubt Jesus is winning. Does Christianity really explain the reality we see? And the answer from the little scroll is: Yes! This is a plan. Expect it to be this way. Expect it to *look* bad. But it is a plan of God. And he will have the triumph. But what this scroll will reveal is that victory will come through the suffering of God's people. There is an oft-repeated illustration that seems helpful. It's that of viewing the world like a tapestry. A rug is held up, but if we look at it from the underside, all we see are these straggly pieces and a rather ratty looking rug with stringy bits hanging everywhere. It looks like a mess. But on the other side we see the beautiful finished tapestry work. The illustration is meant to convey the fact we can't see the other side of the perfection of God's work, it just looks bad to us on this side.

I think we can take this illustration further and picture that tapestry rolled up. In other words, not only do we see the limited (bad) view of the rug, but we also can't see it fully until it's unrolled. God is working *throughout* history and the good he is doing, despite opposition, will only be completed when history has fully rolled out, unfolded, on the Day of Judgment.

And here is the important point. Unless it unfolds, you never get to see the complete tapestry. There is no other way. We can't skip to the end. The things God is doing *cannot* be accomplished without the unfolding of history, including God unfolding what he is doing in your life and all that he is working in you, which includes suffering and tribulations. The tapestry must fully unfold to see all its beauty.

At the end of history that mighty messenger of 10:6 stands not only over the earth and sea and history, but he stands at the end of time and says *there will be no more delay*. When that plan is complete, it will have reached the perfection he is working towards.

In the meantime, we just want to get to the end. Have you ever longed for vindication or justice when people have done you wrong? People criticize you and you look forward to when you will show them! Some people waste their whole lives brooding over something or someone who has done them wrong. Others who have been wronged look for 'closure', which is the current buzzword, but it doesn't happen.

But we are not like that. We can let it go. Why? There is only One who gets the full and final victory. Wait until that tapestry rug is fully unrolled. It will all come out in the victory of the sovereign One. But first there is more of the scroll to be unfolded. John the apostle is still seeing a vision. At first, he is seeing this vision as though he is at the cinema watching a movie on the big screen, but then he takes a step into the movie. Here John is told to actually step into his own vision ...

> Then the voice that I had heard from heaven spoke to me once more: 'Go, take the scroll that lies open in the hand of the angel who is standing on the sea and on the land.' [John steps up to the angel]. So I went to the angel and asked him to give me the little scroll. He said to me, 'Take it and eat it. It will turn your stomach sour, but in your mouth it will be as sweet as honey' (10:8-9).

John goes up to the angel who is big enough to have one foot on land and one on sea and takes the book out of his hand and eats it. How does all that work? But remember it's a vision. John is to devour this book. You've heard that kind of metaphor. When someone reads a book quickly they are said to devour it. In this vision John is literally doing that. He eats it!

> I took the little scroll from the angel's hand and ate it. It tasted as sweet as honey in my mouth, but when I had eaten it, my stomach turned sour. Then I was told, 'You must prophesy again about many peoples, nations, languages and kings' (10:10-11).

A couple of precedents to this are Psalm 119:103, *sweet like honey to the mouth are God's words to the believer*, and Psalm 19:10. So the scroll was sweet to taste, but it turns sour in the stomach. Why would that be? The sweetness of the scroll is the good news. Do you remember when you were first converted how sweet that good news was? You thought telling people about this good news would be the greatest thing. This is sweet. This is good news! You thought all your family and friends were going to love this news because you have the answer to the meaning of life! And you thought this was going to be the sweetest news to the ears of your friends too. Yet not only do they reject you and your good news, it even causes bitter arguments, even persecution. Venomous opposition!

So the scroll is going to taste sweet at first. John has got to devour it. It has to be in him. That's the message. That's what Ezekiel had to do. And John is going to need the message to be in him, because this is the biggest news ever. If we look into the future of what John has to prophesy about, he needed this strengthening, because this is big. He will be prophesying about a titanic future. We have seen the seals and trumpets open, but the seven bowls are still to come. There is this dragon that wants to eat a child. There are beasts coming out of the sea and beasts coming out of the earth. We haven't even met the Antichrist or the great harlot, Babylon, and her final doom, the devil, the 1000 years, or the new heaven and new earth. John is going to have to eat that book because this prophesying is big!

It's a warning the end is coming. Just behind the veil is the end. Is that 'end' in our lifetime? Will it be next year or next week? We don't know, but however long, it will be a time of what? *Tribulation.* Evil will rise. How much more? We don't know. Prophesy John! It will be a time of great enemy fire, a demonic, powerful delusion to deceive even the elect if that were possible. It will be a time of partial judgment and disaster on a condemned world, but it will also be a time of persecution and going through tribulation. Satan wages war against God and his people. The message of Jesus will be opposed even in the church. However sweet it tastes it will cause deep bitterness as it goes down.

Ezekiel had to eat his scroll, which was a message of judgment to a people that would oppose him. John is re-commissioned as a prophet as he was in 1:10 and 4:1-2, which were allusions to Ezekiel's commissioning as a prophet (Ezek. 2:8-3:3). The significance is paramount to John as a prophet to proclaim these things. He can't merely read from a book he copied. It must come up out of his very belly. He has to consume it! Eat it up!

But when you hear these words of judgment and the gospel, do they get inside *you?* Does it have that effect on you? Can you taste how sweet it is? Have you tasted some of the bitterness when it is opposed? If we seriously believe this word, then we have to consume it and the fire of it overflows into our lives. Because now we have these words passed on to us by John. John is dead and gone. He can't proclaim this message any more. John wrote this book of Revelation to the servants of God. John has given this message to you. If you have a Bible, this message is literally in your hands. And you are to pass it on, to *announce* it! (10:7).

It's good news to a world that is condemned. It is unfolding the mystery of life. The mystery of this life is *not* whether you end up living in the right house, with the right spouse or the right job and live happily ever after. It's whether you and your family and friends come to know the Savior and get to live in the new heaven and the new earth that is revealed at the end of this scroll. That is what we have to be proclaiming. That is, if you have tasted it! Unless you have tasted this message, you can't pass it on. It's sweet news, but only a few really find it. Do you really believe this world is headed for judgment, and there is a short time to pass this message on? Do you believe that this is the day we are going to go through suffering and some bitterness for the kingdom? There is meaning in this time of suffering and partial judgments on the world as the tapestry unfolds. Jesus wins and Jesus must win with the proclaiming of the good news until the last of his is in. But it will happen through suffering. The feet of the mighty One are across both land and sea. He is over it all.

A missionary friend of mine returned from China and showed me how in the Chinese language the ancient characters speak of the book of Genesis, Noah's flood and man's eviction from the Garden. The ancient word of God, asleep through those centuries, was there in ancient China. But it comes around again. John is commissioned to proclaim it, *'You must prophesy again about many peoples, nations, languages and kings.'*

The word now goes forward in China today. While there is bitterness in the Western world to this message, it is being received by millions in non-Western countries today. The message is going forth. John himself knew what it was like to proclaim good news only to have it incite hatred and persecution. He could feel that bitterness in his stomach. John was there, praying for his imprisoned brother James (Acts 12:5), who had his head cut off by Herod. John had lived through the deaths of all the other 11 apostles who were executed for proclaiming the good news. John is the last surviving apostle. And where is he while he receives these visions from Jesus? He is in *prison*, in a cave, on the island of Patmos. That's how he began writing down this book of Revelation to the churches, by saying *ours is suffering and kingdom and patient endurance in Jesus* (1:9).

What is the Christian's lot? The sweetness of the good news comes through the bitterness of many hardships, all the way to the end. The more you proclaim the gospel and this sweet sound, good news to those who are being saved, it continues to be bitter and a condemning message to those who reject it, and it will bring bitter persecution as you proclaim it. If you want to proclaim this gospel you too will know it's both bitter and sweet. And after you have tasted this bittersweet gospel, after you have suffered for it and felt the bitterness, what then? You gotta do it again!

... '*You must prophesy <u>again</u> about many peoples, nations, languages and kings*' (10:11).

Study Questions

1. Why might this scroll be a 'little' scroll?

2. What is the significance of the word 'announced'?

3. What are possible reasons for the 'mystery' of the scroll?

4. Give reasons why God delays his Judgment Day.

5. Is there a scriptural precedent for eating scrolls and how does that help explain our text?

6. Why would the scroll be sweet to taste?

7. Why would it turn bitter and can you relate this to your own experience?

8. How does John's commission relate to Christians in general?

ABOUT THE AUTHOR

Bill Medley spent 15 years in the entertainment industry working as a comedian and actor. He was not brought up in a religious home and had no desire to ever become part of any 'organized religion'. In fact, he actually believed "Religion is for fools" and occasionally used religion as the butt of his jokes in his stand-up comedy.

No one shared the gospel with Bill, but he always thought one day he would investigate the religions of the world as an academic exercise. However, by age 32 and some life experience, he was ready to investigate in a deeper way. He set about reading the Scriptures of the five major world religions including the Bible, the Buddhist Scriptures, the Hindu Scriptures and the Koran. The uniqueness of Christ and his claims brought him to faith.

He has been the Pastor of Frankston Presbyterian Church in outer Melbourne, Australia, since 2006. He is married to Diana and they have three sons, Rick, Luke and Joshua.

OTHER BOOKS BY BILL MEDLEY

www.ingramcontent.com/pod-product-compliance
Lightning Source LLC
Chambersburg PA
CBHW050259010526
44107CB00055B/2092